MORAL EDUCATION

MORAL EDUCATION

A First Generation of Research and Development

edited by

Ralph L. Mosher

Library of Congress Cataloging in Publication Data

Main entry under title:

Moral education, a first generation of research and
    development.

    Bibliography: p.
    1. Moral education--United States--Curricula.
I. Mosher, Ralph L.
LC311.M58   370.11'4'0973   80-18607
ISBN 0-03-053961-7

Published in 1980 by Praeger Publishers
CBS Educational and Professional Publishing
A Division of CBS, Inc.
521 Fifth Avenue, New York, New York 10017 U.S.A.

Printed in the United States of America

ACKNOWLEDGMENTS

To Larry Kohlberg, Diana Paolitto, and Joe Reimer, who persuaded me that yet another book on moral education was worthwhile and by their own contributions to it helped prove they were right.

To Dr. Gerri Bagby, Vice-President of the Danforth Foundation, whose moral and financial support made much of the first generation possible.

To the many students and teachers of the Brookline and Cambridge Public Schools, who really wrote the book.

CONTENTS

ACKNOWLEDGMENTS   v
LIST OF TABLES AND FIGURES   xiv

Chapter   Page

PART I: A FRAMEWORK FOR MORAL EDUCATION

1   AN UNCOMMON CAUSE   3
    Ralph Mosher

    WHY MORAL EDUCATION?   3
        Adolescence: A Prime Time for Moral Education   4
        Watergate   5
        Institutional Roots: Boston and Harvard Universities   6
        A New Rationale for Guidance   12
    THE DANFORTH MORAL EDUCATION PROJECT: AN
        UNCOMMON CAUSE   13
    TAKING THE MEASURE OF THE PROJECT   16
    A READER'S GUIDE TO THE BOOK   17

2   HIGH SCHOOL DEMOCRACY AND EDUCATING
    FOR A JUST SOCIETY   20
    Lawrence Kohlberg

        MORAL STAGES   21
        EDUCATING FOR A JUST SOCIETY   26
        HIGH SCHOOL DEMOCRACY   34
        THE CAMBRIDGE CLUSTER SCHOOL   37
        THE SCARSDALE ALTERNATIVE SCHOOL   47
        A NEO-PLATONIC MODEL OF MORAL EDUCATION   49

3   ORGANIZING A SCHOOL SYSTEM FOR ETHICS EDUCATION   58
    Robert Sperber and David Miron

        THE BROOKLINE MORAL EDUCATION PROJECT, 1974-77   58
            The First Year of the Project: 1974-75   59
            The Second Year of the Project: 1975-76   62
            The Third Year of the Project: 1976-77   68

Objectives and Activities of the Project   71
Three Important Issues   71
Summary of the Project: 1974-77   76
HOW THE BROOKLINE MORAL EDUCATION PROJECT
WAS ORGANIZED AND ITS EFFECT ON TEACHERS
AND STUDENTS   77
CAN MORAL EDUCATION AS IT IS TAUGHT AT
BROOKLINE BE REPLICATED ELSEWHERE,
AND SHOULD IT?   81

4   STAFF DEVELOPMENT IN MORAL EDUCATION   83
Henry Zabierek

5   RESEARCH AND MEASUREMENT ISSUES IN MORAL
EDUCATION INTERVENTIONS   92
Ann Higgins

THE MORAL EDUCATION STUDIES REPORTED
IN THIS BOOK   93
Direct Moral Discussion of Real-Life Situations
with Natural Groups   93
Moral Discussion and Education for Personal Development   96
Social Studies Curricula and Moral Development   99
WHAT THE NEXT GENERATION MAY LEARN
FROM THE FIRST   100
Analyzing the Data of Moral Education Curricula   102
The Effects of a Just Community School   104
CONCLUSION   106

PART II: MORAL EDUCATION IN PRACTICE

HIGH SCHOOL CURRICULA

6   COGNITIVE DEVELOPMENT AND MORAL REASONING
IN THE TEACHING OF HISTORY   113
Thomas Ladenburg

A DEFINITION OF HISTORY THAT EMBRACES DEVELOP-
MENTAL GOALS   115
A MODEL FOR TEACHING THAT COMBINES SUBJECT
MATTER WITH DEVELOPMENTAL GOALS   116

A BROADENED DEFINITION OF MORAL DILEMMAS   118
UNITS THAT BRIDGE THE GAP BETWEEN SUBJECT
   AND DEVELOPMENTAL GOALS   120

7   MORAL EDUCATION TO REDUCE RACIAL AND ETHNIC
   PREJUDICE   126
   Robert Alexander

   RATIONALE   126
   LOEVINGER'S THEORY OF EGO DEVELOPMENT   130
   TEACHING THE MORAL EDUCATION CURRICULUM   133
      Phase One: Personal Introductions   133
      Phase Two: The Discussion of Moral Dilemmas
         about Prejudice   135
      Phase Three: Field Placements — Adolescents As
         Moral Educators   138
   WAS PREJUDICE REDUCED IN THE GROUP?   141
   IMPLICATIONS AND SUGGESTIONS FOR FUTURE
      CURRICULUM   144

8   ADOLESCENT MORAL REASONING ABOUT SEXUAL AND
   INTERPERSONAL DILEMMAS   146
   Ann DiStefano

   RATIONALE   146
   SEXUAL IDENTITY IN ADOLESCENCE   150
   ADOLESCENT MORAL REASONING   153
   A PRACTITIONER'S VIEW OF KOHLBERG   153
   THE CURRICULUM   156
   RESEARCH RESULTS   160
   THE CURRICULUM IN RETROSPECT   160

9   MORAL EDUCATION FOR ADOLESCENTS   165
   Paul Sullivan

   PERSONAL INTRODUCTIONS   166
   PHASE 1: MORAL DISCUSSIONS   166
   PHASE 2: COUNSELING AND EMPATHY TRAINING   170
   PHASE 3: MORAL PSYCHOLOGY AND PHILOSOPHY   172
   PHASE 4: ADOLESCENTS AS MORAL EDUCATORS   176
      Creating a Board of Appeals   176
      Leading Moral Discussions with Elementary School Students   179
   EVALUATION   182

10   **THE SOCIAL BEHAVIOR OF STUDENTS AT DIFFERENT STAGES OF DEVELOPMENT**   188
Mark Masterson

DEVELOPMENTAL THEORY   188
EMPIRICAL RESEARCH   189
BALES' THEORY AND MEASURE   191
THE RESEARCH METHODOLOGY   193
    The Sample   193
    Research Procedures   193
    Data Processes   194
    Clinical Observations   194
    Behavior Patterns   194
THE RESULTS   195
    Students at Preconventional Developmental Levels   196
    Students at Conventional Developmental Levels   198
    Postconventional Ego Stages   200
CONCLUSION   201

JUNIOR HIGH SCHOOL CURRICULA

11   **THE MORAL EDUCATION OF EARLY ADOLESCENTS**   205
Diana Pritchard Paolitto

CHARACTERISTICS OF EARLY ADOLESCENT
    DEVELOPMENT   205
THE PROGRAM   208
    Phase One: Understanding Moral Dilemmas   209
    Phase Two: Communicating Moral Dilemmas   209
    Phase Three: Learning about the Moral Dilemmas of
      People in the Community   211
THE IMPACT OF THE COURSE   215

12   **FACING HISTORY AND OURSELVES: HOLOCAUST AND HUMAN BEHAVIOR**   216
Margot Stern Strom

A RATIONALE FOR TEACHING THE HOLOCAUST   216
AN OVERVIEW OF THE CURRICULUM   218
TRAINING TEACHERS FOR THE HOLOCAUST
    CURRICULUM   219
PREPARING STUDENTS FOR THE HOLOCAUST
    CURRICULUM   221

Chapter   Page

    A CASE STUDY OF THE HOLOCAUST CURRICULUM   222
        Anti-Semitism   222
        Victims of Tyranny   228
    EVALUATION   232

ELEMENTARY SCHOOL CURRICULA

13 MORAL EDUCATION IN THE ELEMENTARY SCHOOL: UNCON-
    VENTIONAL METHODS FOR CONVENTIONAL GOALS   237
    David Stuhr and Louise Rundle

    MORAL STAGES AS EDUCATIONAL GOALS   237
    ELEMENTARY EDUCATION AS PREPARATION   238
    CURRICULUM DEVELOPMENT IN MORAL EDUCATION
        IN THE 1970s   239
    A CURRICULUM IN CLASSROOM DEMOCRACY   240
        Planning for the Curriculum   241
        Teaching the Curriculum   242
        Results   242
    ISSUES IN PROMOTING MORAL DEVELOPMENT IN THE
        ELEMENTARY SCHOOL CLASSROOM   243
        Considerations of Teacher Authority and Student
          Responsibility   244
        The Children's Perceptions   244
        The Children's Activity   245
        Implications for Curriculum Development   245
        Teacher Training   246
    BROADENING THE PERSPECTIVE   247
        Parental Involvement   247
        School Implications   248

14 MORAL DEVELOPMENT IN ELEMENTARY SCHOOL
    CLASSROOMS   250
    Roger Aubrey

    CLASSROOM MANAGEMENT AND MORALITY   251
    WHAT'S IN IT FOR ME?   251
        Please Administration   252
        Improved Management   252
        Guilt   253
        Ignorance   253

Improvement   253
New Challenge   253
DEALING WITH DISSONANCE   254
HOW DO WE DO IT?   255
WHAT'S THE RIGHT ANSWER?   256
HOW DO WE GET THEM TO LISTEN AND DISCUSS
     AND NOT TO FIGHT?   257
EVALUATING AND USING MATERIALS EFFECTIVELY   258
WHAT ABOUT PARENTS?   260
HOW DO WE KNOW ANYTHING IS HAPPENING?   261

JUST COMMUNITY AND SCHOOL DEMOCRACY RESEARCH

15   AN ALTERNATIVE HIGH SCHOOL BASED ON KOHLBERG'S
     JUST COMMUNITY APPROACH TO EDUCATION   265
     Elsa Wasserman

     STARTING THE SCHOOL   266
     THE JUST COMMUNITY SCHOOL AND RESEARCH
         ON THE CONDITIONS NECESSARY FOR MORAL
         DEVELOPMENT   268
     THE STRUCTURE OF THE JUST COMMUNITY SCHOOL   270
     THE CLUSTER SCHOOL IN OPERATION   272
     ASSESSING THE CONDITIONS FOR MORAL GROWTH   273
     LOOKING AHEAD   277

16   A DEMOCRATIC HIGH SCHOOL: COMING OF AGE   279
     Ralph Mosher

     PART ONE: COMING OF AGE AS A DEMOCRATIC
         HIGH SCHOOL   282
         Year Three: 1977-78   282
         Year Four: 1978-79   286
     PART TWO: STAGE 5, EVEN IF YOU CAN GET THERE,
         ISN'T ENOUGH   293
         The Good News   293
         Epilogue   301

17   EDUCATING FOR DEMOCRATIC COMMUNITY: SOME
     UNRESOLVED DILEMMAS   303
     Joseph Reimer and Clark Power

          THE MOVE TO DEMOCRATIC SCHOOLS   303
          THE JUST COMMUNITY APPROACH   305
          THE MORAL ATMOSPHERE OF THE DEMOCRATIC SCHOOL   306
          THE EVOLUTION OF NORMS IN THE CLUSTER SCHOOL   310
          THE DRUG ISSUE   311
          INTEGRATION AND COMMUNITY BUILDING   315
          ADVOCACY WITH INQUIRY   317
          THE UNRESOLVED COMMUNAL DILEMMA   319
          CONCLUSIONS   320

18   DEMOCRACY IN THE ELEMENTARY SCHOOL   321
     Thomas Lickona and Muffy Paradise

          THE CASE FOR DEMOCRACY   321
              What Is Democracy?   322
              Why Democracy with Children?   322
              Democracy and Valuing the Child's Point of View   323
              Democracy and Rules   326
              Democracy and Conflict   328
          PROBLEMS OF DEMOCRACY   329
              Lessons for Successful Democracy   331
              Democracy and the Wider School   335
          THE BENEFITS OF DEMOCRACY   336

PART III: PARENTS AS MORAL EDUCATORS

19   THE FAMILY AND MORAL EDUCATION   341
     Sheila Stanley

          THE FAMILY AS A MORAL EDUCATOR   343
          THE COURSE   344
              Phase One: Communication Skills   344
              Phase Two: The Family Meeting   346
              Phase Three: A Democratic Approach to Conflict
                  Resolution   349
              Phase Four: Dissension over Values   350
          EVALUATION OF THE COURSE   352

Chapter	Page

20 PARENTS AS MORAL EDUCATORS   356
Robert Azrak

THE TECHNICAL ASPECTS OF THE STUDY   358
THE COURSE FOR PARENTS   359
   Phase I: Introduction to Moral Development Theory   360
   Phase II: Typical Discipline Issues   361
   Phase III: Promoting Moral Development through Discipline   361
RESULTS OF THE STUDY   362
DISCUSSION OF THE RESULTS   363

PART IV: CONCLUSIONS

21 MORAL EDUCATION: THE NEXT GENERATION   369
Ralph Mosher

THE CASE FOR THE FIRST GENERATION   370
THE SINS OF THE FATHER   373
   On Icarus, and Flying Too High   374
   Was Anyone in Charge Here?   374
   Funny Things Happen on the Way to Commencement   375
   The Frailties of the First Generation in Summary   377
WHAT HAVE WE LEARNED FROM A DECADE
OF APPLIED RESEARCH IN DEVELOPMENTAL
AND MORAL EDUCATION?   378
   Knowledge from Practice   379
   New Understanding of School and Its Effects
    on Children's Development   380
RESOLUTIONS FOR A NEXT GENERATION   381
CONCLUSION   385

BIBLIOGRAPHY   386

ABOUT THE CONTRIBUTORS   411

LIST OF TABLES AND FIGURES

Table		Page
2.1	Definitions of Moral Stages	22
2.2	Examples of Responses at Stages 1 through 4	24
3.1	Objectives and Activities of the Danforth Moral Education Program, 1974-77	72
7.1	Theoretical Relationship of Ego and Moral Stages to Prejudice	128
7.2	Correlation Matrix of Pretest Scores for Experimental and Control Groups	142
8.1	Identity Development in Adolescence	149
8.2	Qualitative Analysis of Change in Moral Reasoning for Experimental Group	162
8.3	Qualitative Analysis of Change in Moral Reasoning for Control Group	162
14.1	Criteria in Reviewing Programs of Moral Guidance and Humanistic Education	259
16.1	SWS — One-Year Change Data, 1977-78	297
17.1	Phases of the Collective Norm	308
17.2	The Modal Phase Scores	312
17.3	Relationship of Modal Phases to Reported Norm Violation	313

Figure		
3.1	Research Development and Diffusion Model of Change	78
8.1	Group Pretest and Posttest Means for Kohlberg Moral Judgment Interview	161
9.1	Group Pretest and Posttest Means for Kohlberg Moral Judgment Interview	184
9.2	Group Pretest and Posttest Means for Loevinger Sentence Completion Test	185

PART I

A FRAMEWORK FOR MORAL EDUCATION

1
AN UNCOMMON CAUSE

Ralph Mosher

To report any continuing event seven years after its inception is a challenge. Indeed, to identify a beginning is somewhat arbitrary. There is the problem of oversimplifying a complex interaction of purposes, people, and events. Bias and selective inattention always push at the pen of the reporter; some things are honestly (or better) forgotten, episodes that seem important in passing are given a reduced proportion in hindsight. A tendency exists to make our purposes more rational or systematic than they were in process, to stress our successes rather than our failures, and so on. The virtues of the academy — scholarship, *veritas*, the creation of knowledge, the scientific method — have their dialectical vices: the business of generating funding for research, academic politics, the egos of professors.

We begin with these acknowledgements not out of a sense of preciousness but because they always operate and undoubtedly have in the project to be reported in this book. There will be an effort on the authors' part to be absolutely honest with the topics and the analyses of what we did and did not accomplish. And this is more than a cosmetic effort to make the hidden curriculum of a book on moral education consistent with its rhetoric. The topic is so important as to merit the most rigorous and reliable thinking possible. If moral education is "sold" to the profession or the public by partial truths, a profound fraud would result.

WHY MORAL EDUCATION?

Such demurrers lead to the rationale for research on moral education. Why moral education, why our research on this matter, foundation support for it, and a book reporting what we have learned? The answers to these questions are complex and we will deal with the several roots of this research in detail. We begin with some of the broader reasons for the study of moral education and then turn to the interests of the particular institutions and individuals who joined in this uncommon endeavor. It is not a contradiction to cite one man as a prime mover. Lawrence Kohlberg of Harvard had devoted some 20 years of psychological research to morality and its development over the human life-span. That research had eventuated in a view of morality as the structure of the individual's reasoning about issues of right and wrong, one's rights and obligations, plus the contention that mature moral judgment is not only intellectually encompassing but based in universalizable principles of respect for each individual and for justice in society. Further, Kohlberg had described, empirically, six stages in the development of our moral reasoning and how morality is stimulated. His theoretical work had received national and international attention. He also had given several years to efforts, both in public schools and in prisons, to stimulate moral reasoning.

Because of Kohlberg's research (and Piaget's as well) education was privy to a new and significant body of psychological knowledge about morality and how it develops. That knowledge is reviewed at length in Chapter 2. One general feature of this psychological explanation of morality made it especially applicable to education. That was its assertion that our thinking about right and wrong is substantially affected by our experience of moral problems and the thinking of other people about the right thing to do. The psychology is an interactionist one. The ethical rules and criteria in our heads mature, become more thoughtful and principled, as we make real moral choices and hear or debate conflicting opinions about what we should do, choose, or think. The nature of the person's experience affects his moral thinking. That is a formula for systematic (moral) education, something that had been eschewed in American public education for a generation because of the failure of earlier programs based on indoctrination.

Adolescence: A Prime Time for Moral Education

Both Kohlberg's research and the long-standing experience of educators indicates that adolescence is a special time for deciding on a set of values by which to order and live one's life. Most people who write about adolescents, for example, refer to the idealism of this age group. Adolescents have to make difficult personal decisions of right and wrong. Their moral concern and sensibility easily may be subverted into rigid political ideology, into new and exotic moralities or religions, or into despair. Under this lies a concern to make moral and ethical sense of their world. Ritual disagreements with authorities (for example, parents or teachers) and an idolatry of unconventional flora (for example, "grass") and fauna (what adult can dig Elton John's costumes?) mask a profound adolescent movement toward the social and moral conventions of the family, the church, and the state. Indeed, if adolescence goes according to the development script it is a rehearsal and perfecting of the lines, roles, norms, and rules of being an adult. In a social sense, adolescence means giving up an exclusive selfishness, a hedonism, and an instrumental use of others. The perspective that replaces this "me firstism" is a gradually enlarging recognition of the rights and feelings of other people, typically friends and family, but there can be a genuine concern, too, for others in the family of man. How else can you explain the idealism of 25-mile walkathons for victims of muscular dystrophy or fasts for African famine relief?

Because of Kohlberg's major theoretical contributions we have a relatively clear blueprint for this aspect of human development. That is we know the characteristics of moral reasoning in childhood and adolescence, its progression, and some, at least, of the experiences critical to its stimulation. A precis of Kohlberg's Stage 2 moral reasoning or of Stage 3 would be premature here; it appears in the next chapter. Yet these stages are powerful characterizations or metaphors for preadolescence and adolescence. The knowledge that the systematic discussion of moral dilemmas, learning to understand the thinking and feeling of other people, action on behalf of social and moral goals, and experiences in democratic rule-making and in creating fairer institutions can stimulate development from Stage 2 to Stage 3 is both less gratuitous to the reader and what we should expect from developmental moral education. Indeed knowledge specific enough to *order* these experiences and others to stimulate consecutive development is an aim and criterion of developmental education. Much of the book deals with this challenge. The general point is that developmental psychology, in Kohlberg's work, has established with considerable validity and specificity "what [moral] tendencies are especially seeking expression at a particular time" (Dewey 1964, pp. 5-6). The evidence of developmental psychology also is that the child and especially the adolescent is less likely to develop any more sophisticated ethical position as an adult if his natural efforts to create a personal moral philosophy are unsupported by systematic moral education. So adolescence is established by developmental psychology as a prime time for values or ethical education of a nonindoctrinative character.

WATERGATE

Watergate and what it has come to symbolize has meant renewed public interest and support for programs in moral education in the public schools. To say that people do not trust the country's political leadership, the agencies of our government (for example, the CIA or state welfare programs), American corporations (for example, the oil companies), the military, the police, and so on, is to repeat the litany of the public opinion polls. One of President Carter's most telling campaign promises was to reconstruct a government as good as the American people. Vietnam had represented a deadly assault on America's belief in the special destiny and decency of its political leaders, foreign policy, and its "boys." Some of the best of those boys were driven into bitter exile for their moral convictions, those who fought in Vietnam are not honored. The fear that other young people will be corrupted by drugs, alcohol, crime, or pornography is pervasive. The erosion of conventional morality (as reflected in crime, abortion, divorce rates, family disorganization, violence, and so on) is widely chronicled. Meanwhile, whole groups in America — women, blacks, chicanos, homosexuals — assert long-denied constitutional and human rights. More parochially, the back-to-the-basics movement in public education is, among other things, an effort by parents to enforce conventional morality in the schools: in discipline, dress codes, study habits, and so on.

Against this background it is perhaps not surprising that a high proportion of Americans (4 of 5 in recent Gallup polls) support moral education in the public schools. What the respondents mean by moral education is, of course, moot. Probably the teaching of virtues such as honesty, respect for adults, moderation in the use of alcohol/drugs, good grades, sexual restraint, and so on. But the development of the public school programs in moral education reported in this book was tolerated or made possible by this complex of public attitudes toward morality and its current corruption at so many levels of the society.

It is important to say also that many of the authors in this book, especially Kohlberg, had been concerned with morality, scholarly research on its development, and with moral education for some time before the polls, press headlines, and public uneasiness made what we were doing topical. Educators would have to exceed Caesar's wife in virtue not to capitalize on an idea whose time appeared to have come. That seems to be the case with moral education. Hopefully this book will also establish that we knew things about morality and how to educate for it — and were to learn much more — (that is, that we were not Johnny-come-latelys). To the contrary this is the report of a scholarly, longitudinal effort to create moral education of genuine substance (an effort that, as a matter of fact, is still on-going).

Institutional Roots: Boston and Harvard Universities

A personal belief that character is absolutely central in human beings and to the quality of their social life was not my only qualification for editorship of this monograph. Norman Sprinthall and I had begun to create education to enhance adolescents' psychological development at Harvard in the late 1960s (Mosher and Sprinthall 1970). Transferred, reasonably intact, to Boston University and the University of Minnesota in the early 1970s, that work was evolving a set of objectives that represent another taproot of the research reported in this book. Those objectives (sharpened, like cheddar, by age) were fivefold:

1. To establish, in two graduate departments of counseling, a program in what was first called psychological and later developmental, education. (This book describes program research at Boston University. The substantial curriculum development and teacher training at Minnesota is reported elsewhere — see Miller 1976). Graduate students, both at the master's and doctoral level, were placed for practical internship experience in several Boston-area public schools, Brookline principal among them. Brookline faculty members reciprocally chose to pursue doctoral study at Boston University. Both gown and town shared common ideological and practical commitments. The ideology will be described shortly. Among the practical agreements was a belief in substantial field-based professional training, influenced broadly by the model of the clinical years of medical education. Important aspects of that preparation for practice were the creation, teaching, and evaluation of innovative curricula to stimulate personal (including moral) development in children and adolescents. Such curriculum development in the schools was seen as a powerful way to prepare graduate students and prospective educational leaders. There was a clearly enunciated professional leadership (and probably elitist) objective in the university program; yet at the same time these students were to get their hands dirty, and were joined by faculty, in the developing and testing of such curricula. The faculty, like the Israeli officer corps or the ablest clinical professor in the medical school, led from the front.

2. To develop knowledge from practice. There is an underlying epistemological view here that is critical to an understanding of the investment in moral education represented in this book. Other educators and I have expressed an epistemological dissatisfaction about the producing of new knowledge concerning classroom teaching and learning. Schaefer's (1967) remarkable John Dewey Society Lecture was precisely on this issue. Schaefer dealt not only with the initial training of teachers (where James Conant in 1963 has begun and ended) but also with the more difficult problem of the intellectual renewal of the experienced teacher and the school as an educational institution. His focus was a comprehensive one: how the school, as a whole, can avoid becoming static, a library of congress for the transmission of knowledge to the young. His bet was on the classic aphrodisiac of the academy: inquiry. But it was to be inquiry of a special kind: focused on the fundamental issues of what is to be taught, how, by whom, where, and with what outcomes for the student.

My only disagreement with Schaefer's analysis had to do with his credulity that added sophistication in "concepts and theories of the social sciences will afford valuable ways of viewing the world of the school" (Schaefer 1967). Means typically serve old, not new, ends. Fully as likely an outcome are further concepts, theories, and findings about the social sciences.

The essential need is for knowledge to direct practice, yet it seems that we know precious little about either our teaching or how to develop curriculum. The problem is especially clear with regard to teaching. Biddle and Ellena's (1964, p. 3) statement that "[after 40 years of research] we do not know how to define, prepare for, or measure teacher competence" is a staggering commentary on the way in which we have been conceiving of and doing research in education.

Similarly, most curriculum development during the 1960s and 1970s in this country has entailed rationalizing the existing courses of study. With few exceptions these new and better curricula in mathematics, the sciences, and so on, have not been produced by educators. Schwaab (1972, p. 81) noted this as one of the signs that the field of curriculum is moribund; "[there has been] a translocation of its problems and the solving of them from the nominal practitioners of the field to other men." Schwaab's view that the field of curriculum is moribund is important in several ways to a central argument of this chapter. I see curriculum development and evaluation as one of the defining characteristics and methods of a new, more applied research in education. Professional study in education has not been oriented, nor has it operated, in this way. The reasons for this are complicated and include deference to the academy, but the field of curriculum itself is culpable. It has preferred to build models rather than to do — that is, to develop curricula. And if education has abandoned to the academy the maintenance of the existing curriculum, the profession's rigor mortis is even more apparent in regard to curriculum reformulation. By this I mean the producing of genuinely new curriculum, courses for which there is no contemporary precedent in the school. Programs to stimulate students' moral reasoning or democratic high school and classroom interventions are examples.

Are there alternatives, any complementary ways to generate knowledge to direct practice? One way to create such knowledge is from practice itself. I have used the term "clinical research and development" to describe this way of working (Mosher 1974). The method is an alternating cycle of reflection and action, hard thinking, careful practice, and evaluation designed to produce a more comprehensive understanding of the educational problem and its possible solutions. This style of working avoids certain possible concomitants of reflection or theory by itself (for example, intellectual structures that do not comprehend the complexity of the educational problem, "poor" theory, disinclination to act) as well as the pitfalls of unexamined action (that is, which tends to be ad hoc and to develop low-order solutions that work).

Underlying this applied educational research and development are some simple but basic assumptions. One is that educational practice (what and how children are taught) is the first business of education. Most schools are overwhelmed with the teaching of children. Basic research in psychology and sociology regards educational practices as a problem for later, or for someone else. A focus on children's instruction and learning and a commitment to improve it are basic to clinical research and development. A second related assumption is that the generic need is for *knowledge* to improve educational practices. Clinical research and development is not simply another name for educational problem solving. Problems in practice will be solved and educational problem solvers will be trained in this way. More significantly, the general knowledge base and professional understanding from which education practice derives will be increased. Without such a capability to study and improve its educational practices, the "profession" will remain largely fixated and dependent for effect on the gifted teacher and for progress on the uncertain commitment and outcome of basic research in the social sciences.

The idea of producing knowledge from the deliberate manipulation and analysis of practice, while radical in one sense, can also connote a slow incremental process. Criticism of what is wrong in our schools in this sense is cheap. A much more compelling and complex task is to conceive of alternative curricula and teaching and to test them out. It is also necessary to train educators with the capabilities and commitment to work this way. A majority of the chapters in this book are written by such professionals.

Clinical research and development, then, is one way in which practitioners can inquire, study, and add to the body of knowledge about the profession. The idea that substantial knowledge can be generated from practice is seemingly the hardest concept to understand. The usual mind set is that practice derives either from theory or from basic research. The idea that we can add both to our conceptualizing and practice in education by validating one against the other is not unique. To my knowledge, the work in moral and developmental education at Boston University, Harvard, and Minnesota since 1969 has been the first to test and act upon this central idea. After seven years of effort, we are still a long way from having plumbed the idea fully. But this book per se is evidence that important professional knowledge can be generated from practice that adheres to this method.

So one source of the programs in moral education reported here was epistemological — the need to create a type of knowledge uniquely necessary to public education. Such knowledge was to be generated by systematic applied research on curriculum and teaching, as core processes in education, informed by pertinent psychological theory of the learner. It was not to be the pale carbon copy of social science research that crowds the pages of educational journals. Assuming educators might reconstruct some of their schooling practices in this way, the question remained: to what ends was this more powerful pedagogy to be applied? How were we to decide what curricula to develop and teach? What knowledge is of most worth?

3. To use development as the aim of education. To say that the most important question the educator faces is that of the aims of education can be a cliché, yet most education goes on unmindful of such questioning, or the answers are assumed to be tacit. When aims are made explicit they have about them the air of real clichés. The curriculum research at Boston University had clear philosophical and ideological premises (that is not as arrogant as asserting them to be right, simply clear). A first was that educational ends are to be taken very seriously, thought about deeply, stated clearly, defended philosophically. Our educational aim, in essence, is the enhancement of the individual's development within a democratic society. Human development, in this definition, is

broadly or holistically understood. It includes at least nine interrelated dimensions of human growth and behavior: cognitive, moral, social, political, ego, affective, physical, vocational, aesthetic. All are considered equally important to the individual's life and happiness. Equality of opportunity for every person to develop them to the full is the hallmark of a democratic society and its institutions (most critically, its educational institutions). Democracy, because of its commitment to the general welfare, to social justice, to citizen participation in deciding public policy, and to the enhancement of individual dignity is the ideal form of governance and way of life. Education thus aims to promote individual development and a democratic society.

This states the ends of education in comprehensive, unambiguous terms. The whole research effort reported in this book is intended to translate the broad aims of individual development and social democracy into consistent, valid educational practices. It is here that the more powerful clinical research and development discussed above join forces with powerful ends. Powerful ideas, after all, are the only ones worth advancing. Nor are these aims new. This is a conception of education as old or as "progressive" as John Dewey. It and its contemporary restatements will be more fully elaborated in Chapter 2. A brief excerpt from Dewey (1964, p. 15) suggests its lineage:

> The aim of education is development of individuals to the utmost of their potentialities. But this statement in isolation leaves unanswered the question as to what is the measure of development. A society of free individuals in which all, through their own work, contribute to the liberation and enrichment of the lives of others, is the only environment in which any individual can really grow normally to his full stature.

4. To translate modern developmental psychology to education. The work at Boston University, Harvard, and Minnesota in "neoprogressivism" has been significantly influenced by modern developmental psychology. A fuller exposition of developmental theory of morality is made in Chapter 2. I have elsewhere (Mosher 1979) reviewed these theories and why they are particularly important to education. It is appropriate to summarize some of that case. Developmental psychologists are engaged in the analysis of human competencies (for example, of logical thinking, morality, and so on). They provide descriptions of the mature characteristics of such competencies (for example, Piaget's formal operations define mature logic; Kohlberg's Stages 5 and 6 describe mature moral reasoning). Even more important, developmental psychology describes how these competencies evolve, the steps or stages in that growth. The stage descriptions are comprehensive; they permit us to locate and understand individuals and, if we are teachers, to plan specific educational experiences and learning to enhance their further development. Developmental psychology is also involved in identifying what it is that leads to the growth or blocking of these competencies.

Finally, developmental psychology can help educators establish where individuals are in the learning of these competencies.

We have already said that developmental psychology is interactionist, that is, it finds human development to depend heavily on the person's experience. Education can be a powerful Socratic prod to growth. Developmental psychology accords to systematic experience a major influence in the construction of human personality and actively seeks a common cause with educators toward that goal. Further, the course of the individual's growth is toward greater rationality and character. This is a psychology of man ascending, and it is perhaps especially American in its optimism about human potential. It describes young people as growing, mutable; progressing to adult intellectuality, morality, identity, and as capable of higher-order human thought, affect, and behavior as they are of barbarism. The demons and unconscious personality employed by other theories are less emphasized; education, properly constituted and practiced, can be a critical humanizing factor. Few psychologies, as a matter of fact, have been as comprehensive and holistic in their view of human competencies, as optimistic about human capability, or as open to an equal partnership with education as has developmental psychology.

5. To provide moral guidance. A concern with the all-around development of every child and generation of educational knowledge and programs to that end is a logical corollary, yet this is a nontraditional view of the proper role of psychologists and counselors in schools. Much of the research on moral education described in this book has been done by counselors. Given its preoccupations over the past several decades, the field of guidance is an unlikely handmaiden to such efforts. Therefore, the criticism of existing psychological services in American public schools and the new rationale for guidance that led to the partnership with moral education needs spelling out.

Guidance has had a long search for its identity. Historically, counselors began by matching man and job. Assessment, in the form of the testing of intelligence, academic achievement, job aptitude, vocational interest, and personality followed. Most recently, the field has been preoccupied with providing psychotherapy or psychological counseling to troubled children, adolescents, and adults. Guidance has had an important influence, both real and symbolic, on education. It has consistently argued the importance of emotional, social, and vocational development in an educational system giving priority to intellect; it has valued the individual against the institution and believed in his potential. Guidance has promised much and delivered too little, yet it remains an important ideology in public education.

As the little red schoolhouse recently has come under increasing criticism, so, too, has the little white clinic in it. Less than half the counselors in the United States have had training in psychological counseling. "Longitudinal studies indicate that these fields [counseling, guidance, and school psychology] failed to successfully prognose, much less cure mental illness partly because they confused mental illness with deviance from the middle class norms of the schools" (Kohlberg 1971, p. 81).

A New Rationale for Guidance

Guidance has been a stepchild; it has derived its theory from other sources: industrial psychology, educational psychology, clinical psychology, and psychiatry. The programs at Boston University and Minnesota reflect a belief that counseling must transcend its derivative status and overcome a passivity and inefficacy in the face of great human pain, confusion, and need. The time is opportune for a reformation of counseling's objectives; indeed, new initiatives are essential. A basic need is for theory that will enable the field to move beyond a primary concern with the treatment or rehabilitation of atypical individuals or subpopulations (for example, school underachievers, the emotionally disturbed, drug-dependent adolescents). John Dewey, as noted, argued that the stimulation of human development is the basic objective of education. Lawrence Cremin has said that guidance is the most characteristic child of the progressive movement in American education. Within a concern for all-around personal development, then, we believe that guidance should provide educational experiences that help every individual grow as a person, specifically in terms of moral, emotional, social, and vocational development. These are the dimensions that historically have concerned and at least implicitly unified the fields of counseling, guidance, and school psychology. Thus we both reassert and reformulate generic objectives in arguing that the stimulation of personal, emotional, ethical, social, and vocational development for all is the basic justification for the professional specialty of guidance.

We believe further that counseling should contribute leadership in educational and psychological programs to stimulate human development on these dimensions. Counselors, as we see it, will work where crucial educational effects on ego, emotional, and moral development occur; in schools, with teachers and students; in the community, with parents and the numerous educational resources that exist there. Functionally, this means the counselor must have the ability to analyze, prescribe, and act for psychological growth with individuals, organizations, and in the community. He will collaborate with others in stimulating development in individuals and in the organizations or social systems that affect their growth.

Obviously, it is presumptuous to suggest that counselors can realize these aims by themselves. We envisage a professional who knows more, does more, and has different priorities than at present. The requisite theoretical and educational programs already exist to make it possible for counselors to be moral educators. We have had at least three reasons for focusing counselors' attention on moral education. The first has already been set out: the basic purpose of education and of guidance is the stimulation of individual development and social democracy. The programs in moral education described in Part II of this book are examples of education designed to enhance personal (more specifically, character) development in children and adolescents. Second, we believe that counselors, just as is true for other educators, should be knowledgeable of the substantial theoretical and applied research now going on in moral education. Third, we believe that counselors are uniquely confronted by the moral dilemmas with which children and adolescents (and, to some degree, parents) struggle and that they have many skills and contributions essential to effective programs of moral education. For these reasons we have trained counselors to act as moral educators. Rather than claiming to be "value neutral" (a claim debunked a decade ago by Shoben's argument that counselors are, in fact, "smugglers" of school and adult — that is, conventional values) we believe that counselors should join teachers, administrators, and parents in the development of systematic programs of moral education in the school and community.

THE DANFORTH MORAL EDUCATION PROJECT: AN UNCOMMON CAUSE

For a complex of contributing reasons, then, the Danforth Project in Moral Education beginning in 1974 was a natural extension of an already existing relationship between Boston University, the Brookline and Cambridge Public Schools, and the Center for Moral Education at Harvard University. We turn now to another taproot of the research and development on moral education to be reported in this book — that is, the objectives of the Danforth project itself. It is important to reiterate that in retrospect it is both easier and harder to sort out and give priority to these objectives than was the case in the beginning. Those readers who have worked in the fluid "natural laboratories" of the public school and have done curriculum development or teacher education there will understand how that could be.

With the tentativeness proper to a nonhistorian, let me suggest that the Danforth project per se had at least the following five objectives:

1. Establish demonstration moral education programs in several public school systems. The Danforth Foundation was interested in exploring the feasibility of moral education in the public school and in supporting pilot projects in curriculum development and teacher training from which the profession and the public might learn. To be able to point to several school systems — Brookline, Cambridge, Pittsburgh, as examples of on-going moral education programs — would be an important building block. It is also essential to note that there is a long history in the Danforth Foundation of commitment to character education.

The focus on moral education in the high school was also a foundation priority. It corresponded with the curriculum development interests of Fenton at Carnegie-Mellon, Kohlberg in Cambridge, and Mosher in Brookline. Subsequently, the curriculum development and teacher education activity in Brookline was extended into the elementary schools and to courses for parents. The reasons for so doing were that much critical moral development was, or was not, happening in childhood and early adolescence and had to be responded to in any comprehensive education program. Elementary school teachers in Brookline also expressed strong interest in moral education; over 100 voluntarily attended an initial series of workshops. Further, Mosher believed that it was important to "give away" to parents, as the natural and historical moral educators of children, whatever special psychological or applied knowledge of children's moral development and its stimulation we possessed.

2. Develop curriculum and staff for moral education. A second objective of the project was, in an analogous way, to give away moral development theory and curriculum development knowledge to teachers and counselors. One of the problems vitiating many of the curriculum reform projects of the 1960s was their elitist origins. Such curricula typically were written by experts: heavily subsidized university scholars, psychologists, or curriculum professionals based either in the universities or research and development laboratories. The curricula which resulted were tried out in various pilot school systems, published commercially, and sold nationally. Teacher training institutes were often given poor-relation treatment in this process. In effect this meant that the curriculum was essentially untouched by practitioners' hands until it reached the Social Studies Department shelves at Jefferson High School in Ames, Iowa. The problem was that it too frequently remained on the shelf.

The Danforth project had, by contrast, a rather touching New England belief in the efficacy of local educational initiative and control. The premise was that teachers and counselors, or a group of them self-selected by interest, could appropriate moral development theory, design their own moral education materials, and be more invested in them by so doing. There was in this a premise of professional respect for, and power to, the practitioner. This in part was attributable to Mosher's earlier involvement with the Harvard TTT (Trainers of Trainers of Teachers) project, where this idea had been tried with some success. An important related expectation was that certain of the teachers and counselors with whom we were to work would become, in turn, the trainers of other teachers. We believed that two things might be expected to get the attention of teachers in general: they were practical courses or programs in moral education and teachers "doing it." In our experience, no university scholar has the credibility with teachers as does one of their own demonstrating, explaining, and indicating enthusiasm for moral (or other kinds of innovative) education. One key product of the Danforth project, then, would be indigenous moral education courses/materials; a second was to be teachers able to train other practitioners in curriculum design and pedagogy for moral education. We have already discussed the underlying epistemological view that significant professional knowledge can be created by the analysis of practice. It is not naive to expect some teachers to contribute to the reconstruction of knowledge about the learner and the craft of teaching; indeed they can be professionally vitalized by such applied inquiry.

3. Develop a town-gown partnership. Another objective or effect of the Danforth project was to create a working partnership in moral education between a foundation, two universities, and two public school systems (one quasi suburban, the other quasi urban) in the Boston area. Harvard was an international center for theoretical research on the psychology of moral development and its measurement. Substantial applied work in prisons and education was also ongoing. Boston University was a national center for applied research in moral and other areas of developmental education plus the graduate education of counselors and teachers. The pupil personnel and guidance services of the Brookline public schools, as noted, were already closely allied with Boston University in graduate training and program development. They joined with the director of social studies and the high school social studies department in bringing the Danforth project to Brookline. Subsequent chapters by the superintendent, Robert Sperber; the director of social studies, Henry Zabierek, and the former director of guidance and health education, Roger Aubrey, discuss the school system's objectives/terms in this partnership.

4. Establish school democracy. From the beginning the effort in Cambridge was to create, sustain, and study the effects on students' moral development of a "just community" high school, the Cluster School.

This project, with Kohlberg as the principal architect and builder, had been operating for one year with support from the Kennedy Foundation. It derived from prior applied research on moral development in a women's prison in Niantic, Connecticut, which involved a group of inmates in the governance and management of their residence and institutional life together. A basic premise was that the "justice structure" of schools (that is, their rules, discipline codes, adjudication of disciplinary infractions, governance, recognition of student and faculty rights, and so on) is their fundamental, if "hidden," moral curriculum. Because it is a largely tacit way of thinking or code it may be even more pervasive and profoundly educative.

Kohlberg believed that this covert moral education was ripe for being rationalized; that moral education within the curriculum of an unjustly administered school or prison was an obvious contradiction. Students and faculty should share in deciding the rules and purposes of their school and educational life together. Each person should have an equal voice and vote in building the school community and in governing it fairly. In that way the "real" moral issues of the school, currently hidden or adjudicated and catechized by teachers or administrators, would become the direct source of the student's moral education. Chapter 15 describes the evolution of the Cluster School during its first three years. Certainly the school represents the most rigorous translation of Kohlberg's ideas of a just community into educational practice.

In the second year of the Danforth project a somewhat parallel study of a democratic alternative high school was begun by Mosher in Brookline. Here the circumstances were different. The School-Within-A-School (henceforth SWS) was not created de novo, as had been the Cluster School, nor was there a central commitment to moral education or the just community ideology.

SWS had been established as an alternative school within Brookline High School in 1969; it had traditions of its own: a more personal relationship between the teacher and student, freedom for the student, relativism about the norms of the larger high school, and so on. There was, however, a concern to involve the students in genuine self-government of the school and to build a greater sense of social cohesion or community. The evolution of SWS toward participatory democracy and what has been learned there about the possibilities and limits of school democracy are described in Chapter 16.

5. Finally, the Danforth project was primarily concerned with educational development – that is, the purpose was to involve teachers in creating and trying out moral education curricula and to develop two democratic or just community alternative high schools. A variety of moral education courses and materials, integral to several subject areas of high school, was seen as needed. Similarly, an examination of what forms a democratic high school might take was an important developmental objective. Research on the effects of the varied moral education curricula was done but it was not the first concern. Indeed, no Danforth monies were allocated to research. It was done as part of the rules of passage of all doctoral candidates and through Kohlberg's interest. The initial priority was to create prototype courses, staff development workshops, and revised institutional arrangements for moral education.

TAKING THE MEASURE OF THE PROJECT

In summary, the Danforth project, in conjunction with established programs at Boston University and Harvard, had as its objective at least three "products." A first was moral education materials and courses to be used in two school systems. These courses would "demonstrate" how moral and ethical issues might be taught within the context of several areas of the high (and elementary) school curriculum. There was no plan that pilot materials for all areas of the high school curriculum would be produced; indeed, significant subject areas – mathematics and the sciences – were not involved. The reasons for that omission were purely situational to Brookline and Cambridge, such subject areas are obviously rich in moral content. (The Tacoma Public Schools' "Ethical Quest" project is furthering curriculum development in these subject areas, for example.) Nor was there the hypothesis that moral education materials produced in Brookline or Cambridge would be of use nationally, although that has, to some degree, proved to be the case. The aim was modest: local moral education materials and programs, created and used by teachers or counselors within the school's regular curriculum and likely, for that reason, to survive the project.

A second product was to be practical knowledge of how the school as an institution affects the moral development of students and how that effect might be altered by school democracy. It was assumed that the school, in the way it operates as a whole – its governance, discipline, authority, and so on – educates children's moral thinking and behavior. To the extent that tacit curriculum could be made more democratic; to the degree that students and faculty could openly debate and decide the school's policy and rules, its discipline: the terms that would govern their social and academic life together and do so against considerations of fairness and the common good; to that degree moral education would become both very real and influential. During the life of the project a beginning was made in elaborating these ideas conceptually and in practice.

A third "product" was to be practitioners and professional leadership for moral education programs, both locally and nationally. The latter, more ambitious, aim was reinforced during the project's life by the requests, both for workshops and permanent leadership, made of its personnel.

For example, Ladenburg, Mosher, Paolitto, and Sullivan made substantial early staff development contributions to the Tacoma "Ethical Quest" project. Sullivan, at that point a research associate with Danforth, was appointed director of the Tacoma project late in 1975. The training of educational leaders was a particular aim of the Boston University program and a pressure on the Center for Moral Education at Harvard. The extent to which people originally involved with the Danforth project have moved to positions of educational and academic influence is apparent from the About the Contributors section of this book.

The Brookline Dissemination Center for Moral Education was not explicitly anticipated in 1974, although this kind of role for a school system and for some of the teachers and counselors associated with the project was nurtured very deliberately. Related to this was an effort to coordinate the research and development activities in moral education in Brookline and Cambridge with other parallel programs funded by the Danforth Foundation, for example, Fenton's work in Pittsburgh; Quigley's "Law in a Free Society" project in Santa Monica. Kohlberg gave much attention to this effort.

We close this introductory chapter with a statement of two more personal or idiosyncratic objectives. For Kohlberg, the Danforth project represented an opportunity to see a further application, in education, of his highly seminal theoretical study of morality. His assistance was vital to two educators, Fenton and Mosher, interested in the furtherance of that application. For me, the Danforth project was an opportunity to contribute to an area of education to enhance human development that seemed particularly well-framed by Kohlberg's psychological research. The juxtaposition of resources was promising; and character is of the essence to me. Coupled with the Dewey tradition of education for rationality and character, the professional challenge was to plan a diverse education for a central strand of human development, that is, the moral domain, but always as one further example of what, ultimately, an education for whole human development might be.

A READER'S GUIDE TO THE BOOK

The book is divided into three principal parts. The first five chapters provide a framework for the programs in moral education described in Parts II and III.

It probably is not excessive or parochial to regard Boston as the hub of the moral education movement in the American public schools during the past decade. This chapter has examined the several roots from which the research and development in moral education in Brookline and Cambridge grew. It also is fitting to cite one man as a prime mover. Lawrence Kohlberg, in Chapter 2, summarizes his 20 years of seminal research on morality, its development, and how to promote it by education. Robert Sperber, superintendent of the Brookline Public Schools, then describes in Chapter 3 why and how he incorporated the teaching of morality in public education. He also presents the history and the sequence of the research in Brookline — who developed what curricula, when, and so on. Henry Zabierek, codirector of the Danforth Moral Education Project, explains in Chapter 4 how the Brookline faculty was prepared to teach this "new" subject. Finally, in Chapter 5 Ann Higgins summarizes the data as to the effect on childrens' moral development of the many school and parent educational programs reviewed in Parts II and III.

Part II describes moral education in practice; and there were a lot of practices; 15 chapters' worth in all. High school programs, as they were the first to be developed, are the first to be reviewed. Many roads were taken to Stage 6. Classroom simulation of the constitutional and moral debate of the Founding Fathers in Philadelphia (Ladenburg in Chapter 6); the discussion of racial and ethnic prejudice at Brookline High School in a psychology class (Alexander in Chapter 7), and adolescents teaching moral education to young children (Sullivan in Chapter 9) are examples of the varied forms of moral education studied.

Programs in the junior high schools and elementary schools of Brookline also are reported in separate subsections of Part II. Again the diversity of moral education is represented in chapters on teaching the Nazi Holocaust (Strom in Chapter 12) and Rundle's pioneering study (Chapter 13) of school democracy in a fifth-grade classroom. The "bottom line" issue for some teachers, that is, whether developmental stages in students' thinking have any consequences for their behavior in the classroom, is the subject of a seminal chapter (10) by Masterson.

That John Dewey's shadow loomed longer and longer as the decade progressed is apparent in four chapters that constitute the last section of Part II: "Just Community and School Democracy Research." It describes major formative efforts by Kohlberg to educate for justice (Chapters 15 and 17); by Mosher to increase student participation in self-governance and building of school community (Chapter 16), and by Lickona to promote teachers' understanding and practice of classroom democracy in Brookline's elementary schools (Chapter 18).

One of the splendid fables brought low by our experience was that we could give away to parents, as the "natural" moral educators of their children, our "professional" knowledge of moral development and instruction. However, involving parents in our common cause was very hard to do. The idea remains as logical and compelling as ever. Where we *were* successful in including parents, we found important effects on their children's moral thinking. Nor were the parents themselves unaffected. Part III: "Parents As Moral Educators" reports both the high hopes and the paradoxes of this phase of our research.

2
HIGH SCHOOL DEMOCRACY
AND EDUCATING FOR A
JUST SOCIETY

Lawrence Kohlberg

The first lecture I gave on "Education for a Just Society" was given in 1968, shortly after the death of Martin Luther King (Kohlberg 1970). In it I advocated the Platonic vision of moral education that commenced with the execution of Socrates and ended with the assassination of Martin Luther King. Socrates and King attempted to stimulate a higher level of morality, a level of principles of justice, by questioning and confrontation. I called their level of morality a sixth and highest stage of moral development, a stage of universal principles of justice, of equity and respect for human personality. In this chapter, after reviewing our moral educational efforts directed toward the highest or principled stages of moral judgment, I will focus on our more recent efforts oriented toward creating a sense of justice and community in students at the intermediate or conventional stage of moral judgment. Before elaborating this shift in focus, we will review the moral stages and their implications for moral education. The stages of moral judgment were arrived at from extensive longitudinal and cross-cultural research guided by what I have called the cognitive-development paradigm in psychology and education.

The cognitive-developmental approach was fully stated for the first time by John Dewey. The approach is called cognitive because it recognizes that moral education, like intellectual education, has its basis in stimulating the active thinking of the child about moral issues and decisions. It is called developmental because it sees the aims of moral education as movement through moral stages. According to Dewey (1964, p. 213),

> the aim of education is growth or *development*, both intellectual and
> moral. Ethical and psychological principles can aid the school in the

greatest of all constructions: the building of a free and powerful char-acter. Only knowledge of the *order and connection of the stages in psychological development can insure this.* Education is the work of *supplying the conditions* which will enable the psychological functions to mature in the freest and fullest manner. (Emphasis added.)

Dewey postulated three levels of moral development: the premoral or pre-conventional level "of behavior motivated by biological and social impulses with results for morals"; the *conventional* level of behavior "in which the individual accepts with little critical reflection the standards of his group"; and the auton-omous level of behavior in which "conduct is guided by the individual thinking and judging for himself whether a purpose is good, and does not accept the standard of his group without reflection."*

Dewey's thinking about moral stages was theoretical. Building upon his prior studies of cognitive stages, Jean Piaget (1965) made the first effort to define stages of moral reasoning in children through actual interviews and through observations of children (in games with rules). Using this interview material, Piaget defined the premoral, the conventional, and the autonomous levels as follows: the premoral stage, where there was no sense of obligation to rules; the heteronomous stage, where the right was literal obedience to rules and an equation of obligation with submission to power and punishment (roughly ages 4-8); and the autonomous stage, where the purpose and consequences of following rules are considered and obligation is based on reciprocity and exchange (roughly ages 8-12).†

MORAL STAGES

In 1955 I started to redefine and validate (through longitudinal and cross-cultural study) the Dewey-Piaget levels and stages. The resulting stages are presented in Table 2.1; examples of interview responses are presented in Table 2.2.

We claim to have validated the stages defined in Table 2.1. The notion that stages can be validated by longitudinal study implies that stages have definite empirical characteristics. The concept of stages (as used by Piaget and myself) implies the following characteristics:

Stages are "structured wholes," or organized systems of thought. Individuals are consistent in level of moral judgment.

---

*These levels correspond roughly to our three major levels: the preconventional, the conventional, and the principled. Similar levels were propounded by William McDougall, Leonard Hobhouse, and James Mark Baldwin.

†Piaget's stages correspond to our first three stages: Stage 0 (premoral), Stage 1 (heter-onomous), and Stage 2 (instrumental reciprocity).

TABLE 2.1
DEFINITIONS OF MORAL STAGES

I. Preconventional level

At this level the child is responsive to cultural rules and labels of good and bad, right or wrong, but interprets these labels either in terms of the physical or the hedonistic consequences of action (punishment, reward, exchange of favors) or in terms of the physical power of those who enunciate the rules and labels. The level is divided into the following two stages:

Stage 1: *The punishment-and-obedience orientation.* The physical consequences of action determine its goodness or badness regardless of the human meaning or value of these consequences. Avoidance of punishment and unquestioning deference to power are valued in their own right, not in terms of respect for an underlying moral order supported by punishment and authority (the latter being Stage 4).

Stage 2: *The instrumental-relativist orientation.* Right action consists of that which instrumentally satisfies one's own needs and occasionally the needs of others. Human relations are viewed in terms like those of the market place. Elements of fairness, of reciprocity, and of equal sharing are present, but they are always interpreted in a physical pragmatic way. Reciprocity is a matter of "you scratch my back and I'll scratch yours," not of loyalty, gratitude, or justice.

II. Conventional level

At this level, maintaining the expectations of the individual's family, group, or nation is perceived as valuable in its own right, regardless of immediate and obvious consequences. The attitude is not only one of *conformity* to personal expectations and social order, but of loyalty to it, of actively *maintaining,* supporting, and justifying the order, and of identifying with the persons or group involved in it. At this level, there are the following two stages:

Stage 3: *The interpersonal concordance or "good boy – nice girl" orientation.* Good behavior is that which pleases or helps others and is approved by them. There is much conformity to stereotypical images of what is majority or "natural" behavior. Behavior is frequently judged by intention – "he means well" becomes important for the first time. One earns approval by being "nice."

Stage 4: *The "law and order" orientation.* There is orientation toward authority, fixed rules, and the maintenance of the social order. Right behavior consists of doing one's duty, showing respect for authority, and maintaining the given social order for its own sake.

III. Postconventional, autonomous, or principled level

At this level, there is a clear effort to define moral values and principles that have validity and application apart from the authority of the groups or persons holding these principles and apart from the individual's own identification with these groups. This level again has two stages:

Stage 5: *The social-contract legalistic orientation,* generally with utilitarian overtones. Right action tends to be defined in terms of general individual rights, and standards which have been critically examined and

TABLE 2.1, continued

agreed upon by the whole society. There is a clear awareness of the relativism of personal values and opinions and a corresponding emphasis upon procedural rules for reaching consensus. Aside from what is constitutionally and democratically agreed upon, the right is a matter of personal "values" and "opinion." The result is an emphasis upon the "legal point of view," but with an emphasis upon the possibility of changing law in terms of rational considerations of social utility (rather than freezing it in terms of Stage 4 "law and order"). Outside the legal realm, free agreement and contract is the binding element of obligation. This is the "official" morality of the American government and constitution.

Stage 6: *The universal-ethical-principle orientation.* Right is defined by the decision of conscience in accord with self-chosen *ethical principles* appealing to logical comprehensiveness, universality, and consistency. These principles are abstract and ethical (the Golden Rule, the categorical imperative); they are not concrete moral rules like the Ten Commandments. At heart, these are universal principles of *justice,* of the *reciprocity* and *equality* of human *rights,* and of respect for the dignity of human beings as *individual persons.*

Source: Reprinted from Lawrence Kohlberg. "The Claim to Moral Adequacy of a Highest Stage of Moral Judgment." Journal of Philosophy 70, no. 18 (October 1973): 631-32.

Stages form an invariant sequence, under all conditions except extreme trauma, movement is always forward, never backward. Individuals never skip stages; movement is always to the next stage up.

Stages are "hierarchical integrations." Thinking at a higher stage includes or comprehends within it lower-stage thinking. There is a tendency to function at or prefer the highest stage available.

Each of these characteristics has been demonstrated for moral stages. Stages are defined by responses to a set of verbal moral dilemmas classified according to an elaborate scoring scheme. Validation studies include

A 20-year study of 50 Chicago-area boys, middle and working class. Initially interviewed at ages 10-16, they have been reinterviewed at three-year intervals thereafter.

A small, nine-year longitudinal study of Turkish village and city boys of the same age.

A variety of other cross-sectional studies in Canada, Britain, Israel, Taiwan, Yucatan, Honduras, and India.

With regard to the structured whole or consistency criterion, we have found that more than 50 percent of an individual's thinking is always at one stage, with the remainder at the next adjacent stage (which he is leaving or which he is moving into).

TABLE 2.2
EXAMPLES OF RESPONSES AT STAGES 1 THROUGH 4

In Europe, a woman was near death from a very bad disease, a special kind of cancer. There was one drug that the doctors thought might save her. It was a form of radium that a druggist in the same town had recently discovered. The drug was expensive to make, but the druggist was charging ten times what the drug cost him to make. He paid $200 for the radium and charged $2,000 for a small dose of the drug. The sick woman's husband, Heinz, went to everyone he knew to borrow the money, but he could get together only about $1,000, which was half of what it cost. He told the druggist that his wife was dying, and asked him to sell it cheaper or let him pay later. But the druggist said, "No, I discovered the drug and I'm going to make money from it." Heinz got desperate and broke into the man's store to steal the drug for his wife.

Tommy at age 10 (Stage 1)
Heinz shouldn't steal; he should buy the drug. If he steals the drug, he might get put in jail and have to put the drug back anyway.
But maybe Heinz should steal the drug because his wife might be an important lady, like Betsy Ross, she made the flag.

Tommy at age 13 (Stage 2)
Heinz should steal the drug to save his wife's life. He might get sent to jail, but he'd still have his wife.
("Tommy, you said he should steal the drug for his wife. Should he steal it if it were a friend who was dying?") That's going too far. He could be in jail while his friend is alive and free. I don't think a friend would do that for him.

Tommy at age 16 (Stage 3)
If I was Heinz, I would have stolen the drug for my wife. You can't put a price on love; no amount of gifts make love. You can't put a price on life either.

Tommy at age 21 (Stage 4)
When you get married, you take a vow to love and cherish your wife. Marriage is not only love, it's an obligation; like a legal contract.

Source: Compiled by the author.

With regard to invariant sequence, our longitudinal results are presented in the Heinz Werner Memorial Lecture at Clark University (1979) and indicate that on every retest individuals were either at the same stage as three years earlier or had moved up. This was true in Turkey as well as in the United States.

With regard to the hierarchic integration criterion, it has been demonstrated that adolescents exposed to written statements at each of the six stages comprehend or correctly put in their own words all statements at or below their own stage but fail to comprehend any statements more than one stage above their own. Some individuals comprehend the next stage above their own; some do not. Adolescents prefer (or rank as best) the highest stage they can comprehend.

To understand moral stages, it is important to clarify their relations to stage of logic or intelligence, on the one hand, and to moral behavior, on the other. Maturity of moral judgment is not highly correlated with IQ or verbal intelligence (correlations are only in the 30s, accounting for 10 percent of the variance). Cognitive development, in the stage sense, however, is more important for moral development than such correlations suggest. Piaget has found that after the child learns to speak there are three major stages of reasoning: the intuitive, the concrete operational, and the formal operational. At around age 7, the child enters the stage of concrete logical thought. He can make logical inferences, classify, and handle quantitative relations about concrete things. In adolescence individuals usually enter the stage of formal operations. At this stage they can reason abstractly, that is, consider all possibilities, form hypotheses, deduce implications from hypotheses, and test them against reality.

Since moral reasoning clearly is reasoning, advanced moral reasoning depends upon advanced logical reasoning; a person's logical stage puts a certain ceiling on the moral stage he can attain. A person whose logical stage is only concrete operational is limited to the preconventional moral stages (Stages 1 and 2). A person whose logical stage is only partially formal operational is limited to the conventional moral stages (Stages 3 and 4). While logical development is necessary for moral development and sets limits to it, most individuals are higher in logical stage than they are in moral stage. As an example, over 50 percent of late adolescents and adults (all formal operational) display principled (Stages 5 and 6) moral reasoning (Kohlberg 1979).

The moral stages are structures of moral judgment or moral reasoning. Structures of moral judgment must be distinguished from the content of moral judgment. As an example, we cite responses to a dilemma used in our various studies to identify moral stage. The dilemma raises the issue of stealing a drug to save a dying woman (see Table 2.2). The inventor of the drug is selling it for ten times what it costs him to make it. The woman's husband cannot raise the money, and the seller refuses to lower the price or wait for payment. What should the husband do?

The choice endorsed by a subject (steal, don't steal) is called the content of his moral judgment in the situation. His reasoning about the choice defines the structure of his moral judgment. A moral choice involves choosing between two (or more) values as they confict in concrete situations of choice.

The stage or structure of a person's moral judgment defines what he finds valuable in each of these moral issues (life, law), that is, how he defines the value, and why he finds it valuable, that is, the reasons he gives for valuing it. As an example, at Stage 1 life is valued in terms of the power or possessions of the person involved; at Stage 2, for its usefulness in satisfying the needs of the individual in question or others; at Stage 3, in terms of the individual's relations with others and their valuation of him; at Stage 4, in terms of social or religious law. Only at Stages 5 and 6 is each life seen as inherently worthwhile, aside from other considerations.

EDUCATING FOR A JUST SOCIETY

While my thinking and research on moral stages and moral education were rooted in Piaget and Dewey, in 1968 I traced their roots in an older vision of education in a just society, the vision of Socrates and Plato. I claimed our research on moral development, both cross-cultural and in Blatt's (1969) experimental program of moral discussion in American schools, supported the Socratic vision of education for justice. I claimed the research supported the following elements of the Socratic view:

> First, virtue is ultimately one, not many, and it is always the same ideal form regardless of climate or culture.
> Second, the name of this ideal form is justice.
> Third, not only is the good one, but virtue is knowledge of the good. He who knows the good chooses the good.
> Fourth, the kind of knowledge of the good that is virtue is philosophical knowledge or intuition of the ideal form of the good, not correct opinion or acceptance of conventional beliefs.
> Fifth, the good can then be taught, but its teachers must in a certain sense be philosopher-kings.
> Sixth, the reason the good can be taught is because we know it dimly all along or at a low level and its teaching is more a calling out than an instruction.
> Seventh, the reason we think the good cannot be taught is because the same good is known differently at different levels, and direct instruction cannot take place across levels.
> Eighth, then the reaching of virtue is the asking of questions and the pointing of the way, not the giving of answers. Moral education is the leading of men upward, not the putting into the mind of knowledge what was not there before.

The 1960s was no more safe for Stage 6 exemplars than was Socrates' Athens. The quest for justice and a concern for what I called the sixth stage of universal principles moved in the land.

In 1976 the bicentennial led me to a reassessment of education for justice in light of the contemporary scene (Fenton 1976). I gave a bicentennial lecture entitled "The Quest for Justice in American History and Education" at, among other places, Kent State. Even indirect reference to the martyrs of the 1960s and the Platonic vision that moved them met with embarrassed silence in a student body that did not want to be reminded of the conflicts of the past.

My 1976 lecture on education for justice reasserted not the Platonic vision I had called Stage 6 but the vision of Jefferson and the founding fathers I called Stage 5. Stage 5 is the morality of the social contract and the rights of man that generated the Declaration of Independence and the Constitution. Our longitudinal research solidly confirmed that this was a natural stage of development found in Israel and Turkey as well as in the United States. While a natural stage, only a small minority of adults, even of college graduates, reached the fifth stage. In 1976 I said Stage 5 was, as ever, in some danger because it was in the possession of a minority.

Watergate supported this claim. President Nixon's willingness to violate the civil rights of his fellow citizens, I pointed out, was not sheer expediency but was at least partly moral ignorance or lack of civic and moral education. I said that Nixon's public utterances displayed no clear usage or comprehension of fifth-stage thought. In this he was little different from the American majority that every year votes down the Bill of Rights when presented to them unlabeled in the Gallup Poll. Watergate supported the founding fathers' wisdom in constructing a system of checks and balances to support human rights. It also showed, I thought, the founders' wisdom in proposing that public education should focus on education for citizenship.

In this vision public education was civic education and the graduate of the public school would be a free citizen. A free citizen was someone who could sign our social contracts, the Declaration of Independence and the Constitution, with informed consent to their Stage 5 premises.

In 1976 Watergate provided the scenario to reassert the Stage 5 vision of the founding fathers. In addition, further research by my colleagues and myself also dictated a retrenchment from Stage 6, Platonic idealism, to Stage 5, rational liberalism. Empirical research between 1968 and 1976 did not confirm my theoretical statements about a sixth and highest stage (Kohlberg 1979). My longitudinal subjects, still adolescents in 1968, had come to adulthood by 1976 but none had reached the sixth stage. Perhaps all the sixth-stage persons of the 1960s had been wiped out, perhaps they had regressed, or maybe it was all my imagination in the first place.

More accurately, the ideas of justice I called Stage 6 are now the subject of slow scholarly philosophic dispute, revolving largely around John Rawls' (1973) Stage 6 restatement of the liberal social contract. This restatement generates universal principles of social justice that include not only our familiar Stage 5 civil libertarian assumptions of procedural justice and equal opportunity but also the more radical and substantive Stage 6 principle of justice as equity in the distribution of income and respect.

My 1976 call to the schools to make the world safe for Stage 5 democracy reflected not only rhetoric but a developing practice of civic and moral education supported by the Danforth Foundation (Fenton et al. 1974). This practice linked together the new social studies curricula with developmental moral discussion. Fenton at Carnegie-Mellon University and the Pittsburgh schools tied high school curriculum in civics and history to developmental moral discussion. Mosher at Boston University and the Brookline schools tied high school curriculum in social studies, psychology, and human relations to developmental moral discussion. Quigley and Clark in Los Angeles related new social studies law curriculum to developmental moral discussion.

This linkage between the new social studies curriculum and moral discussion around the goal of understanding the Stage 5 premises of our society was a natural one in terms of educational theory. The new social studies had taken the Socratic inquiry method as the basis for reasoning about matters of social fact in relation to value issues in problematic cases. Our developmental moral discussion extends the Socratic method to systematic moral dialogs about values. The new social studies of the 1960s had assumed high school students could reason about social facts at Piaget's stage of formal reasoning and that they could reason about moral values and justice at my fifth stage of social contract. Developmental psychology suggested that stimulation to these cognitive levels, rather than assuming them, was a more reasonable goal of secondary civic education. But these differences between the new social studies of the 1960s and our cognitive developmental curriculum of the 1970s represented minor differences in instructional means, not differences in educational ends. Both postulated as ends an understanding of the liberal principles of constitutional democracy in the context of reasoned discussion about controversial social and moral problems.

This new education for Stage 5 that I advocated in 1976 looked attractive in comparison with available alternatives. Aside from neglect of civic education, the principal alternative was the old-fashioned indoctrinative civic education for Stage 4, teaching respect for law and order, authority, nation, and the free enterprise system on the value side and straight facts on the cognitive side.

In summary, my 1967 lecture on education for justice stressed a retrenchment from my 1968 Platonic Stage 6 to a Stage 5 goal and conception of justice. This chapter reports a further retrenchment to Stage 4 goals as ends of civic education. It discusses my civic educational efforts for the last four years at Cambridge High School's alternative Cluster School. Our Cluster approach is not merely Socratic and developmental, it comes close to the indoctrinative in its use of teacher advocacy. Its goal is not attainment of the fifth stage but a solid attainment of the fourth-stage commitment of being a good member of a community or a good citizen. Its philosophy of civic education is, in a certain sense, then, conventional or fourth stage. Only its educational approach is unconventional and new. The approach is the governance of a small school community by participatory or direct democracy. Rules are made and enforced through a community meeting, one-person-one-vote whether faculty or student. Later in this chapter, I will report one such meeting. First I need to briefly indicate why I have been led to advocate such a form of civic education from the point of view of contemporary social needs, research, and theory.

The central rationale for representative constitutional democracy is still the founding fathers' rationale that democratic governance best protects justice or individual human rights. There is a second and somewhat different rationale for participatory or direct democracy, the rationale of community as something more than justice. Direct democracy promotes participation in society and a resulting sense of community. Athenian direct democracy was not as good as American representative democracy at protecting justice, Socrates' right to life, and free speech. Athenian direct democracy, however, was very good at creating that sense of participation and community that keeps a society alive and free of the death called privatism. Today the major problem in developing youth is privatism; its major educational solution is participation.

In 1978 a national conference on civic education was held in Santa Monica. A central theme was civic education through action or experiential learning, rather than curriculum improvement in the sense I discussed as education for Stage 5. The focus of experiential learning in new thrusts in civic education was participation — either participation in the governance of the school through school democracy or participation in the outside community through service projects or projects working on community problems. Why the emphasis on participation? Partly because that is where developmental education theory takes participants in the conference like Fenton, Mosher, Hedin, Newmann, and myself. What appeal would education for increasing participation have had in the 1960s when half the country wanted students to stop participating and making trouble, to get them to settle down in the classroom? On the other hand, today participation represents an educational response to a growing privatism of youth.

Each younger generation in America is diagnosed by its elders in academe in terms of its moral character, usually from a psychoanalytic perspective. In the 1950s David Riesman (1952) diagnosed the coming generation as "The Lonely Crowd," Whyte (1956) as "The Organization Man." In the 1960s Keniston diagnosed the coming generation first as "The Uncommitted" and then as the "Young Radicals." In the 1970s the diagnosis is given by Lasch (1978) as "The Culture of Narcissism," or more popularly as "The Me Generation." At the top of the best-seller list is Ringer's (1977) *Looking Out for Number One.* These diagnoses and slogans are reminiscent of our second stage, of instrumental hedonism and exchange. Ringer's book starts with a preface explaining that you can trust the book's advice because he wrote the book to make money but gives a fair dollar value. The best-selling ideological or theoretical fad is sociobiology, featuring "the selfish gene." These signs and portents and diagnoses do not mean that today's youth are fixated at a second moral stage or a narcissistic level of ego development. This is no more true of them than of their "new conservative" elders who are doing the diagnoses. Rather the youth, like their elders, are responding to an overwhelming national mood of privatism.

"Privatism," the ideology of "look out for number one," is exactly the attitude behind the new-conservative elder's demand for more discipline in the schools and more "back to the basics." Behind the back-to-the-basics movement is the basic of California's Proposition 13, money. In terms of outcomes of education the recent Gallup Poll indicates the most endorsed educational outcome is the ability to write a job application letter with correct grammar and spelling. In terms of educational input, the most endorsed input is not spending money. This is the privatism underlying the back to the basics.

The new privatism unites the cynical or disillusioned liberal with the cynical or disillusioned conservative, "the new conservative." Until Nixon and Watergate, the conservative private property ethic was what Barry Goldwater called the conscience of the conservative, a Stage 4 moral commitment to maintaining American society or a Stage 5 commitment to liberty and democracy threatened by Marxist socialism. The more recent new conservative ideology stresses not moral Stage 4 but "look out for number one." It calls into question not only the Stage 5 premises of the Declaration of Independence but the Stage 4 societal maintenance ideas that I took for granted as safe in 1976. Perhaps under Nixon's Stage 4 rhetoric of law, order, and nation we suspected a Stage 2 "look out for number one," but at least the rhetoric was Stage 4. For the rhetoric of the new conservatism that does not even pretend to Stage 4, let me cite the (1978) Massachusetts Democratic candidate for governor, Edward I. King. I quote the Boston *Globe* (October 21, 1978):

> King yesterday denounced his Republican rival, Hatch in a press conference reiterating his support of the death penalty, a 21 year drinking age, and an end to tax-funded abortions. He said these views were not extremist, they were moderate. "If you're a millionaire living off inherited wealth in Beverly like Mr. Hatch, you may think that those who care about capital punishment to deter murder are part of a hate group. But if you live in Winthrop like I do, you want capital punishment, and you don't do it out of hate, you do it out of fear. Up in Beverly, the crime rate is low. Maybe Hatch hasn't been mugged or doesn't know anyone who has."

King's Archie Bunker reasoning is not Stage 4; it is Stage 3. It asserts that what's right is right because it's what my group thinks is right or what's good for my group. Since King's group, the lower middle class, is more numerous than Hatch's group, the rich, King thinks not only that he will get elected but that he is right. If he were fourth stage, he'd worry about what was best for the total community in Massachusetts.*

---

*Stages in thinking about capital punishment have been empirically studied, (Kohlberg and Elfenbein 1975). If King were fifth or sixth stage, he would respond to the John Rawls

Whether King's reason is morally right or not it seemed to be right by the criteria of "look out for number one." It got him elected governor. It appealed to the disaffection of the voters, not only from our Stage 5 civil-libertarian constitutional premises, but from any Stage 4 conception of government as rule by law, not by men, in the public interest. Here is this disaffection in the words of Laura, a senior graduating in Cambridge High School. She comes from a stable working class family and is part of our research sample.

> I don't know whether I'll go to college next year or take a year off to work. What I want out of life is to have a good job, I want to be happy at my job. I would like to be a stewardess and travel and learn about people and things. To a certain extent I want to travel to escape, the world depresses me and the government depresses me. I don't want to hear the truth about what my country is like. I know it is corrupt; they say it is a way of life and I'm still young enough to be a little frightened that I'll be like that. We say we have a democratic government but I don't think it treats people fair at all. In a way I think the government hates people, in a way I think it tries to bribe people. If we had a democratic government we wouldn't have ghettos and people on welfare and riots. But maybe that isn't there, it's a big world out there and I don't expect it to run smoothly. I don't understand it but in a way I don't want to understand it.

Our research criterion indicated her moral reasoning was mostly Stage 3, though a far more idealistic or "moral" Stage 3 than that appealed to by King. She says: "I was brought up to be good but I chose on my own not to become selfish, to be considerate. It is okay to think of yourself but also you should give space to others and have your mind open to others and the world." She also shows some beginning fourth-stage thinking about hypothetical moral dilemmas. She doesn't apply her beginning fourth-stage capacities to her perception of government and the larger society; her disaffection, she says, is such that she doesn't really want to try to understand. She also does not approach government in terms of public issues; she approaches it as failing to meet her third-stage moral expectations that it be a government of good people concerned about helping other people, and she is disappointed.

How can we fault her third-stage privatism as a citizen when her privatism can be seen as a disillusioned response to the third-stage privatism of political "leaders" like King?

---

idea of universal justice. From the Rawls view, a law or punishment is just if it would be the result of a social contract made by the people trying to choose impartially. They go behind a "veil of ignorance" as to their actual position in society, as rich or poor, as a possible victim of crime or a possible felon. As a possible victim of murder, as well as a possible felon, you would want punishment to deter murder. But as a possible felon, you would not want capital punishment. If you did not know who you were to be, the additional gain to deterrence would not be acceptable if you had the chance of being killed.

In the 1960s we seemed to see youth groping toward principled fifth- or even sixth-stage reasoning, and recoiling from fourth-stage political leadership while being misunderstood as immoral and lawless. Today the misunderstanding is a stage down. The youth groping toward some fourth-stage conception of a political community are alienated at the personal and institutional or collective egoism of institutional leadership and are branded "the Narcissistic generation."

The purpose of our comments is not to seriously diagnose the times but to point to the current need for the American high school to take some active steps to help students like Laura to positive Stage 4 conceptions and attitudes toward citizenship.

In a sense, then, our goals in high school civic education are old. Our approach, however, is very different from the old civics education prevalent in the 1950s. That approach was one of indoctrination of fourth-stage values, with a conservative slant (Kohlberg 1973). An example is the text, *Civics for Americans,* written by Clark, Edmonson, and Dondineau in 1954. They say:

> *Civics For Americans* is a book designed to help young people develop the characteristics of good citizenship. Primarily these characteristics are devotion to the Constitutional government of the United States, respect for law and appreciation of the advantages of a free-enterprise economy, faith in God and man and in the tenets which distinguish our way of life. Willingness to assume the responsibilities of school citizenship is essential to developing these characteristics.

Clearly, too, this requires more than the integration of developmental moral discussion of dilemmas in history, civics, and human relations with new social studies analyses that we described as the education for Stage 5 of the curriculum projects of Fenton, Mosher, and myself (Fenton 1976). The additional educational experience required is the experience of civic participation, the focus of the Danforth conference on civic education.

The first form of participation discussed in the conference was participation in the outside community represented by the projects of Fred Newmann in Madison and Diane Hedin in Minneapolis. The second form of participation is real power and democratic participation in the governance of high school itself.

The general educational rationale for both is still best given by Dewey's (1966) theory as this has been elaborated in the psychological theory of Piaget (1965). According to both, the fundamental aim of education is development and development requires action or active experience. The aim of civic education is the development of a person with the structures of understanding and motivation to participate in society in the direction of making it a better or more just society. This requires experiences of active social participation as well as the learning of analytic understandings and moral discussion of legal and political issues.

A paper by Newmann (1978) provides the rationale for participation experience in terms of the basic psychological theory and research of Piaget (1965),

David Hunt (1973), and myself. My own theory argues, following Dewey and G. H. Mead (1934), that if sociomoral development is the aim of social education the central means of social education is the creation of opportunities and experiences for social role-taking and participation. In an earlier review of the research literature (Kohlberg 1969) I conclude that both active power and decision-making responsibility and more passive belongingness in secondary groups correlate well with and stimulate social and moral development. Social development (or stage of social cognition, of moral judgment, of self-perception) is correlated with socioeconomic status, with participation in formal and informal voluntary organizations, with occupational status and responsibility. From this point of view, the primary "problem" of disadvantaged street youths is that they have no sense of power and participation in the wider organized society, in the secondary institutions of high school, of work, of government. Their world is the world of Stage 2 instrumental exchange or of Stage 3 informal loyalty or caring. The Stage 4 world or organized society is not a world they can understand or identify with since they and their families have no roles of power and participation in that world. Newmann's paper reviews the research literature and comes to similar conclusions.

I have showed the educational need for experiences of political participation in terms of the stage psychologies of Dewey and Piaget. John Stuart Mill (quoted in Newmann 1978) makes the same claim from a different, perhaps more common-sense, psychology:

Freedom has an invigorating effect upon the development of character. Character develops very differently when a human being feels himself under no other external constraint than the necessities of nature or of a society in which he has a share in imposing and the right to publicly dissent from and alter if he thinks them wrong. The effect of freedom on character development is only obtained, however, when the person is, or is looking forward to becoming a citizen as privileged as any other. What is still [more] important than this feeling is the practical discipline from the demands made upon the citizen to exercise some social function.

It is not sufficiently considered how little there is in most people's ordinary life to give any largeness to their ideas or sentiments. Giving them something to do for the public supplies in a measure, these differences. If circumstances allow the amount of public duty assigned to them to be considerable, it makes them an educated person. The practice of the assembly raised the intellectual standard of an average Athenian citizen beyond that of any other mass of people. An intellectual benefit of the same kind, though far less, is produced in Englishmen by their ability to be placed on juries and to serve parish offices. Still more salutary is the moral instruction afforded by participation in public functions. One is called upon while so engaged to weigh interests not one's own, to be guided in conflicting cases by another rule than one's private partialities, principles that have their reason for existence in the common good. Where the school of public spirit does not exist, scarcely any idea is entertained that private persons owe any duties to society except to obey the law and submit to the government. There is no unselfish sentiment of identification with the public, thought or feeling is absorbed in the individual and in the family. The man reasons thinking not of any collective interest, of any objects to be pursued jointly with others but only in competition with them.

So, 100 years ago Mill made the statement for participation as necessary for what we call the fourth stage of civic attitudes as well as for the fifth stage, and he pointed to it as the remedy for what we have called privatism.

Newmann's paper presents the Dewey-Mill psychology as part of the "participatory-idealist" philosophy of democracy. This classical ideal is embodied in the Stage 5 educational and moral philosophies of human development and perfection running from Aristotle to Dewey. These philosophers assert that the educational aim of full individual human development can be reached only through an education for full participation in society or in a human community. Development to a fifth or sixth stage of human personality and experience, in this vision, cannot take place except in and through experiences of participation. Whether one's exemplars of human development are sixth-stage exemplars like Socrates or Martin Luther King, or fifth-stage exemplars like Aristotle and Dewey, their development was inextricably tied to participation in their political communities. Education by, and for, participation is not simply a concern of a "citizen education," it is a concern for human development education.

HIGH SCHOOL DEMOCRACY

Given the importance of actual experiences of participation in a political community, why does it rest upon the high school to provide it? Why not leave it to spontaneous experience after high school? The answer is that unless a person leaves high school already at the fourth stage and with corresponding interests and motivations, he or she is unlikely to be in a position to have the capacities and motivation to enter positions of participation and public responsibility later. They will, as our graduating student says, avoid such situations, not seek them.

I cited Newmann's and my own review of the research literature correlating participation to higher stages of cognitive, moral, and ego development. The correlations are both cause and consequence. Experience of participation causes development; but higher stages of development are also causes or conditions of being in a position of participation (Candee et al. 1978). Opportunities for participation, then, are given to the mature in our society. Representative democracy, like our economic system, tends to give growth experience to those who don't really need it, to those already advanced.

The high school's expectation and help in entering participatory roles is required, especially for those students who would not seek them later. This, at least, is required of high schools or educators who take seriously the "developmental," "progressive," or "participatory idealist" philosophy of education and citizenship. It is almost universally accepted by educational sociologists that an informed definition of the school as an agency of social education rests on seeing it as an intermediary between the family and the society. The bridging role of the school is conceived of in a system-maintaining, or what Newmann (1980) calls an "elitist pluralist," perspective by functional sociologists such as Durkheim (1961) and Parsons (1964). In this perspective, the school is, like the government, a bureaucratic or impersonally rule-governed organization stressing competitive merit or achievement. Through it, rather than directly through the family, children learn to respect general and impartial rules and to be concerned about collective goals.

In the developmental or "participatory idealist" view of Dewey, the school was a necessary bridge between the family and the outside society in providing experiences of democratic community. Already in Dewey's day, the town-meeting forms of democractic community most amenable to creating experiences of participation were becoming rare. Today they are practically unknown for most adults and adolescents alike. The schools and universities need to help create roles of responsible participation as vehicles because the civic and vocational roles that graduates enter are typically not roles of responsible participation. Furthermore, the school is needed to encourage rational and moral reflection and discussion of participation roles if participatory experience is to lead to growth. Otherwise such experiences may simply confirm the ignorance or alienation with which Laura, our graduating student, approached her civic role.

The most basic way in which the high school can promote experiences of civic participation is to govern itself through a process of participatory democracy. The learning and development required for democratic governing must come from doing or making a government, from being an active member of governance with the power to influence government to be more just. The only way school can help graduating students become persons who can make society a just community is to let them try experimentally to make the school themselves. The school can offer a chance for experience in making a just community immeasurably easier, safer, and less frustrating than the experience of adult participation in society. It provides the adolescent with direct power and responsibility for governance in a society that is small and personal, like the family, but that is complex, rule-governed, and democratic, which is a Stage 4 or 5 society like the society in which the student is to be a citizen.

I have made the Socratic argument for school democracy in terms of participatory experience for development to a fourth-stage citizenship role orientation, as well as for developing some awareness of our fifth-stage principles of constitutional democracy. The negative argument is perhaps even more compelling. This is the argument that bureaucratic-authoritarian high school governance actually teaches alienation and ignorance about a democratic society. In this argument, while the high school social studies curriculum teaches equal liberty and due process, the high school "hidden curriculum" (the governance and informal social relations of the school) teaches something very different. Newmann (1977) states this as follows:

> Public education should teach students to function in a political-legal structure of representative democracy. This means there has to be a consistency between the principles of democracy being taught and the actual process of education or the student will rightly come to distrust both the democratic principles taught and the process of education. Education must authenticate these central principles of democracy and apply them to the educational process. Equal liberty and consent of the governed are the two most fundamental principles behind representative democracy. These principles of equal liberty and consent can be embodied in the educational process by providing freedom of choice, intellectual openness, and active participation.

In the projects of Fenton, Mosher, and myself, school democracy is the central experience of participation necessary for moral and civic development. In the projects of Newmann and Hedin, internship and project experience in the community are the central experiences of participation for civic development. I question whether community internship and project experiences in themselves have either the intensity and duration, the democratic form, or the chance to combine action and reflection that school democracy can provide for stimulating civic development.

At the same time, participation in a democratic school is not enough to guarantee a development or transfer of fourth-stage understandings and attitudes to the out-of-school society. Laura attended a democratic school we shall discuss, the Cambridge Cluster School. Laura attributes much of her third- and fourth-stage moral concern to this experience of community in the Cluster School:

> I learned more or less on my own to be considerate, not to be selfish, though also from my mother and from the Cluster School. Cluster has signified that in this democratic school people should respect one another and care. That is what a community is, people caring for each other and watching out for each other and helping each other grow. In Cluster we all try to work together and when someone has a problem we try to approach it in a good way. Cluster is a democratic school within Latin High School, but it is different than Latin. I'm not saying Latin teachers aren't fair. It's just you come in, the teacher is in front, saying "Now you do this," and you just listen. In Cluster, you come in and the teacher says "How should we approach our lesson" and people try to work as one. So I have tried to be a good community member, to voice my opinions even when people don't agree with me. I think

I'm respected and that makes me feel good about myself and I think I've helped the school.

Laura's moral and positive attitudes of participation in the democratic school, then, have not transferred to the larger civic world in the absence of a parallel process of participation in the larger community.

Our conclusion is that a civic education for civic participation ideally should include two experiences: the direct democracy of a smaller school community found in the alternative school for the development of fourth-stage concepts and attitudes of community; and the experience of participation in the larger community governed by a mixture of representative democracy and rule-governed bureaucracy for the generalization of such attitudes to a participatory attitude to the wider society.

THE CAMBRIDGE CLUSTER SCHOOL

Let us now look more closely at alternative schools with governance structures of direct or participatory democracy. These schools were founded in the late 1960s and early 1970s largely directed to the needs of adolescents who were alienated from bureaucratically governed high schools. When founded, all put high stock in democratic governance and in creating a spirit of school community. In our view, however, all started with inadequate theory to direct their practices of democratic community.

Most explicitly the ideologies involved the romantic "let them grow" maturationist ideology of A. S. Neill's British open school and American humanistic psychology. Less explicitly, these 1960s alternative school ideologies involved a radical political search for justice for minorities at home and "colonials" abroad. Thus there was a fusion between educational libertarianism in the sense of free school "do your own thing" and a radical impulse toward participation in terms of justice for the oppressed. The radical impulse kept free-school libertarianism from being examples of "do your own thing" privatism and kept alternative schools alive as viable communities.

The death of the radical concern for justice in suburban youth, however, revealed the emptiness of romantic educational libertarianism. It left, that is, no way for the alternative school to engage students or to pull them out of the privatism endemic in youth. Privatistic liberty in an alternative school tended not to attract enough students in the mid-1970s to outweigh the reputations of many such schools — that the students were weirdos who would graduate with inadequate college entrance credentials. One of the best and the longest-established of the alternative schools, Newton's Murray Road in Massachusetts, closed in 1978 because a drop in enrollment presented the necessity of movement back into the regular high school building, which the students' sense of community did not surmount.

Four years ago the staff of Brookline's School-Within-A-School sensed similar problems and decided to try a new solution, a systematic participatory governance structure like that of Cambridge's Cluster School. They asked Ralph Mosher to consult with them in establishing such a process. The staff thinks that their adoption of the process is the cause of the fact that currently the school has a waiting list and high student morale. Two years ago the Scarsdale Alternative School decided to work with the Cluster School's theory and governance for similar reasons.

I have discussed the shift of my concern for education for Stage 5 justice to a concern for education for Stage 4 participation and community in terms of changes in the times. In reality my developing concern for community has come from changes in my basic theory that have resulted from a serious effort to relate theory to practice in five years of daily involvement in the Cluster School. My earliest efforts to relate a stage theory of moral development to education were based on the usual one-way vision of the relation of psychology to teacher practice. This vision I now call the "psychologist's fallacy." This is the belief that the theory that guides psychologists in their research should be the basis for what is important and true for guiding teachers' decisions in practice. An example is the Skinner approach to education. I would not dispute the idea that Skinner's laws or theory of reinforcement learning are true and useful when applied to habit learning of animals and children. This does not, however, mean that the theory is a good guide for teacher practice. Skinner may quite properly find human freedom and dignity useless concepts in ordering data about bar-pressing. That does not mean that the many manuals for teacher practice derived from Skinner's theory are educationally valid. Valid teachers' decisions must be based on the assumption of the growing freedoms and dignity of the child. Valid theories of educational practice, then, cannot be simply based on psychological theories for ordering value-neutral psychological data motivated by pure research.

At first, I did not recognize this clearly and started in education in the manner of Skinner. My student, Moshe Blatt (1969), did a dissertation study showing that Socratic discussion of hypothetical moral dilemmas led to one-third of the students moving to the next moral stage, with no movement in the same year's time in control groups. From the beginning, my colleagues and I developed more and more complex derivations of the theory in terms of curriculum and manuals for practice to help students reach the next higher stage of reasoning. This is, indeed, one phase of the civic education for Stage 5 developed in the Danforth project. At the very beginning of the project, however, Fenton, Mosher, and I knew there was something wrong with this approach. We knew it because Fenton and I conducted a study in which we trained 40 social studies teachers in Boston and Pittsburgh to do Blatt-type dilemma discussions. In more than half of the classes in which the Blatt effect occurred, one-third of the students moved a stage. Control classes by the same teachers without dilemma discussion led to no moral stage change. The operation was a research success but the educational patient died. One year after the study, only one of the 20 teachers involved in the research in the Boston area was doing moral discussions, a teacher who has now gotten her own grant.

My involvement in Cluster grew out of dissatisfaction with curriculum experiments leading to stage change significant to the researchers, Kohlberg, Mosher, and Fenton, but of no significance to the teachers and students in question. I concluded two things. First, I had to start with goals that were meaningful to teachers and students, not goals derived from a theory. In the moral area, this meant, among other things, setting goals in terms of real-life moral behavior and attitudes, not reasoning on hypothetical dilemmas. Second, it meant a two-way collaboration with teachers in constructing theory, not a one-way street based on deduction of prescriptions for teaching by the psychologist from his theory. This collaboration was the contract I proposed in 1973 to the six teachers planning to start the Cambridge Cluster School. The school's inception was decreed when a group of parents, largely academic, petitioned the school committee to start an alternative school with classrooms in the regular high school. The school was to have 70 students, ninth through twelfth grade. It would teach English, social studies, and electives, the remaining classes to be taken in the regular high school. It was to be representative of the Cambridge population in class and race. This meant that about 25 percent of the students would be black. It would operate with volunteer teachers from the regular high school.

The superintendent, knowing of my interest in working with teachers, suggested that I attend the planning meetings for the school. Largely because of the enthusiasm of the students asked to attend the planning meetings, my suggestion that the school governance be one of participatory democracy was accepted. I proposed to the teachers that I act as an unpaid consultant to the school. I would attend school and staff meetings as an active participant as well as observer as long as the teachers found it useful. In return, I asked only that the teachers commit themselves to maintaining participatory democracy, however rough the road. I said I thought my theory would be useful but I didn't know just how, nor did I ask for a commitment of the teachers to work with the theory. I thought the theory we would jointly build would codify the intuitive good practices the teachers already used, would help to organize questions of how to proceed as we came into such problems, and would help to evaluate progress toward our goals.

The first involvement of theory with the school was an application of already existing stage ideas to pragmatic problems of process and procedure in community meetings. The teachers' initial conception of school democracy was the usual romantic Summerhill alternative school conception of power to the people — the idea that adolescents were basically capable of responsibility and self-governance if only given a chance. I had seen this romantic conception work quite well in affluent suburban alternative schools like Newton's Murray Road. I had also seen it fail where students were largely street kids, as were a large proportion of the Cluster students. Many of our entering students, as research subsequently demonstrated, were largely at our second stage of moral reasoning, the stage of reasoning in terms of egoism and exchange. Two years later, one of these entering Stage 2 students expressed his Stage 3 perspective on the past. He was discussing admissions policies in a community meeting. He said, "We need to select more good kids. We can't take any more kids like I was when I came in. I suppose you couldn't find many kids as bad as I was for that matter."

Stage theory told me that entering students such as this one were as basically concerned about fairness as were Newton students, but that their Stage 2 conception of fairness was different. The first need, said the theory, was to deal with issues that were very concrete Stage 2 issues of fairness, not abstract issues of curriculum and administration of interest to Newton students.

The second need was to expose students to reasoning about these school issues at the next stage up through small group discussions in which Stage 2 thinkers would hear Stage 3 thinkers reasoning and teachers would express their own Stage 3, 4, or 5 views.

The teachers bought these implications of stage theory after the community meeting the second week of school. The issue was curriculum, what electives could be offered. The teacher chairing the meeting listed on the board six electives the teachers were prepared to teach and several additional offerings that students were willing to teach. He asked for a vote on each elective. A student said he would not vote for any of the electives; he didn't like any and proposed that students would not have to attend classes. Before the faculty quite knew what was happening, a vote was taken, compulsory afternoon school was abolished, and the bell rang. I yelled that that was only a straw vote, and the next day the teachers explained that the school could not vote to violate a state law.

At this point the staff agreed to a set of procedures based on the points about Stage 2 just made. The staff would meet with me prior to a community meeting to select an issue of fairness, of concrete concern to the students, and to sort out their own positions and reasoning on the issue. The next day the staff would discuss the issue in their classrooms of 10 to 20 students, clarifying proposals and engaging students in listening to one another's reasons. Only then would the community as a whole make a decision on the issue. Slowly a viable democratic process evolved. Now, in the fifth year of the school, a responsible attitude to democratic process, internalized by most of the students, is clearly evident.

As an example, Mike, one of the active leaders among the students, was apprehended with marijuana in his possession by a policeman outside the building. The police took him to the school headmaster who suspended him from school for three days. He was relatively defiant toward the police, the headmaster, and his father in relation to the episode. He did feel a certain degree of guilt toward Cluster School, however, since the school had its own democratically made rule about dope that he had violated. Like most Cluster students, he believed it was all right to smoke dope, and his only reason for refraining from getting high was that he recognized that it hurt the Cluster School community if students came to class high. After he returned to school from his suspension, there was a heated discussion of the issue in a community meeting. Afterward at lunch I sat in on a conversation between the student involved and two others. The student said, "This shouldn't be a community that people give their all to. It's too hard, too idealistic. I'm going to smoke pot no matter what; it's too hard to give it up. That doesn't mean I won't follow all the other rules, the cut rules and the rest of them." Another student said, "You're right, I've tried to give everything to the school, like planning the retreat, and it didn't work out. You just get exhausted. It's all right for Arthur and Brian [two teachers] to give everything to the school, it's their life. We're young and we need to grow; it's too exhausting."

The community meeting they were discussing had concluded with a student's proposal that the meeting be continued the next week but that the faculty not be present during the first hour of the meeting so that the discussion could be more frank. The final vote on any proposal about drugs would be taken after the staff joined the meeting. While the staff waited in mild panic and apprehension, my researcher's heart was eager for this controlled experiment. Without staff present, would the students' sense of the democratic process regress to Stage 2 of the first year of the school, to an agreement easy on everyone? In fact, when we entered the room we found that the student who had been caught with pot and a black student had chaired the meeting. The students had proposed and voted a drug rule that had some teeth in it. On the first offense, a student was to go to the student discipline committee, receive a warning, and write a paper on the abuse of pot. A second offense would lead to the parents coming in and three days' suspension from school. On the third offense, a student would be automatically expelled from Cluster School and go back to the regular high school, with a chance to reapply the following year. After this proposal was reported, I asked whether the proposal meant that the teachers would report offenders to the discipline committee or the students as well. After some discussion, the students said that the rule meant that students were responsible for the rule as well as teachers and that they should report other students. Whether they would remained to be seen.

The way in which the drug issue was handled at Cluster School illustrates two parts of its evolving theory, one mildly controversial, the second very controversial. The mildly controversial part of the theory is the part focused on Dewey's and Piaget's ideas of school democracy for individual stage development. According to Dewey and Piaget, children learn or develop through doing; the child is an actor not a passive learner. The task of social education is to develop a person with the ability to make a democratic society — with the skills and motivation to make our society more just, and more of a community than it now is. Not surprisingly, our Cluster students, mostly Stage 2 on entrance, are almost all Stage 3 and Stage 4 thinkers upon graduation, a growth less likely in comparison group students in the regular school (Power 1979).

The second part of the Cluster School theory is more controversial and is not shared, for instance, with Ralph Mosher and the Brookline School, because it raises many philosophic problems. The Dewey-Piaget theory dictates a staff role as process facilitator, as inquiry-question asker, reflective-active listener, and facilitator of democratic procedure. Cluster teachers advocate. They advocate for the same reason that they hope the students will advocate. They advocate in the name of making the Cluster School more just or fair and more of a community. They hope, and have found, that if they advocate in this manner, so will many students. They apply pressure or expectation for the students to make rules and agreements that represent a concern for fairness and community.

They act more like Durkheim's priest of society or the Israeli kibbutz group leader advocating collective responsibility than as pure process-facilitators. In advocating, they may be seen as indoctrinating by authority. They do not try to indoctrinate students by telling them by their own personal authority that marijuana is wrong. Not only is that a hopeless task psychologically, but they think it philosophically objectionable since it cannot be done through the means of democracy and appeal to reason. But they do try to advocate by the use of democratic group authority, arguing not that smoking marijuana is wrong, but that actions rationally or demonstrably bad for the community are wrong. They try to link agreed-on rules and norms to students' growing sense of community.

The Cluster School staff illustrated this advocate role during a fourth-year meeting over the black-white division in the community. Let us look at this meeting in more detail to illustrate the staff's advocacy around the value of school community. Because the issue is one of integration, staff advocacy is much more controversial and "political" than is advocacy for observing the no-drug rule discussed previously.

As background it should be noted that initially the school was 25 percent black, the ratio in Cambridge. In the second year of the school, the blacks said they felt uncomfortable as such a small minority in a white school and requested in a community meeting a small measure of reverse discrimination in the admissions for the next year. After heated debate the white majority agreed. In the fourth year of the school, when the following tape was made, the school was more than one-third black, but many of the black kids were still practicing black separatism, overcrowding the classes of the one black staff member.

In the meeting this teacher confronts the school with the black-white division in the community. White staff join in to urge the need to agree to a norm of integration, both in classes and in feelings between community members. They do not see themselves as adults indoctrinating black and white students with their liberal trip. They see themselves as advocates of true community in a racially divided community. The reader may not agree or think the distinction is a real one, but we will argue that it is.

Bill (black staff member)
> There are at least two groups that I know of, I mean it looks that way, maybe it is just that they are intellectually different, but there is a group which includes Colin; there is another group which includes Leslie, and maybe Phyllis and maybe Bill and they don't want to have anything to do with each other. They have different interests and I don't see how you can have a community if you have people separate, and I think maybe in that group. I wonder why no one wants to talk about why they feel they want to be in one group and not in a whole group. Do you feel like that is sort of private, and you don't want to talk about it?

Betsy (white student)
> There is a certain atmosphere in certain places in this school. Like I know that a lot of white people have said to me, "Oh, I feel uncomfortable going into the building, I am not wanted in there." And I know that a lot of blacks feel weird in Diane's group, like they are not wanted in there, but lately I have gone to Bill's, gone in there, and feel better about it. Bill's room is where the black kids hang out. Diane's room is where white kids hang around. If we just spent a little time in each other's rooms, we might get along better.

Jenny (white student)
> I think Bill is right about the fact that there are two groups.

John (black student)
> We talked about this for the last two weeks and it is boring me.

Bill (black staff)
> It's boring because you are not involved in it.

Arthur (white staff member)
> We are not just talking about integration right now, we are talking about the very nature of community.

Betsy (white student)
> There are two groups and there are at least some in one group who refuse to even consider anything that the other group says. There is no ground that we can meet these people on. If there was a way for all the groups to get together and to interact, that would be much better. Some people said that we should have had a retreat by now, we should have. You can't meet these people, they go to different classes, they are different groups. There is no common ground yet.

Joe (black student)

That's true, the only time that people get together in a group is on a retreat, when we are high.

Larry (white consultant)

That is the problem that this community meeting is supposed to be working on, but I don't think that we can say we can't work on it at a community meeting and go off on a retreat and get high or something. We've got to work it through to some extent here. I would like Tema to say why not.

Tema (white student)

It isn't that people don't understand each other, but they never talk to each other. They just assume that people are prejudiced in their ideas or viewpoints and that is ridiculous because they never even talk to these people.

Arthur (white staff)

I can see why maybe getting high on a retreat makes it a lot easier to relate to some other people in the community. But I also am being pulled the other way in saying we have to learn to confront one another's innermost thoughts and being and communicate without the extra help of a drink to be sociable or a reefer or whatever it is that makes the barriers start to fall down. There ought to be other ways, too, of doing that, during the school day. When my core class split up into two groups, some people stayed with Betsy and some people came with me, originally some of the black kids in the group were staying with Betsy, but when they saw that they were going to be the only two or one or three black kids in that group, they got up and they all went on with me.

Charlie (black student)

I am like that too. I am not prejudiced, but I went in the class over there, I was the only black one in there, and I wasn't scared to be there, but I'm not going to be the only chocolate chip in a vanilla cone. I have to be in a class that is mixed, I can't be in a class with all whites and one me.

Ann (white consultant)

I wanted to ask Billy about his idea of community — that you'll go your way and I'll go mine.

Eddie (black student)

What do you mean, I don't understand?

Ann

What does community mean to you if everyone goes their own way?

Eddie

They are humans, that's what it is supposed to be like. You want me to come in here, right, say "Hi Karl, how are you doing, how are you feeling?" Well, I don't care. It is just ridiculous, and you will never get it like that.

Ann

Why not?

Eddie

You want to know why? If I knew why then I could solve all the problems in the world.

Before trying to theoretically defend the Cluster staff, let me comment on the meeting and a sequel of the meeting. In the videotape two black adolescents felt the staff's use of community pressure to integrate behavior and resisted it. As Charlie (a black student) replied to Arthur (a teacher), "I'm not going to be the only chocolate chip in a vanilla cone. I have to be in a class that's mixed, I can't be in a class with all whites and me." Charlie understandably fears loss of his identity in an all-white class. We might say he resists the expectation of positive integration not because it isn't part of Stage 3 ideas of "being a good community member," which he accepts, but because the sacrifice may be too great. In contrast, Eddie takes a more Stage 2 position. He says, "You go your way, I'll go my way, I won't interfere with you if you don't interfere with me." He refers to Karl, a white student he doesn't like, not just because Karl is white but because of his barefoot hippy style, which is anathema in the black subculture. Eddie says to Ann, a white consultant: "You want me to come in there and say, 'Hi Karl, how are you doing, how are you feeling?' Well, I don't care. It is just ridiculous and you'll never get it like that." Asked why not, he answers, "If I knew why I could solve all the problems in the world." Eddie may not be able to answer the question that would solve all the problems in the world, but he soon can answer the question that can solve the problem of Karl.

A few months later, Karl came before the community meeting because he had registered for only two courses during the day, the two Cluster core courses. The Cambridge High School requires a minimum of four courses. Karl needed the four courses and three more to graduate that year. Karl says he does not care if he graduates and doesn't see why Cluster School is bothering him when the principal and the high school don't care. Karl said, "I don't care about graduating and I'm not interested in high school. I'm only here for Cluster."

Eddie: If you don't like high school, why don't you take the seven courses so you can graduate?

Karl: I can't graduate this year — it would be too many courses.

Eddie: Why didn't you take more courses last year so you could graduate this year?

Karl: I didn't think about it, I didn't care.

Eddie: If you don't care about yourself, we have to care about you for you. What are you here in school for now? What are you going to do after high school?

Karl: I don't need to graduate to do what I want to do, to play rock.

Eddie: Do you think you're being a good example in Cluster?

Karl: No. Do you think you are a good example?

Eddie: I guess we're even. I guess if you're not going to worry about yourself I'm not going to worry for you. But you should think about it.

For our theoretical point of view, the staff was advocating not its political ideology of integration but the fundamental principles or values of a just school community. In other words, they were advocating the ideals of justice and community immanent in the school itself. They were advocating justice and community at the fourth and fifth stage in which these ideals should be manifest in the entire community and not simply be manifest in cliques of friends and racial compatriots. Between the two meetings, Eddie's thinking about community had moved up a stage in response to community expectations at the third and fourth stages.

In sum, staff concern about integration in Cluster School functions not as political indoctrination but as part of building a higher-stage small community. Its dangers include not only Eddie's exhortation but also rebuff in a larger unintegrated society. So far Cluster's graduates, almost all now in college, think it's worth it.

What is the value of the kind of stage development we strive to create? It is valuable insofar as the creation of a particular just community is valuable. Where individuals are lifelong members of a community, advance in the stage of justice and community in a group is obviously worthwhile. Insofar as students in a kibbutz or the kibbutz as a collectivity moves or grows toward fourth- or fifth-stage shared norms of trust, concern, and collective responsibility, then life is moral, people do treat each other morally.

What is the situation, however, where students have a school community with fourth- or fifth-stage collective norms of justice and community and then go out to the world where these norms are not shared? Hopefully, what is retained is a higher stage of individual moral reasoning, a history of action in terms of these norms, and the ability to help make or move groups of which the person is a member to a higher stage. We don't know if that will be the case but that was John Dewey's vision for the schools: that schools would make citizens who were more just and democratic and who would then make schools and the society more just in a progressive spiral. Whether Dewey's noble vision can become more real or not, I do not know. It is at least a worthwhile enough vision to justify the small experimental effort my colleagues and I have mounted in striving to produce small-school just communities.

THE SCARSDALE ALTERNATIVE SCHOOL

Let me add an example of the process among a group of students more intellectual and introspective, the students of the Scarsdale Alternative School. Sensing the weakness of "do your thing" relativism as a basis for alternative school community, the Scarsdale Alternative School turned to me for help in terms of moral development.

The remedy we prescribed was participatory democracy. The school had always been democratic in the sense of having a schoolwide meeting to discuss issues and policies. We suggested it become rigorously democratic with all rules and disciplines being formulated by the whole community — one person-one vote. We further suggested that these issues be very explicitly discussed as issues of fairness or morality, in small student-teacher groups or classes, as well as in the community meeting. Finally, we suggested that teachers very explicitly appeal to a developing sense of community and to the need for the individual student to have defined obligations to the community, rather than leaving a sense of community to spontaneous good fellowship.

One part of our approach is to use democracy as the construction of a Stage 5 social contract to procure individual rights and, hence, get beyond adolescent "do your thing" relativism. A more basic part, however, is to help the adolescent construct a Stage 4 moral community that can stimulate and support altruism and the sense of conscientious obligation. Both sides come together in dialogue about the limits of the community's authority over the individual and the limits of the individual's freedom vis-à-vis the community.

Let me illustrate by reporting events in the Scarsdale Alternative School that fall. The staff and two students attended a Harvard summer workshop to plan ways of making the school a more just community. The staff agreed to full power-sharing with the students, and with the need to formally make and enforce rules by the democratic process rather than depending upon informal teacher authority to handle issues. The first event of the fall was the schoolwide outing or retreat to plan the year and to build community. A meeting discussed the issue of drugs and alcohol on the retreat. The students agreed not to use dope on the retreat. The staff urged that students, as well as staff, have responsibility for enforcing the rule, not just for obeying it. After much discussion, the students voted that in the abstract, they had the responsibility to enforce the rule, they should enforce it, but that in practice they couldn't be expected to police their friends, that while they *should* enforce the rule they wouldn't vote that they *would* enforce the rule.

After the retreat I raised the question as to whether students had observed the rule they voted on. A mild discipline was agreed upon in case anyone wished to admit violations. Soon, 20 students spoke up admitting they had violated the rule. Their attitudes ranged from the feeling that they were civilly disobedient heroes of individual rights to penitence at letting down the community. Some of the upright students castigated the sinners; other upright students castigated the moralists for hurting the feelings of the sinners. In the end, the dominant feeling was that everyone, saint and sinner, cared about one another and the community.

The next week, the students and staff went on to make a rule about coming high to class. In previous years, this issue had been dealt with by teachers, who would suspend a student for the day if they thought he was obviously high. Some students said a person had a right to get high, it was an unwarranted restriction of his freedom. This led to a lengthy metaphysical excursion to get a definition of the word "rights." The staff and many students agreed that being high was a violation of the obligation to participate in the school community and in the class, it was not just the individual student's own business. Some individualistic students did not see the point. One said, "I don't see how it's different than making a rule against picking my nose in class. Picking my nose is offensive to others, but I should still have a right to do it." A student said that picking one's nose didn't hurt the community or the common good, but coming high to class did. In the end, the rule was approved.

What are the benefits of the emphasis on democracy, fairness, and moral community? We can give hard answers for the working class black and white students in Cambridge. For them it is registered in movement from preconventional to conventional morality, and concomitant changes in life style, in the ending of delinquent behavior, college attendance, and so on.

What we hope to help achieve in Scarsdale is best expressed by the students themselves commenting on the changes democracy has brought to the school and themselves. Judith says:

> The school is definitely better this year, it's dealing much more with real issues and it's more democratic. Last year a lot of the decisions were in the hands of the teachers and there was some antagonism. There's more of an atmosphere where people react to each other and feel a connection and a caring of what happens to us all together.

"What's so good about all this democracy, anyhow?" the interviewer asked.

> It makes you deal with things. People complain about rules that other people make, but then you can break them because I didn't make them or because they were unjust, anyhow. That's the message you get in the main high school, or I did. You walk in and it's a pig sty and no one cares and I didn't care when I was there about dropping garbage because that was just a dumb rule, and had nothing to do with me. There's a lot of change going on in my thinking now. I don't know whether it's good or bad, but there is more thinking about other people, but also more of a questioning attitude.
>   Like in community meetings, I know there is a big difference. Before, I thought about what was good for me in the meeting. I didn't think consciously selfish, I just thought we each should vote for what

we each wanted and then you combine them and then the best comes out somehow. Now, I try to distinguish what I think is best for me from what I think is best for all of the students or all of the community and I usually try to think of what's best for the community. So I think of that as more caring of other people. I'd never thought of seeing things in terms of my part in the whole group.

"Does the group have a limit on what it should expect of you?" asked the interviewer.

I think if you're being into the school, you're being into something that you give up certain rights or freedoms for the chance of belonging here. But, there are definite limits, there is no way the community should decide everything, many things should be left to individual decisions. I don't think people should give up all their rights but there is a certain amount of obligation that's part of being here. Some rights for decisions you have placed in the hands of the group, but not totally.

Judith expresses a movement in her thinking toward our fifth stage, toward an explicit thinking through of a social contract, protecting individual rights in the context of a conscious thought for the public interest. Perhaps of more importance, she feels herself a member of a moral community. In this age of privatism and the "me generation," this is perhaps the greatest need for developing youth.

A NEO-PLATONIC MODEL OF MORAL EDUCATION

Let me now theoretically review the drift of my argument outside the immediacies of American alternative schools in 1980. My work in alternative schools started with accepting the many criticisms of our pre-1973 moral education practice based on Socratic dialogue about hypothetical dilemmas. It assumed that a more complete moral education would deal with real moral dilemmas and actions, not hypothetical ones. It assumed that the teacher would deal with the content of morality and not simply its form. Such dealing with content as well as form introduces the danger of indoctrination of students by the teachers' favored moral content. It introduces the danger of teachers' preachings they do not fully practice. The only way to prevent these dangers, I thought, was through a governance structure of direct democracy. Formal equality of teacher and student would prevent teacher advocacy of moral content from resting on indoctrinative appeal to authority as opposed to the rational giving of reasons. It would prevent teacher hypocrisy in advocating standards he was not obliged to live up to himself. In collaborating with teachers who advocated ideal community, my theory shifted from a neo-Socratic to a neo-Platonic model of moral education. Readers will be familiar with what I am calling the neo-Socratic model of moral education illustrated by the eight Socratic points commencing this chapter. This model arose from the intersection of Socratic and Piagetian theorizing around the findings of Blatt and Kohlberg (1975).

Moshe Blatt was the first graduate student of mine to actually lead me into new forms of moral education. Blatt came as a graduate student to the University of Chicago psychology department in 1965. He said that I had researched moral stage development long enough (ten years) and that it was time to do something about it educationally. He proposed a dissertation in which he would lead classroom discussions of hypothetical moral dilemmas like those I used in research interviews. He would then compare moral stage change over the year in these experimental classes with development in control classes that did not participate in moral discussion. Blatt proposed, then, an instructional method based on arousing controversy about choice and on Socratic questioning about reasons to justify conclusions about dilemmas on which students disagreed. His research-based premise was that students would comprehend and assimilate reasoning by peers at the next stage up while discarding reasoning by peers at the stage below.

I was skeptical that Blatt's proposed verbal discussion of purely hypothetical dilemmas would lead to genuine moral stage change. But Blatt persisted in spite of my pessimism and found "the Blatt effect." The Blatt effect was the finding that one-fourth to one-half of the students in one semester of such discussion groups would move (partially or totally) to the next stage up, a change not found in control groups (Blatt and Kohlberg 1975). Blatt's venture launched cognitive-developmental moral education in a series of projects that have consistently replicated the Blatt effect. One major replication of the effect was the Stone Foundation project, planned by Edwin Fenton (Colby, Fenton, Kohlberg, and Speicher-Dubin 1974, 1976) and this writer. The project engaged over 20 high school social studies teachers in the Boston and Pittsburgh areas in a developmental moral discussion of hypothetical dilemmas that was incorporated into Fenton's Carnegie-Mellon social studies curriculum in ninth-grade civics.

Students were pretested and posttested on moral stage over an academic year. Change was compared to that in control classes that used the same social studies curriculum and were taught by the same teachers but took no part in moral discussions. As in the Blatt study, no upward moral change in the control classes was found in the nine-month period. There was also little change in half of the experimental classes. In the remaining experimental classes, however, the Blatt effect was found; that is, one-quarter to one-half of the students in these classes moved significantly toward the next stage during the academic year. The fact that the Blatt effect was found in half of the social studies discussion classes indicated that it was not dependent upon any particular dilemma curriculum or upon intensive psychological and theory training and motivation such as Blatt possessed. (It is also our impression that the Blatt effect was not contingent on personality qualities of the teachers, such as being at the highest, or principled, stage themselves.)

The Stone project not only replicated the Blatt effect in 20 schools, it also demonstrated the significance of the three central elements of the Blatt approach to moral education. Any approach to education involves defining variables in curriculum, in student and classroom composition and character-istics, and in teacher instructional behavior. The essential curriculum element of the Blatt approach was controversial moral dilemmas in areas that would arouse disagreement between students of "cognitive conflict" in choice. The central element in student or classroom composition was a mixture of students at different stages, thus exposing students to peers at the next stage above their own. The central element in teacher behavior was an open but challenging position of Socratic probing.

The Stone project indicated that each of the three elements had to be present if any change were to occur. With regard to curriculum, the Stone project demonstrated the necessity of controversial dilemmas. In the control classes without dilemmas, no change occurred. In the experimental classes with dilemmas, more change occurred in the classes that discussed 20 dilemmas than in those that discussed only 10.

With regard to student and classroom characteristics, the Stone project comparison of "change" and "no change" experimental classrooms indicated one significant difference. The "change" classes all had mixtures of students at two and usually three stages; the "no-change" classes did not.

With regard to teacher instructional behavior, the Stone project indicated the significant difference between teacher behavior in "change" and teacher behavior in "no change" classrooms. All teachers in the classrooms in which students changed used extensive or Socratic probes of reasoning; they asked for "why's." Most of the "no-change" class teachers did not. This difference in use of Socratic probes was the only item in a 100-item observation schedule of teacher behavior that differentiated the "change" and "no-change" classes at a statistically significant level. Socratic probing, then, was central to teacher behavior in cognitive-developmental moral education.

The import of these Stone findings may be clarified by another finding from the original Blatt study (Blatt and Kohlberg 1975). This finding represented the positive counterpart of the negative findings of Hartshorne and May (1928-30). Hartshorne and May found that didactic instruction and preaching about honesty or services (altruism) in "character education" classes had almost no lasting or significant effect on either student moral judgment, or "knowledge," or on student moral behavior.

The positive counterpart of the finding in the Blatt study was that moral judgment did change relatively significantly and lastingly (still present in one-year follow-up) without teacher preaching or lecturing. In addition to his own groups, Blatt studied groups in which students were to discuss dilemmas with one another and in which their regular teacher was present only to keep order. In a few of these groups, as much change occurred as in the Blatt-led groups.

The characteristics of the "no-change" leaderless groups were instructive. Most of these no-change classes were classes without stage mixture; in particular, they contained groups of students who were young (age 11-12) and at a relatively low stage. Compared to the Blatt-led classes, these classes usually suffered because peers did not probe each other's reasoning as Blatt's classes did, and no next-stage reasoning was presented as Blatt did if no peer would. In one case I observed, however, the class suffered not from the above but from the pressure of teacher instructional behavior. A class without such probing may be cited. The class was one of the control classes in which teachers were handed dilemmas and asked to have the students discuss them but in which the teachers were given no exposure to developmental aims and methods in dilemma discussions. In that class, the teacher presented a Blatt dilemma to a group of junior high inner-city students. The dilemma was this: Which is worse, stealing from a small store or stealing from the government? A lively discussion ensued between students who said that stealing from the government was worse because you could get in big trouble (presumably a first-stage response, reasoning in terms of punishment and obedience) and other students who argued equally vehemently that stealing from a small store was worse because the storeowner didn't have that much to begin with (a second-stage response, reasoning in terms of individual instrumental need). Rather than allowing the students to carry the discussion, as instructed by Blatt, the teacher remained active, though not in the Blatt manner. After briefly listening to the student discussion, the teacher turned to the board and wrote, "Stealing is wrong," underlined it, and said, "Yes, class, but the real point is that they are both stealing and they are both wrong." He handled the remaining dilemma in a similar way. There was no upward stage movement in this particular "leaderless" class.

In summary, both the Blatt and the Stone students demonstrated the following assumptions of cognitive-developmental moral education:

> Moral education is best conceived of as a natural process of dialogue among peers rather than as a process of didactic instruction or preaching.
>
> The teacher and the curriculum are best conceived of as facilitators of this dialogue through presenting challenging dilemmas or situations, through probing for student reasoning and listening to reasons, and through presenting reasoning at a higher stage.
>
> While no change occurs without any one of these elements in the discussion, the teacher may not be required to supply any of these conditions if the students supply them themselves.

I think it is clear that the psychology of the practice arising from the Blatt effect is the psychology of Piaget with its emphasis on dialogue between students arousing cognitive conflict, overcoming egocentrism of thought through the need for intersubjective argument and through exposure to the next stage up. I call it neo-Socratic not only because the teacher has the role of Socratic questioner, but because the teacher, like Socrates, is assumed to be a moral philosopher animated by a concern for the ideal form of the good or of justice. It assumes that the teacher, and ultimately the student, can be concerned about the universal form of justice or of moral reasoning and promote that, as distinct from a concern about the content of morality embodied in conventions that change in each social time and each social space or culture. It assumes, then, that the teacher can free himself from advocacy and indoctrination for the sake of philosophic dialogue. It assumes that the teacher can have faith that the pursuit of the philosophic good will settle the more immediate questions of conduct or behavior – as Socrates assumed. Socrates could ignore a concern about his student's behavior because he himself was a just or moral man in his behavior, as he demonstrated by example rather than by preaching or by trying to control his student's behavior. For Socrates to know the good was to do the good. His example did not lead all his students to practice their highest conceptions of justice but it informed the intellectual quest for justice with dignity and fascination. Implicit in the faith of Socrates in the power of free dialogue about justice was his faith in Athenian democracy. Even when Athenian democracy condemned Socrates to death for teaching justice, Socrates retained his faith in Athenian democracy and allowed himself to be executed to maintain the social contract.

While the execution of Socrates did not dispel Socrates' own faith in Socratic moral education, it did shake Plato's faith in both democracy and in a purely Socratic approach to moral education. In place of Athenian democracy, Plato envisioned a Republic guided by guardians or philosopher-kings. Only the guardians were to receive a Socratic or philosophic moral education, and then only in adulthood after exposure to indoctrinative moral education, in the context of a communal life with all goods shared to build a spirit of sacrifice for the good of the republic or of the republic or of the total community.

A modern or neo-Platonic vision of moral education I found in an Israeli kibbutz researched by myself (Kohlberg 1971) and by Reimer (1977). The psychology underlying kibbutz moral education was not that of Piaget, but that of Durkheim.

While collective education theory has often been grounded in Marxist social theory and ideology, the same basic theory of collective education has also been developed by completely non-Marxist social scientists. Its most classic intellectual statement was made by the great "bourgeois" French sociologist, Emile Durkheim (1961). According to Durkheim, morality is respect for the rule and altruistic attachment to the social group. He says (1961, p. 148) that

> although family education is an excellent preparation for the moral life, its usefulness is restricted, above all with respect to the spirit of discipline. That which is essential to the spirit of discipline, respect for the rule, can scarcely develop in the familial setting, which is not subject

to general impersonal immutable regulation. But the child must learn respect for the rule, he must learn to do his duty because it is his duty, even though the task may not seem an easy one. Such an apprenticeship must devolve upon the school. . . . School discipline is not a simple device for securing superficial peace in the classroom, it is the morality of the classroom as a small society.

Durkheim holds that altruistic concern or sacrifice, like the sense of duty, is always basically directed toward the group rather than to another individual or to an abstract principle. Durkheim reasons that altruism is always sacrificing the self for something greater than the self, and another self can never be greater than the self except as it stands for the group or for the society. Accordingly, a central part of moral education is the sense of belonging to, and sacrificing for, a group. He says, (1961, p. 239):

In order to commit ourselves to collective ends, we must have above all a feeling and affection for the collectivity. We have seen that such feelings cannot arise in the family where solidarity is based on blood and intimate relationships since the bonds uniting the citizens of a country have nothing to do with such relationships. The only way to instill the inclination to collective life is to get hold of the child when he leaves his family and enters school. To instill in the child a feeling for collective ends, the class must really share in a collective life. Such phrases as "the class," "the spirit of the class," and "the honor of the class" must become something more than abstract expressions in the student's mind.

On this basis, Durkheim suggests that one of the logical innovations in moral education is the use of collective responsibility, collective punishment, and reward.

A means to awaken the feeling of solidarity is the discreet and deliberate use of collective punishments and rewards. Collective sanctions play a very important part in the life of the classroom. The most powerful means to instill in children the feeling of solidarity are to feel that the value of each is a function of the worth of all.

Let me illustrate this Durkheim psychology at work in the kibbutz by a quotation from one of the madrichim or adult leaders of the adolescent group whom I interviewed (Kohlberg 1971). With regard to ideology, this hashomer hatsair (ideologically left wing) madrich tells us: "I demand high values. What I mean by high values are certain social values. I am not talking about the kibbutz, socialism or some other generality. I am talking about living within a society." The iron of kibbutz education, then, is not kibbutz ideology but the iron of the welfare of the peer group and of the kibbutz in which it is embedded. There are certain arbitrary rules related to the ideology, but these rules are not sacred to the madrich. Nevertheless, our madrich tells us that he sometimes rigidly enforces arbitrary rules because it is necessary for the maintenance of the solidarity of the group. The hashomer code prohibits smoking, drinking, and social dancing for the youth. This is not because such actions are believed to be sins according to a Puritan ethic. As our madrich explains these rules (Kohlberg 1971, p. 358):

> I myself can't believe smoking or social dancing are crimes. All over the world children dance and here not. Originally it was part of the youth code, like the Scouts: no smoking, drinking, social dancing to be pure in every respect. It was to symbolize that we are different that we reject those other values. But now it is something else. The "no dancing" may be the only way to keep one within the society, here, to keep the youth society together. Because if a boy wants to be with a girl on more than friendship terms and have sexual intercourse or at least a real sexual life, they withdraw from the group, it destroys the social life of the group. In my own response to the sexual life in the group, I may close my eyes to it, it depends upon which couples and upon the total picture of the group life.

His sternness in behalf of maintaining group solidarity is due to his view that solidarity is one of the two conditions that are essential to his task. (The second condition is simply that the group accepts the guidance of the madrich.) Without this condition, our madrich says, he is powerless to educate, since the incentives for education and socialization are based on the principle of collective responsibility:

> Our methods of education depend upon the group. For 24 hours the adolescent lives with other members of the group. He has to be affected by the group if we are to succeed.
>
> Examples? For instance, do you know about the system of studying here? The system is not examinations, no punishments. Note also that we don't punish, because in itself punishment by the adult has no meaning, it is nothing. The most we can do is to throw a ward out, and that only really happens when he wishes to be thrown out, when he doesn't want to belong to the group anymore, when he doesn't fit in. So we have no real punishment if the child doesn't study or learn. We can come to a person and tell him, "go and study, go and learn." He says, maybe not in these words, but he can say to me, "if I don't study, what are you going to do to me?" And I say, "nothing, what can I do to you?" So I have to use the group. I can go to the group and say, "look, this one, and one or two others, they don't study, they don't participate in class, they are slowing down the progression of the whole group in learning." And so he can say to me, "I don't care," but the group can put the pressure on him. If he cares for the group and has a good relationship with the others, he might change his ways. Now this works in some groups, it doesn't work in others, it depends on the group. If the group is strong, if it has solidarity, it works. If the group is not, it doesn't work. In one of our groups, it works very well now. In another it doesn't work at all (p. 360).

I call the kibbutz form of moral education neo-Platonic as well as Durkheimian because its teachers constitute an analogy to Plato's guardians. The kibbutz is more democratic than Plato's Republic since all adults acceptable as kibbutz members are guardians like the teachers. The adults too all hold things in common and deliberate on the public good. The adults, as parents and especially as teachers, however, practice an indoctrinative moral education of the young based on example as well as preaching. Like the Platonic Republic, only a minority of adults reach the fifth or sixth stage of principledness or of philosophic morality. But like Plato's Republic, all its adult citizens are active in thought and deed on behalf of fourth-stage conceptions of the common good. Even the children from disadvantaged and troubled backgrounds who go to the kibbutz high school eventually attain and practice fourth-stage good citizenship as kibbutz members. In working with alternative teacher advocates, our practice evolved into something closer to the theory of the Republic, of Durkheim, of the kibbutz than of the Socratic theory. By practicing full formal direct democracy, we hoped to avoid possible indoctrinative tyranny by the Platonic guardians or the kibbutz madrichim. As our example of the Cluster community meeting illustrated, formal direct democracy still allows teachers to wield authority as better representatives of the spirit of community or of the common good.

There are weaknesses and dangers in the teacher's role in our neo-Platonic practice, even though it avoids some of the indoctrinative manipulation sometimes found in the kibbutz. These stem largely from the fact that our school is not the larger intergenerational community represented by the kibbutz (Kohlberg 1971, p. 361):

> There is a second basic principle of collective education employed in kibbutz youth groups. It is the principle that the madrich and the wards relate to each other in terms of the membership of both in a permanent kibbutz community which the wards are to enter. As Wolins points out, the madrich says "Be like me" not in the sense of being a teacher, but in the sense of being a member of the kibbutz. The madrich represents the kibbutz to the adolescent, and the adolescent is to grow up to be a member of the kibbutz. There is a permanent community and a permanent way of life which define the aims of kibbutz education for the wards, for the madrich, and for the community. The hashomer madrich tells us "Our education of the youth from the city only works because the kibbutz needs the youth, because the adult members feel they are, when grown up, to be members of the kibbutz. Our maximum goal is that each city youth becomes a member of the kibbutz to share at the same level. Our minimum goal is to reach the level to be good citizens of Israel. But that is a compromise.

Our just community alternative school is not a kibbutz lifelong community, it is only a six-hour school. Our remedy of wider community volunteer projects is a weak solution in comparison to the kibbutz. It can be no more unless teachers, students, and parents are to live a common life as part of a larger intergenerational community. As a result, like Plato's Republic, our just community school is as much an incomplete Utopian ideal as it is a reality. Its reality is sufficient, however, to engender in both students and teachers some of the aspirations and competences a just society requires.

3
ORGANIZING A SCHOOL SYSTEM FOR ETHICS EDUCATION

Robert Sperber
David Miron

THE BROOKLINE MORAL EDUCATION PROJECT, 1974-77

In the spring of 1974, Professors Lawrence Kohlberg of Harvard University and Ralph Mosher of Boston University approached Dr. Robert Sperber, the Superintendent of Schools in Brookline, Massachusetts, to explore his interest in collaborating with them to establish a demonstration project in teacher training and curriculum writing in moral education at the high-school level. Their proposal was to explore similar objectives at the middle-school level (grades six

This chapter is from David C. McClelland, editor. *Development of Social Maturity.* Copyright 1980 by Irvington Publishers, Inc. Reprinted by permission.

The authors wish to acknowledge the important contribution of the Danforth Foundation in supporting the program of ethics education in the Brookline Public Schools. Specifically, they would like to thank Dr. Geraldine Bagby, Vice President, for her understanding and her strong advocacy of this program.

Acknowledgement is also due the members of the Brookline School Committee for authorizing this project; and to Dr. Henry Zabierek, Director of Social Studies; Mr. Carmen P. Rinaldi, Headmaster of the High School; Dr. Ann F. DiStefano, Coordinator of School-Within-A-School; and Ms. Margot Stern Strom, a teacher who trained other middle-grade teachers, for their role in making the project work and for serving as resources to the authors in the writing of the chapter.

Special thanks are also due Professor Ralph Mosher of Boston University, who represented the Center for Moral Education as overall coordinator of the Brookline project.

The authors also wish to acknowledge the contribution of Miss Lillian U. Ford for her expert editing of their material.

through eight); and to develop a one-semester course for Brookline parents in the psychology of the child's moral development and the parents' role in moral education. This demonstration project was to be underwritten by the Danforth Foundation of St. Louis, Missouri. Sperber, offered resources to help teachers deal with questions regarding the state of morality in America, responded enthusiastically to Kohlberg's and Mosher's proposal. In order to begin the program, particularly one that could be considered controversial, Sperber suggested that a presentation be made to the Brookline School Committee to ask for its support.

In presenting the idea for the project to the School Committee in June, 1974, Sperber stated:

> People are dissatisfied with their society. They are distrustful of people in responsible leadership positions. Life is grim; examples of immoral behavior abound (Watergate, etc.); and there is fear of a crumbling economy. In short, our society is frightened and groping for direction. With the decline of the two-parent nuclear family, there is a void that has to be filled by the schools to help youngsters sort out issues of right and wrong and to learn about their responsibilities as citizens. Improvements in our society, however, cannot occur globally. They must be undertaken in small pieces, effort by effort, with small groups of people, particularly among families and on the local scene. With little evidence of other local institutions indicating commitment to solving the pressing social issues of our times, the public schools must step in. The only concern I have is that ethical education not be perceived as an integral part of English, history, science, mathematics, and the arts. We must also look upon it as a way of teaching, and personnel in the schools must be guided by the principles enunciated by Kohlberg and others in terms of their own personal conduct as adult models.

The Brookline School Committee voted tentative approval of the project in June, 1974. They asked that a progress report be made in January, 1975, following the seminar for a group of volunteer High School teachers which would present information about Kohlberg's theory and the teaching of moral education.

The First Year of the Project: 1974-75

The First Workshop for High School Teachers

The workshop met twice monthly from early October, 1974, through January of 1975. Participants included ten social studies teachers, ten guidance counselors, the High School Headmaster, an English teacher, and the Coordinator of Independent Studies. The workshop reviewed the psychological research on moral development conducted by Professor Kohlberg over the past twenty years; examined curriculum materials on moral education available in social studies, English, and psychology; considered the methodology of teaching ethical reasoning; and began to create curriculum materials within the content of Brookline High School courses in American history, World history, literature, psychology, and independent studies. Although the faculty members were volunteers, two-thirds of the group indicated they would continue developing these course materials during the spring semester. The focus on making moral education an integral part of the High School's curriculum was a key decision and one that would lead to positive acceptance of this project by certain High School faculty and the community in the months ahead.

In January, 1975, the Superintendent presented a progress report to the School Committee on the work to date and asked for permission to continue the project for the next two and a half years, or the life of the grant. Critical to the authorization given by the School Committee was the report of the Headmaster of Brookline High School. He indicated that although he had originally been concerned that the material would indoctrinate and the teaching of moral education concepts might intrude on the work of the church and the home, he was now convinced (having participated in the seminar) that the teaching of moral education was a legitimate function of the schools. This was particularly true since the teachers were adapting the methodology of teaching moral dilemmas as part of the regular curriculum.

The School Committee's support of the moral education project was consistent with the results of the eighth annual Gallup Poll of Public Attitude Toward Education, released in the fall of 1976, which indicated that 69 percent of the parents of pupils thought the schools should assume a share of the responsibility for the moral education of youth. The same poll gave a list of qualities important in the development of a child, and "high moral standards" was mentioned most often.

Spring Semester Activities

The unanimous support of the School Committee made it possible for Professors Kohlberg and Mosher to proceed vigorously with the three major objectives for the project: (1) pursuing teacher training and curriculum writing through existing courses offered at Brookline High School in social studies, psychology, and independent studies [see Chapters 6, 7, and 8 for full examples of various curricula using this approach] ; (2) initiating a teacher-training program at the middle-grades level; and (3) developing and conducting a seminar for Brookline parents.

Teacher Training and Curriculum Development

On their own initiative and without funds, following their participation in the introductory seminar in the fall of 1974-75, several of the social studies teachers wrote and tested two dilemmas for each of twelve units in the standard American history course. An honors course was revised to emphasize ethical issues in certain major periods of the history of our country [see Chapter 6]. Similar adaptations were made in a course in Russian history, a law course, and a course entitled "America Through Its Media: 1910-1970." Parallel curriculum development was done for courses in psychology, guidance, and independent studies. The text for all Psychology I classes, taught by the guidance staff, included a chapter on "Moral Development." Several pilot courses in the psychology of moral development were tested in this period. One of these courses involved twenty students from Brookline and Boston. A guidance counselor taught a Psychology II course, "Cross-Cultural Experiences and Value Systems," to a Brookline High School class of recent immigrants representing fourteen different countries. Two curriculum projects were planned during the spring of 1975 for further development during the summer and the next school year, 1975-76. One course focused on racial and ethnic prejudice, and a second interdisciplinary course for freshmen and sophomores involved social studies, English, and guidance.

Work in the Middle Grades

So many Brookline elementary school teachers wished to participate in the 1974 fall workshop that the Project staff decided to respond with a three-session workshop in the spring of 1975. It covered: (1) an overview of the psychology of moral development; (2) various materials and methods of teaching moral education; and (3) moral and social development in children. An average of 75 elementary school teachers attended each session and the discussions were very lively. Clearly the interest in moral education was not limited to the High School. Tentative dates were set during the spring for a fall workshop which would parallel the objectives of the High School workshop of 1974. With so much interest generated at the middle school, the age group between eleven and thirteen years was identified as a group to teach. This made theoretical sense since Kohlberg's research suggested that a critical change in moral development from pre-conventional to conventional moral reasoning occurs at this age level.

The Parent Seminar

During the spring, plans were made to offer a one-semester course in 1975-76 for parents interested in learning about the moral development of children. While the seminar would give a priority to parents whose children and adolescents were in moral education classes, it would also be available to other interested citizens.

The reasons for the seminar were threefold: (1) the Brookline school system and the project staff believed that parents are the primary moral educators and thus they should be given knowledge to help the moral development of their children; (2) they believed that parents and citizens should understand that the theory and practices of moral education were rational and the curriculum was non-indoctrinating; and (3) in order for moral education programs to be widely disseminated, they would require broad community understanding and support.

Summer Curriculum Workshops

During the summer of 1975, significant curriculum development activities took place. Sixteen High School teachers and counselors produced the following courses or additions:

Social Studies
(1) Thirty-five dilemmas were developed for incorporation in the standard American history course, which is a required course for all students.
(2) In the honors American history course, three units were developed entitled, "The Revolution," "Making the Constitution," and "The Federalist Era," plus a teachers' guide.
(3) Moral education content was integrated, in the form of written dilemmas and film, in two courses: "Law and the Individual" and "America Through Its Media: 1910-1970."
(4) An elective in the School-Within-A-School entitled, "The Psychology of Ethics in Relationships," was offered [see Chapter 8].
Psychology/Guidance
(5) "About Prejudice," a semester course for freshmen, which treated racial and ethnic prejudice as moral issues.
(6) A course for the High School students in the psychology of moral development which included a practicum in moral education in the elementary schools.
(7) "Cross-Cultural Experiences and Value Systems"
(8) "Counseling and Communication Skills"
English
(9) "Adventure Literature: Readings and Moral Dilemmas"

The Second Year of the Project: 1975-76

The three major goals for the second year of the Danforth-Brookline Moral Education Project, as it was called, included consolidating the High School teacher training and curriculum development program; offering a teacher training program for interested middle-grade teachers; and actually conducting the parent seminar which had been in the planning stage during year one (1974-75). To these three goals was added a fourth goal of great importance, involving the project staff as consultants with the students and faculty of the School-Within-A-School. This is an alternative high school program discribed more fully later in the chapter. A final goal for the second year was disseminating the results of the work to date and some efforts at acquainting the community with the importance of the program. Let us examine each of these goals to see how they were met during the course of the second year.

Curriculum Development at Brookline High School

The essential process at the High School involved teaching material developed during the previous year and in the summer curriculum workshops. Curricula had to be developed, initially in workshops when teachers could concentrate on that task alone, and then each year the material would be painstakingly taught, critiqued by both the teachers who developed it and by colleagues who were given some released time to observe and offer critical comments. This process was followed in two departments, Guidance and Social Studies, as well as in School-Within-A-School and in the seminars taught in the Independent Studies Program. The process was then repeated when the courses developed in the summer of 1975 were further revised in summer workshops in 1976, to be taught again, with modifications during the school year 1976-77. It was planned that careful evaluation would be made as to the effects of these courses on moral reasoning when they were taught in 1976-77. For example, students taking a moral education course on prejudice offered by the Guidance Department showed statistically significant gains in moral reasoning and ego development when tested at the end of the course.

Moral Education Programs in the Middle Grades

The desire for a moral education workshop for middle-grade teachers came about as a result of interest shown by elementary school teachers in a similar workshop offered to the High School staff in the fall of 1974. As indicated above, 75 elementary school teachers, in the spring of 1975, responded enthusiastically to the three-session workshop introducing moral development theory.

A Fall workshop, which was planned during the summer of 1975 by Henry Zabierek, Director of Social Studies, and Margot Strom, an elementary teacher, had several goals. These goals included: (1) teaching and discussing Kohlberg's theory of moral development; (2) examining moral education curricula suitable for the pre-adolescent; and (3) identifying curriculum interests which certain teachers would develop in detail during the spring semester.

The two workshop consultants also identified three goals for the elementary teachers in the workshop: (1) they wanted participation from as many schools and from as many subject areas as possible to develop a network of informed teachers throughout the system; (2) they wished to encourage communication between the High School staff to present their work at several sessions; and (3) they desired to offer a forum and support group for the middle grade teachers who have more formal responsibility for the moral climate in their classrooms.

The first semester workshop was structured along lines similar to those of the High School workshop of the previous year. Bi-weekly meetings consisted of large-group presentations with follow-up discussions, and small-group informal discussions of assigned readings and events tying together the material learned in the workshop with the life of the school.

The goal of attracting a widely representative group of teachers was met. Teachers came from seven of the eight Kindergarten-Grade 8 schools and represented the following disciplines: art, guidance, health education, English, science, social studies, foreign languages, special education, the multicultural program, and the library. Three principals also attended some of the sessions. (Participation of the principals was a critical element as it was in the case of the High School Headmaster, who attended the previous year's program.)

The 28 participants focused on issues relating to justice in the classroom and school as well as learning about stages of moral development, applicable curriculum material, and how to lead moral discussions. An informal evaluation completed at the end of semester one indicated that the teaching goals had been met, but the participants desired more time for small-group discussions.

To accommodate the desire for small-group discussion, the seminar members decided to break into two groups. One group concentrated on developing curriculum materials related to role-taking and moral reasoning to be integrated into the regular classroom subject matter. A language arts and social studies teacher, who taught a unit on heroes and heroines, developed role-taking opportunities through role-playing, writing, and discussion as the children learned about Martin Luther King and Tamsen Donner. A teacher of multicultural materials presented, in moral discussion format, a unit on the myths and folktales of different cultures. Guidance counselors helped the teachers devise strategies to solve moral dilemmas arising from their classrooms. This group shared the results of their work at a parent-teacher meeting.

The second discussion group was devoted to developing the school as a democratic institution. The participants designed activities based on their school roles and their particular relationship with their students. For example, a librarian developed a weekly program for eighth-graders in which they talked about their experiences helping younger children as tutors, discussed films they saw together, and helped develop discipline procedures for their school. A home economics teacher worked with her principal and other teachers in creating role-playing techniques for solving moral conflict situations arising from the classroom and within the school.

Despite the excellent work that was accomplished in 1975-76 with the teachers of the middle grades, there was no summer curriculum workshop to follow through and no further consultation from the project staff to these teachers during 1976-77 because of a lack of funds. Some of these teachers, however, incorporated the techniques and materials into their teaching on their own.

Parent Education Seminar

There were three major goals of the parent education seminar: (1) to help the parents, as the primary moral educators of children, became familiar with Kohlberg's theory; (2) to help them understand how this theory was used in specific curricula of the Brookline Public Schools; and (3) to help them apply the theory so that they could conduct effective family discussions about moral issues. The Superintendent of Schools was very much interested in this phase of the Project and attempted to aid the Director of Adult Education, Harry Lent, and the Director of Guidance, Roger Aubrey, who were collaborating in offering this course, by announcing it in one of his regular meetings with all the Parent-Teacher Organization presidents. In addition, flyers were sent to all the teachers urging them to contact interested parents; mailings were made to community organizations; a special mailing to community people was made by the Director of Adult Education; and a press release was sent to the local paper.

Eight sessions were held. Early classes, through lectures, films, readings, and discussions, focused on the theory of moral development. Moral dilemmas were introduced and became the essential focus of the course. The parents were taught to understand a moral dilemma, how it was used in classrooms and how it can be used in leading family discussions, and how discussing moral dilemmas can contribute to the development of the child. The course illustrated the value of differences of opinion in discussing moral issues since these differences promote a confrontation between people who reason at different levels of development. Moral issues which were discussed focused on social norms, property, life, truth, matters of personal conscience, and civil liberties. By session four, the parents not only had discussed particular dilemmas but also were practicing the reasoning of an assigned moral stage. A Brookline teacher explained how she taught moral dilemmas in social studies. First, she presented the dilemma and asked questions to elicit the childrens' reasons for taking one position or another. Then, if the original dilemma did not engage the children, she presented an analagous or alternative dilemma and encouraged them to expand on it. Finally, the teacher asked the students to summarize the discussion in the light of factors which could influence their decision, such as the law, or personal responsibility, or the value of life, etc. Parents were taught how they could apply these steps in leading moral discussions with their own children. In the last four sessions, the parents discussed actual family dilemmas, for example, bullying, allowances, part-time jobs, and dating. Some parents in the class volunteered to lead discussions of these issues at home and then shared the tapes of these discussions in class. The taped interviews confirmed that parents were able to present a high level of reasoning with their children.

Although the attendance at the seminars was low (eight parents and three adolescents), the evaluation of the course by the participants was positive. Most of the seminar members had begun to use the Kohlberg methodology with their children at home, and there was indication that parents would inform others about taking the course the following year.

Developing a Just Community Concept at the School-Within-A-School

The fourth goal of year two was to establish a democratic, self-governing program at Brookline's alternative high school. The School-Within-A-School (SWS), was first created in 1969 in response to the needs of students who wanted more of a say in their own education and who were looking for a more personal relationship with their teachers. The school originally recruited a voluntary group of about 100 students, who spent part of their day in a fourth-floor wing of the main high school taking special courses, created by the SWS faculty of four persons: a coordinator, who was a guidance counselor; and teachers of social studies, mathematics, science, and English. The remainder of the students' day was spent in courses with the rest of the school taking the laboratory sciences, foreign languages, and arts. The students' extracurricular activities were also centered around the alternative program. Unitl 1974, the staff made decisions regarding the rules of this special community, although SWS students attended faculty meetings and expressed their points-of-view. A desire on the part of the SWS faculty to explore the role of students in governing SWS and the exposure of SWS faculty to the original moral education seminar for High School faculty led the staff, some students, and two staff members from the Center for Moral Education to come together in the spring of 1975 to begin planning the establishment of the Just Community concept for SWS for the fall of 1975. After outlining the direction of a self-governing community, in the spring of 1975, the SWS students and staff voted to participate.

The initial focus of the students was how to change the governance structure of SWS. There were many meetings to establish the rules of order and to ensure fair practices. Attention was also directed towards ways to establish an agenda and how to select a chairperson.

The vehicle that was chosen to carry the major effort in domocratic government was the town meeting, which had been used in SWS since 1970. There was much debate among the students and the faculty as to whether attendance at the town meeting was to be voluntary or mandatory. This particular issue continued to be raised throughout the 1975-76 school year and represented the tension arising from switching the community from one which gave attention to the individual to one which focused both on the freedoms of the individual and the requirements of being a member of a community. The group wrestled with the question of how much freedom must be sacrificed by the individual on behalf of the community. The consultants from the Center encouraged the SWS staff to turn over as many issues as possible to the town meeting. Gradually the students shared in deciding such important issues as curriculum, rules of discipline, classroom attendance policies, and admissions procedures.

Initially, the students were more comfortable talking about abstract questions and avoided discussing individual staff or making judgments about fellow students. For example, as they discussed the concept of "the violation of another person's rights," they were reluctant to talk about peers who were acting in an unruly manner in the quadrangle of the High School. However, when the SWS group was denied the right to put up a poster announcing a meeting on a controversial issue, they wrote a letter to the newspaper and the High School Headmaster outlining very forceful arguments dealing with freedom of speech. As a result of this letter, the Headmaster agreed to form a committee, which included students, to establish criteria concerning the display of posters.

Other issues which the town meeting voted on included whether students from the regular High School would be permitted to elect an SWS course; the process for appointing new staff members; how to select students for SWS membership; dealing with SWS students who were "cutting" classes; grading procedures; and racism in the High School.

One of the Center consultants took basic responsibility for the conduct of the town meetings, which were held twice weekly. The town meeting decided to form an Agenda Committee of five students, which served as the governing body of the town meeting. This committee, chosen randomly from a list of volunteers, established topics to be discussed at the town meeting. The consultant helped the students on the Agenda Committee, a position which rotated quarterly. Since the Chairman of the Agenda Committee also chaired the town meeting, the consultant helped with leadership skills, parliamentary rules for conducting a meeting effectively, and moral discussion skills.

The other consultant worked with the teachers to help them make their classrooms more democratic. The SWS teachers were not only concerned to teach more democratically, but also to apply moral development theory to their curriculum planning and their teaching. The consultant performed his role by being a participant-observer in the classroom and sharing his observations with the staff. At the town meetings he played a similar role by serving as a catalyst looking at issues from many different viewpoints. After each town meeting the consultants and the Co-Director from the Center helped interested staff and students analyze the content and process of the discussion from a theoretical viewpoint.

The 1975-76 year was spent creating a new governing structure, and the students and faculty were pleased with the results. They voted unanimously to continue the town meeting form of government in 1976-77. The major focus in 1976-77 would be to improve the skills necessary to maintain this form of government. There was also interest expressed in evaluating whether or not participation in the democratic school could lead to a significant increase in the students' ability to reason ethically and whether there was any perceptible improvement in the "moral climate" of SWS.

Dissemination of the Project Results

The final goal of year two of the Danforth-Brookline Moral Education Project was to disseminate the results of the work to date. One of the important objectives of the project was to make the results of the Brookline experience known not only locally but throughout the state and nationally, in order that the program's outcomes might be generalized.

Many presentations were made, over fourteen locally (i.e., within Massachusetts), twelve nationally (e.g., at the American Personnel and Guidance Association), and one at an International Conference of Israeli Educators.

In addition to the local, national, and international discussions of the project, there was interchange, consultation, and collaboration among the Brookline, Cambridge, and Pittsburgh-Carnegie Mellon projects. The teacher training emphasis and the curriculum development experiences of the three centers (Brookline, Cambridge, and Pittsburgh) were brought together so that ideas could be exchanged.

Curriculum material developed in Brookline was distributed widely in the United States and to Israel. Also, the work of the individual teachers was published in a number of journals and magazines. These included: *School Education, The School Counselor, Kaleidescope* (Massachusetts State Department of Education Journal), and *Theory into Practice.* This last publication gave extensive coverage to the subject.

In addition to articles which teachers have contributed about the project, *Newsweek, McCall's,* and *Glamour* magazines reported on the work of the program. The Guidance Associates organization created a filmstrip based on the program for use with high school teachers.

The Third Year of the Project: 1976-77

In the third and final year of the project, six objectives were formulated: (1) further writing and use of moral education curricula in the High School; (2) continuation of curriculum development and staff training in the middle schools; (3) continuation of the moral education seminar for interested parents and adolescents; (4) further development of the School-Within-A-School as a democratic community; (5) dissemination of the project results; and (6) the beginning of the design and implementation of research to measure the effectiveness of the moral education curriculum.

Curriculum at the High School

Consultation with Professor Mosher and Dr. Zabierek continued for high school teachers and counselors using the moral education curriculum. One guidance counselor taught a psychology course on moral development to juniors and seniors. Although the foundation's support ended in June, 1977, two sections of the course were continued. This was significant since it indicated a commitment of the Brookline Public Schools to continue the curriculum begun with foundation support.

The "About Prejudice" course, which was first taught to ninth-graders in 1976-77, was incorporated as part of the freshman orientation seminar in 1977-78 so that the entire class would be exposed to this new curriculum.

In the Social Studies Department, three teachers taught the moral dilemma history units they had been developing and testing for the past two years.

The Middle-Grade Program

The 1975-76 middle-grade moral education workshop had developed a core of teachers who were interested in making the upper grades a more democratic institution, a goal somewhat parallel to the aims of the SWS faculty. During the summer of 1976, a questionnaire had been sent to all seventh- and eighth-grade students at the Runkle School. The questionnaire was concerned with issues of governance and life in the school community, including course scheduling, locker placement, and snowball rules. The rate of response was high – 80 percent.

At the start of the 1976-77 school year, the school principal put into effect a majority of the suggestions resulting from the questionnaire. In addition, a student advisory group was organized, consisting of forty seventh- and eighth-graders plus teacher representatives, including some from the preceding year's workshop. The advisory group's purpose was to examine school community issues and decide how to make decisions. They met four times and the forty students had to demonstrate their commitment by attending all four meetings. They did.

A new moral education curriculum on the Nazi Holocaust was prepared for the eighth grade. This curriculum was generated by two teachers' enthusiasm as a result of their attendance at two Greater Boston meetings of professors and teachers dedicated to developing a new curriculum on the Holocaust and other acts of genocide [see Chapter 12].

The commitment of the Brookline Public Schools to continue their work in moral education at the expiration of the grant was further demonstrated by a decision of the Brookline Teacher Center to conduct workshops for elementary teachers on human development and classroom management techniques related to the work done by middle-school teachers in moral education.

Moral Education Seminar for Parents

For the second year in a row, the Brookline Adult Education Program offered the seminar, "Parents as Moral Educators." Sixteen parents, whose children ranged in age from preschool to college, as well as a few adolescents, took the course over the two-year period.

School-Within-A-School

The major work of the Danforth-supported staff in 1976-77 was to continue to refine the democratic community operating within the SWS at the High School. A history of student reluctance to take action against any peers who broke the rules of the community and hesitancy to restrict anyone's freedom by establishing such policies as making attendance at town meetings mandatory has been noted.

Also during 1975-76 the students had been content to let the staff deal with each discipline case rather than establish policies to govern the behavior of the group. As a result of consultation with the SWS faculty and the Danforth staff, the students gradually began to realize that the faculty was fallible and reacted on the basis of personalities. They also recognized that it wasn't fair to put all responsibility for enforcing appropriate conduct on the staff. While the students hoped philosophically that each student would goven himself properly, in reality this was not occurring; and thus the entire SWS community had to pass a set of appropriate rules to govern behavior.

This realization led to the SWS town meeting passing a rule at the end of the 1975-76 school year that each student would have to take two courses in SWS and leave class periods open for the town meeting.

Thus, during the first semester of 1976-77, with the help of their teachers and the Danforth consultants, the students began to assume greater control of the town meeting system and of running the acutal meetings. They made changes in the way the meetings were structured and introduced changes in the rules of order which had originally been suggested by the consultants. They also asked the consultant who had previously coached the chairperson during the town meetings not to do so but rather to be available only as a resource.

Nonetheless, by the second semester, SWS was running out of topics for the town meeting. Attendance was down and there was a general sense of lack of community. The students had some good discussions about cliques, which led to an effort to orient new members and discussions about how it felt to be excluded from a group. A meeting at which attendance was requested was held to find out why town meeting attendance was declining. This meeting led to revisions in policies which had been hampering attendance. Picnics and other socials were held, and a sense of community began to grow.

By the end of the school year, the students had voted to make town meeting attendance mandatory. They also decided to form advisory groups to help students discuss issues of common concern. SWS had passed a crisis, with everyone making an increased personal commitment to the town meeting structure. The students had learned that building a sense of community was difficult, that it required hard work, and that the town meeting structure alone could not carry the whole responsibility for the success or failure of their school as a democratic community.

Continuing Efforts at Dissemination

The major effort at dissemination in the third year of the project for Brookline was a workshop for teachers in the greater Boston area. The workshop, held in May, 1977, was attended by about 170 elementary and high school teachers from all over the Greater Boston area. Almost every Brookline teacher and administrator who had been working with the program presented his/her experiences, techniques, and materials. The purpose of the workshop was to attempt to interest teachers and administrators from other school systems in adopting moral education programs; to discuss the steps to be taken in introducing the program; and to show how teachers, with appropriate training in understanding the theory, can write, produce, and teach moral education curricula. The reception was good, and a decision was made to establish a dissemination center. Fifteen thousand dollars of seed money was contributed by the Danforth Foundation.

On the state and national levels during 1976-77, Brookline teachers participated in 21 moral education programs. In addition, the work of some key teachers on the project was documented in five educational films and videotapes, including one broadcast by the Public Broadcasting Service.

Objectives and Activities of the Project

The summary in Table 3.1 of the objectives and activities of the Moral Education Project in Brookline from 1974 to 1977 will be helpful in understanding the work that has been described in the case study.

Three Important Issues

As one analyzes the project described in the case study, three important issues arise.

Challenges

First, at any time during the introduction of the project or as the program developed, were there any questions raised or challenges made by staff, the parents, or community organizations? If there were challenges, how were they dealt with?

Earlier in the case study, reference was made to the Headmaster's concerns about the wisdom of introducing Kohlberg's moral education material to the Brookline High School program because he felt it was indoctrinative and intruded on the work of the church and home. He also felt at that time that good teachers were already employing moral dilemmas as a teaching methodology, so why introduce a new vocabulary or knowledge of Kohlberg's particular methodology? Finally, his initial opposition was based on the fact that questions

TABLE 3.1
Objectives and Activities of Danforth Moral Education Program, 1974-77

Date	Objectives	Teacher Training	Curriculum Development	Specific Courses	Democratic Community	Outreach Activities
10/74-1/75	To establish a demonstration project in teacher training and curriculum writing	23 High School faculty. Twice monthly				
1/75-6/75	To explore similar objectives at Middle-Grade level. To develop one-semester course for parents	75 elementary teachers. Three sessions	Some social studies programs: Psychology I & II Cross-Cultural course	American History Law and the Individual America Since 1945 Eighth-Grade Social Studies	Planning spring, 1975, 75 students voted to participate	
5/75-9/75			Some social studies programs: Honors History Psychology & Guidance Freshman Orientation Counseling and Communication Seventh- and Eighth-Grade Social Studies	Women in Society Criminal Justice		
9/75-6/76	To consolidate High School teachers and curriculum development work. To conduct teacher training and Curriculum Development for High School teachers. To conduct courses for parents	23 middle grade school teachers. Twice monthly. 16 middle grade teachers and others. Twice monthly		Parents' course; 11 people	Town meeting voluntary/mandatory discussion; new governing structure emerged.	14 local presentations, 12 national presentations, 1 international

	To disseminate results of work to date		
5/76-6/77	To continue developing and using curriculum in High School		21 presentations
	To continue SWS consultation	Parents' course; 16 participants	Student control of meetings asserted
	To disseminate		
	To design research Evaluation		

Source: Compiled by the authors.

regarding morality and ethics are so diverse that the school, being already over-burdened with expanding curricula, was scarcely in a position to assume, too, training in morality or ethics.

These are common objections which could be raised not only by professional staff but by parents or groups in the community.

The key to overcoming these objections was the participation of the Headmaster (as previously noted) in a training program along with volunteer staff from the Social Studies and Guidance Departments. After school seminars focused on orientation, explanation of Kohlberg's theory, and detailed decussion on how the theory might be translated into curriculum and how it might be taught in classrooms. The Headmaster's personal description of his experience gained from participating in the seminars is particularly insightful and helpful to any superintendent thinking of introducing similar material into his school system:

> I participated in all of these seminars and came away with a modified position from the one expressed earlier. Any doubls which I had had respecting Kohlberg's theories being promulgated as a new religion were dispelled. The processes and steps Kohlberg described were substantially wide and flexible so as not to limit the mode of instruction in particular classes. The objectives to heighten awareness and to develop the ability to recognize levels of understanding were realizable. The outcome of using moral dilemmas in teaching would not affect or impair the regular teaching process or preempt the materials normally required in each course. The fact that individual teachers could prepare their own dilemmas for presentation reassured me further.

Similar objections and questions were raised by a small number of parents at one of the elementary schools. Their major concern was that the parents should be responsible for their children's training in morality. The principal of the school and a teacher who was using the material and had become a trainer of other teachers met with the parents. They explained that they were teaching moral development as part of the curriculum rather than "doing Kohlberg."

After the parents had attended the moral education program being taught under Adult Education, were supplied with readings, and had many long discussions, the real issue eventually emerged. The parents, in fact, were opposed to a group guidance program in which the counselor was attempting to help children sort out their feelings and values. (This group guidance program was introduced independently of the Moral Education Project.)

Despite the staff's attempts to supply information, two parents remained adamantly opposed to the moral education program on the grounds that they felt they were totally responsible for their children's moral development. Their children were therefore allowed to be withdrawn from the classroom moral education programs.

The final challenge to the moral education program came from a League of Women Voters' study completed in 1976. This study raised four issues as a result of its comprehensive inquiry:

(1) Should the High School not indicate in its Catalogue that certain social studies courses used moral dilemma methodology? It was agreed to do so although discussion of right and wrong has always been a part of every social studies course.

(2) The League felt that certain dilemmas were contrived. It was pointed out that the dilemmas in our social studies courses are drawn from issues in the curriculum in all cases, based on historical facts, and were not contrived.

(3) The League indicated in its report that the moral dilemma technique was "not an easy or simple one to use." This was acknowledged and attention was called to the extensive training seminars for teachers on theory, techniques, and materials.

(4) Finally, the League stated that "there seems little willingness among school department personnel involved in their use to consider possible shortcomings in Kohlberg's theory or technique." This reaction was surprising, and the League was assured that it was not so, and that the Social Studies Department had adapted the theory of Kohlberg to conform to the philosophy of the social studies program.

Total Impact

A second major question arose about the total impact of the moral development program in terms of numbers of children and faculty and the programmatic impact on students' moral development. It was estimated that twenty trained High School faculty had taught moral development curriculum to 450 students. At the elementary and middle school grade levels, approximately thirty teachers were involved along with 650 children. In terms of programmatic impact, the High School Headmaster felt, based on impressions of admittedly "soft data," that there was "increased awareness, sensitivity, and understanding among High School students and the staff involved and that ultimately the school community and society will benefit."

The coordinator of SWS reported her impressions of observable changes in students' attitudes towards the democratic school. Since the student body voted to mandate town meeting attendance for all members as a vehicle to make decisions, students had a much stronger ownership in the alternative school. Previously, only a small group volunteered to do the necessary tasks to keep SWS going. Now, as a result of the moral development program, all students, randomly selected through a jury selection process, shared responsibility for the community's welfare. Students talked openly about the difference in environment between SWS and the rest of Brookline High School. They spoke about what should happen in a democratic school and what their role should be vis-à-vis the faculty and SWS.

Institutionalizing the Program

A third major issue related to how Brookline was planning to institutionalize the moral development program as the Danforth Foundation funding ended in 1977.

Institutionalizing the program was to be accomplished primarily through teacher training and by adopting curriculum which had been modified as a result of workshops. The Director of Social Studies made plans to utilize in 1978 a core of teachers, who were originally trained by Kohlberg, Mosher, and Fenton in 1974, to teach other members of the department. These training workshops for both high school and elementary school teachers were supported by local workshop funds. As a result of the curriculum workshops, the following courses which include moral development material had become part of the official social studies curriculum: eighth-grade social studies, "Law and the Individual," United States history, "America Since 1945," "Women in Society," and Criminal Justice.

Summary of the Project: 1974-77

As the project ended, most of its objectives had been realized. Several dozen Brookline teachers had developed skills in incorporating moral education in social studies, English, and guidance curricula and had learned the pedagogy as well. Although the grant had ended, the Brookline Public Schools were committed to continuing these courses at the middle-school level and at the High School. A new course in the teaching of the Holocaust was developed and adopted for grade eight with other outside support funds. A group of parents had been exposed to this program. Some evaluation activities had taken place and a new grant from a different foundation (Ford) had been secured to evaluate the democratic community of the SWS. In the words of the Project Center (Kohlberg and Mosher 1977) "A major thrust not fully anticipated in the original proposal was the development of an alternative school democratic community (The School-Within-A-School) oriented to moral development goals. This has represented a more intense and theoretically interesting non-academic or experimental emphasis in moral education than was projected in the original proposal."

The report of the Project Center also stated, "The Danforth Project in Brookline has been successful, we believe, in being the first example in America of the official and effective commitment of a public school system and of a working group of teachers to an approach to civic and moral education which is a reasoned application of research knowledge and scholarly thought to the area."

HOW THE BROOKLINE MORAL EDUCATION PROJECT WAS ORGANIZED AND ITS EFFECT ON TEACHERS AND STUDENTS

As indicated earlier in this chapter, three innovations were promoted by the organizers of the Brookline Moral Education Project: (1) a curriculum designed to increase moral reasoning among high school and middle-school students; (2) the establishment of a "just community" concept in the Brookline alternative high school; and (3) teaching parents to be better moral educators. A great deal of activity was generated in support of these three innovations, and this section will examine the principles behind this activity.

At the outset, the consultants from the Center for Moral Education worked with the Superintendent of Schools to establish a climate for change and to solidify the support of the Brookline School Committee. With the Superintendent's critical backing and with additional support from other key people, the School Committee gave its approval. Organizational theorists such as Argyris (1962) and innovation experts such as Miles (1964) identify support from the top decision makers as key to a change strategy. To quote Mosher (1977) "Critical to the success of the project has been an administrative climate of support."

As with many innovations, funding and intellectual stimulation came from an external source. In this case, the source was the Danforth Foundation via the Center for Moral Education at Harvard University and Boston University. The overriding objective was to establish, in one or more school systems, a moral education demonstration program in the High School and then be able to point to this as a model. A demonstration program would provide research results as well as experience at the middle-grade level and with parents. Both of these last two objectives were priorities for the Center staff.

The strategy was to give teachers and counselors some knowledge of moral development theory and existing curricula in values education, and then to have each teacher develop his/her own curriculum and materials which would complement his/her courses. In this way a significant number of practitioners would become curriculum developers. Those teachers would become trainers of other teachers. With a core group of teachers and counselors having the necessary theoretical knowledge, curriculum development skill and teacher training competencies, the conditions would be right for a vital center to continue efforts started by external forces.

This strategy, described by Mosher in Chapter 1, comes close to the classic Research Development and Diffusion model of change identified by Havelock and Guskin (1969). It is useful to use the R, D, and D model to review the activities undertaken in Brookline. The steps in the R, D, and D model are diagrammed in Figure 3.1.

There are a number of similarities between the model and the activities performed in Brookline. Basic research on moral development was conducted

FIGURE 3.1

Research Development and Diffusion Model of Change

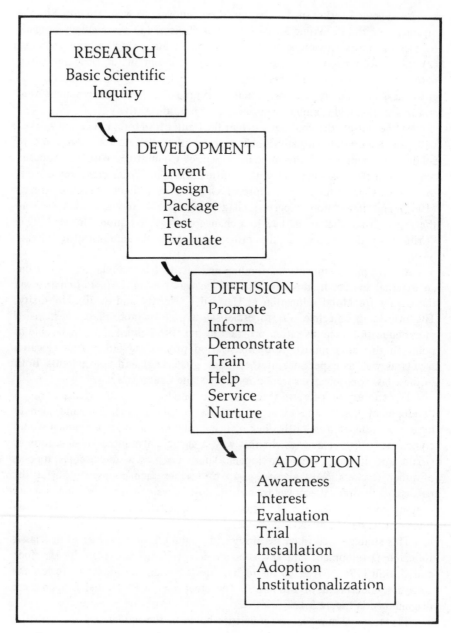

by Kohlberg and his colleagues. Curriculum materials were developed over the years in the form of dilemmas which illustrate stage thinking. Some experience was available in establishing "just communities" in correctional institutions. Information and materials on both of these developments were available at the start of the Brookline program.

The workshop conducted for the High School teachers in the fall of 1974 was the first major attempt at diffusion of the "20 years of research" in moral development. Efforts at diffusion led to adoption of the idea, thus leading to the development of curriculum materials and courses for students, as documented above. Essential to the Brookline project was the Brookline teachers' taking a major role in designing, packaging, testing, and evaluating curriculum materials for use in classrooms. All these activities can be entered under the rubric of development in the R, D, and D paradigm. Therefore, while a major effort was made at diffusion and adoption, the teachers who participated in the Brookline project were actually developing the innovation as they adopted the idea.

Institutionalization of the democratic community of the SWS followed a similar pattern. While the innovation was being diffused and adopted, the Brookline teachers and students, with Mosher, were developing it and giving meaning to the idea.

The attempt to reach the parents and increase their ability to be moral educators can be seen as a third innovation tried in the Brookline project. Here the results seem quite clear: institutionalization was not needed. The course for parents was not continued due to lack of interest in the particular course offered. It appears from hindsight that reaching the parents was really an effort in and of itself, and to have tried to accomplish more than what was attempted at Brookline was beyond the scope of the project. A number of alternative approaches to the course offered might have been more successful. Perhaps the ability of parents to serve as moral educators must be promoted in conjunction with the moral education of the students. When parents were involved, as was the case in one middle-school course, an increase in moral reasoning did take place.

The strategy of encouraging the teachers to develop their own curricula had as its logical conclusion the publishing of their materials for commercial sale. One publishing house has already reviewed many of the courses, and commercial publication seems inevitable for some of the materials. An assumption made by the organizers was that the teachers who were good at developing curricula would elect to become part of the project. This in fact is what happened. Enough people volunteered so that the program could be initiated: Approximately one-half of the counselors and social studies teachers participated actively in the project. An important organizing principle was the national focus this project was to have in order to satisfy the main objective of the funding agency. An impressive amount of publicity was generated as well as interest — enough to persuade the funding agency to grant more money solely for dissemination. The consequence of publicity and exposure of such a program is that people who are at the core of innovation get job offers to go to other places. This in fact happened to at least seven of the key actors in the Brookline project.

A critical question continues to be: Can the center of this project in Brookline remain vital and self-sustaining? Though the answer appears to be "yes," this issue was still a concern as the project entered its fourth year.

The cornerstone of any diffusion effort is the training and equipping of teachers or counselors to practice the innovation. It is critical to any self-sustaining effort that this training and equipping be conducted on an ongoing basis. Selman and Jaquette (1978) have identified certain skills, such as the ability to lead a probing discussion, as being critical to the success of teaching Kohlberg's approach through the method of moral dilemmas. Mosher estimates that it takes an hour a week for approximately twelve weeks of audio and/or videotape review with the teacher to supervise his/her progress in this area adequately. Each teacher participating in the project received about three to four hours of supervision. As the project continued and the more experienced teachers left, such supervision became increasingly important.

Equally important is the issue of the effect of the project on the participating students and teachers. Has the program produced any measurable results on either moral reasoning or behavior? A number of doctoral theses written by present and former Brookline teachers on various aspects of the project are reported in later chapters of this book. They offer detailed evidence of the effect of the project on students' moral reasoning and behavior.

Taken in conjunction with other efforts in other school districts, the Brookline project perhaps raises more research questions than it answers. Obviously, it is one purpose of this book to present a comprehensive report of the research data generated by the project. Scharf (1978), in a recent review of research undertaken to date, identifies three areas that need to be researched to close the gap between developmental theory (Kohlberg and others) and broad-based educational practice. The first deals with what Scharf calls the "social ecology of moral change." There is the question of which specific strategies, tactics or dilemmas are likely to affect moral thinking. Social role-taking, moral dialogue, exposure to higher stage thinking, and a "just community" seem related to moral change. The relative effectiveness of these educational strategies, however, has not been as thoroughly researched as it could be. More is needed especially in the area of measuring the moral environment of a democratic school such as in SWS; and more is needed to link empirically such environmental measures to moral changes.

A second question raised by Scharf is, "How and to whom can developmental teaching competencies be successfully transferred?" The research literature cited here identifies studies where the teaching was done by university professors or doctoral candidates. Their training and selection are unusual. So the question remains as the Brookline project continues with a new generation of teachers: Will similar gains in moral change be found among their students?

Finally, Scharf raises the question of the relationship between education and moral action. Reimer and Power [see Chapter 17 of this book] are attempting to ascertain whether a change in moral reasoning in a classroom or school setting has any effect on moral action. At the moment, efforts to understand this relationship are just beginning. Evidence from the coordinator of SWS cited earlier shows that students are taking more responsibility for their own governance and are able to see the contrast between their own method of making decisions and the more traditional high school process.

This capacity for assuming responsibility was recognized also by the administration. For example, when the matter of replacing the Coordinator of SWS arose in 1977, the Director of Personnel for the Brookline Schools sent a letter directly to the town meeting and asked if the students wanted to reopen interviews or to recommend the appointment of the Acting Coordinator who had been serving during the sabbatical leave of absence of the Coordinator. The students voted overwhelmingly in favor of the latter procedure, and ultimately DiStefano was appointed by the School Committee. This acknowledgement of their responsibility helped to further the students' respect for the process, and when the Coordinator resigned in order to become a professor at Washington University, eighteen students volunteered to serve on the committee to find a replacement to begin September, 1978.

The Coordinator noted also the degree of responsibility and trust which has developed among the students so that there was no vandalism and virtually no stealing. Teaching areas and office areas are student areas. When a backgammon set which a student brought in disappeared after several weeks of use, there was a general conviction that it had been taken by someone outside SWS.

The responsible attitude of the students has made suspensions unnecessary since whatever problems might arise can be handled within the democratic framework of the SWS. In addition, absenteeism in the SWS is lower (7.13%) than in the rest of the High School, which is itself at a comparatively low rate (8.17%).

CAN MORAL EDUCATION AS IT IS TAUGHT AT BROOKLINE BE REPLICATED ELSEWHERE, AND SHOULD IT?

It is easier to answer the second part of our question. Given the alternatives of indoctrination and values-clarification, yes! As it should be clear by now, however, adopting the cognitive development approach of Kohlberg, as was done in Brookline, puts a heavy demand on administrators, teachers, and students. Administrators need to be as knowledgeable as teachers about a sophisticated approach that invariably raises concerns with school boards, community groups, parents, and other teachers. For teachers, it demands a commitment to conscious inquiry about oneself as well as mastering a philosophic approach. It asks in the words of Scharf that the teacher be "a social philosopher and psychologist as well as master of the educational craft." That is no easy task in our experience. Of students, the process involves more vigorous thinking and higher performance in areas where it is easier to lie back.

By way of summarizing, twelve important steps appear to us to be key to any attempt to begin a system-wide moral education program:

(1) Get the formal support of the school board before beginning, and obtain dollar support for training and dissemination throughout the district.

(2) Conduct an instructional session or demonstration of the moral education program approach for key opinion leaders in administration, the community, and the teaching staff.

(3) Use the available resources of already-funded programs, including outside experts, to assist in training a local cadre of teachers.

(4) Participation in the program should be voluntary for students.

(5) Establish a well-thought-out rationale for making moral education a part of regular curriculum, not an add-on.

(6) Allow sufficient time to develop curriculum and to pilot-test material with divergent student populations.

(7) Empower an internal well-trained cadre to disseminate findings and train others. Free this group to work a substantial amount of their time on the project.

(8) Form a community and staff advisory committee to educate and to develop an adherence group. Delegate to them the responsibility for on-going evaluation. Include social data as well as evidence of ego development and moral development.

(9) Link the local resource center with others in nearby regions or states. Encourage the resource center to aid in the professional growth of teachers.

(10) Provide teachers with all available resources: books, films, curricula from other districts, etc.

(11) Keep informing the school board and involve administrators to maintain their support and interest.

(12) Organize efforts to train teachers on a regular basis (both old and new ones); earmark local summer curriculum funds to allow teachers to write new curricula.

4
STAFF DEVELOPMENT
IN MORAL EDUCATION

Henry Zabierek

Why moral education? Why staff development? Why still another addition to the ever-lengthening litany of public-school undertakings? Before any discussion of methodology can take place, there is a compelling need to articulate the reasons for moral education or there will be only madness to our method.

The Danforth Moral Education Project originated in Brookline because we in the social studies were seeking ways to help students cope with a society in which all of its institutions — government, business, law, medicine, education among them — were being questioned. We recognized the inadequacy and the escapism of special courses in citizenship, and we shuddered at the dangers and immorality of indoctrination. In the social studies we were challenging students' reasoning on issues of is/ought and right/wrong, but we had no theoretical or systematic base for what we were doing. Society's children reflected the deep spiritual malaise that had gripped American society even before Watergate. As one student lamented, "It's hard to say who's right and wrong these days about anything."

We were concerned with the disjunction between what the society advocated to be taught in school and what that society practiced beyond the school's borders. Students were to perform things intellectual, but their parents sought things material. The Bill of Rights was mandated for schools, but there were too few demonstrations of justice in the wider world. Lessons to save the environment were trendy and numerous in classrooms, yet corporate America appeared intent only on its riches.

The list of problems foisted on schools appeared interminable. American society expected its schools to provide the whole of education, as other institutions increasingly forfeited their roles. The schools could not and should not try to do all things. The fact that schools were required to do so much was a clear indicator that the society did not know what either schools or society should be doing. The emergence of boomlets such as that for career education signalled an economic emphasis for schools, all pointing to personal gain rather than civic responsibility.

We sought a return to the original mission of schools, and to education that aimed to prepare students to deal rationally with public issues rather than prepare them for a cog-in-the-wheel existence.

The concern for a return to citizenship education was illustrated by the formation of national task forces on citizenship. Even here the starting point was often one of alarm rather than of clear direction. Lamentations over how embarrassingly little knowledge students had of their government clouded the wider view. Those who despaired for the young seemed unmindful that only 55 percent of the eligible adult voters chose to cast their ballots in the presidential election of 1972. And they elected Richard Nixon. What should we expect of our students?

The view both from within and outside the schools was and remains sobering. Recent studies by the National Science Foundation (Weiss 1978) on the status of social studies education demonstrate that the predominant goal of these classroom teachers remains a slavish adherence to factual information alone. Instruction is seen as lecture and recitation. Students are asked to regurgitate not only the textbook facts, but also they are required to reproduce the exact language of the text itself. Student interest is sublimated to the quest for grades and approval. Historical decisions and historical events go unquestioned. In the wake of the mass suicides in Guyana, hints of genocide in Cambodia, and a world hesitant to acknowledge its moral obligations to the boat people of Vietnam, advocates of moral education have that sense of feeling of "pinched Puritans in a house of prostitution."

Given the compelling need to provide an education where students would be asked to clarify their reasoning around issues of fairness and justice, we sought to pursue staff development and curriculum development simultaneously. We wanted to profit from, rather than to be seduced by, the mass flow of curricula during the 1960s. These efforts have borne the criticism of elitism, where experts in the disciplines adhered to Bruner's (1960) thesis of educating students in the structure of the disciplines. Only with rare exceptions, some of the work at Carnegie-Mellon University in Pittsburgh serving as a notable example, were card-carrying classroom teachers in the role of authors. Where teachers' training was ignored in the 1960s and where teacher-training institutions were not involved in the new developments, in the Brookline Moral Education project we sought to train teachers who would train others. We recognized that credibility was paramount in teacher education, and that classroom practitioners were persuaded more by those who labor in the trenches of the classroom rather than those who dwell in the plasticity of the command posts of publishing mills.

An equally vital imperative was the need for a collegial town-gown partnership. The objectives of the project had to conform to the philosophy of the school system. The "Sheepskin Curtain," that barrier between schools and universities that has been all too "basic" to American education, had to be withdrawn. The professor majors in research and minors in teaching. The public school teacher majors in teaching; research for the teacher is too often a luxury that neither teacher nor school system can afford. We sought a respectful mix of theorists and practitioners with vigorous support from the Center for Moral Education at Harvard and from Boston University.

A careful analysis of the organization of the moral development project has appeared in Chapter 3. Curricula were produced in such amounts as to create the need for a dissemination center. Teacher training extended beyond the classroom to local, regional, and national meetings. Media attention came from television programs, radio interviews, national magazine articles, and newspaper accounts, local and national. Others were interested in what we were doing, why we were doing it, and, most frequently, how well we were doing.

Our experiences substantiate the fact that no one should enter the field of moral education who merely "wants to get on the bandwagon" or who seeks outlets for pent-up missionary zeal. Moral education is not easy or necessarily fun. It is more than an exercise in "warm fuzzies." Moral education is not bland; it has a "bite" to it because it is an attack on neutral behavior. It should not be a separate subject of a particular program. Rather, it should be part of every subject and pervade the whole range of what constitutes school life.

It is crucial that schools examine what they are now doing before they embark on plans for moral development. Are they indoctrinating, inculcating, or prescribing values? Do they wish to relinquish any of these practices? Are administrators more willing to be upset by Standard Aptitude Test Scores or by the quality of student citizenship? In short, are they really interested in moral education or do they wish merely to know more about it?

If educators are interested in not only what students know, but also what kind of citizens they will become, then citizenship education mandates that students inquire systematically into values. The times require a stimulation of present citizens; there is no such thing as a neutral recapitulation of facts. The twin follies of the outright indoctrination of students or a neutral recapitulation of facts must be exposed as both dangerous and fruitless for any claims to citizenship education. Social studies education for too long has been a vehicle for the simple indoctrination of national loyalties. The mere transmission of the culture, where students are not allowed to think until they have learned a given basic knowledge and prescribed modes of behavior, is anathema for preparing students for democratic citizenship. Attempts at neutrality are doomed to failure; the teacher, the teaching style, the materials, and the curriculum are all value-laden and the results of such teaching leave students totally unprepared to deal with citizenship in a pluralistic society. Every historical event harbors moral overtones and its leading characters are beset with decision making. To study the issue of slavery in the United States or the policy of genocide in Nazi Germany without a systematic inquiry into the attendant moral issues is unconscionable.

Systematic inquiries into moral questions that are inherent in the curriculum add a depth of knowledge to student understanding. Students are allowed to identify more closely with historical figures and the time in which they lived. Students recognize that history is not a well-organized city; rather it is a jungle.

Any analysis of school goals or purposes must be predicated on the fact that the time of a common value system shared by home, church, and community is history in itself. Factors such as industrialism and immigration have neutralized the school's role of overt moral educator, where one set of values is understood and prescribed for all. Indoctrination is for preachers, not teachers. Public schools should seek to promote the moral autonomy of students as the essence of democracy and to recall the words of Plato: "In order for education to achieve its purpose, reason must have an adequate emotional base."

Chief among the pitfalls of moral development programs is that such efforts are seen as a panacea for the full range of school and community difficulties. Such high aspirations almost ensure dashed hopes. A case in point can be illustrated from a session on "Affective Education" at the American Association of School Administrators (June 1979) meeting in Denver. Here school leaders seemed united on the proposition that values or morals education was fruitless. Their evaluation was taken from such measures as the continual high incidence of broken windows in their school plants, and the constant percentage of youthful citizens who posed problems for their educators. They decried the lack of traditional measures to evaluate affective education and viewed this as sufficient reason to discard the entire notion as yet another short-lived innovation.

Such scenarios are the fault of the practitioners and the uninitiated alike. The former claim too much; the latter expect too much. Far from any cure-all, moral education is limited. It deals with thinking, a necessary but not sufficient factor for improving moral behavior. The task of a teacher posing a moral dilemma is to search for "right reasons," rather than "right answers." The point of moral development is akin to that of philosophy: "The point of philosophy is not to change the world. It is rather to get things into proper perspective, to grasp better what reasons are good reasons for changing or keeping things as they are" (Peters and Hirst 1970, p. 131). To extend this thinking into the actions demanded of the crestfallen educators at Denver requires dramatic changes beyond the single classroom that will be discussed later in these pages.

Before any educators embark on programs in moral education, they must be prepared to make a commitment in time and money. The temptation is to underestimate both the concept and its implementation. Shrugs of "We've been doing it for twenty years" ensure that "we" have not. Eight to ten formal sessions on the theory and practices of moral education are mandatory. Training leads to the production of materials; materials without training guarantee failure.

Training teachers in moral education demands a civic courage of its own. Teachers must be convinced that there is both intellectual stimulation and practical application that will improve their overall teaching. Theory, materials, and practice must be combined so that theorists and practitioners move forward in mutual respect. Teachers must serve as students and as teachers to internalize the nature of a particular dilemma and the techniques for classroom application.

Teacher training for moral education has been found to be invaluable beyond the realm of the classroom dilemma. Moral and ethical thinking are not separate from cognitive development, but an essential part of it. Morality is based on reason, not revelation. Indeed, our concern that Brookline social studies teachers engage in more lively, searching discussions with their students was one of our primary aims in pushing the moral education project at its inception.

Moral education has led to a rediscovery of the Bloom taxonomy* and its increasingly many variations. The development of a proper cognitive structure to deal with moral problems is vital. Cognitive stimulation, not didactic lessons, is essential for moral development. Traditional classrooms too often are scenes of textbook regurgitation of facts, yet students are called upon to evaluate particular issues on test days. Such "quantum leaps" are examples of poor teaching and teacher injustice toward students. Training in moral education dramatizes the necessity of stage-by-stage learning.

No program in moral education can endure without a superintendent who is committed to the need for it and who is politically competent to "sell" it to the school board and the wider community. Proposals for the adoption of moral education programs are often much misunderstood and exceedingly susceptible to the rigors of majority rule. Continuous support must come from school leaders from the launching through the sailing. They must demonstrate true leadership and be willing to persevere in the face of divergence. Honesty to the community is essential and the true nature of the beast must be unmasked; the issue is moral education and should not be couched in the banal language of decision making, inquiry, or brainstorming. Support for programs in moral education calls for stout hearts.

Continuous sustenance of moral education programs must also take the form of providing frequent opportunities for teachers to share their experiences and to provide support for one another. Curriculum innovation strikes horror into the minds of many citizens because of the sorry history of too many projects and grants that were bravely launched but cravenly nurtured. Staff development implies continuous attention and frequent reexamination of teacher practices. Theorists and practitioners need to confront unanticipated issues and to revise impracticable techniques.

---

*Bloom has provided detailed logical taxonomies of how students' cognition and affect become more complex as guides for curriculum development and instruction.

The crucial role of the teacher in staff development has too often been ignored or unrealized. Once such a program is underway, the teacher is the key to staff development. Training sessions should be free of the administrative urgencies of many meetings, where products must be produced and progress must be demonstrated. The by-product of successful staff development is good teaching, and this can be achieved only if teachers have frequent opportunities to freely exchange their successes and failures. By providing such opportunities we dignify teachers as persons and contribute to a camaraderie the benefits of which extend far beyond the intended goals of any program.

Since the ultimate support for moral education programs must come from the community, educators need to provide education and information under the aegis of adult education programs, parent-teacher meetings, church groups, and to other interested community groups. Educators must acknowledge that "School curriculum has always been Belgium in our war over values" (Goodman 1979). Moral education programs risk disturbing long-held beliefs, attitudes, and methods.

Adult education courses furnish the most attractive forums for providing information because they offer opportunities for parents to learn both the theory and practice of moral education. The theory of moral development is not the exclusive province of professional educators. Parents are the initial and sustaining moral educators. Moral education courses for parents benefit both teaching and parenting. A union of these groups is crucial to dissolve the territorial claims for moral education.

Meetings with other community groups where some citizens have preconceived questions and preconceived answers place greater burdens on educators. Only those school personnel who are knowledgeable in theory and experienced with practice are qualified to participate. Careful preparations for such sessions must be made so that they do not assume the nature of adversarial encounters.

Reassurance and candor are much in order. Parents should know that the discussion of moral issues is not another addition to the school curricula. Dealing with moral dilemmas necessitates knowledge of content and ensures studying issues in depth. Reading, writing, and other "basics" are not shunted aside but enhanced as student interest is provoked. But as educators we need to return parents to one of their children's educators. I paraphrase Fred Rogers of "Mr. Rogers' Neighborhood": It's easy to convince people that children need to learn the alphabet and numbers. How do we help people realize that what matters is how a person's inner life finally puts together the alphabet and numbers of his outer life? What really matters is whether he uses the alphabet for the declaration of war or for the description of a sunrise, and his numbers for the final count at Buchenwald or for the specifics of a brand new bridge. Other common concerns call for answers with reason and candor. The comfort that "morality is a private matter" serves in part to explain the morality of Richard Nixon. The presumption that knowledge of governmental structure and the identity of its leaders insure a sound civic education must be confronted with the fact that Howard Hunt was one of the great inadvertent civics teachers of our generation, just as Fannie Fox became one of the most effective parliamentary reformers that the House of Representatives ever knew.

The specter of students deciding the bases of right and wrong alarms many parents. They view such thinking as a form of anarchism and forsee the resultant disintegration of the society. Yet students must have experience in autonomy or they will use it badly when it is available. Fairness, autonomy, and reason are basic to citizenship education and the validity of moral rules are not determined by appeals to majority agreement.

Chief among the other anxieties of parents is the view that moral dilemmas are "contrived" or "melodramatic." Where this proves to be true, such lessons should be reviewed and revised or discarded. However, these claims are usually predicated on the notion that the world functions smoothly. Examples abound that render this idealistic yearning rather than sheer reality. It should be apparent, for instance, that neither democracy nor capitalism survive in pure forms in this country, yet should we label them as "contrived"? Conflict and change are the "stuff" of the historians, and their textbooks embolden these events in special type. One person's view of melodrama becomes another person's view of reality.

Educating parents and the community about the issues of moral development should not preclude their active consideration in other areas of teaching and learning within the confines of school life itself. Justice is not limited to one or two disciplines or a handful of classes. Single-minded disciplines, often myopic in their educational view and tenacious in pursuit of their known truth, must be enlisted for their aid. For instance, science taught without systematic consideration of moral issues may be frightening to contemplate. The richest literature of English classes sustains its credibility because it addresses the eternal questions of mankind. Moral education encompasses universal issues and these issues have their place in the total curriculum.

Recent efforts in establishing democratic classrooms, such as the work of Mosher currently in operation in Brookline, are intended to implement the theory of moral and social education into classroom reality. They are particularly significant in that they address the issue of student responsibility, a much-neglected issue in the wake of the student movement since the 1960s. They also seek to develop the concepts of tolerance, as well as social commitment, empathy, and compassion, in the face of the single-minded pursuit of individual issues practiced frequently in the larger society.

Our experiences in Brookline affirm the fact that the moral education and the intellectual growth of our students will be developed best by the constant sharing of ideas and practices by theorists and classroom practitioners alike. We must not leave the field to the theorists alone, or we invite that condition that can best be described as "the Leisure of the Theory Class." Books and articles already abound on the wonders of the new medicine, for example, cognitive developmental moral education. Associations have been formed and they meet regularly, both regionally and nationally. No social studies conferences can be considered complete until the infamous Heinz Dilemma (see Table 2.2) is at least mentioned. One could go on mercilessly, but to be merciful is to be at a higher stage.

None of what has been described above is either dishonest or evil. Quite to the contrary, it is the beginning of something "good." Books, articles, associations, and conferences on the subject are to be applauded; but classroom teachers must be more involved in readying their students for moral education and in reporting their findings. They need to continually explore and discover the entry points for moral discussions and to be able to recognize what engages the student. In short, they must ensure that the theorists are not left with the leisure of talking to one another. Classroom practitioners are equal partners in the task of improving the cognitive and moral development of students.

Teacher reports, too often unpublished, do not concentrate on claims of ever-spiralling stage changes. The heat of classroom teaching stands in stark contrast to the cool dispatch that emanates from much of the literature of the published facts of moral education. Teacher-created dilemmas often prove not to be dilemmas in student's minds. A classroom lesson on the Fugitive Slave Law of 1850 proves to be a disaster; no eighth-grade student will take the position that slaves should be turned over to authorities for their ultimate disposition to their masters. Few, if any, students will argue that Washington's soldiers at Valley Forge are more entitled to a cache of food than a woman and her children. Genuine, workable historical dilemmas do not come cheaply; teachers must know their students equally as well as they know their history.

Developmentally appropriate dilemmas and probing questions to challenge students at higher level of thinking are not enough. Teachers of moral education can be as easily seduced by stage progressions as cultural transmitters can be by their prescribed factual and behavioral truths. Good teaching takes place in an atmosphere suitable for it: open, challenging, and supportive. Prior to the introduction of moral dilemmas, teachers must work, even sweat, to consciously develop listening skills, the ability to question one another, and willingness to acknowledge the wisdom of another person's view. Work in moral education has brought teachers back to basics: establishing a classroom atmosphere more appropriate for teaching and learning, choosing materials more carefully, and acknowledging the developmental level of their students so that teachers are not captivated either by the course content or the promises of upward mobility through the stages of moral development.

Teachers have found that traditional measures for student achievement are insufficient in measuring cognitive developmental growth. Much classroom time in moral education is devoted to developing working definitions of new vocabulary words and to promoting student usage of these words in the context of class lessons. Increased attention is given to drawing analogies, recognizing similar themes, and referring to previous lessons. These strategies are fundamental for students to grasp the meaning of a moral dilemma.

More formal or substantive measures for measuring moral development are also required. Subjective judgments can be made from classroom observations: for example, improvement in children's social perspective-taking and the taking of more perspectives into account on social issues; positive student evaluations of courses that include moral development; and greater student participation in classroom activity. Yet teachers continue to seek the foundations that students require as a basis for moral discussions.

None of this is said to discourage others from either beginning work in moral reasoning or stopping work already begun. It is rather a plea for more teachers to begin now to ensure that they and their students will be sufficiently prepared for it.

A union of theorists and practitioners is essential at the creation and mandatory during the implementation. Before the former rush to judgment, teachers must remind them that there are more than six stages to moral education. We need to lay the foundations for moral reasoning by becoming involved in issues of fairness, autonomy, reason, and justice in circumstances that engage students so that schools may more often produce moral beings rather than adult conformists. Heinz must wait.

5
RESEARCH AND MEASUREMENT ISSUES IN MORAL EDUCATION INTERVENTIONS

Ann Higgins

In this chapter we review the findings of the studies described in this book, offer some substantive and methodological conclusions, and discuss implications for planning further research and intervention projects. This review concentrates upon the discussion of the effects upon moral reasoning development of the various curricular interventions, since all of the studies measured moral judgment change and all of the interveners defined enhancing the moral reasoning of their students as an explicit goal. However, these interventions offered rich and multiple experiences to their participants and each intervener had several goals, important and worthy of discussion. The multiple goals and the ways in which they were assessed will be documented but discussed only in relation to moral judgment development.

Lockwood (1978) recently reviewed and critiqued the effects of 11 moral education programs and curricula upon the participants' moral reasoning. It should be mentioned that two studies included in this book, Paolitto's (Chapter 11) and Sullivan's (Chapter 9), were reviewed by Lockwood. It seems instructional to summarize both Lockwood's conclusions and suggestions for further research to indicate the knowledge gained and the areas still in need of clarification and expansion.

Lockwood concluded that adequately designed studies of the direct moral discussion approach showed mean increases of one-half stage and those of the deliberate psychological education or psychological awareness approach consistently showed development of about one-third stage. He pointed out that in both programs some students advanced and others stayed the same from pre- to posttest. Furthermore, he thought it reasonable to conclude that there was evidence of more change in subjects using lower-stage reasoning, especially Stage 2, than in those using higher-stage reasoning, Stage 3.

The five methodological suggestions for improving research in this area originally offered by Lockwood can be reiterated today despite major advances in the test instrument and knowledge of its validity and reliability. These suggestions are briefly noted here and will be explicated in the section on methodological conclusions.

The Moral Maturing Score (MMS) should not be the only moral developmental variable reported.

Any average change of less than one-third of a stage should not be regarded as indicating substantial or meaningful development.

Further research on the impact of educational interventions should employ more rigorous designs.

The use of the moral judgment interview as a written questionnaire is ill-advised.

Double-blind scoring procedures should be employed whenever possible.

Lockwood's ideas for further research remain a challenge for us today. Specifically he recommended investigation of the stability of long-term treatment effects; the effects of particular components of a curriculum upon moral judgment development; the possibility of promoting development from the conventional to the postconventional level; and the associated changes in behavior, thinking, and attitudes that accompany gains in moral judgment. In other words, what additional indexes of success can be provided for teachers?

THE MORAL EDUCATION STUDIES REPORTED IN THIS BOOK

This section categorizes the studies and summarizes the moral judgment change results. The categories by stated purpose and the nature of the treatment intervention are enhancement of moral reasoning through direct moral discussion of real-life situations with natural groups, deliberate psychological education and direct moral discussions, and moral discussion integrated in academic social studies and history curricula.

Direct Moral Discussion of Real-Life Situations with Natural Groups

As stated above, the studies have been divided into three major groups, which are defined by the kind of intervention employed. The first category consists of three studies using direct moral discussion of real-life situations with natural groups. In one of these studies (see Chapter 13) Rundle cotaught a fifth-grade classroom in which moral issues were discussed within the context of classroom democracy. Classroom rules were discussed and modified using democratic procedures with the emphases upon consideration of the good of the whole and making consensus decisions. There were two control groups, one regular classroom with no moral education program, and one direct moral discussion classroom using hypothetical moral dilemmas. This traditional moral discussion classroom was cotaught by Rundle and the regular classroom teacher, untrained in developmental moral discussion.

The democratic classroom showed a mean change of one-half stage, from a mixture of Stage 1 and 2 to solid Stage 2 or a mixture of Stage 2 and 3. The traditional moral discussion classroom and the control classroom showed no change, remaining a mixture of Stage 1 and 2.

Rundle used additional measures to assess the level of cooperation among the children and the moral atmosphere of the classroom. The democratic classroom significantly increased in cooperation on a bridge-building task (cooperation task). At the end of the course a subsample in the democratic classroom resolved a set of classroom moral dilemmas at a stage higher than did a subsample in the traditional moral discussion classroom. The Rundle study, then, suggests that the discussion of real classroom dilemmas in a democratic setting is a powerful stimulant to moral growth both in the classroom group and in thinking about hypothetical moral dilemmas. Her research does not allow us to determine whether this powerful effect was due to the democratic process of decision making. However, to conduct discussions of real classroom dilemmas without empowering the students to a say in their resolution would be a very artificial exercise.

The second study in this group was done by Grimes (see Chapter 13). She was interested in the effect on students of developmental moral discussions between fifth- and sixth-grade children and their mothers. She, like Rundle, had a comparison group of children who discussed hypothetical moral dilemmas as well as a regular control group with no moral discussions.

In three pretreatment sessions the mothers in the experimental group were introduced to the concept of moral stage development and the technique of developmental discussion of moral dilemmas. Then the mothers and children met together and discussed dilemmas presented by Grimes and later wrote and discussed their own dilemmas. The group concluded with a series of "morality" role plays enacted primarily by the children.

All except one child in the mother/student group advanced between one-third and one whole stage. The mean change was one-half stage development from Stage 2 to Stage 3. The student moral discussion group got the typical Blatt effect of one-third stage upward change from Stage 2 to Stage 2(3). The control group showed no change, remaining at Stage 2.

The inclusion of the mothers seems to have had a strong effect going beyond the effect of hypothetical moral discussion in the classroom. Presumably, the experimental discussions of mothers and students continued in the natural setting of the home. In addition to the increased amount of moral dilemma discussions between the children and mothers in the daily life of the family, this natural grouping seems to have given the children added motivation to engage intensively in the moral discussions.

Stanley (see Chapter 19) conducted a study at the high school level somewhat similar to Grimes' study. Her treatment group included both parents and their adolescent children. The families were taught listening and discussion skills and practiced family fairness discussions in the workshop meetings. At home they held weekly family meetings in which they were encouraged to reach fair decisions through consensus and to make family contracts to implement those decisions.

Stanley had two comparison groups. One group, of parents only, attended a workshop with the same purpose of enhancing the effectiveness of family decision making as the experimental parent/adolescent group. The adolescents of this parent-only group were pre- and posttested on the Moral Judgment Interview. A third group of adolescents comprised the regular control group.

Only adolescents in the parent/adolescent group showed moral growth. The group mean increased one-third stage from Stage 2 to Stage 2(3). While the mean change was not great, every adolescent moved up one-third stage. Neither comparison group showed any mean change. There was less change in this study than found in Grimes' and Rundle's studies in which the interventions increased the moral development of the participants one-half stage. It is striking that Stanley's adolescents were at the same initial stage as Grimes' and Rundle's eleven and twelve year olds. Other studies (Blatt and Kohlberg 1975) suggest that movement from Stage 2 to Stage 3 is easier at a younger age than at an older age where Stage 2 reasoning has become crystallized or "fixated."

In addition to assessing the moral judgment of the adolescents, Stanley assessed the parents' attitudes toward egalitarian family decision making and their skills at conducting family meetings, taped at home. She found that the parents who met alone espoused more egalitarian attitudes than the parents who were in the workshop with their children. However, the parents meeting with their children were rated as conducting family meetings with more empathy and active listening, and with making fewer authoritarian statements than the parents in the other group.

On the one-year follow-up Stanley found all the families in the parent/adolescent group were still holding weekly family meetings. Only two of six families in the parent-only group were doing so. The Stanley study adds to the conclusion of the Grimes study that initiating a discussion process between parents and children created a continuing motivation for such discussion beyond the time of the intervention. It also offers a partial replication of Grimes's finding of marked upward stage change.

Azrak (see Chapter 20) conducted a study designed to evaluate the effect of a parent education workshop upon junior high school students' moral judgment development. Only parents attended the ten-week workshop in which they were taught moral developmental theory, how to lead moral dilemma discussions, and how to apply such knowledge and skills to the discipline issues that arose with their early adolescent children. Homework assignments involving the children together with the parents were assigned. There was one control group of parents. The early adolescent children of the treatment group parents advanced a mean of one-fifth stage (17 MMS points) on moral judgment, moving from Stage 2 toward Stage 3.

This study is the only one we reviewed that did not create an intervention program for children or adolescents; hence, its results should be compared with the results of other parent education programs rather than with the results of other studies in this survey. However, we speculate that the effectiveness of Azrak's program would have been greater, comparable to Stanley's or Grimes', if the natural unit of the family had been the target of the intervention.

In summary, the "real-life" studies suggest that the most powerful interventions for stimulating moral stage change are those that involve discussion of real problems and situations occurring in natural groups, whether the family or classroom, in which all participants are empowered to a say in the discussion.

Moral Discussion and Education for Personal Development

The second category consists of six studies that combined direct moral discussion with deliberate psychological education. The techniques of deliberate psychological education included peer counseling, having adolescents conduct moral discussions with younger children, and introducing to students developmental psychology themes including moral stage theory. The fundamental purpose is to promote the general ego development of children and adolescents.

The study combining these methods that showed the greatest moral stage change in adolescents was that of Sullivan (see Chapter 9). Sullivan taught a year-long course offered as a social studies elective to high school juniors and seniors. This course included five phases: personal introductions, moral discussions, counseling and empathy training, moral psychology and philosophy, and a practicum experience as moral educators. There were two control groups in this study, one psychology class and one science class.

The experimental group gained one-half stage (45 MMS points) on the average, indicating movement from Stage 3 to Stage 3(4). There was essentially no moral judgment growth in either control group. Sullivan also administered the Loevinger Sentence Completion Test and found a mean increase of one stage, typically from the conformist to the conscientious stage, for the experimental-group students. Neither control group showed any upward stage change on this measure of ego development.

The large amount of change on both the measures of moral judgment development and ego development indicate the power of combining direct moral discussion with deliberate psychological education and of offering a long and richly varied course.

In a one-semester moral education seminar concerned to reduce prejudice (see Chapter 7), Alexander included all the components of the Sullivan intervention except the peer counseling phase. The moral dilemma discussion phase focused on situations raising issues of prejudice. He had one regular high school class control group. All students in this study were juniors and seniors.

Alexander obtained the Blatt effect of a mean upward change of one-third stage (28 MMS points) in moral growth. The upward change represented movement from Stage 2(3) to Stage 3. This group showed a mean increase of one-half stage in ego development. The group moved from slightly above Loevinger's conformist stage to slightly below her conscientious stage. The control group showed no growth on either developmental dimension.

Alexander used three content measures to assess attitudes of prejudice. Only one of these showed significant differences between the two groups in the expected direction.

In the third study in this category, Arredondo-Dowd (1978) was interested in the effect of a course exploring "cross-cultural experiences" on the development of immigrant adolescents. Her four groups were comprised of eleventh and twelfth graders, two included only immigrants and two, American-born. All immigrant students spoke English as their second language.

The one-semester intervention of the experimental group included moral discussion of dilemmas throughout five units or phases; personal introductions, social issues, adolescence, developmental moral psychology, and socialization experiences. The mean moral judgment score increased about one-third stage (26 MMS points) for this group. Movement was primarily from Stage 2 (3) to Stage 3(2). This group showed no development on the ego measure, remaining at Loevinger's conformist stage. None of the control groups showed significant change on either developmental measure. A one-year follow-up of the two immigrant groups showed that both had moved from the conformist stage (I-3) toward the conscientious stage (I-4) on the ego development measure. The mean score was I-3/4. No moral judgment follow-up was carried out.

The fourth study in this category is that of Felton (1974). She taught a counseling course to two groups: adults and adolescents together, and adolescents alone. A high school psychology class served as the control. Her treatment did not involve direct moral discussion but focused on role-playing and communication and discrimination skills in order to develop empathy and respect. She did not find any moral judgment development in her adult/adolescent combined group, and there were decreases in moral judgment scores in the adolescent-only and control groups.

DiStefano's study, the fifth in this category (see Chapter 8), involved a one-semester senior-level course called the "Psychology of Ethics in Relationships." It focused primarily on developmental moral discussions of situations involving relations between the sexes. The course commenced with personal introductions and descriptions of significant relationships in each of the students' lives. There was no peer counseling or cross-age teaching in this intervention. The students were members of a democratic alternative school program and the control group also came from this program. The alternative school program included weekly community meetings involving moral discussion and democratic decision making.

The experimental course group had a mean increase of almost one-half stage (42 MMS points) in moral judgment development. Similar changes were found on a set of dilemmas addressing sexual issues as were found on the standard moral judgment interview form. The control group showed an upward change of one-fourth stage (26 MMS points) on the standard interview form and a bit less upward change on the sexual dilemmas task. The common alternative school experience being shared by both groups indicates that it may account for half of the development noted in the experimental group. Generally both groups move from Stage 3 to Stage 4.

The last study in this category (see Chapter 11) was carried out by Paolitto and focused on the development of moral reasoning and social perspective-taking. The one-semester health class for eighth-graders involved moral dilemma discussion as a preparation for understanding and communicating moral dilemmas faced by adults in the community. The students wrote dilemmas for the adults as well as heard the adults present their own moral dilemmas. A second health class served as a control group. Both were taught by the same teacher. The experimental group did not show significant increase in either moral judgment (the pre-post MMS mean change was 12 points) or social perspective-taking as measured by the Selman and Byrne Role-Taking Assessment (Selman 1973). The students were mostly Stage 2 on the moral judgment interview and Stage 3 on the social perspective-taking measure. It may be that the students were already at their ceiling on social perspective-taking, so the course could not stimulate perspective-taking advance. If this were the case, then more direct discussion of controversial moral dilemmas might have been more effective in promoting moral growth.

A study by Harris (1976) helps to illuminate the relation of deliberate psychological education interventions to the moral growth of the participants. Harris studied three groups to which subjects were randomly assigned. The first treatment group was a class of 15 high school juniors in a values education course emphasizing moral discussion throughout an 18-week semester. The second treatment group was a class of 15 high school juniors enrolled in a values education course that emphasized deliberate psychological education for the first nine weeks followed by moral discussion during the second half of the term. The control group was composed of 15 juniors in a high school economics course. Each of the three groups was administered the Moral Judgment Interview three times: as a pretest, as a nine-week midterm test, and as a posttest at the end of the semester.

The results of Harris' study show that there was an equal amount of upward moral development over the semester for the two experimental groups, changes of 46 and 47 MMS points. This change was spread out evenly across the semester for the moral discussion class, which gained 24 MMS points in the first nine weeks and 22 MMS points in the second nine weeks of the semester. In contrast, the class that received deliberate psychological education in the first half and moral discussion in the second half of the semester showed essentially no moral judgment increase during the psychological education phase but gained 41 MMS points from the midtest to the posttest, the moral discussion phase. The psychological education phase, then, apparently facilitated more rapid growth during the moral discussion phase. It also suggests that the optional placement of the psychological education component is prior to the moral discussion phase.

The Harris study suggests that deliberate psychological education affects moral development only as a precondition to direct moral discussion. However, two studies employing deliberate psychological education without explicit direct moral discussion did obtain the usual one-third moral stage change. These were Sprinthall's (1976) study of high school curriculum in the psychology of counseling and Erickson's (1975) study of deliberate psychological education for high school women. Their curricula differed in several ways from the Harris and Felton curricula in psychological awareness, which produced no direct moral stage change. In the Sprinthall study, the experience went beyond learning, listening, and counseling skills through role-playing exercises to a phase of actual reciprocal helping through counseling one another about real problems and to counseling friends and acquaintances not in the course. This included a discussion of the moral responsibilities of someone who takes on a counselor role.

In Erickson's curriculum a focus on listening skills through role playing and interviews was followed by experiences of exposure to personal moral dilemmas both through literature and through interviewing women outside the class. In the course of this experience the students were taught something about moral stage theory itself.

In summary, the Harris and Felton studies suggest that a restricted focus on listening skills will not lead to direct moral judgment stage change, though it may facilitate experiences of a more explicit moral nature. The Sprinthall and Erickson studies suggest that these experiences may include moral reflection on the role of the counselor as well as discussion of hypothetical and real personal moral dilemmas in the adolescents' lives.

In summary, the studies we have reviewed in this category suggest the value of integrating deliberate psychological education with direct moral discussion for stimulating moral growth.

Social Studies Curricula and Moral Development

The third category includes social studies curricula that employ moral discussion but whose primary aim is growth in understanding of historical or social issues.

The Lieberman (1979a) study looked at the effects upon moral growth of the ten-week unit called "Facing History and Ourselves: The Holocaust and Human Behavior," developed by Strom and Parsons (see Chapter 12). This social studies unit was taught to one class of eighth graders in two different schools, with a control class from each school. The unit included moral discussion, films, interviews with Holocaust survivors, and discussions of the students' feelings and reactions to the material.

Lieberman administered pre- and posttests measuring moral judgment development, interpersonal awareness as assessed by Selman (1973), and ego development (Loevinger 1976). The experimental group (both intervention classes) did not increase in moral judgment nor on ego development significantly more than did the control group (both control classes combined). These groups were primarily at Stage 2(3) and 3 on moral judgment. However, the experimental group did show a significant increase in interpersonal awareness stage, moving mostly from Stage 2 to Stage 2(3).

The Harvard Center for Moral Education as part of an evaluation of Danforth-sponsored projects assessed the moral judgment development over one semester in two U.S. history classes in Brookline High School, one honors-level course taught by Ladenburg, and one standard-level course taught by Oakes. Students from a history class without moral discussion served as the control group. Ladenburg taught units in American history as described in Chapter 6. Role play of historical situations is an integral aspect of some of the units. Oakes engaged his students in both historical and hypothetical direct moral discussion of the Blatt variety. Neither class nor the control groups showed any substantial moral growth.

These two studies allow us to suggest tentatively that the enhancement of moral judgment development may be more difficult when the teacher has strong curricular priorities and when the moral dilemmas are defined by, and focus upon, a particular academic content. In some cases it may be that the idea that there are social and historical "facts" and "right answers" to tests inhibits full involvement by the students in the moral dilemma discussions.

WHAT THE NEXT GENERATION MAY LEARN FROM THE FIRST

In this section we will offer, for general use, certain methodological recommendations based on troublesome points in some of the studies just reviewed. Although the examples given relate to specific studies, the recommendations suggested are general ones that we feel should be considered for future research. Common problems in data collection and suggestions for improvements will be discussed first, followed by problems and recommendations for data analysis and presentation.

It is important to reiterate Lockwood's suggestion that the Moral Judgment Interview be given as an oral interview and not as a written questionnaire. The written format has a low test-retest reliability in comparison to the interview.

For example, in DiStefano's study, which used the written format, several subjects in the control group and one in the experimental group dropped a whole stage from pretest to posttest. This finding can be reasonably explained as due to the known unreliability of the written format in conjunction with another commonly found phenomenon, that of boredom on the posttest in control group subjects.

A second consideration in collecting data is suggested by the boredom factor, that is, that alternate forms be used from pretest to posttest. Because Form A and Form B are not of exactly equal difficulty, it is important that half the subjects receive Form A on the pretest and Form B on the posttest and the other half of the subjects receive Form B on the pretest and Form A on the posttest.

Third, no experimental or control group (design cell) should have fewer than 10 to 12 subjects. This is about the size necessary for the Blatt effect of one-third stage change to be statistically significant using a t-test to measure pre to post change.

Fourth, if at all possible, subjects or groups should be randomly assigned to interventions and control or comparison groups. Paolitto's study that randomly assigned the treatment to the classroom is an example of this procedure at the group level since randomization of individuals between classes is usually not possible.

A fifth important point is that studies designed to test innovative and hopefully powerful treatments should have as one control group a Blatt-like, traditional direct hypothetical moral discussion group as did Grimes and Rundle.

The fact that this comparison group in Rundle's study showed no change points out the importance of having a trained moral educator lead such a group. The effectiveness of innovative treatments can be assessed only against the standard Blatt effect (one-third stage increase) rather than against the no change, null hypothesis.

The Harris study points to a sixth recommendation for data collection and for the planning of interventions. Curricula and teaching strategies should be designed with hypotheses about the possible effect upon moral growth of their different components. It may be that in a complex and varied treatment one component would be singled out for study and optimally placed in the intervention so that moral judgment interviews could be administered upon its completion as well as before and after the entire treatment.

Seventh, taped recordings of the classroom treatment processes should be made to document that the desired conditions of the intervention actually exist.

Eighth, it is desirable to collect data that assess or document other processes or goals of the intervention beyond direct moral discussion. The use of assessment measures with established levels of reliability and documented validity would add the most information to the field of moral education in two ways. Such an accumulation of data provides knowledge very useful for interpreting the meaning and effect of interventions. Also, cumulative empirical data on the relationship between moral judgment and other often-used measures (for example, Loevinger Sentence Completion Test) aids in expanding our theoretical understanding of the relationship between moral development and development in other domains.

Last, we encourage long-term follow-ups such as were involved in the original Blatt and Kohlberg study (1975). The reason for a long-term follow-up is not only to show that the treatment effects are relatively lasting but also because gains due to some treatments would be expected to continue after the formal termination of the project. Two examples of this are the Grimes and Stanley interventions that produced new patterns of family interactions that might lead to the expectation of continued gains after the posttest.

Analyzing the Data of Moral Education Curricula

We now turn to considerations and recommendations for data analysis and their presentation. First, moral judgment protocols should be blind scored as regards both treatment group and time of testing. Also the same scorer should score all the protocols of any one subject to avoid confounding scorer error with treatment effects. Second, both interrater and test-retest reliability should be calculated and reported. Test-retest reliability should be determined on the control group correlating the pre- and posttest scores as a measure of instrument stability in the population being studied. For instance, in the DiStefano study using the written format, there was very little test-retest correlation in the control group population. Presumably this is evidence of the lack of reliability of the written instrument but also could have been caused in part by the "alternative school treatment" common to both the control and intervention groups.

A third and important recommendation is to distinguish between development and group differences in data analysis. A test of the change from pre to post, typically a t-test, in the experimental group should be done to assess the change of that group. Analysis of variance on posttest scores covarying for pretest and other relevant variables also should be done. The results of the DiStefano study indicate why an analysis of covariance needs to be done as well as a pre-post test of change. In that study the control group went up as well as the experimental group indicating factors other than the treatment were causing part of the change in the experimental group. The Felton study is an example of the opposite problem. Since her control groups scored lower on the posttest than on the pretest, the covariance analysis showed a significant effect even though there was no upward change from pre- to posttest in the experimental group.

Fourth, the data need to be fully reported in the original write-up of any intervention study. As well as tests of significance, descriptive statistics on the experimental and comparison groups should be presented in full detail. Most readers will want to compare the experimental findings with the results of other experimental studies, for example, the Blatt and Kohlberg study. For this purpose inferential statistics or tests of significance do not provide information. Major and minor stage as well as mean MMS points should be given both for individuals and group means. Mean change, proportions of subjects moving from one stage to the next, and proportions of subjects demonstrating new stage thinking are examples of data presentation that allow comparison across studies.

Besides reporting descriptive data, Lieberman (1979b) recommends the use of nonparametric tests of significance rather than parametric statistics (t-test, ANOVA) to maintain the integrity of qualitative data.

Before the studies reported in this volume were completed there were a few well-established points about cognitive moral developmental education (reviewed in Kohlberg 1977 and Lockwood 1978). The first conclusion is that cognitive developmental moral discussion leads to about one-third to one-half upward stage change in experimental groups during a period of time (one academic semester or year) in which there is essentially no change in control or comparison groups. This change occurs in classrooms in which the students' reasoning is at a mixture of two or more stages. Another necessary condition for enhancing moral growth is that the teacher use Socratic probing for the students' reasons during moral dilemma discussions. The last necessary condition is that there be moral discussion that creates controversy and divided opinions among the students in discussing a minimum of 10 to 20 hypothetical dilemmas.

The studies reported in this volume confirm these conclusions and suggest additional ones. One of the probable conditions for optimal growth through moral discussion is a climate of openness, trust, and active listening. The studies that used psychological awareness activities were, in part, effective for this reason. However, psychological education that does not include real-life counseling experiences in which the students actively consider the moral responsibility of being a counselor does not seem to directly promote moral judgment growth. The studies by Harris (1976) and Felton (1974) are evidence of this point. Research (Walker 1979, Colby 1975) has shown that the levels of social perspective-taking or psychological awareness as reflected in Loevinger's sentence completion and Selman's and Byrne's interpersonal awareness assessments are necessary, but not sufficient, for the attainment of parallel levels of moral judgment stage. It may be that psychological awareness activities similarly promote personal stage growth, which is a prerequisite for advance in moral stage.

What new conclusions come from the present set of studies? They suggest that the most powerful moral education interventions involve discussion of real dilemmas in the context of a natural group: parents and children or an elementary school classroom group. This emerges as the probable conclusion from the Grimes, Stanley, and Rundle studies (see Chapters 13 and 19). Reasonable corollaries of discussing real situations in a natural group are the cultivation of democratic decision making, by giving to each participant a share in the decision and also the making of family or classroom contracts for implementing those decisions. Research on such interventions in the school should now employ the methods for observing and assessing group moral atmosphere discussed by Reimer, Power, and Kohlberg in this volume (see Chapter 17). Moral atmosphere research assumes that democratic moral discussion and decision making tend to promote shared or collective norms of community at a relatively high stage compared to the moral judgment stage of some of the individuals in the group. Such a relatively advanced moral atmosphere is, in turn, a stimulus for the moral growth of the individual students. It is also probably a mediator between the moral judgments and the moral actions of students in the group and between the decisions and actions taken by the group as a whole.

The Effects of a Just Community School

A longitudinal study of the effects of democratic governance and direct moral discussion was done over the last few years in Cambridge and Brookline. Alternative programs based on an explicit philosophy of enhancing the ideas of justice and community exist in the public high schools of these two communities, the Cluster School in Cambridge and the School-Within-A-School in Brookline. These schools, comparison alternative programs, and control groups in the high schools were studied. Yearly individual moral judgment interviews and individual interviews of the program or high school moral atmosphere were administered. In addition the weekly town meetings of the two focal "just community" programs were taped and transcribed for a three-year period. The report of this research is now being written. At this time only data from the Cluster School have been analyzed (Power 1979). The individual moral judgment change data on the Cluster School will be reported herein.

The Cluster School had a yearly enrollment of between 55 and 70 students in grades nine through twelve. Most students who entered the program remained in it until graduation. Considering moral stage change greater than one-third of a stage, 18 percent of the students showed some development over a one-year period for any year in the school. The mean moral judgment stage change for all one-year data is 15 MMS points; over two years the mean change is 35 MMS points; and over three years it is 53 MMS points. There is an overall pattern of upward change without stage skipping. Most students entered the school reasoning primarily at Stages 2 and 3 and most left using some Stage 4 reasoning.

Two aspects of the alternative school experience are related to greater upward movement. First, regardless of grade or age, the students showed greater gains in their first year in the program than in subsequent years of attendance. The mean upward change for the first year of tenure in the school is 22 MMS points for those who entered in years I through III. For any year of the Cluster School, 28 percent of the students in their first year of tenure showed upward stage movement between one-half and one stage and 33 percent advanced between one-third and one-half stage. The fact that almost two-thirds of the students advanced more than the expected one-third stage change corroborates the interpretation of the Rundle and Grimes studies that moral discussion in natural groups with democratic decision making are powerful effectors of development. Second, the year of the school was an influential factor. Looking at moral judgment growth over a one-year span, the mean change of the students during year III was 14 MMS points, whereas during year IV it was 26 MMS points. A subsample of seventeen students who entered in year III showed an upward stage change of 46 MMS points from the beginning of year III to the end of year IV. Another illustration of the impact of the year of the school upon students' reasoning is that in year II, 44 percent of the development was to Stage 4 and in year IV, 90 percent of the development was to Stage 4.

The interaction of these two variables also had an impact on moral growth. Although the mean change is 22 MMS points for a student's first year in the school for years I through III, those who entered the Cluster School in year IV advanced 41 MMS points in that one year.

Data from the Cluster School offer some evidence that the moral atmosphere seems to be a stimulus for the moral growth of individual students. Stage scores on four school values (the values of community, democracy, fairness, and order) were clinically assigned on material from the moral atmosphere ethnographic interviews. These four scores were averaged to arrive at a school values stage score. A comparison of the school values stage scores with the moral judgment scores showed 61 percent of the time students scored lower on school values than on moral judgment. However, an examination of the scores of students who were retested the following year show that the gap had closed. In other words, on a one-year retest these students scored at the same stage on both measures (moral judgment stage = 2.95 and school values stage = 2.93). Very briefly these data seem to indicate that horizontal development (decalage) across moral issues was occurring and perhaps that the content of what students considered to be moral expanded to include issues in their school lives.

A further investigation of the relation between moral judgment and school values change showed that all students who showed upward moral development also showed upward development on school values. Students who did not increase on school values stage also did not show upward change on moral judgment.

These findings, although tentative and on a sample of only 21 students, seem to indicate that there may be a necessary but not sufficient relationship between understanding the ideology and goals of the school at higher stages and change in moral stage. Students who developed higher-stage reasoning about school community issues increased on their moral judgment scores. Thus it does seem, as we suggested earlier, that a more advanced moral atmosphere seems to be a stimulus for the moral growth of individuals in the school community.

CONCLUSION

The studies we have reviewed that integrate moral development objectives with innovative social studies and history curricula do not appear to generate substantial moral judgment change. At this time there remains a question why this is so. A slightly cynical reader might note that these social studies curricula were developed and taught by full-time teachers who did not have a doctoral dissertation resting on their efforts. A less cynical reader might note the complexity of simultaneously integrating in the classroom regular social studies' objectives with effective direct moral discussion. Pursuit of social studies' knowledge and understanding may lead in a different direction than pursuit of direct moral discussion goals. Our observations suggest that effective Socratic moral discussion requires a teacher's rather single-minded focus on generating sustained moral controversy and probing for reasons.

The genre of the studies we have reviewed (with the exceptions noted above) is that of the doctoral dissertation developing an innovative curriculum and testing its effects on individual student development. This type of study is a magnificent learning experience for the person conducting the study, leading to the mastery of not only curriculum development but also of moral development assessment and research methods. As contributions to the field these studies are basically formative research evaluations of experimental curricula that are not always followed up by further curriculum refinement. These studies often do not build systematically upon each other in the sense that contributions of one curriculum and any additions or deletions are not spelled out in a subsequent curriculum. It might be a good idea for future curriculum studies to replicate one prior curriculum in one comparison group and to teach a hopefully improved curriculum to the treatment group. What is perhaps the greatest challenge would be to design studies that give us new knowledge about the process of moral development. Such studies would probably require a more microscopic analysis of classroom interactions and moral atmosphere. It also would require greater attention to the characteristics of the students who change and of those who do not change as a result of the intervention. Studies cited earlier (Colby 1975, Kohlberg 1977, and Walker 1979) suggest that many students fail to change in response to moral education because they lack either the logical prerequisite or the social perspective-taking prerequisite for the next moral stage. It could be worthwhile to routinely assess these variables on a pretest when conducting a moral development intervention.

More microscopic analyses of the outcome measures of moral and interpersonal awareness development offer a third way of beginning to look at the process of moral development. The relation between the particular content of a curriculum and the content or issues on the developmental assessment measures in which students showed the most change has been done by Lieberma Lieberman (1979a) when analyzing the effects of the Holocaust curriculum (see Chapter 12). The issues of interpersonal awareness on which there was the most change were consistent with the content focused upon by the course.

In reviewing recent moral education interventions we have categorized them into three types: direct moral discussion of real-life dilemmas with natural groups; direct moral discussion and deliberate psychological education; and direct moral discussion in social studies curricula. Because we reviewed only two studies in the last category, no conclusions will be made, but we offer the observation that enhancement of student's moral judgment development through discussion of moral dilemmas defined by an academic content seems particularly difficult. It may be that it is confusing for students and difficult for teachers to discuss and study the same subject area both as knowledge and as fact and as the basis and content for Socratic dialog about moral issues. Studies in the second group that combined direct moral discussion with psychological education that had a real-life, experiental component demonstrate that substantial moral growth of one-third stage movement or more can be expected with this type of intervention. The research results in interventions using natural groups, those in the first category, showed the most moral judgment change, usually upward movement of one-half stage. These studies suggest that when teachers consciously work to accomplish the dual goals of having direct moral discussions of real life dilemmas, within a natural group in which all participants are empowered to a say in decisions, the moral growth of the students is almost insured and is certainly dramatic.

Following the review of this generation of research, we offered recommendations for the design of future studies, for analysis of data, and presentation of results. Clearly, significant work has been done and we feel that researchers and educators should learn from and build upon the solid results of this generation.

PART II

MORAL EDUCATION IN PRACTICE

HIGH SCHOOL
CURRICULA

6
COGNITIVE DEVELOPMENT
AND MORAL REASONING
IN THE TEACHING OF
HISTORY

Thomas Ladenburg

The idea that human development should be the aim of education was first stated by John Dewey (1916)

> The aim of education is growth or development both intellectual and moral. . . . Only knowledge of the order and connection of the stages in psychological development can insure the maturing of psychic powers. Education is the work of supplying the conditions which will enable the psychological functions to mature and pass into higher functions in the freest and fullest manner (p. 207).

While Dewey envisioned the development of intellectual capacities as a goal, he did not have the "knowledge of the order and connection of the [various growth] stages" or the conceptual tools to measure them. The groundwork for that discovery was produced by Jean Piaget and his colleagues in the 1930s. Through their studies, they learned to distinguish different mental capacities which were involved in reasoning about concrete data and in the ability to think about thought or formal operations. Human development, Piaget informed us, is a process in which one acquires the means to progress from one kind of thinking to another. Building on Piaget's discoveries, Professor Lawrence Kohlberg identified six distinct stages of reasoning when dealing with

Reprinted from *The History Teacher* 10, no. 2 (1977): 183-98. Copyright by The Society for History Education, Inc., 1977.

moral issues differentiated by increasing complexity and inclusiveness at each stage. They begin with primitive obedience to authority and the avoidance of pain and move progressively on to the egocentric realization of reciprocal exchange, and from the recognition of the need for loyalty to family and peers to the incorporation of a societal perspective, and finally to a recognition of global or universal principles of human dignity and equality.

Professor Kohlberg found that progressing to different stages of reasoning requires the incorporation of previous stages; indeed, a stage cannot be omitted. Moreover, the process is not influenced by cultural factors. Kohlberg's great contribution to developmental education was his (and his colleagues Moshe Blatt, Ralph Mosher, and Norman Sprinthall's) revolutionary discovery that educational interventions could stimulate the development of moral reasoning from lower to higher, more complete, and holistic stages. This discovery has made it possible to realize Dewey's dictum that the aim of education is the growth and development of both intellectual and moral faculties.

Courses designed to stimulate the ability to reason about moral issues typically include two components. First, they involve students in exploring moral dilemmas, generally short, hypothetical case studies in which choices must be made between equally compelling alternatives. Secondly, students are involved in an affective component such as leading moral dilemma discussions with younger students or counseling elementary school youngsters. By employing these rich and varied techniques over a period of but one academic year, developmental educators have been able to stimulate moral reasoning by as much as a full stage.

While this effort has served as the cutting edge of a new curriculum movement, it has failed to gain widespread acceptance in schools throughout the country. Most schools generally see their roles more in terms of intellectual rather than developmental education, if we are to define "intellectual" as mastering traditional subject matter and "developmental" as stimulating increased capacity for moral reasoning. However, there is no need to continue maintaining these artificial distinctions. Since Kohlberg and his colleagues have provided the tools and data which can enable us to realize the full potentials of Dewey's insights, developmental education can and should be integrated into the traditional curriculum in general and into the teaching of history and social studies in particular.

This work has already begun. Several school systems — Tacoma, Washington; Brookline and Cambridge, Massachusetts; Pittsburgh, Pennsylvania; and Minneapolis, Minnesota — are all in the process of producing and distributing experimental materials designed to stimulate development. Moshe Blatt and others have published a collection of hypothetical dilemmas for classroom use, and Edwin Fenton has produced a series of filmstrips for Guidance Associates. Thomas Jones and Ronald Galbraith and Barry Beyer have written carefully constructed guides to help teachers lead discussions of moral issues.

The work produced and made available by the social studies educators, however, has not been as rich in its conception or as varied in its execution as the course materials generated by developmental educators. In general, the social studies materials have been modeled after the dilemmas used by Kohlberg in his experiments to test and validate his theory of moral reasoning. Typically they involve contrived moral conflicts cast in hypothetical, historic settings, in which individuals are left to choose between only two courses of action. Writing in *Social Education,* Barry Beyer (1976) gives the rationale for this design. He suggests that the moral dilemma "be as simple as possible," involving "only a few characters in a relatively uncomplicated situation" (p. 196). However, Jack Fraenkel in the same issue of *Social Education* criticized this approach. If students "are to find out about the nature of the world in which they live," he argues, "they must be exposed to a wide variety of different kinds of issues and dilemmas" (p. 221). I heartily concur with Professor Fraenkel. Social studies educators must improve upon the techniques espoused by Jones, Galbraith, and Beyer. Otherwise, they run the risk of reducing the study of history, with its recurrent moral themes, to simplistic case studies devoid of the discipline's rich complexities.

In addition to the hypothetical dilemmas, the history curriculum can and should include dilemmas as rich and varied as those faced, for example, by the Founding Fathers in writing the Constitution, by Congress in ratifying the Jay Treaty, or by Franklin Roosevelt in proposing the Social Security system. Dilemmas of this character have the potential of developing into a new "new social studies" effort that can achieve the cognitive and affective goals of the developmentalists as well as the traditional intellectual objectives of education.

The central purpose of this chapter is to present a model that will help teachers and curriculum writers begin this necessary task. In order for history teachers to reach this ambitious goal, it is essential that:

1. The high school teacher be provided with an acceptable definition of his subject area which also embraces developmental goals.

2. This definition be translated into a model for teaching history and developing social studies curriculum that combines subject matter with developmental education, and that allows cognitive development and moral reasoning to be used as a means of teaching the discipline as well as an end in itself.

3. The concept of a moral dilemma be so broadened as to include a continuum ranging from simple, hypothetical dilemmas on one end to complex, moral development units on the other.

4. Specific examples of units that bridge the gap between teaching subject matter and stimulating growth be provided to enable teachers to apply principles inherent in the model to their own curriculum.

A DEFINITION OF HISTORY THAT EMBRACES DEVELOPMENTAL GOALS

In his book, *The Aims of Education,* Alfred North Whitehead (1956) defines education as "the art of the utilization of knowledge." He reminds us that "ideas which are not utilized are positively harmful" (pp.15-16). Unless they become more concerned with the reasons certain decisions are made rather than with the decisions themselves, it seems that history teachers are particularly open to the accusation of imparting information which is no longer usable. True, the new social studies have placed more emphasis on process and discovery than on isolated facts. Nonetheless, history does not become alive for most students unless they are somehow involved in the vicarious process of making or rethinking historic decisions. Indeed, it is this idea of process that provides a link between the past and present.

By taking part in the effort of making and evaluating decisions, students become participants in a continual drama. Through simulations, discussions, and debates, they learn to use facts and concepts in order to buttress an argument, support a point, or reason to a new conclusion. These dialogues with the past impart knowledge that can be applied to current problems or to analogous cases. As students become conversant with history in this manner, they incorporate new ideas and facts into their thought processes. If the subject matter is carefully chosen, they become active participants in the historical-political culture which has shaped our past and now defines our present.

Man operates within a time frame or context. He perceives problems and makes decisions from alternatives open to him. At some future moment he may look back and more clearly analyze the reasons for his decisions. The model of man as a decision maker operating within the context of time, and of man standing apart from the decision, reflecting back on it, helps us to understand the many and diverse activities of the historian, as well as the nature of the discipline and the four types of questions historians try to answer. These questions are: What was the historical context in which the dilemma occurred? What sequence of events preceded the decision? Was the decision that was reached a correct one? Why was the particular decision made at that time?

In posing the first question, historians are guided by their interest in the past as a unique and singular example of man as a universal entity. Their search into specific kinds of history, the social, economic, political, and intellectual, gives rise to specialties in these areas. In seeking answers to the second question, historians probe into events with the skill of trained detectives and attempt to learn exactly what transpired. Whether consciously or not, historians pass judgments on events, sometimes using standards which even they can or do not define, and thus in the role of moral philosophers answer the third question, on ethics. Finally, historians seek answers to the fourth question: why did it happen? Here they uncover the motives of men and women, wrestle with the problem of inevitability, and uncover causes in social, economic, and political-ideological circumstances.

A MODEL FOR TEACHING THAT COMBINES SUBJECT MATTER WITH DEVELOPMENTAL GOALS

In posing these questions and involving students in the search for their answers, the high school history instructor can impart a small but representative sampling of the total import of the discipline he teaches. But he can also encourage cognitive growth by stimulating the ability to reason at higher and more complex stages. This is possible because the questions posed in the classroom are both sequential and consequential; students learn about the general context of any period; this information allows them to understand the events; they then resolve the decision maker's dilemma by participating in a reconstruction of the decision-making process; and they reflect back on their own deliberations as they analyze why the decision was made. At each stage, the student seeks answers which he can understand only at his level of reasoning, and each set of conclusions is therefore tailor made (as Dewey would have it, with his own "hands") to his intellectual ability. As he progresses from one stage of questioning to the next, his level of understanding will grow and deepen, and his ability to master facts or comprehend concepts will be similarly expanded.

The four-stage model can be applied to the American Revolution. First, the teacher explores the first question by asking what the climate of the times was and leads his students through an examination of the social, economic, political, and ideological background to the Revolution. Youngsters study the class structure of colonial America, the mercantile policies of England, the relationship between colonial governments and the British Parliament, and the colonists' conceptions of "liberty" and power." Secondly, classes inquire into the events that actually took place at the time, occasionally using the historian's inquiry tools in sifting through conflicting source materials. Here they learn of the French and Indian War, the problems of ruling an empire, the Stamp Act and the protest it aroused, the Boston Massacre, the Tea Party, the Battle of Lexington, and the Declaration of Independence. This is traditional fare. But interlaced with descriptions of these events, products of economic and social conditions, students are involved in the third level of questioning. They make moral judgments about decisions that were reached or were about to be made. They may be asked whether the Stamp Act riots were justified, whether British soldiers had the right to fire at colonists on King Street, and whether the British were justified in imposing the Intolerable Acts as punishment for the Tea Party. Finally, and only after completing the earlier stages of questioning, students are required to reflect on the series of events they had studied and are asked what caused the Revolution or, more simply, why disagreements were not resolved peacefully. Here they are forced to seek adequate explanations for events they have studied within the context of their own times and which they have measured against their own structures of moral reasoning.

This model — requiring sequential development of four different types of questions — can form the blueprint governing the construction of most history courses. The planning involved, of course, is extremely complex, and the ideal may not always be attained. But the payoff in terms of developmental and traditional intellectual education can hardly be exaggerated. Every question prepares the way for the next, and the final exercise allows the dilemmas built into the unit to provide evidence for the analysis required at the end.

A BROADENED DEFINITION OF MORAL DILEMMAS

Besides linking the "what" and the "why" questions, moral dilemmas also have the unique quality of "turning students on." The query, What should _____ do? Was _____ justified? or Who was right? whether asked in the context of the Stamp Act, the Tea Party, or the Battle of Lexington, has always been in my experience the question that excited the most interest, discussion, and debate. The reasons for its power to elicit a response are partially a matter of speculation, but seem closely connected to Piagetian and Kohlbergian theories. Every student has formulated a mental construct uniquely his own, concerning issues of justice, fairness, or right and wrong. A contrary opinion, or one argued at a higher stage that serves to jar this construct or attack the structure of the reasoning, is opposed as long as there are intellectually valid grounds to combat it. In defending their views against alien ideas, students are forced to dig deeply into their own resources and ultimately modify their own structure of moral thought. Facts become weapons that are used to reinforce their own ideas or eventually to batter down their citadels. As the mind is exposed to reasoning which it recognizes as more complex or complete, it alters or modifies its views, incorporating these newer and more adequate concepts. Thus dilemma discussions are the means by which we encourage students to deal with new ideas and to modify their own patterns of thought. Moral dilemmas have more power to accomplish this change than abstract discussions of causality because they summon immediate feelings of right and wrong which are always with us and which press uniquely on adolescents.

Since moral dilemmas necessarily play so central a role in cognitive development and moral reasoning, it is important to distinguish among several kinds of dilemmas that may be used. At one end of the scale are the cases involving hypothetical dilemmas. They deal with universal principles of right and wrong, devoid of considerations of either time or place. The classic in the Kohlberg literature is the case of Heinz whose wife will die of a rare disease because he cannot afford to pay the druggist's exorbitant price for the necessary medicine [see Table 2.2]. "Should Heinz steal the medicine?" the subject is asked. This dilemma was a central one used by Kohlberg to discover and validate the character of the six stages of moral reasoning. The value of this and similar dilemmas involving fictionalized case studies is limited from the standpoint of the history teacher because the ethical questions they raise lack a historical context. Heinz's dilemma is equally perplexing whether he lived in Europe at the turn of the century or in America in the 1970s. It reveals nothing about the nature of any particular point in time and does not force students to come to a deeper understanding of any historical period.

The second mode is the historical dilemma. Like the former, it deals with a person caught in an ethical problem, but this time the situation contains another dimension because it includes consideration of the nature of the time period within which the decision must be made. An example of the historical dilemma is the case of Helga who is asked by her friend Rachel to hide her from the Nazis. This dilemma is similar to one involving a man who must decide whether he will hide a runaway slave and violate the Fugutive Slave Act. Both dilemmas can be reasoned at several different levels. The former involves conflicting claims of loyalty to friend or family, the danger to self (what if the Nazis discover Rachel?), and the morality of the German laws against the Jews. The latter involves a parallel conflict between duty to another human being and the morality of slavery and the laws protecting property rights.

In an article appearing in *Social Education,* Ronald Galbraith and Thomas Jones (1975) clearly elucidate a strategy to teach this type of historical dilemma. It involves reviewing the facts of the case, clarifying alternatives for the decision maker, and eliciting reasons for each opposing course of action. Discussions are to focus on the reasoning employed. If the class does not divide naturally into opposing camps, the terms of the dilemma are changed somewhat by the teacher. What if Rachael were only an acquaintance instead of a good friend? What if the punishment for hiding Jews were imprisonment in a concentration camp? Once a clear division is found in the class, opposing arguments are presented, and student discussion is focused on reasons rather than solutions.

While these strategies may meet the needs of the developmental psychologists, it is doubtful whether they are equally useful in teaching history. If dilemmas are to serve as a means for teaching subject matter as well as developing moral reasoning, more complex examples must be used. And with the wealth that historical events afford, there is ample reason to require that the dilemma be real rather than hypothetical. The case of the slave mother who kills her child rather than permit the master to sell it as he has the other three is one example. So, too, is the case of Jonathan Harrington who must choose between his loyalty to family and his allegiance to friends and the Revolution, when he decides whether or not to stand with the Lexington militia in the face of superior British forces. Both of these dilemmas are real and reveal something of the nature of the conditions surrounding them.

More complex historical dilemmas can be drawn from cases of actual decision makers faced with crucial decisions that affect the lives of others. Several examples easily come to mind: Abraham Lincoln agonizing over the Emancipation Proclamation, Harry Truman debating whether to drop the atomic bomb on Hiroshima, or a juror at the trial of the soldiers involved in the Boston Massacre. The reasoning needed to engage in these dilemmas must of necessity become interlaced with a consideration of the historical factors which played a role in the decision.

A single historical dilemma can easily be made the basis for a two- or three-day activity and involve many of the thinking and reasoning skills necessary to the learning of history. For example, students can be given the information to stage a mock trial of the British soldiers accused of murder in the Boston Massacre. During the trial, youngsters may act out the parts of witnesses, defendants, lawyers, judges, or "impartial" jurors. The decision rendered will most likely depend on the skill of opposing lawyers in presenting the case, and in the process of preparation, opening statements, cross-examination, and summation students will learn a great deal about our advocacy system of justice. Jurists and witnesses, too, can learn much about courtroom procedure and are required to think through some complex legal issues.

The enterprising teacher can build this lesson on the Boston Massacre into a dilemma miniunit, the third kind of moral dilemma useful to the history teacher. He could follow the mock trial with a reading on the Kent State incident and ask who were the people most clearly to blame, the British soldiers or the National Guardsmen. This discussion may be continued, using the Battle of Lexington as another example; students could add the militia's stand on the Green, the shot from an unknown source, and the subsequent killings of New England farmers as a parallel case to follow the Boston Massacre and Kent State discussions. These three lessons could form the basis of the miniunit and would undoubtedly evoke controversy, hard thinking, and a search for some general principles regarding dissent and protest. By this time, the students should be sufficiently immersed in history as process, making decisions they will later stand away from and try to analyze.

Historical miniunits can be built around a number of other events. One which works very well examines the issue of how to deal with a great wrong such as slavery. Rather than involve students in the hypothetical case of the runaway slave, teachers can have youngsters re-create the Lincoln-Douglas debate over how the nation should resolve the question of slavery in the territories, followed by a discussion of John Brown's dramatic raid on Harper's Ferry, and ending with an analysis of Lincoln's decision to put priority on saving the Union rather than ending slavery.

UNITS THAT BRIDGE THE GAP BETWEEN SUBJECT AND DEVELOPMENTAL GOALS

It is hoped that teachers will not stop with the dilemma miniunits. They should construct entire units designed to stimulate cognitive development and history courses using moral issues to promote the desired development. The basic pattern for such units has already been described. It revolves around the four questions historians most frequently ask. A sample of such a unit on the writing of the United States Constitution was developed by the author and refined as part of the Brookline, Massachusetts, Moral Development Project. It has been taught to over 350 students and meets most of the established criteria for a moral development unit. This unit is described here in the hope that it will encourage other teachers to try similar enterprises.

The heart of the unit is a simulation requiring that youngsters assume the roles of the Founding Fathers and resolve five major issues before the Constitutional Convention. Each student delegate prepares for his role by analyzing the Articles of Confederation, debating the justification of Shay's Rebellion, and reading excerpts from Madison's Federalist Paper Number 10. Following this exposure to the social, economic, and political-ideological background to the convention, he is given an explanation of the issues to be resolved and a political biography of the delegates, which includes their views on the issues.

The mock convention opens with delegates attempting to resolve the conflict between the large and small states over representation. Students spend roughly equal amounts of time hearing prepared speeches, debating the issues as a "committee of the whole," jawboning with students during "caucuses," and analyzing or voting on conflicting resolutions. On succeeding days, the mock convention considers how power should be divided between the national and state governments, what powers should be given the President, the Congress, and the people, what should be done about slavery and the slave trade, and whether to write a Bill of Rights. After each of these issues is resolved through simulation, students read the Constitution and learn how these same questions were resolved in 1789. Now, aware that the solutions of 1789 were not necessarily perfect, they debate ratification and read several historians' interpretations of the Founders' motives. Thus prepared, they reflect back over the historical context of the times, the problems faced by the Founders, their solutions as embodied in the Constitution, and the experience of the simulation itself in an attempt to determine why the Constitution was written.

On the surface, discussions focusing on such issues as dividing power between the national and state governments may not appear to involve moral dilemmas. Certainly, they involve questions far more complex than those raised in the Heinz or Rachel cases. But behind all political decisions lies the fundamental question of justice, which is central to the resolution of all moral dilemmas and at the very heart of the political process. It is impossible to separate moral questions from political issues, and, indeed, any attempt to do so would deny the latter their essential character. In writing of Stephen Douglas' miscalculation in framing the Kansas-Nebraska Act, historian Allan Nevins (1947, pp. 108-09) made essentially the same point:

> He did not remember that it is the essence of democratic government that a temporary majority shall not abuse its power, nor shall cardinal changes be forced in national policy except after full and free discussion. ... These were all at bottom moral considerations, and his apprehension of them was cloudy and limited.

The exercise of writing a constitution is really an experience in arriving at a social contract. Students are required to go beyond simple obedience to the law; they must decide what the fundamental arrangements governing our political institutions should be. This would obviously require some application of what Professor Kohlberg labeled as Stage 5 reasoning, the "official morality of the American government." However, in arriving at this stage many lower stage arguments are used. The following dialogue was recorded during the mock convention and illustrates distinct stages of reasoning used by students in discussing the issue of dividing power between the national and state governments:

> Luther Martin: The purpose of these United States was because we needed to protect the state government from bigger powers. Before they were the United States they had to be protected from the British Power and now you want to just impose the power of the national government on each state. The state of Massachusetts should have the right to take care of any law itself. . . .
>
> Gouverneur Morris: Do you realize what might have happened if Shay's Rebellion had occurred in another state? It might have been taken care of in a completely different way. They might all have been executed — maybe they would have been tarred and feathered. We don't know. We can't have that type of disorder going around. We have to have a unified type of law that will affect everyone in every state; that they will get the same punishment no matter what state the rebellion took place in.
>
> John Lansing: I really disagree with that statement. That is saying that each person's feelings and each person's ideas are the same throughout the whole country, and people in New Hampshire, say, are going to have different issues and are going to feel differently about things than people in Georgia which is about 900 miles away — so we can't say that in one country each person is going to feel the same way and going to want to react the same way; so you can't have one law govern all those people.
>
> Charles Pinckney: What has been stated as an idea is that all men are equal. If all men are equal, they deserve to have the same rights, the same laws governing them. . . .
>
> John Lansing: You are saying that all men are robots — that's what you're saying.
>
> Charles Pinckney: I'm not saying that! I'm saying they deserve to have equal rights; they deserve to be treated equally; which means they must have equal laws.

Assumed in this author's definition of history is the premise that students must be involved in the process of making historic decisions and that there is no fundamental conflict between teaching subject matter conceived as decision making and stimulating cognitive development or moral reasoning. By playing the roles assigned them in the convention, students not only partake in their nation's political-historical culture; they gain the ability to see a situation from another point of view which is an essential factor in cognitive development. Perceiving problems from a reponsible adult perspective also provides the adolescent with conditions that promote the confidence, self-esteem, and sense of mastery so important to psychological development. Thus, the young man who argues against the national government on the basis that its power may be excessive learns something for himself about the relationship between authority and freedom. So does the young woman who, as Gouverneur Morris, tells the convention that because of Shays' Rebellion "we obviously need a stronger federal government."

As Madison and Wilson could cite their Aristotle, Sidney, Locke, or Hobbes and make references to Greek city-states and European constitutional monarchies, so the veterans of the mock convention are able to refer to Federalist Number 10, the theory behind England's unwritten constitution, the ineffectiveness of the Articles of Confederation, and Hobbes's concept of the state of nature. In becoming conversant about the problems confronting the Constitution makers, students begin to incorporate into their own thought processes the political science concepts and factual information necessary to understand the complexities of framing the Constitution. They are prepared not only to discuss the Constitution intelligently, but to participate in discussions of analogous problems confronting the nation today. Thus, the convention, in Whitehead's words, teaches utilizable knowledge.

It is possible to design an entire history course which continues the dialogue begun at the convention and to use many of the same techniques. The Federalist era, for instance, can be seen as the working out, through concrete policy decisions, of the broad and general conceptions of government discussed at the convention. Debates over funding the national debt, establishing the Bank, suppressing the Whiskey Rebellion, supporting the Alien and Sedition Acts, and the Virginia and Kentucky Resolutions, after all, raise issues and problems very similar to those decided at the Convention. The issues raised by the Tariff of Abominations, the Bank veto, the compromises of Henry Clay, the Dred Scott Decision, and secession continue the dialogue, involving students in reasoning through the underlying dilemmas posed by our conceptions of majority rule and minority rights. Resolving the problem of justice for black Americans may start with debates over the extension of slavery and continue in arguments over balancing the need to preserve the Union against the moral necessity of ending slavery. Related issues can be raised in a unit on Reconstruction, debating the relative merits of Lincoln's and Stevens' plans for dealing with the South, simulating the trial of Andrew Johnson, examining the opposing arguments in the Plessy decision, and considering current manifestations such as the cases for and against compensatory treatment and busing.

The rise of industrial America raises other perplexing dilemmas, pitting the freedom of businessmen against the needs of consumers, the rights of workers against the prerogatives of employers, and the plight of immigrants against the obligations of society. Foreign policy is similarly laced with fundamental moral concerns regarding true national interests and obligations, the moral restraints on pursuing those interests, and the necessity of foreign involvements. Finally, the 1920s and the Depression raise issues concerning the obligation of the national government to the plight of the unemployed and disabled within the context of fiscal and monetary policies geared toward encouraging economic expansion or combating inflation.

In all of the units outlined briefly above, it is possible and desirable to continue involving students in the dialogue initiated at the convention, to teach the economic and sociological concepts that make the present understandable, and finally, to involve students in the process of making decisions as well as requiring them to analyze the reason they were made. Knowledge thus obtained well never be inert, but will create citizens competent to take part in the political process which is, after all, the outgrowth of our historical experience. Students thus equipped will undoubtedly reason at higher moral and cognitive levels and will, in Dewey's words, "mature and pass into higher functions in the freest and fullest manner."

Involving students of low academic ability in discussing moral issues is more difficult than working with honors students. Nevertheless, the same principles that govern the successful use of hypothetical dilemmas, historical dilemmas, mini- and full dilemma units for the talented will work in teaching the less talented. With students who are not motivated dilemmas often induce discussion where other more traditional methods fail. The challenge is to develop or find material at the correct reading and conceptual level. The Constitution unit described here has been rewritten for low ability students, and a sample version has been developed for fifth graders. Since youngsters cannot discuss ideas they do not understand, it is important to translate problems into familiar terms. The fifth-grade class discussed the issue of secession rather than the question of power between national and state governments. One student translated the issue into his own words: "If you join a club, you can't quit and take the clubhouse with you."

Other units described here also work well with less able students by employing reasoning at lower stages. The mock trial of the soldiers involved in the Boston Massacre was a great success. In debating the Kent State incident, several youngsters argued that the dead students deserved their fate because "they would not have been shot if they had not done something wrong." Several viewed the situation from the Guardsmen's point of view, claiming that they were shooting in self-defense. Others adopted the victim's perspective and asked, "How would you like to be shot (like Sandy Sheuer) for looking for a lost dog?" Taking a more philosophical outlook, others argued "it all depends on who you were."

Although the level of discussion seldom reaches Stage 4, teachers should avoid despair. Instead, they should realize that the best way to raise the level of reasoning is by continued exposure to arguments at higher levels that will eventually cause the more complete and developed sentiments to become incorporated into the youngster's reasoning structure, thus advancing his capacity for logical, structured thought. The field studies by Professors Kohlberg and Mosher and their students have clearly demonstrated this point.

In general, units used with students of low academic ability seem to work well in proportion to the extent that the material presented is about "people" rather than "things." A unit on slavery can be particularly successful because cases like that of the woman who killed her child, a girl severely beaten for avoiding work, and Frederick Douglass besting his master are real dilemmas and illustrative of a society which systematically repressed human rights and dignity. Other successful units revolve around the plight of Indians and immigrants, areas equally rich in human interest stories and illustrative of fundamental issues involving the conflict between individuals and society.

This is not to say that moral dilemmas that pose significant political problems cannot be raised within the context of an American history course designed for the nonacademic student. A unit on the "limits of war" is generally successful. It employs the Lusitania case, the "final solution," Hiroshima, and the My Lai massacre. Similarly, the New Deal raises important political and economic issues in an ethical context. Students of all ability levels can and should be involved in discussions of postwar foreign policy questions such as the Truman-MacArthur controversy, the Cuban missile crisis, the Berlin blockade, and the Marshall Plan. Nor should the curriculum avoid discussions of civil rights, feminism, the counterculture, and so forth.

Teachers should not be discouraged if some youngsters are not facile with sophisticated concepts. Too many of us have tried and failed to teach the distinction between the protective and revenue tariff, learning the lesson that we cannot teach what the student is unwilling or intellectually unable to absorb. Rather than be defeated by this experience, teachers should concentrate on understandable concepts and design historical materials and miniunits that involve their classes in the process of confronting the dilemmas of history. One must rely on the reasoning processes revealed in the classroom to stimulate cognitive and moral growth. History can be taught in significant ways to students of all ability groups; the limiting factors are not the youngsters themselves, but the time and imagination of the teacher and the availability of materials.

The time has arrived for social studies educators to apply the developmental educators' knowledge, insights, and techniques to their own disciplines. Unfortunately, the work done to date, although a necessary beginning, has been too simplistic to encompass or exploit the rich and varied cloth of historical experience. Social studies people must develop moral dilemma units which present man as a decision maker operating within a context of time. Students can then experience historical dilemmas by participating in the decision-making process and then analyzing the reasons those decisions were made. Only after this difficult but necessary challenge to create a new "new social studies" is accepted, can the social studies teacher claim his rightful and central role in stimulating both cognitive development and moral reasoning.

7
MORAL EDUCATION TO REDUCE RACIAL AND ETHNIC PREJUDICE

Robert Alexander

RATIONALE

Americans have traditionally ignored racial or ethnic animosities until they exploded into riots, demonstrations, assasinations, and urban upheavals. The Kerner Report (National Advisory Commission 1968, p. 407) concluded: "Our nation is moving toward two societies, one black, one white — separate and unequal." A contemporary societal response to this problem is exemplified in the role that government has assumed, for example, passing equal employment opportunity laws, "affirmative action" programs, housing legislation, court-ordered busing, and other educational integration plans. Clearly, the long-range effect of such approaches has not been fully measured. In addition, one might question whether these remedies systematically affect individuals and their racial attitudes.

Not surprisingly, a microcosm of this human relations problem existed in Brookline High School where this curriculum was developed, though the bases of prejudice were not limited to race but included ethnicity, handicapped people, and one's social class as well. For example, this high school has a de facto segregated cafeteria, problems of control of "turf" in bathroom and gym areas, disagreements between "Jocks" and "Greasers," and accusations of prejudice in the choice of athletic teams and cheerleaders. As a result, students learn in an environment that is potentially explosive. Although crisis situations in the past have been defused temporarily, the fundamental issues of prejudice have not been dealt with in a consistent, rational way.

An analysis of the psychology of prejudice suggested that it is a learned response. In the 1940s and 1950s, when many significant studies were completed (in part a response to the Jewish Holocaust in Nazi Germany), it was held that prejudice was a personality trait, defined during early childhood, and fixed throughout later development. One of the first studies to explore in depth the full range of the interrelated ego functions that contribute to prejudiced personality types and syndromes was *The Authoritarian Personality* (Adorno et al. 1950). The results of this study indicated that highly prejudiced people showed greater similarity in responses than their counterpart, people with low prejudice. The significant differences between the groups clustered around attitudes toward the current self and in cognitive structure. Adorno characterized the highly prejudiced group as conformists, stereotyped in their thinking, and given to moralistic condemnation of those who did not adhere to conventional mores. Their interpersonal relations with other people were often exploitative or manipulative and concerned with things rather than feelings.

Subjects scoring low in prejudice were often conformist. They regarded individual differences as a desirable quality and were tolerant of people construed as different. Interpersonal relations were based on companionship, reciprocity, and mutual affection. A subsequent inquiry by Frenkel-Brunswick (1951) was aimed at Adorno's original assumption that those high in prejudice were in no way less mature than those persons low in prejudice. In studying rigidity in the personality of children high and low in prejudice, the personality test items that correlated with prejudice were the same items that differentiated younger from older children. "Some of the trends which are connected with ethnocentrism are thus natural stages of development which have to be overcome if maturity is to be reached" (Frenkel-Brunswick 1951, p. 406). Erikson (1959), for example, pointed out that prejudice might be a psychological need during the process of identity formation. Loevinger (1976), from a developmental perspective, made a logical comparison of ego stages to Adorno's prejudiced and unprejudiced personality types. Davidson's (1975) research, which correlated stages of respect to Kohlberg's stages of moral reasoning, added empirical support to this developmental interpretation of prejudice. Furthermore, Piaget and Weil (1951) delineated cognitive developmental stages that resulted in prejudiced conclusions or eliminated such attitudes based on rationality. These theoretical relationships of prejudice will be discussed subsequently and are outlined in Table 7.1. Moreover, to increase a student's knowledge about issues of prejudice is insufficient (Trager and Yarrow 1952; Clark 1955; Kleg 1971). Rather, the principal purpose of the moral education program described in this chapter was to stimulate change in the structure or way the person thinks about issues of prejudice. Thus the person may develop both more complex and principled ways of thinking about race, ethnicity, or social class.

TABLE 7.1
Theoretical Relationship of Ego and Moral Stages to Prejudice: Adorno's Types; Piaget's Cognitive Stages; And Davidson's Stages of Respect

Loevinger's Ego States	Adorno's Types	Piaget's Cognitive Stages
Presocial Symbiotic: Determination of self from non-self.	—	—
Impulsive: Interpersonal relations exploitative.	—	*Stage 1:* Egocentric perspective of others. Prejudice a result of rigid thought structure.
Self-Protective: Impulse control an issue, manipulative, exploitative, takes advantage of others.	Crank, Manipulator, Authoritarian.	*Stage 2:* Attempts to "role-take" individual perspective results in strong ingroup loyalties.
Conformist: Conformity to external rules, need for social approval, identification with welfare of family-peer group, basic trust.	Conformist (Prejudiced). Rigidly unprejudiced.	*Stage 2:* (Transitional) "Role-takes" family or group perspective. Limited abstract ability, little questioning of approved norms.
Self-Aware: Self-awareness, appreciation of multiple possibilities in situations, self-confidence. Attitudes may differ from group norm.	Easy-going. Unprejudiced.	*Stage 2:* (Continued) Abstract thinking, "role-takes" societal perspective, objectivity may reduce prejudice.
Conscientious: Self-evaluated standards and issues, goals, achievement, self-respect.	Protestor. Unprejudiced.	*Stage 3:* Cross cultural-international perspective. Advanced abstract ability. Prejudice rejected by rationality.
Individualistic: Respect for individuality.	Genuine. Liberal.	*Stage 3:* (Continued)

Kohlberg's Stages of Moral Reasoning	Davidson's Stages of Respect
Stage 1: Punishment and obedience orientation.	Respect interpreted as obedience to authority.
Stage 2: Right actions based on satisfaction of one's own needs. Fairness interpreted pragmatically.	Respect described as permission for peers/groups to pursue their own aims permitting prejudice.
Stage 3: Good behavior is that which pleases others and conforms to majority view.	Respect is an apparent obligation to display concern for others. Sympathy mitigates prejudice.
Stage 4: Fixed rules, maintenance of social order. Right behavior consists of doing one's duty.	Respect based on seeking objectivity.
Stage 5: Social contract, right action based on individual rights agreed upon by society. Democratic principles of American Constitution.	Respect a result of moral principles, e.g., justice, individual rights, fairness.
Stage 5: (Continued)	(Continued)
Stage 6: Universal principles of justice, reciprocity, and equality.	

Source: Robert C. Alexander, "A Moral Education Curriculum of Prejudice," Ed.D. dissertation, Boston University, 1977, p. 24.

LOEVINGER'S THEORY OF EGO DEVELOPMENT

Loevinger (1976) refers to ego as the "master trait" in personality around which the edifice of personality is constructed. This conception of ego development relies on a pointing definition outlining typical behaviors at each stage that clearly delineate persons at lower and higher stages. Ego development is not the same as development of all functions exercised by the ego and, specifically, intellectual and moral development are not a fair measure of ego development. In Loevinger's definition, the term is reserved for what is typical to a certain developmental sequence and a certain characterology that delineates people by stage. Consequently, ego development applies almost independently of age level. Loevinger refers to "milestone behaviors." These are behaviors that tend to rise and fall in prominence, that is, become reintegrated into a new structure at the next stage, as one ascends the scale of ego development. These "milestones" may be described as a set of core issues or focused concerns that characterize the individual's essential way of interacting with the environment.

For example, the issue of conformity becomes a central concern at the I-3 stage (conformist) then gradually tapers off as the person's ego structure assumes a more complex form. People at the conformist stage of ego development are frequently at Kohlberg's conventional level of moral judgement, that is, what is socially approved by the group, government, or religious system is right. The cognitive structure of the conformist is simple, that is, although able to recognize group differences, he is insensitive to individual differences (Piaget's Stage 2). He sees everyone within groups (for example, "jocks," "hippies," and so on) as essentially alike, or at least he thinks they should be. Thus, such people may be either rigidly unprejudiced or hold real negative feelings that are expressed as prejudices about strangers. The beginning of introspection, however, signals movement to the next stage.

Loevinger's self-aware ego stage is characterized by a transition from conformity to group norms and standards to an "increase in self awareness and appreciation of multiple possibilities in situations" (Loevinger 1976, p. 19). This new sense of individuality enables the person to recognize that she may have feelings and attitudes that are contrary to those endorsed by her friends or family. This may lead to criticism of the group because of an increase in self-confidence and a greater sense of what ought to be. Adorno's (1950) easy-going, low-in-prejudice type assumes a similar attitude, that is, live and let live. While the conformist lives in a conceptually simple world with rigid views of in-groups and out-groups, the person at the self-aware level has the ability to comprehend a broader societal perspective. This more advanced cognitive structure seems to be a necessary condition for subsequent moral development. Transition to the next stage is characterized by the development of conceptions of purpose, goals, and long-range expectations.

A person at the conscientious stage is preoccupied with self-evaluated standards and issues of responsibility. The major elements of the mature adult conscience are present. They include self-determination of goals and ideals, differentiated self-criticism, and a sense of responsibility. Achievement is a central issue but the focus is on improvement of the real self in response primarily to internal standards. Guilt is a common phenomenon yet the source of guilt is not from breaking societal rules, rather it is derived from the consequences of one's own actions, particularly those involving other people. The internalization of societal rules is completed at the conscientious stage but motives and consequences are viewed as more important than rules alone. Such moral reasoning is found in Kohlberg's Stage 4 and more principled thinking typically found at Stage 5. Clearly, social rules may be subject to question, that is, exceptions and contingencies are recognized. The conscientious person "may even feel compelled to break the law on account of his own code, a fact recognized in the status of the conscientious objector" (Loevinger 1976, p. 21). Adorno's (1950) "protesting" low in prejudice type is similar, that is, he wants to correct the injustices caused by prejudice.

The cognitive structure of the conscientious stage is more abstract than at previous stages, because many possibilities are now seen and alternatives are more obvious. Distinctions are made between moral standards and social manners or between moral and esthetic standards. Things are no longer rigidly conceptualized as right or wrong, in-group versus out-group, and so on. "A conscientious person thinks in terms of polarities, but more complex and differentiated ones; trivial versus important, love versus lust, dependent versus independent, inner life versus outward appearances" (Loevinger 1976, p. 21). At this stage the person feels a responsibility for other people to the extent that he may feel obligated to shape another's life or prevent him from making an error. Related concepts of privileges, rights, and fairness imply that the conscientious person sees himself and others as capable of determining their own destiny. Piaget's Stage 3 (cross cultural-international perspective) is similar in cognitive structure, that is, the logical, moral, or value judgments necessary for such an objective perspective are present. The person recognizes that other countries or groups may have different values and beliefs but these differences are acceptable based on principles of justice, fairness, and equality. Prejudice at this stage may be rejected on the basis of rationality. Loevinger suggests that "the ability to see matters from other peoples' view is a connecting link between deeper interpersonal relations and a more mature conscience" (1976, p. 22). The line of development becomes more fully integrated at the next stage of ego development.

The individualistic level is a transitional stage from the conscientious to the autonomous stage and is characterized by a heightened sense of individuality and a concern for emotional dependence. "To proceed beyond the Conscientious Stage a person must become more tolerant of himself and of others. This toleration grows out of recognition of individual differences and of complexities of circumstances at the Conscientious Stage. The next step, not only to accept but to cherish individuality, marks the Autonomous Stage" (Loevinger 1976, p. 22).

Interpersonal relationships at the individualistic stage may become antagonistic to striving for achievement and the sometimes excessive assumption of responsibility for self and other characteristics of the conscientious stage. "Moral ism begins to be replaced by an inner conflict" (Loevinger 1976, p. 22). The heightened awareness of inner conflicting emotions, previously ascribed to the external world, may cause new experiences of uncertainty. However, persons at the individualistic stage of ego development demonstrate increased cognitive complexity in part by an awareness of psychological causality.

Adorno's genuine liberal, low-in-prejudice type appears to have similar characteristics. "Subjects in this group have a strong sense of personal autonomy and independence. They cannot stand any outside interference with their personal convictions and beliefs, but they do not want to interfere with those of others either. One of his conspicuous features is moral courage, often far beyond his rational evaluation of a situation. He cannot keep silent if something wrong is being done, even if he seriously endangers himself" (Adorno 1950, p. 44). Adorno's research found that the genuine liberal type consistently demonstrated the lowest level of prejudice within the total sample. It is likely that these characteristics described by Loevinger and Adorno become solidified in the next two stages of ego development.

The autonomous stage derives its name because the person is now able to recognize that other people have a need to be autonomous. The limitations of autonomy are understood in that emotional interdependence is inevitable. Conceptual complexity is an outstanding characteristic of this stage. Rather than projecting inner conflict onto the environment, the autonomous person has the courage to cope with conflicting needs, conflicting duties, and conflict between needs and duties. Social stereotypes are distinguished from realistic views of people. There is an increased toleration for ambiguity and a general departure from a dichotomized view of life.

"The autonomous person takes a broad view of his life as a whole. He aspires to be realistic and objective about himself and others. He holds to broad, abstract, social ideals, such as justice" (Loevinger 1976, p. 26). The existence of prejudice at the autonomous stage is unlikely because there is no longer a psychological need to displace hostility or project negative feelings. Conceptual complexity would tend to mitigate faulty generalizations, and moral principles of justice and fairness between groups would reject prejudice within society.

A new element that transcends the autonomous stage is consolidation of the sense of identity. It characterizes the integrated stage. However, I will not attempt to elaborate the other characteristics of this stage since they are similar to the previous stage and realistically the possibility of finding a person at this stage of development would be rare indeed, particularly in the adolescent population of this study.

The theoretical relationship of Loevinger's ego stages, prejudiced thinking, and moral development seems to follow a course that is often parallel. As the cognitive complexity characteristic of each ego stage increases, there may be a subsequent increase in moral reasoning and decrease in prejudice. This may be a result of less rigidity of thought, increased ability to role-take, or a broader societal perspective, and greater objectivity, respect, and fairness that the person will accord to others. Clearly, ego development is a major contributor of individual differences in any age cohort, and it seems to be related to the problem of prejudice. The following statement made by a high school student exemplifies these developmental issues:

> When I was in the eighth and ninth grade I used to have a lot of different friends and they used to call me a Tom. Then, I didn't like to be black. That was really hard. My friends were trying to hold me back, they were trying to make me feel guilty. They would always say you're always in the library with your white friends and you never spend any time with us. At first I felt guilty and stuck with them, but then I started to break away.

The previously outlined theoretical relationships were used as a conceptual basis for this moral education curriculum. It was designed (and evaluated) to determine the effect of education on the problem of prejudice in adolescents. Furthermore, it attempted to avert the hysteria of a crisis situation through "preventative" and developmental educational experiences. Specifically, the curriculum was designed to reduce prejudice in adolescents in two ways: through the stimulation of moral reasoning to higher stages, and through the stimulation of ego development to advanced levels.

TEACHING THE MORAL EDUCATION CURRICULUM

The Moral Education Seminar was scheduled one evening each week for three hours and included a total of 15 sessions. Participants received one-half of an academic credit for their work. We met in the students' homes for several reasons. This arrangement provided the necessary block of time to have in-depth discussions, enabled students with full academic schedules during the day or jobs after school to participate, and allowed parents to observe the activities of the seminar. The class was representative of the larger school population in regard to racial and ethnic background, religious affiliation, and socioeconomic status. Student teaching placements were arranged in a freshman guidance program called "About Prejudice." Participants in the seminar were assigned in teams of these classes to teach moral education materials in conjunction with regular faculty members.

Phase One: Personal Introductions

At the beginning of the seminar, I asked the students to introduce themselves. I explained the need to develop trust within the group so that we would be able to deal with difficult personal and social dilemmas involving issues of prejudice. Also, it seemed important to model empathic listening and support so that people would feel they could talk without fear of rejection or criticism by the group. Moreover, the purpose of the introductions was to stimulate communication, listening, and to begin to engage the students in moral discussions of these personal experiences. To my surprise several people volunteered. It was not a particularly uncomfortable experience getting started after all.

Kirstin introduced herself by talking about a summer work experience in which she was employed as a gas station attendant. In reality, the job responsibilities consisted of house cleaning tasks around the gas station, which she considered stereotyped women's work. Thus Kirstin felt that she was being "exploited." Following this introduction, other students asked questions regarding Kirstin's interests, hobbies, and so on. However, I stressed that this experience may have been an example of sex-role stereotyping so that other people might include similar experiences in their introductions. Ann picked up this theme in her introduction. She gave an interesting family history that raised many questions for people in the seminar. Ann's parents were married shortly after World War II, and her father was unable to return to Russia with his wife for fear of losing his job as a photographer with a newspaper. She elaborated the many difficult political, interpersonal, and economic decisions that her parents had to face. The students found this story compelling and began to struggle with the issue of making decisions that involve conflicting responsibilities.

In the next introduction, Joe made reference to his style of clothing and the fact that people had called him "a junky" because of his appearance. I asked the group how reliable first impressions are and mentioned the need for information about people before one makes a judgment. The following discussion occurred:

Joe: But people only see what they want to see.

Kirstin: But a lot of that goes back to what your parents taught you, that is your morals and attitudes towards people that are different.

Joe: When I was twelve, I was a bigot, but not because I wanted to be. You have a tendency to feel the same way that your parents feel when you are young. Now, if your father is a bigot and he is telling you that people are bad, you believe that people are bad because you think that he is right. When I entered the high school, I started to change a lot. I learned that people are people, but I don't see it through blurred eyes. I see reality. I don't think that because a person is black that I am going to get jumped.

Elizabeth: Joe, wasn't that a case of rebellion against your father?

Joe: No, it is a part of growing up.

Jamine: I think it's important not to make judgments about people until you get to know them.

Elizabeth: For example, if you walk down the hall and see a group of kids you have to think about fears or stereotypes that you have

learned from your parents. I guess you have to think about your
values toward those people.

Brenda: As you get older your values change. You start to raise a lot
of questions about what your family and friends have told you.

Several important things were illustrated in this brief discussion. First,
students began to recognize that prejudice may be caused in part by irrational
generalizations about people and groups. Second, they seemed to grasp the
notion that prejudice may be faulty learning. The students didn't directly equate
prejudice to a moral question. They did seem to be struggling with the idea
that attitudes toward people may have something to do with other factors like
moral values, the development of personal standards that may be different from
family and peer-group standards, and in general the formation of fair value
judgments about people. Further, the students were able to share personal
information without feeling uncomfortable. Also, group norms such as listening
carefully, responding empathically, and raising questions of others were being
established. Finally, students became aware of the moral issues implicit in their
introductions and began to formulate their own definitions of what a moral
conflict was.

Phase Two: The Discussion of Moral Dilemmas about Prejudice

The aim of phase two of the course (involving seven class sessions) was to
discuss issues of prejudice. They were introduced in two ways. First, the
students were asked to keep a log noting personal observations or experiences
of prejudice they encountered at school, in the community, or at work. Class
time was reserved for discussion of such personal dilemmas. The second resource
was a variety of films that presented open-ended, hypothetical moral dilemmas
related to prejudice, for example, *Should We Go to the Movies, Veronica, Bill
Cosby on Prejudice, The Bill of Rights in Action: Equal Opportunity,* and
Black History: Lost, Stolen, or Strayed? Two additional films were presented
from the Learning Corporation of America's series: *When Parents Grow Old,*
and *Trouble with the Law.* Their content will be described subsequently.

These curriculum materials were organized with the following objectives
in mind: to create moral conflict in the students' thinking, to provide opportunities for the students to "role-take" (in a cognitive sense), and to have
students listen to peers reasoning at higher moral stages. The first teaching goal
was to engage the group in moral discussions and, when appropriate, to have
students reasoning at adjacent stages discuss the issue together. Although I
encouraged students to challenge the reasoning of other people, I felt it was
equally important to support the idea of respect among students in the class.
I wanted students to be able to talk openly about their opinions and to reason
through issues of prejudice without feeling that they were being attacked. I felt
it was my responsibility to intercede if the discussion got "out of hand," but
that simply did not happen.

The second teaching goal was to have the students "role-take" or assume the position of other people in the class, in the moral dilemmas, and from a broader social perspective. By modeling this kind of empathetic behavior I found that other students not only began to do this but encouraged their peers to put themselves in the other person's position as well.

For example, Elizabeth talked about her difficulty getting into the weight room in the gymnasium. Following the instructions of her swimming coach, Elizabeth went to the high school weight room but found no times available for women on the schedule. "Women were not given equal opportunity to use the athletic facilities." This personal dilemma stimulated an active debate.

As the discussion continued, Cyndee pointed out the cultural impact that school programs, textbooks, and the media have on sex-role stereotyping. Everyone started talking and arguing simultaneously. It was a very impassioned debate about equality between people regardless of sex. Since no one was listening, I felt that if I interrupted the students, the behavior of the group could be used as an immediate example of a moral issue. It took several minutes to restore order. Then I asked the group to think about what they had been doing. "Is it fair to cut each other off regardless of how excited and anxious you may be to talk?" Several people commented that each person had a right to talk and that we should try harder to listen to what was said. I considered that this teaching method had been worthwhile because it focused the responsibility for maintaining social control, respect between people, and good listening and responding skills on the students. Thus, the seminar gave students a natural opportunity to put into practice the moral principles which they discussed.

When we returned to the issue of sex stereotyping, several interesting comments were made. For example, Cyndee noted that "women should have a right to equal opportunities so that they can make their own choices." Elizabeth said, "I have a right to go there. My parents pay taxes and I should have an equal opportunity to use the weight room facilities. A lot of people don't have enough guts to challenge it." Elizabeth was making a very sincere but dramatic argument for women's rights at the end of this discussion. Nevertheless, the structure of her moral reasoning seemed to be at Stage 2, that is, I have rights in exchange for the fact that my parents pay taxes. However, her remark about having enough "guts" to challenge inequality when she faced it may have been significant in terms of ego development. Certainly behavior of this sort, in which students put their moral reasoning into moral action, had a profound influence on Elizabeth and indicates moral and ego development.

In the second half of this particular class, we viewed the film, *Should We Go to the Movies,* which presented the dilemma of whether a young couple should have sex. The moral issues were focused on trust, individual expectations within relationships, and fairness in interpersonal decisions. During this discussion a student made the following comment: "Boys do talk about their sexual exploitations but girls are different." Elizabeth picked up on this faulty reasoning and noted: "That's a stereotyped statement that you shouldn't make. I think that boys are stereotyped as blabbing around about their sexual exploitations in locker rooms and things, but I don't think that is fair or true." This discussion gave me an opportunity to reinforce the idea that prejudice is a moral issue, that is, it may be based on lack of respect, faulty reasoning, or generalization.

In the next seminar, I presented the film, *The Bill of Rights in Action: Equal Opportunity*. In this film, a black factory worker was promoted over a white, even though the white person had seniority with the company. The personnel director stated: "When two or more people of equal qualifications present themselves for advancement into supervisory positions, it would be the policy of this company to advance the person of minority background in order to take a positive step to undo, if possible, two hundred years of discrimination." The white worker protested, saying that, in fact, he was the one who was being discriminated against. The case was argued in depth before an arbitrator, but the conflict was not resolved. The students were asked to debate the issue.

> Brenda: They were just using minority people to protect themselves according to the law. But, I think they should have hired the black man even though he didn't have seniority.
> Ann: I disagree. The issue of color shouldn't come into the decision.
> Joe: I disagree. The union's argument that the Constitution was color blind was false. The Constitution was made for 80 percent of the white population so the union argument, which was based on the contract, was wrong. Sol Jones didn't have an even break before. How could he have seniority? He wasn't getting an even chance now. In order to correct that problem they had to step on someone's toes and give Sol the job. (Applause)
> Dan: I am saying that the black man should have a chance because the white man had gypped him before when he didn't have a chance to get into the company and establish seniority. But if you're going to do that I think you have to do it by changing the contract.
> Joe: That's right, make an amendment or something.
> Elizabeth: If they want to have equal rights, giving the black man the job without seniority was not fair in relation to other people who have seniority. If they give Sol the job, only because he is black, that is reverse discrimination. I don't think that race should be a factor at all because prejudice will keep on going. But if they treat everyone equally, right from the start, that would be fair.

Leaving such discussions unresolved is an effective teaching strategy. Certainly the U.S. Supreme Court continues to struggle with such difficult issues. Thus the seminar leader should not feel compelled to force students for closure. Rather, encouraging students to be open minded may produce the necessary tension to stimulate their development to more advanced ways of thinking about such issues.

In the next seminar I used the film, *The Trouble with the Law*, from the Learning Corporation of America's Searching for Values Series. The principal character, William Popper, an adolescent, was involved in an automobile accident that caused the death of an elderly woman. The accident occured during a heavy rain storm that created hazardous driving conditions. Information submitted in the accident report reflected negligence on the part of the driver, that is, no appreciable tread on his tires, faulty brakes, and numerous unpaid parking violations. In fact, William's conviction was based largely on his negligence and contempt for the law. Consequently, he rejected the standard by which the judge found him guilty. On impulse, William escaped from the court house before he could be escorted to jail, and then fled to Canada.

Following the film, I asked the students for their reactions. The first moral question discussed was whether or not it was right for William to take the law into his own hands.

> Barnie: No. But, at the end he said he had tried it their way and he felt that he had been treated unfairly. He thought the court and the lawyer had discriminated against him because he was young, wore blue jeans, no socks, and had long hair.
>
> Brenda: They really based the decision on everything other than the accident. But if I were the judge, I would not have sent him to prison. This is too severe. I would have fined him $500 and suspended his license for a year.
>
> Barnie: But Bob [the teacher], put yourself in William Popper's position. If you were driving down that street and a lady stepped off the curb and you hit her, would you think it was fair to be put away?

I felt the striking aspect of this discussion was the role-taking that had occurred at two levels. First, students like Brenda began to see the issue from different viewpoints, for example, that it indicated a more complex for of thinking relative to the dilemma. Also, the fact that the statement was made without probing by the teacher may have indicated a change in the way Brenda perceived the issue. The second noteworthy aspect was the dramatic increase in the frequency with which the students asked other people, including the teacher, to "role-take" characters in the film. This capability is essential to the development of a broader social perspective.

Phase Three: Field Placements — Adolescents As Moral Educators

Field placements were arranged to give seminar members an opportunity to lead moral discussions with younger students in a freshman guidance program called "About Prejudice." This phase of the course extended over six weeks. Adult staff members provided supervision of these ninth-grade classes at all times. In addition, students from the seminar were paired to provide support for one another. Assuming additional responsibility for leading discussions, writing dilemmas, or bringing in appropriate curriculum materials were encouraged. Giving adolescents such responsible roles seems to be a powerful learning experience. Not surprisingly, however, the students' foremost concern was, "Can I do it?" A similar concern came up in the following class discussion of control and classroom management within a democratic format.

> Barnie: What we should do is immediately set up a discipline. The teacher should say that you are a student teacher, then we should lay down the rules. The discipline should be very strict. Otherwise they will ignore you. (Laughter) When you were a freshman, did you listen to the teacher?
>
> Kirstin: That's nasty.
>
> Cydnee: I don't think that's right. It will inhibit the kids. I think we should really get to know one another and open up to one another. If they can relate to one another they may gain respect in the meantime.
>
> Ken: When I walk into the class, the teacher should say, "This is Mr. X." They respect the teacher and that would help.
>
> Ann: I'm not comfortable with that. I would rather have the kids use my first name.
>
> Joe: I disagree because if you allow the kids to call you by your first name they will think you are on the same level as a friend, and then you'll have trouble.
>
> Teacher: Are you saying that if you get too casual with the freshman, you will lose control of the class?
>
> Joe: Right. Here it's O.K. You can't say, "My name is Joe," because then they'll think you are a friend. Then, "Look man, I don't agree with you." Boom, then everyone will start disagreeing with you.
>
> Teacher: But Joe, do you anticipate going into the class with a set of right answers to the dilemmas, or do you envision a dialogue between you and the students? The discussion should be open ended so that the freshman has to make his own decision.
>
> Joe: No, I would rather have them state their reasoning and I will be the leader. But you have to set the rules down in the beginning that you are the boss.

Barnie and Joe seemed to be very concerned about, or threatened by, the freshman students, but they were also raising a crucial issue relative to the justice structure of the classroom. During the process of discussing this issue, the students realized that it was a moral question and subsequently examined their reasoning in greater detail. I wanted to pursue this line of debate to point out the logic behind their different viewpoints.

> Teacher: Barnie, what is the basis of respect if we follow your line of reasoning?

Barnie: Fear. What do you want? Do you want them to respect you because you are a big person? That's the only thing that will work unless they already respect you.

Teacher: Your reasoning is similar to the authoritarian approach exemplified in Wiseman's film *High School*. Wiseman's high school students must conform frequently to certain standards because of fear of being punished. Although this technique may work, does it seem logical in a classroom that is focused on moral development where the goal is to discuss issues of individual rights, justice, and respect between people?

Barnie: It works but only to a certain extent. It works because the person has to do it. But it doesn't produce the results you are looking for. In fact, it might be worse.

Teacher: Is it fair to treat the kids that way?

Joe: No. You have to get the kids to understand that you want them to relate to one another humanely. The way you can maintain control is by listening carefully to what each person says, giving your own ideas but stopping right before the issue is decided. That way you can let everyone have a chance to state their opinion. But in no way should you try to play God with the kids in your classroom!

During this discussion, the students struggled with questions that related to the basic goals of the curriculum. For example, does the justice structure of the classroom promote moral development? How, as teachers, do we treat other people? What assumptions do we make in so doing? What is the place of authority, respect, fairness in relations between people? The juniors and seniors had previously examined hypothetical questions of this sort. Now they sought to evaluate their field placements. The important aspect of this process was that the students began to recognize the importance of the teacher's role in determining the justice structure of the classroom. Since they were in a position to affect other people, they seemed to be very concerned about handling issues and responding to the freshmen in a way that was fair. This provided a natural introduction to the pedogogy behind stimulating moral reasoning and the theoretical foundations of Kohlberg's cognitive developmental conception of morality.

First, the students read an outline of Kohlberg's three levels and six stages presented in the pamphlet, "Moral Reasoning" (Lockwood 1972). Then I explained that the theory was based on the way people think about moral issues that involve conflicts between rights, duties, and responsibilities. The idea of development is that people go through a fixed sequence of steps somewhat like climbing a ladder from lower stages to higher stages. No one can skip a stage, and a person can understand stages lower than his current stage and in part one stage above. Thus, a central teaching strategy is to encourage students at adjacent stages to express their reasons, to listen to other people, and to extend their thinking to analogous dilemmas. Several students had noticed the difference in social perspective that was implicit at the conventional level and asked how they could help freshman students understand issues at that level. I suggested that they encourage the freshmen to look at dilemmas from the other person's viewpoint, to withhold judgment until they had taken everyone's situation into consideration, and to involve students in role-playing activities.

I also wanted to help students identify the differences between moral stage responses and to articulate stage appropriate responses. For this purpose, I presented the film *Moral Reasoning,* based on the Milgram Experiment in which teachers punished learners with electric shocks. In the film, the experimenter asked each teacher why he continued to administer shocks or why he refused. Subsequently, these responses were compared to each stage of moral reasoning in Kohlberg's theory.

To expand students' ability to recognize stages, I presented a written moral dilemma. Then I asked the students to formulate responses to this dilemma at Stage 1, 2, and 3. Thus, students were able to identify the differences between moral stages and gauge their responses appropriately. The teacher's role should be to encourage students to examine issues in detail and draw their own conclusions or remain undecided. In this way the teacher functions as a facilitator by encouraging and expanding the conflict in thinking between the students. Moreover, the goal was to work toward reasoning based on fairness, and justice between people and groups. During the following weeks, students in the seminar were encouraged to use these skills in their actual teaching of ninth graders.

WAS PREJUDICE REDUCED IN THE GROUP?

A statistically significant change in moral reasoning and ego development and a subsequent decrease in prejudice suggested that the Moral Education Seminar was an effective educational means to reduce racial and ethnic prejudice (see Chapter 5 for a detailed presentation of these data). Specifically, the mean stage of moral reasoning increased from Stage 2 to Stage 3. The most dramatic change was observed in the data on ego development. The average gain for participants in the seminar was slightly over a full stage, that is, from somewhat beyond the conformist stage (Mean 5.64) to slightly below conscientious stage (Mean 6.82). Within the experimental class (n = 14), eight students reached at least the conscientious stage and three of these students advanced to the individualistic level (a transition stage from the conscientious to the autonomous level).

As noted earlier in this chapter, at the conscientious stage, the major elements of an adult conscience are present (Loevinger 1976). This is certainly an advanced level of ego development for adolescents to attain. The reader may recall that people at the conscientious level understand that other groups or countries have different values and beliefs and accept such differences on the basis of principles of toleration, fairness, and equality. Therefore prejudice may be rejected as "unthinking." At the individualistic stage a person must become more tolerant of himself and others. Not only are individual differences recognized, they are cherished. Such thinking in the students was reflected by a general decrease in negative attitudes measured by the Reactions Test, the Social Problems Questionnaire, and the Association Questionnaire (Schuman and Harding 1963).* However, only the data from the Social Problems Test reached levels of statistical significance.

Another treatment of these data was designed to examine the concept suggested earlier in this chapter (Table 7.1), that is, high stages of moral reasoning and ego development may be associated with low frequencies of prejudice. Those relationships, at least for older adolescents, had not been examined statistically. Therefore, the researcher correlated pretest moral stage scores on the prejudice instrument (see Table 7.2). The findings tentatively supported speculation that moral stage and ego stage were related to prejudice.

TABLE 7.2
Correlation Matrix of Pretest Scores for Experimental and Control Groups

Kohlberg	Loevinger	Social Problems	Reactions	Associations
	**.446	-.256	*-.417	*-.393
		.180	-.076	-.142
			** .448	.284
				*** .490

*   P < .05
** P < .01
***P < .005

Source: Compiled by the author.

The pretest moral maturity scores were positively correlated with ego stage scores (p < .01 level) and negatively correlated with prejudice scores as indicated by the following instruments: Reactions Test (p < .05 level); Associations Questionnaire (p < .05 level). A negative correlation was reported for the Social Problems Questionnaire. However, those data did not reach a statistical level of significance. Nevertheless, high moral stage scores seemed to be associated with low scores on the prejudice instrument.

The Loevinger correlation data showed no relationship with the prejudice scores, yet those data seemed to be consistent with the theoretical relationships

*The Reactions Test measures the respondent's ability to choose a response that describes how a minority person feels or how he would react in a dilemma situation. The Social Problems Questionnaire measures the respondent's willingness to discriminate against minority groups. The Association Questionnaire was used to measure personal distance from minorities.

outlined in Table 7.1. On the pretest ego scores, three subjects were at the I-3 conformist level and 19 subjects were at the I-3/4 self-aware level. Consequently, the lack of variation in ego stage levels and specifically the consentration of subjects at a transitional ego stage would account for the scatter in prejudice scores. Clearly, further research is needed to examine the relationship of prejudice to ego stages at both high and low extremes.

What caused such changes in the adolescents' thinking about issues of prejudice? In general, a combination of experiences including moral discussions, social relationships with the other students and the teachers, a classroom environment and teaching approach based on democratic principles, peer group pressure, and opportunities to assume adult roles were contributing factors in stimulating the observed change.

For instance, in relation to the moral discussions, Steven commented: "The moral and ethical dilemmas really made me think." A substantial number of students found that the curriculum stimulated conflict in their thinking and enlarged their social perspective. This helped them to see their own behavior or thinking from another person's viewpoint. Laura was an example; "The seminar put me in contact with students who opened my mind to new perspectives. I learned things about myself and others." Loevinger (1976) has indicated that transition from the conformist stage of ego development to the conscientious stage may be characterized in part by an increase in self-awareness and an appreciation of the multiple possibilities in situations. The preceding remarks by students were concrete, personal translations of this theoretical shift.

My role in the seminar was to focus discussion on the moral issues, encourage the students to listen to and take the role of others, and to advance higher moral stage arguments when appropriate. Consequently, I functioned as a catalyst for change by gradually increasing the complexity of the curriculum materials, by encouraging students at adjacent stages to interact in discussions, and by advancing slightly more complex questions. These teaching methods, both in theory and in terms of the experimental findings of this study, seemed to have been associated with actual growth in individuals' thinking. Kirstin characterized this process at least for her. "The class was able to speak among itself, but more important with the teacher on an equal level. We learned about ourselves mostly but also we learned how our behavior affects others. When we made a decision, or formed an opinion we had to analyze why. We were forced to think about our reasoning. Eventually, we were able to voice the opinions we might not have been able to put into words before."

Students were encouraged to make democratic decisions that affected the seminar. For example, weeks after the seminar began, a member of the group asked about inviting a guest. This request was discussed in relation to the ethical questions that it raised, for example, whether or not the request was fair to those students who had not been allowed to join the class late; whether or not new people would distract from the group's cohesiveness; whether or not it was morally right to exclude people from a seminar. Eventually, a motion was developed and put to a vote. During this decision-making process students were encouraged to consider different viewpoints, listen to one another's moral reasoning, and evaluate the merits of possible solutions in regard to principles of majority will, interest, and fairness. Experiences of this sort that encouraged students to assert themselves in an environment structured by democratic principles are likely to contribute to the students' moral development.

The influence of peers who believe in different group norms and values in theory may have a positive effect in stimulating adolescent development away from the conformist stage. For example, during the discussion of the film, *Should We Go to the Movies,* Howie noted: "They shouldn't have let their friends influence them. They both shared personal information about their relationship with other people and that was wrong." Support for thinking of this sort seemed to be facilitated by the curriculum.

The last factor in stimulating moral and ego development in the experimental class was the experience of coteaching moral dilemmas in ninth-grade classes. Laura evaluated her experience thus: "It was quite a challenge to change roles from student to teacher and try to stimulate a group of freshmen into a moral discussion." Specifically, the students were given an opportunity to put their moral thinking into moral action. Consequently, they had to deal with many role conflicts that were implicit in being a teacher. The teaching experience prompted students to take the perspective of the freshmen into consideration and to behave in more "adult" or formal ways.

Giving adolescents such adult responsibility at a time when they are in transition from the conformist stage of ego development to the higher ego stages may indeed provide the necessary motivation for such advanced development.

IMPLICATIONS AND SUGGESTIONS
FOR FUTURE CURRICULUM

In summary, the findings imply that the experimental curriculum had a substantial effect on the moral and ego development of adolescents and seemed to be one effective educational way to reduce prejudice. I am confident that it can continue to produce these effects. In addition, giving students meaningful roles within the school and an opportunity to discuss such difficult institutional and interpersonal conflicts focuses responsibility for maintaining equal rights between individual students and racial, ethnic, or social class groups precisely where it should be lodged.

As an extension, the students could set up a rumor clinic to deal with issues of prejudice within the school. This would not only provide a service to the school but also give students first-hand experience in discussing misunderstandings between people. A Human Relations Committee aimed at decreasing prejudice within the school and designed to engage students in discussions with other people their age and with adults may provide substantial developmental experiences. Placements in government agencies, community groups, and metropolitan agencies such as METCO (Metropolitan Council for Educational Opportunity) could provide exciting options for students. Such first-hand experiences could be discussed by students throughout the seminar in combination with the existing curriculum to broaden the scope of its content. Moreover, it is important to construe the curriculum as a preventative approach to prejudice. The democratic teaching approach provides a forum to discuss, openly, issues of prejudice. Further examination of such potentially explosive problems in a rational way based on principles of social justice and fairness seems to be a promising way to prepare students to cope with these issues. Finally, the facts that the experimental curriculum stimulated both moral and ego development and reduced the degree of prejudice in adolescents are minimum and critical tests for educational programs intended to affect so sensitive an area of human relations.

8
ADOLESCENT MORAL REASONING ABOUT SEXUAL AND INTERPERSONAL DILEMMAS

Ann DiStefano

RATIONALE

The curriculum described in this chapter was designed to assist adolescents in their social development. Of more specific interest was how adolescents make ethical decisions in their interpersonal relationships, and how they understand themselves. This curriculum is based on theories of identity formation, sex-role development, and moral reasoning.

Adolescence has been singled out as a critical period in what Erik Erikson called "identity formation." One reason for the adolescent's preoccupation with the question "Who am I?" is the development of the capability for formal operations, as described by Jean Piaget. Formal operations is the ability of the individual to think abstractly (versus concretely), including the ability to think about one's self, one's values, and one's future. This capability does not appear in individuals until adolescence, at the earliest. Other influences that make adolescence an important formative period are these: it is a time of rapid physical maturation; there is heightened sexual awareness of one's self and others; and there are signs of achieving young adult status. Among the indexes of coming of age in America are the issuance of driving licenses, the eligibility to work, to serve in the Armed Services, to consume alcoholic beverages, and the choice of remaining in or leaving school.

A related question is, "Is the identity development central to adolescence a change in structure or of content?" "Content" refers to the substance of the issues that occupy our attention, that is, am I physically attractive? popular?

146

should I go to college? which college?; "structure" is the way our thinking about that content is organized, that is, by what rules, criteria, principles, points of view. The core of cognitive-developmental psychology lies in the concept of structure. For the present, it is sufficient to understand that the cognitive-developmentalist is asking if identity is a new structure or merely the further elaboration of a previous one. And the answer is that identity is a new set of ideas and understandings of oneself made possible by new intellectual capabilities, in particular, abstract thinking.

One developmental theory useful in providing a framework within which to examine identity formation in adolescence is that offered by Loevinger and Wessler (1970). They see the ego progressing through structural changes that encompass both content and the manner in which content is considered. The seven stages are:

I-1 Presocial: This is the stage of the new-born infant, oblivious to everything except gratification of physical needs and attachment to mother or her surrogate.

I-2 Impulsive: At this stage, behavior must be controlled by immediate rewards and punishments; world views are egocentric and concrete.

D Self-Protective: The individual calculates self-interest rather than simply acting on impulse; relations with others are manipulative; this is the lowest level that can pass for adulthood.

I-3 Conformist: At this stage, there is a desire, above all, to be loved, to be approved of, and to belong; thinking is in terms of stereotypes, clichés, generalizations, and injunctions.

I-4 Conscientious: For the individual at this stage problems are seen in longer time perspective and broader social content; there is awareness of cognitively differentiated feelings in oneself and in others; social interaction is seen as emotional interaction, as expressive of enduring traits and as motivated.

I-5 Autonomous: Here there is a toleration of those who make choices different from one's own; the personal search is for fulfillment of one's own best self.

I-6 Integrated: At this stage, inner conflicts are reconciled; in interpersonal relationships, individuality is cherished; one is conscious of one's completed identity.

Throughout each of the stages of development, the essence of the ego is the search for coherent meanings concerning Who am I? and What kind of world do I live in? Progress in that search is measured by offering individuals the opportunity to project their own frames of reference onto common human situations. The person's development is evaluated in terms of those projections. In other words, where individuals "are," developmentally, can be ascertained by asking them to consider certain contrived situations and to share their thoughts about those situations; the manner in which they organize their considerations reveals the developmental stage of ego formation. The Sentence

Completion Test (SCT) stems offer respondents an opportunity to react to topics that include interpersonal relations, feelings about self, perceptions of problems and social situations, and perceptions of some social institutions. Two examples are "Raising a family . . ." and "My conscience bothers me if . . . ."

In connection with this study, it should be observed that many adolescents generally perform at the delta (self-protective) and I-3 stages with a few adolescents moving to I-4. Their thoughts about self evolve from definitions of self-interest at the delta stage to those of acceptance by others (conformist) and on to considerations of the self as one among equals (the conscientious stage).

An idea of Goethols and Klos (1970) offers an analogy. For them, adolescents move through three steps: turning inward (alienation and introspection), turning outward (doers), and turning outward while looking inward (self-conscious searchers). These steps are compatible with growth from Loevinger's delta stage to the beginnings of the conscientious (I-4) stage. The perspectives are different, but there is similarity in the movement from self-interest through other-directedness to a more balanced attention to both others and the self.

The concept of role-taking is helpful in discussing identity development in adolescence. By role-taking is meant the ability to understand the thoughts and feelings of other people. Byrne (1973, p. ii) postulates a sequence of five stages in role-taking in the age range of ten to adulthood.

> At the stage 1, there is recognition of the separateness and uniqueness of self and other, that self and other may see a social situation in different ways. At stage 2, the discovery is made that the other can view the self as a subject just as the self can view the other as a subject. Perspectives at stage 3 are taken in a mutual and simultaneously systematic way rather than in a sequential manner. The realization is made that both the self and other can consider each other's point of view simultaneously. At stage 4, one discovers that both self and other understand that both can remove themselves hypothetically from mutual role-taking and view its dynamics from a third person perspective. At stage 5, the realization is made that the self and other can remove themselves from the stage 4 perspective, that both self and other can understand that both can observe the third person perspective.

The relationship of role-taking to a wider range of social behaviors (for example, problem-solving ability, empathy, the ability to communicate, understanding of fairness and justice), has been documented by Selman (1975). It is useful in discussing identity development, especially as defined by the cognitive-developmentalists; further, it is helpful in understanding *how* adolescents think, that is, from what point of view. A synthesis of these theories is represented in Table 8.1.

The preadolescent can understand social situations and relationships only from one perspective — his or her own. Other people are what they do to him or her. Decisions about how to respond to others have as a primary consideration

TABLE 8.1
Identity Development in Adolescence

Identity Stage	Typical Adolescent Considerations	Role-taking Stage	Direction of Perspective
A	Is it important what I do/think?	Stage 1: separateness and uniqueness of myself and of other persons	Inward: self-awareness
B	What do others think/do?	The self and another person may see a social situation in different ways	Outward: one's self conforms closely to an external reference group
C	Is what I do/think more important than what others do/think?	Stage 2: other person can view one's self as a subject and vice-versa	Inward-outward: emphasis is on autonomy in relation to the rest of the world
D	What effect does what I do/think have on what others do/think and vice-versa?	Stage 3: perspectives of one another taken in a mutual and simultaneously systematic way	Outward-inward: emphasis is on the inter-relatedness of self with other persons
E	Where does what I do/think fit in with what others do/think?	Stage 4: both I and another person can view our relationship from a third-person perspective	Outward-inward: The personal search for identity is integrated with the stream of outer group

Source: Compiled by the author.

the effect on, and the importance of the decision to, the self (Stage A). During Stage B, the adolescent shifts his emphasis from self-interest to evaluation by others; he begins to be concerned about what others think of him and in conforming to what they expect. The self is deemphasized. Indeed, adolescents can be lost in the crowd or dependent on it. During the next two stages, adolescent thinking reflects less polarity of perspective. The clear-cut choice based on what the self wants and then what the group wants evolves into a *tension* involving both perspectives. At first, major consideration is given to self-interest (Stage C), then the focus shifts to interpersonal responsibility (Stage D). The shift is highlighted in Byrne's different role-taking perspectives; the self-interest of the young adolescent gives way to the mutuality of thought of the older adolescent. During the final step (Stage E), the exchanges between the self and other people become intensive and equal in importance; the individual's identity remains flexible, but not so changeable as to be significantly threatened by the opposition or loss of other people.

Such a process of identity formation begins in an individual's life before adolescence. Nevertheless, physical and sexual maturation and the emergence of abstract thought make the adolescent process qualitatively significant. For instance, transition to Step C is dependent on the presence of formal operational thought and Step D highlights the exaggerated sense of self-importance associated with adolescents (Kohlberg and Gilligan 1971). Furthermore, such a process finds substantiation in the work of many theorists; for example, H. S. Sullivan's (1953) ideas on chumship fit nicely with the initial stages of this identity formation process.

The outline above is not intended as the formulation of a new stage theory. It is a combination of the work that preceded it. When taken with the information on sex-role development, moral reasoning, and education, this view of identity development provides the basis from which this curriculum evolved. Identity formation, reflected in the individual's manner of thinking, is but a piece, albeit an important one, of the background against which the curriculum was taught.

SEXUAL IDENTITY IN ADOLESCENCE

One aspect of identity that assumes greatest importance during adolescence is sexual identity. The question becomes: "What does it mean for me to be a young man/woman?" Here sexual identity will be considered as distinct both from gender identity and sex-role development. At very young ages, children categorize themselves and others easily and clearly as either boys or girls (gender identity). Throughout their childhood and into young adulthood (and beyond), they are also faced with society's expectations of men and women (sex-role development). Thus, persons forge a sexual identity out of a very concrete reality and a more changeable set of social roles. For example, a young adolescent boy decides whether to apply his developing physical strength to the football team (a traditionally male endeavor) or to a modern dance troupe (considered a more feminine activity by many).

For the cognitive-developmentalist, learning is a life-long experience as well as a series of stage-specific tasks. This is certainly the case when the task is learning to be a man or a woman (Havighurst 1948). In addition, the learning of sexual identity is cognitive in that it has its foundation in a child's concepts of the bodies of herself and others; the child then takes those concepts and evaluates them in terms of how society tells her to think and behave as a girl (Kohlberg 1966).

While gender identity remains fixed for most people, sex-role attitudes change over time. Sex-role development in young children progresses through three separate phases according to Kohlberg. During the first, children are most influenced and impressed by the qualities of power and prestige; these qualities are defined in their most basic and literal senses as strength, size, and social importance. The second phase of attitudinal development brings the qualities of aggression and exposure to danger to the fore; activity directed toward inter-actions with alien others, especially those strangers posing even minimal threat, are valued; an example of this would be the "courage" demonstrated by parents who venture into the job world or who lead family "negotiations" on vacations. It is in the third phase that the ability to nurture and take care of children becomes most important. It is not clear to what extent the sex-role patterns already present in society influence the association of each of these qualities with one sex to the exclusion of the other. There is a greater emphasis on the development and maintenance of physical strength in males; they are encouraged, perhaps even required, to assume more aggressive postures than women in social situations; nuturance is very much considered a "motherly" function performed by the female parent. It, therefore, seems that it is not only sex-role attitudes that are developing but also sex-role stereotypes.

Does this occur as a function of societal attitude or of cultural universals? Kohlberg affirms that the social order "makes functional use of sex categories in quite culturally universal ways" (1966, p. 82). He only fleetingly addresses himself to the inadequacies of the social order that inequitably distributes inter-est, prestige, and models between males and females. This disinterest reduces Kohlberg's hypothesis to descriptive statements of a less than optimal use.

Another major limitation in Kohlberg's writing is the almost total emphasis on the boy's experience, to the exclusion of the female's. "The boy prefers and imitates masculine roles and models, first, because he feels they are 'like self' and second, because he awards superior prestige, power, and competence to them?; the child's sexual identity is maintained by motivated adoptation to physical-social reality and by the need to preserve a stable and positive self-image" (Kohlberg 1966, p. 88). Does the female prefer and imitate feminine roles and models because they are "like self," or does she imitate male models because of their superior power, prestige, and competence? Is it assumed that if she does the former, she will have no difficulty in developing a positive self-image? If she chooses the latter (imitation of male models), there seems to be the danger of sexual identity conflict at that time or later in development. In any case, Kohlberg appears to leave it to society to arrive at what is a suitable environment in which a female is to develop her sexual identity; if, however, it is in the interest of the cognitive-developmentalists to see and promote full development for both males *and* females, the limitations of that social order must be recognized. A society in which both sexes serve as models of prestige, power, aggression, and nurturance would seem to offer a more just environ-ment in which to grow.

In an impressive paper that outlines the strengths and weaknesses of the various theories regarding sex role development, Ullian (1973) offers three hypotheses:

> Sex-role attitudes are a function of the nature of the child's level of
> cognitive organization, which in turn determines the child's
> conceptions of masculinity and femininity.

Sex-role development is closely related to moral development. The level of the individual's moral judgments would therefore be reflected in his sex-role concepts and values.

The end point of development may be defined by the application of universal principles of equality and justice in determining the ways in which men and women ought to differ.

Therefore, how a child defines masculine or feminine is a result of the stage and structure of his/her thinking: that structure is also reflected in the value judgments he/she makes about the worth of being a male or female. This cognitive view, however, need not mean that sufficient attention to the female experience must wait until the higher stages where principles of equality and justice operate. Obviously, it is possible to think about and discuss the role of men and women and their respective rights and obligations to one another at any stage of cognitive or moral development. Such a rethinking would delineate alternative ways of defining power and aggression, and it would discuss how young girls, as well as young boys, develop an adequate sense of themselves and others.

Ullian's hypotheses are interesting and impressive in that they reflect the interrelationships among cognitive capability, sex-role development, and moral development. Also, they do not minimize the cognitive-developmental emphasis; at the same time, she recognizes the importance of the ethical background within which the environment assigns and then rewards differences and similarities.

Thus, the cognitive-developmentalists do not deny the importance of the physical reality of a person's sex. They include it as a critical starting point. They attempt to reconstruct the dynamic process through which that reality is brought into correspondence with a social order. Some, like Kohlberg, do so with a too-ready acceptance of the status quo, an acceptance that results in an analysis that is inadequate in describing the female experience. Nevertheless, there is too much merit in this approach to discard the structure it offers. With the cognitive-developmental approach, there is no need to squander time and energy deciding which came first: physical reality or social reality; the relationship between the two is the source of understanding and the focus for intervention.

An interesting way to summarize may be to examine the ideas of Jeanne Humphrey Block (1973) as she has related them to the work of Jane Loevinger. Block summarizes the relationship of sex-role development to Loevinger's ego development stage as follows:

Stage	*Conception of Sex Role*
I-1 Presocial/symbiotic	
I-2 Impulse ridden	Development of gender identity, self-assertion, self-expression, self-interest
D Self-protective	Extension and enhancement of self

Stage	Conception of Sex Role
I-3 Conformity	Conformity to external role, development of sex-role stereotypes, polarization of sex roles
I-4 Conscientious	Comparison of self with internalized sex-role ideal
I-5 Autonomous	Differentiation of sex role, coping with conflicting masculine-feminine aspects of self
I-6 Integrated	Achievement of individually defined sex role, integration of both masculine and feminine aspects of self, androgynous sex-role definition

This approach also is consistent with the identity formation sequence postulated earlier. Between Loevinger's delta and autonomous stages, Byrne's role-taking shifts occur, as do the changes in perspective outlined by this writer. The developmental approach to ego and sex role development, role-taking, and identity formation is impressive in its consistency and compatibility.

ADOLESCENT MORAL REASONING

As an individual matures, his/her relationships with others increase in number and deepen in quality. The child's circle of relationships evolves from the relatively narrow sphere of parents and siblings into the many and more varied groupings in which the adolescent involves him/herself. Especially in the adolescent's intensified two-person relationships, there arise conflicts that bring moral and ethical considerations to the fore (Lickona 1973). These questions include far more than the often-noted decision whether or not to have intercourse; other issues involved are the changing relationships with one's parents, the conflicts between friendships and more intimate relationships, the selection criteria for boyfriends/girlfriends, and so forth. Adolescents realize that they are required and free to make more of these important choices for themselves than ever before.

A PRACTITIONER'S VIEW OF KOHLBERG

Anyone who works with young people, particularly in school settings, needs to respond in some way to their questions. Teachers and counselors can serve as adults with whom a young man or woman explores the pros and cons of ethical conflicts. They can create classroom opportunities for students to explore these issues with one another. In Kohlberg's theory of moral development, any moral issue may be supported or opposed at each stage. Thus, adolescents may find themselves on the same side of an issue in a discussion for very different reasons. This deemphasis on content fosters productive dialogue regarding moral issues. Moral discussion no longer becomes simply a matter of who believes what, but also of the reasons behind the position one holds. This strength may also serve as a flaw, however. Lack of ability to verbalize one's thoughts may impair an accurate appraisal of an individual's moral reasoning, or it may compromise the posing of a higher-stage argument.

Furthermore, some stages seem predisposed to evaluating ethical issues in particular ways depending on the content of the issue. Interpersonal issues, for example, seem particularly susceptible to this problem. It is difficult to talk of caring and love and passion in other than Stage 3 terms — except, perhaps, in the much loftier context of Stage 6 thinking. It is true that these factors are *included* in Stages 4 and 5, but in a much less important and valued manner. For example, how does one decide whether to accept a new job in a distant location? How does one balance considerations of family, professional future, personal wants, and the importance of the work? If one decides that her parents (or spouse or children) would be happier if the move were not made, is that a Stage 3 conclusion? Can (or need) it be camouflaged in societal or contractual terms?

In addition, it is difficult to discuss the value of human life in both a pro *and* con manner, especially at the principled level of thinking. A woman thinks it's her decision alone whether or not to have an abortion because she believes she should retain primary control of her body. How does one evaluate her respect for her own human dignity vis-à-vis her decision to destroy the fetus? Nevertheless, these are flaws in the delineation of a theory that focuses on structures of thinking, on the development of principles; the flaws can and should be addressed and attended to without sabotaging the basic, overall view of moral development.

As a teacher, this writer has found that Kohlberg's theory of the development of moral reasoning is a useful, coherent approach to one aspect of ego development. It provides a way to understand the changes in thinking among children, adolescents, and adults. It is a model that minimizes neither the importance of the environment nor of the active individual. Basically, it is no more than a revealing, useful tool with which to examine human thought regarding matters of ethical importance. Furthermore, it is for the most part nonprescriptive, yet it does not fall into the trap of equalizing all values. Such an egalitarian view could serve merely to camouflage the hidden moral agenda of a particular system.

In any case, as the debate among theorists takes place, adolescents face difficult decisions about their relationship with others. At no time in their lives are they more concerned about values (Mussen, Conger, and Kagan 1969). To whom *can* they turn? To whom *do* they turn?

Partly because they need to forge a separate identity, adolescents are suspicious of the answers that served their parents well, answers that came from the church, the school, or cultural tradition. More than rebellion, however, spurs young people to eye their moral heritage critically. Many adolescents question everything. Indeed, Kohlberg and Gilligan (1971) assert that a prerequisite for questioning conventional morality (Stages 3 and 4) may be the questioning of one's identity. Thus, stimulating growth in one area of ego development may stimulate growth in another area; similarly, hindering movement on one dimension may hinder movement on another.

Challenging conventional morality is, however, difficult for adolescents (Douvan and Adelson 1966). If it was difficult for the adolescents of the 1950s, about whom Douvan and Adelson were writing, to rebel, it was to become much less so for the adolescents of the civil rights, Vietnam, women's rights era of the 1960s. But the late 1970s are much more like the 1950s. There is the danger that the anxiety generated by challenging prevailing standards may subvert an otherwise serious attempt at new answers and result in "simple-minded moralism" (for example, "It's none of parents' business what their children do").

The developmental process during adolescence is a paradoxical one. To move beyond conventional morality (and few do), adolescents must first understand, and even accept it. If, however, advocates of conventional morality are also primary authority figures for adolescents, as they often are, an unstable situation is likely to result. This instability is very much in evidence in adolescents' sexual decision making.

A study done by Gilligan, Kohlberg, Lerner, and Belenky (1970) examined the moral reasoning of junior and senior high school students regarding sexual dilemmas. They found "that while the level of moral reasoning on sexual issues was comparable to that on the standard Kohlberg dilemmas for about half the sample, it was lower for 80 percent of the remainder." The authors suggest that these results may stem from any or all of three factors: a reflection of a particular cultural condition, the relationship between strong emotions and private thought, and the nature of the transition from conventional to principled morality. Dealing with adolescents, therefore, in more helpful ways might involve exposing them to higher-level resolutions of dilemmas involving sex, or, in any case, providing educational attention to the issue.

In sum, reasoning about sexual dilemmas may differ from some other aspects of moral reasoning because of the extreme self-consciousness of the adolescent. In addition, society's response to adolescents' sexual experimentation and/or questioning often has been fearful and prescriptive. Contrary to its avowed intentions, therefore, society *fosters* relativism in moral reasoning; it does so rather than allowing (let alone encouraging) the "free-thinking" that is necessary for cognitive-developmental growth. Transitions from one level or stage to another are incompletely understood and yet are obviously critical to developmental growth. New experiences (intellectual and otherwise) surely cannot but help in making those transitions, for example, from preconventional to conventional thinking. What is advocated in this study is different from irresponsible permissiveness; it suggests more freedom of thought and action (not license to do as one wishes) that might result in some mistakes, but without which moral development is retarded. This position pertains to all of adolescent moral reasoning, not only to sexual ethics. It is society's differing responses to each, however, which is a major source of confusion. Adolescents are encouraged to assume more and more responsibility in their families and schools, yet in the area of intimate relationships, restraint is encouraged (if, indeed, anything at all is said). More consistency seems to be in order as well as more open discussion.

THE CURRICULUM

"The Psychology of Ethics in Relationships" course, which in retrospect sounds like a forbidding experience, was cotaught by the writer and a male teacher. The presence of both an adult male and an adult female seemed desirable in terms of perspective and support for the participating students. The writer held a full-time teaching position in the Social Studies Department of Brookline High School; the other teacher was a math/science teacher who had also taught a pilot version of the same curriculum. Both teachers sought to model several behaviors; they hoped to demonstrate an understanding of the complexity of interpersonal ethical issues; they sought to be sensitive and attentive to the thoughts and feelings of class members; they directed their thinking to the moral dilemmas contained in movies, case studies, and the like. In addition, during class discussions, the writer attempted to ascertain the stage of moral reasoning being used by the students and to offer arguments one stage higher; this effort was directed at the Turiel finding that the higher-stage argument would be attractive to the listener. In any case, the normal collection of students resulted in the presence and interaction of at least two to three stages of moral reasoning.

The students were asked to be discreet in what they shared with the group: further, everyone was to consider class discussions confidential (which everyone did). Also, to that end, students were asked not to bring guests. Interestingly, there were no drop-outs. The group met once a week from 1:30 to 4:30 P.M. with a 15-minute break. The setting was a high school classroom.

Course materials were selected according to several criteria. Readings or films had to contain an ethical conflict set in the context of a relationship. An example is the case study, "Longing for Johanna," in which Martha chooses to sleep with her boyfriend Paul but does not choose to have intercourse with him. In addition, the work had to be a fairly modern one so as to maximize student interest; concurrently, it had to be available sometime during the semester in which the course was taught. Availability was an especially troublesome factor in including commercial films (for example, *A Streetcar Named Desire*) and television specials (for example, *Brief Encounter*). Another factor in material selection was an effort to balance case studies, movies, music, and written dilemmas.

The effort was to construct a course rich in format; nevertheless, the focus was on the dilemmas contained in the materials. The movies chosen were not necessarily "the best," nor the television programs "outstanding"; all materials, however, were relevant and available.

The first two sessions of the course were given to personal introductions. The students were asked to share one significant relationship in each of their lives. The next two classes were based on a case study ("Longing for Johanna") and a short movie with no dialogue (*Trilogy*). Then students each were asked to devise dilemmas and bring them in for group discussion. The sixth class was devoted to an explanation of moral development theory. Discussion of dilemmas resumed the seventh week with *Brief Encounter* (a television movie) as the topic for discussion. The next week was spent discussing the dilemmas found in popular songs.

The following class, which dealt with the movie *A Streetcar Named Desire*, offers a representative sampling of the kind of content and the atmosphere in class discussions. The questions raised were: (1) Should Stella have asked Blanche, her sister, to leave when it became clear that Blanche was jeopardizing Stella's marriage to Stanley? When? Would it have made any difference if Blanche and Stella were friends rather than sisters? (2) Should Stella have stayed with Stanley even though he physically abused her? When, if ever, is such abuse justified? (3) Does Blanche's behavior in any way justify Stanley's rape of her?

Class members clearly were involved empathetically with Stella as exemplified by the following comment:

Sally: Stella was really caught in the middle. At the very beginning, it's obvious how much she loves Stanley and how much she missed him if he was gone for the day. Then, Blanche came and she [Stella] obviously loves Blanche, and she was supportive of Blanche. And so she's getting ripped right in half.

Several times during the discussion, students became very upset and said that sometimes knowing what someone should do didn't make it any easier to follow through on it. One student seemed particularly conflicted when the class was discussing responsibilities to one's family vis-à-vis responsibilities to a lover or spouse.

Jean: (In response to the teacher's question, "Does Blanche's being crazy justify her behavior?") Is it justified or is it explained?
Lucy: [The explanation] is in their relationship. I don't think it was all that healthy. I just think that for years Stella had been the younger sister and Blanche the very revered older sister of the family and that that was the Southern kind of way it was.
Jean: I think also, though, there's a really important relationship between sisters that . . . uhm, not necessarily good — not necessarily friends, but like a bond that would make it hard to turn against her. And also I thought that Stella was pretty strong in her own way and capable of handling something like that to a

certain point and she was not at the breaking point yet . . . Maybe she felt a little bit guilty for it . . . maybe feeling guilty that she was so much better off.

later,

Teacher: When should Stella have asked Blanche to leave?

Miriam: (Painfully; slowly; long pauses) I *don't* know. I just don't know. It's a very hard thing to do — ask someone to leave your life.

Jean: That's the whole problem. It *is* her sister. Should or shouldn't. In a way, that's kind of not even important. It's like a family responsibility in a way, but a really big responsibility — a feeling of obligation if you're a sister.

Elaine: But you have to be practical, too. I see what you're saying now. But I don't think people have to destroy themselves by putting up with that behavior . . . I mean, just because you're related to someone, if they're a lousy person, you don't have to . . . uhm, accept . . . uhm . . . .

Jean: I'm not saying that I disagree that maybe that's what she should have done. But — should, should, should! But if you put yourself in the position of a sister who feels a very close tie — *really* close to another sister. I just see it as such an incredibly, *incredibly* difficult thing to do — to commit your sister to a mental institution.

Miriam: It's all very easy to say — we should do what's right for that person, but sometimes it's hard.

Lucy: It's not a good reason not to do something just because it's hard.

Elaine: Right. It's not an acceptable crutch.

This excerpt illustrates the sense of frustration that surfaced again and again for the remainder of the semester. The frustration was of two related types. First, there was frustration in dealing with issues that the students seemed unable to solve by their existing moral points of view or experience. Examples of this sort of acute dissonance were conflict between family members and friends or sexual partners and choices between the good of family members and personal gain for oneself. This type of frustration led to the second type, which was aimed at the apparent source of the first, that is, at the course materials and discussions. Students grew more and more restless with talking and seemed to want to *do* something, if only to have a dinner together or go to the movies as a class.

As for the discussion of *Streetcar,* it went on to deal with the issue of violence between Stanley and Stella. The students generally seemed willing to justify the violence as a social class phenomenon and a form of communication understood by the people involved.

Week ten used two dilemmas from a collection of hypothetical situations published by the Center for Moral Education at Harvard University. The first dilemma posed the question of the right of retarded people to procreate: Should they be allowed to have families? The second dilemma asked whether it was right for a wife to have an affair for money if her sick husband needs it for medical expenses.

The eleventh week discussion of *The Glass Menagerie* went very well. The students questioned the ethics of the mother's behavior as a parent. She was very anxious for her shy daughter, Laura, to be socially successful and, therefore, pressured her son, Tom, to bring home a friend, Jim, for dinner. Although Jim and Laura liked each other, it turned out that Jim was already engaged. Shortly thereafter, Tom lost his job and followed in the footsteps of his father by leaving his family without an explanation.

Ernie commented upon the air of unreality created by the mother. Students responded by noting how awful they thought the mother was.

Teacher: What was so terrible about the mother's behavior?

Miriam: She was too dominant . . . .

Lisa: Yeah, but she must have gone through a lot when her husband left her and everything. She must have had guilt feelings having to depend on her son. . . . She was just living in the past.

Lucy: Her biggest fear was that her daughter would be an old maid.

Miriam: I really feel the mother is trying to relive her life through her daughter. . . .

Teacher: But what was wrong or what was right, about the mother's behavior?

Jean: She was being really selfish in the whole way she was treating her daughter. She was pushing her daughter . . . and was completely enclosing her own values in trying to make her daughter a success, leaving absolutely no room for her daughter's feelings or growth or anything.

The discusison turned to the topic of abandoning the family, as the father had done, and finally, as did Tom.

Teacher: How does someone go about making that kind of decision?

Susan: I'd see what effect it would have on me if I left.

Teacher: What if it had a good effect on everyone else but not on me?

Susan: I'd leave.

Michael: I think they [father and Tom] should have at least talked it over before they left.

The discussion ended with mention of society's (people's) unfair behavior toward shy people like Laura.

The last three meetings revolved around a movie (*Cries and Whispers*), a case study ("Courtship and Marriage"), and another movie (*Elvira Madigan*).

RESEARCH RESULTS

Students were pre- and posttested with the Kohlberg Moral Judgment Interview and the Sex Dilemmas Test, as well as with two other measures not directly related to moral education. The results are presented quantitatively in Figure 8.1. Tables 8.2 and 8.3 present a more qualitative analysis of individual change within each group.

An unusual situation occurred with the Kohlberg data. The experimental group increased 42.5 Moral Maturity Points; this increase is one of the largest ever measured for a semester-long course in moral education. Yet the analysis of covariance in this study did not yield statistically significant results. Two points can be made with regard to these data. First, the control group was an unusual one and its experiences included very powerful alternatives to the standard high school curriculum and to a course in moral education. Second, when compared to Alexander's and Sullivan's results (see Chapters 7 and 9), this study's experimental group grew more in a shorter period of time. In addition, more members of the experimental group finished with higher stage scores than control group members.

The results of the Sex Dilemma Test were significant only at the 0.1 level. As with the Moral Judgment Interview, more people increased their scores in the experimental class than in the control group.

On both the Kohlberg Interview and the Sex Dilemmas Test, it is obvious that some portion of the increase in scores is due to normal developmental growth. It is not clear, however, if a developmental ceiling exists and if the students were close to possible upper limits to their growth for their age groups or in terms of their own personal histories.

Self-selection was an issue for both experimental and control groups. What kinds of students sign up for a relatively new course called "The Psychology of Ethics in Relationships?" Although they may be of average or mixed academic abilities and from various socioeconomic backgrounds, they probably possess intellectual and emotional qualities that predispose them toward participation in such a course or in an independent study program.

As part of a clinical evaluation of the program, the students ranked discussion issues according to importance; interpersonal issues (obligations to other people and to self) and honesty in relationships emerged as the most compelling. The students also suggested that the personal introductions take place after one or two dilemma discussions. Finally, they thought the course was too short and recommended that it should be expanded to a full year.

THE CURRICULUM IN RETROSPECT

The curriculum was intended to offer adolescents the opportunity to discuss interpersonal and sexual dilemmas. It sought to do so without prescription or

FIGURE 8.1

Group Pretest and Posttest Means for
Kohlberg Moral Judgment Interview

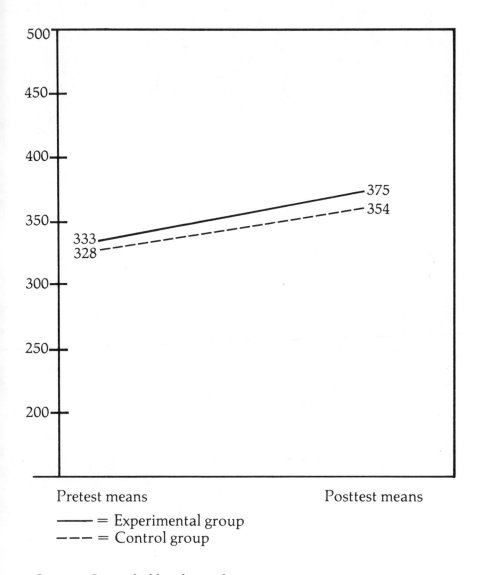

Pretest means   Posttest means

——— = Experimental group
– – – = Control group

Source: Compiled by the author.

TABLE 8.2
Qualitative Analysis of Change in Moral Reasoning for Experimental Group

Pretest Score	Posttest Score				
	2(3)	*3*	*3(4)*	*4*	*4(5)*
2(3)			1		
3		1	1	1	1
3(4)			2	2	
4					
4(5)				1	

75-125 Moral Maturity Points = a pure stage (e.g. 3)
25-75 Moral Maturity Points = a transitional stage (e.g. 2/3)

Source: Compiled by the author.

TABLE 8.3
Qualitative Analysis of Change in Moral Reasoning for Control Group

Pretest Score	Posttest Score				
	2(3)	*3*	*3(4)*	*4*	*4(5)*
2(3)		1	1		1
3			3		1
3(4)		3	1		
4		1			
4(5)				1	

Source: Compiled by the authors.

false relativism. It was not intended as a substitute for sex education, but as a complement to it.

Clearly, students need to know the facts about sex before they can discuss the many issues that arise from intimate relationships. The more informed they are, the fewer irrelevant or untrue issues they will be tempted to introduce into discussions of interpersonal, ethical issues. Therefore, a curriculum such as the one developed in this study builds on good, adequate sex education curricula; it can and should exist separately from such courses, but their purposes are, at least, congruent.

The class discussions often included more than the ethical issues found in the movies or case studies. Generational and cultural differences were talked about. The quality of the film or play was touched upon. The power of organized religion was referred to. Specific instances of shared experience were related. All these methods of participation may have diluted the intensity or extent of moral discussions. They, however, also gave the course its breath and its personality. Students felt able, within reason, to steer the discussion to issues of interest to them, even if it was occasionally "off the subject." This attitude seems perfectly consistent with the goals of this kind of curriculum development and with this course in particular. The students, after all, were living complex and "whole" lives. The educational experiences in which they were involved needed to be reflective and embracing of those lives. Moral discussions, especially, can benefit from the fullness of human experience – from emotion, humor, esthetics – rather than becoming exclusively directed toward intellectual debate.

It has been mentioned that a mixed group of males and females seems essential. Further, the importance of having both male and female teachers should be stressed. Several times during the semester a female class member would look to the male teacher for his opinion (expected to be different from her own); while this might not seem unusual in this predominantly female class, there were also times when a male class member turned to the female teacher for a similar opinion. Students choose to seek the opinion of the adult male or female even in the presence of male and female peers.

With regard to changes in the curriculum sequence, the first change that could be made would be waiting to do the personal introductions until the second or third weeks. The first week or two could be spent discussing dilemmas in a case study or a play. Thus, the initial "ice would be broken," and the discussion would form a backdrop against which course participants would introduce themselves.

Segments of the curriculum that should be modified or replaced are the music tape, *Cries and Whispers,* "Hypothetical Dilemmas for Use in the Classroom," and "Courtship and Marriage." *Cries and Whispers* is, perhaps, too intense a movie for most adolescents and, in any case, its issues are more removed from their lives than those found elsewhere. The dilemmas devised by Harvard's Center for Moral Education were too contrived or farfetched. Furthermore, students perceive them as "homework" and boring.

Some material might be added to the curriculum. The use of poetry should be explored. Finding the right selection for use with certain kinds of students might be very worthwhile. Also, individuals who have experienced interpersonal dilemmas they would be willing to share with the class might be invited in to do so. These people could be nonclass members who are either familiar or unknown to students. For example, a teacher or administrator who had made the decision to divorce might talk about that experience, or a parent or other community member might share a moral dilemma from his/her young adulthood.

More than anything else, the use of student-devised or -selected dilemmas should be expanded. Clearly, students are the best judges of which issues are most relevant to them. This method also allows the curriculum planner some flexibility in structuring a course appropriate for students from different backgrounds. These dilemmas could be entirely of the student's creation, or they could be adapted or extracted from other sources (for example, plays, books, movies). In addition, after two or three discussions, students could be given responsibility for identifying the moral dilemma(s) in the homework assignment and for producing two or three probe questions for class discussion.

The relevance of the issues raised in "The Psychology of Ethics in Relationships" suggests that they be included in a number of subject areas; the materials used lend themselves to inclusion in the teaching of English, social studies, health, and psychology. The status of the issues and the materials should not be seen as supplementary or as some sort of fringe benefit. They are intrinsically present in the academic disciplines offered to all high school students; they are so central and personal to adolescents to warrant the attention of teachers, counselors, and administrators.

9
MORAL EDUCATION
FOR ADOLESCENTS

Paul Sullivan

The curriculum described in this chapter was taught to high school juniors and seniors for one year as an elective course in psychology. On the basis of previous experience with similar one-semester courses, I felt that a full-year course would allow for a broader range of stimulation and would provide more time for the basic reorganization of thinking patterns involved in moral and ego development.

Due to flexible scheduling patterns at the high school, the class was able to meet for three hours one evening a week in various students' homes around the city. During the last part of the course students also led moral discussions in elementary schools for approximately one hour per week. Meeting for a single block of time was a decided advantage. We did not have to terminate productive discussions at the end of a class period and try to resume them the next day. Concentrated attention could be focused on moral issues. Meeting in students' homes created a more relaxed and casual atmosphere for the class. This made it easier to nurture a climate of respect for individuals and their points of view.

The course itself was divided into four basic phases that were preceded by personal introductions of all class members. Phase 1 of the course involved moral discussions. Phase 2 focused on developing counseling skills and the capacity for empathy. Moral psychology and philosophy were the topics in Phase 3. Finally, during Phase 4 the students became involved in practical applications of what they learned. They led moral discussions with elementary school students and created a board of appeals for their high school. Excerpts from actual classes are used to illustrate how each phase worked.

PERSONAL INTRODUCTIONS

Since the students and I were going to spend an entire year together and would be discussing value-laden subjects, we needed to get to know one another. In my experience with previous psychological education courses (Mosher and Sprinthall 1971), introductions had always served to put people more at ease with one another and to facilitate interaction among class members. I felt that to be true for this course as well.

Students were asked to talk generally about themselves — their interests, families, friends, hobbies, and so on — and to discuss an experience from which they had learned something of personal value or importance. I also suggested that this personal experience might be one that involved a moral or ethical issue, a question of right and wrong. My function as the teacher was to respond to the feelings expressed by the students, to be empathic. Such responses enabled the students to go into personal material in their introductions and modeled for the other students a helpful discussion skill.

The introductions for this class were personal without being excessively drawn out. Each ranged in length from 10 to 20 minutes. For example, Ellen talked about the moral issues she encountered working as a volunteer at a local social agency where she did paraprofessional crisis counseling with other adolescents. She described talking to a 17-year-old girl who was pregnant and wanted to marry her boyfriend. Ellen was torn because she felt it was the wrong thing for the girl to do, but as she put it: "Who am I to tell her that?" So she just tried "to talk it through" with the girl. Other students responded and discussed the ethics of how one deals with people in situations like this.

Not all students spoke directly about ethical issues. Some confined themselves to their interests and activities. The moral issues were more implicit than explicit. The introductions did serve the purpose for which they were designed. Students got to know one another; they experienced being heard by others; they began exploring moral issues; they established a sense of group support and caring. In a later curriculum evaluation questionnaire, all students except one felt the introductions had been very helpful in getting the class started and establishing relationships among group members.

PHASE 1: MORAL DISCUSSIONS

It may be misleading to label one particular part of the curriculum as the "moral discussion phase," since moral discussions occurred throughout the course. In this case, however, we deliberately focused on the formal discussion of ethical issues. The range of potential curriculum materials to stimulate discussion was limited only by the imagination of the teacher. Films, novels, plays, television shows, and so on, all provided rich sources of moral conflict. With experience and knowledge of moral development theory the teacher can learn how to choose appropriate materials. I used films extensively and they proved to be powerful stimulants of thinking and cognitive conflict.

A major portion of this part of the course was based on films from the Searching for Values series produced by the Learning Corporation of America. These are excerpts from feature-length films specifically edited to focus on value issues or dilemmas. Blatt (1970) established that moral discussions based on short written moral dilemmas were effective in stimulating moral development. Previously I used films as curriculum materials and found them to be a very powerful stimulus to discussion, for example, *The Godfather, Deliverance, On the Waterfront, Serpico,* and so on, in addition to the film segments in Searching for Values.

The films seemed to capture the attention and imagination of students. Film dilemmas were easily understood by students who had reading difficulties. For a generation that has been brought up on television, video material is especially attractive and potent. I also used written case materials like Lockwood's (1972) booklet *Moral Reasoning: The Value of Human Life,* which has a series of dilemmas built around the moral issue of the value of life.

The objective of this phase of the course was to have students discuss moral dilemmas, examine their own reasoning about these issues, and to interact with other students and the teacher's thinking. As a result of discussing moral issues individuals may come to see inadequacies in their own thinking when they interact with more complex arguments made by other people. Similarly, they may see the limitations of their reasoning when they try to apply it to varied moral dilemmas. The Piagetian processes of equilibration, assimilation, and accommodation cause a very gradual but fundamental reorganization of the way individuals think about moral issues.

A very important aspect of the moral discussions and of the whole course was my role as teacher. In a sense, I acted as a "first among equals." It was clear that I was the leader of discussions, but at times the students would interact for as long as ten minutes without my intervention. There were two relatively distinct types of teacher behavior that I used during these discussions. Both were important in stimulating moral development.

The first set of behaviors was that employed by any good discussion leader: listening carefully to the students' arguments, restating and clarifying them, encouraging interaction among all the members of the class, keeping the discussion focused on the moral issue. This is the minimal level of skill required of a moral educator. Developmental theory suggests that if the teacher, using these skills, can sustain a discussion of an ethical issue the natural interaction of the students' varying levels of reasoning will produce cognitive conflict and change.

The second set of teaching behaviors involved creating arguments at a particular stage of moral reasoning, encouraging those students using one stage of thinking to interact with the students at an adjacent stage, probing for various aspects of the students' moral thinking; posing analogous moral dilemmas, asking students to take the roles of people in the dilemma, and so on. In order to do these things teachers must have some understanding of moral development theory. Using these techniques they can sharpen the cognitive conflict produced by the discussions. Assistance in learning to do this is increasingly available to teachers through books, published curriculum materials, teachers' guides, and workshops.

As the teacher I also had to decide the extent to which I would present my own views and thinking on the moral issues being discussed. In the first few classes I refrained from stating my point of view, feeling that it might inhibit or change the nature of the discussion. Gradually I gave my opinion more frequently, particularly as I came to feel the students were not simply trying to find out what the teacher thought so they could agree. I was careful not to dominate the discussions, but it was important for me to present my ideas because it showed the adolescents that adults also struggle with these issues – and I often did struggle. I was modeling how a person deals with moral issues. It also helped to establish me as a person with my own thoughts and feelings. The students wanted to know where I stood and asked quite directly what I thought. It was essential, however, that I not present my arguments as the only way to resolve the issue, and the "right" answer. In fact, students consistently challenged my thinking throughout the course.

I encouraged free expression of views on the issues by all class members and tried to make the students secure in challenging each other's and my own reasoning. The students needed to feel their ideas were being considered seriously and their views respected even when others disagreed with them. This feeling can be developed if the teacher does this himself and directly intervenes if he feels this is not happening in a discussion. The whole moral discussion process can be more effective if it is seen as a "thinking together" about issues rather than a threatening process of attacking one another's reasoning.

One of the discussions in this phase was devoted to a Learning Corporation of America film, *The Right to Live: Who Decides?* This film is about a group of 26 passengers on a ship who are thrown together in a lifeboat when the ship sinks. The boat is built for 9 and will stretch to hold 14 even if heavy weather is encountered. Some of the people cannot get in the boat because it is so overcrowded and they are holding onto the sides. Mr. Holmes, the first mate of the sunken ship, is looked to for leadership, especially as a storm approaches. He is at first reluctant to assert his authority but eventually makes the decision that all the people will die if some are not put over the side to drown because he believes that the boat will swamp in the coming storm. Holmes backs up his decision with the only gun on the boat when others object. The Social Darwinist criterion of the survival of the strongest is used to decide who is to be put over the side. He wants to keep only the "fittest" so they can row 2,000 miles to Africa if necessary. Other members of the crew are ordered to put various sick, weak, injured, and old people into the ocean. Those left in the boat are eventually picked up by a ship after the storm has passed.

I began the discussion of this dilemma by asking whether what Holmes did was right. This issue was considered at some length but the focus of the discussion broadened to include what other decisions were possible in that situation and what decision would have been the most just and fair. An interesting aspect of the early discussion is shown in this excerpt:

Teacher: The last thing that Holmes says in the movie is, "You're alive. It was right." Certainly one question would be: Was it right?

George: I don't think it was because he was putting himself in the place of God.

Joan: But didn't somebody have to?

Jim: Do you think he was right, Joan?

Joan: I'm not going to give my opinion (laughter). I'm tired of giving my opinion. I'm not going to give my opinion until the end because it always changes from the beginning to the end of class. So I'm going to wait until the end this time (more laughter).

Joan had been a very active participant in class discussions and this statement indicated she was experiencing cognitive conflict as she gave her reasoning and heard that of others. This, of course, is one of the prime objectives of moral discussions. Joan did, in fact, take an active part in the discussion of this film. Again, as the discussion proceeded Joan found her ideas changing. At first she defended Holmes on the grounds that someone had to assume authority and make a decision:

Joan: I think maybe his timing was off, but someone had to take the authority. The authority had to be taken and the only reason I would say it wasn't right is the very idea of taking that much responsibility is sort of hideous. But I'm saying he had to take it.

Bob: When I watched the film it bothered me that it was happening but at the same time it had to happen because everyone would die or 12 or 14 or whatever would live and he had to decide was it worth it. Should everyone die or should 12 people live, especially when you know which 12 people will live. I guess I kept feeling he shouldn't be doing it but I began to realize I think that what was bothering me was that the people weren't doing it on their own. He had to do it for them.

Joan: The whole idea (pause) I think (pause) again my opinion is changing, but I'd say maybe he really could have left it up to God. When the storm comes and the boat goes over, whoever is supposed to hang on will hang on and whoever doesn't, doesn't. But the captain took that responsibility and he wouldn't take that responsibility (pause) OK (pause) it's sort of (pause) . . . That's why it's so hard for me. If he was really going to take the authority of doing that and the people let him, in a way they really let him do that.

Bob: How many people would have changed his choice of people?

Joan clearly was in conflict about her judgment of Mr. Holmes' decision. At first she was fairly sure of her judgment of the situation. But as the discussion proceeded she began to question her initial reasoning as a result of the various arguments raised. Unfortunately, Bob led the discussion in another direction before Joan came to terms fully with the conflict. This would have been a good point for the teacher to highlight the conflict she was experiencing and to encourage her to find some means of resolving it.

As the discussion proceeded we touched on a number of related issues. I asked what other options Holmes had instead of the decision he made. Several suggestions were examined and then implications explored, for example, all stay aboard, some people hang onto ropes in the water, wait and see how bad the storm was, ask for volunteers, vote on what should be done, draw lots, and so on. We also looked at such questions as What other ways might there be to make the decision? Does the person who is physically strong have a greater right to life than a person who is weak? Should Holmes be punished for what he did after they get to shore? Where does the right to life come from? The last question precipitated a discussion about when and how an individual loses the right to life. That in turn led to a discussion of when, if ever, killing is justified. Several situations involving killing were briefly examined — Vietnam, the Arab-Israeli war, the use of atomic weapons against Japan, the fire-bombings of Dresden.

A major emphasis of the discussion was how a fair, just, or equitable decision could be made in this situation. I tried to get the students to examine the basis on which they made decisions and whether there were fairer or more just ways to make a decision. This is especially important in developing principles of justice. I also had students put themselves in the place of various people in the boat, for example, Mr. Holmes, an old woman who is put over the side, the young boy, and so on, and to try to reason out the fairest solution, taking all of these positions into consideration simultaneously.

Phase 1 of the course lasted approximately eight weeks. Student involvement was very high in these discussions. They constantly brought up situations in which they were personally involved and that were related to the moral issue being discussed. The connection between moral issues and their personal lives became clearer. I encouraged students to examine *how* they made moral decisions during the discussions as well as probing for *why* they were taking a particular point of view on a moral issue.

PHASE 2: COUNSELING AND EMPATHY TRAINING

The second phase of the course involved teaching counseling skills to high school students. Dowell (1971) had demonstrated that learning to counsel could have an important impact on the moral reasoning of adolescents. Kohlberg's theory also argues that the enhanced capacity for empathy is one of the key elements in moral development (Kohlberg and Turiel 1971). Learning to listen and hear what another person is really saying was also an important skill for these students to learn. In the final phase of the course they led discussions with elementary school students. They needed to be able to listen carefully to the elementary students in order to conduct a good moral discussion.

I would like to illustrate, briefly, how role-play counseling involves moral or ethical issues. Counseling that involves moral issues can encourage the person who is being the counselor to put herself in the place of the person in the dilemma (the counselee) and see the situation from that person's point of view, which is clearly a form of cognitive role-taking.

This phase of the course was limited in time compared to a regular counseling course that would last for an entire semester. Thus relatively didactic methods were used to teach the students about empathy and how to respond to another individual's feelings. Several of the training methods described by Carkhuff (1969) were used to get the students to be able to recognize and reflect the feelings of others. The analysis of role-play counseling tapes was the focus of the remainder of this phase.

A number of the counseling tapes did involve moral dilemmas. Susan talked about the problem of seeing some adolescents vandalizing the high school and not knowing what she should do. Should she tell them to stop? Would that make them stop? Should she tell the school officials? What might happen to her? Julie related how her boyfriend had been stopped and arrested by the police who found a stash of marijuana in his car. In fact, the dope belonged to his friend but he would not tell the police that because of a sense of loyalty. Now he faced a court appearance. Should she tell his parents whose marijuana it really was? What could she do to keep her boyfriend from having a court record? Here were problems with clear ethical implications about which the students had to think carefully.

The counseling segment was too brief to do justice to the complex process of learning to counsel. For students to become adequate counselors they would need to make several "generations" of tapes so they could learn from the supervision of each successive tape and refine their counseling abilities. Practice and "doing" are the keys to learning this way of thinking and responding, especially when careful supervision can be provided.

This phase did encourage students to put themselves in the place of others, to see the world — and moral dilemmas — through the "eyes" of another person. This enhanced their capacity to empathize, an important element in role-taking and moral development. Discussing the personal moral dilemmas that arose in the role plays may also have had impact on the students' thinking. Finally, the adolescents developed listening skills that were useful in the final phase of the course when they led moral discussions with elementary school students.

PHASE 3: MORAL PSYCHOLOGY AND PHILOSOPHY

The students next learned about the psychology of moral development and how individuals develop in their moral thinking. Primary attention was devoted to Kohlberg's theory since the students used this theory later in leading moral discussions with elementary school children. We did, however, look briefly at other theories. Students read chapters in the book *Ethics* by Clive Beck (1972), Mosher and Sullivan (1974, 1975), and a section on Kohlberg's theory in Lockwood (1972), *Moral Reasoning: The Value of Human Life.*

After considering Piaget's study of moral development in younger children we examined Kohlberg's theory. Each of the stages was studied as well as the mechanisms of development. The readings were elaborated through discussion and questions asked by the students or myself. Students began answering each other's questions as their knowledge of the theory increased. Here is a sample of their many interesting and perceptive questions:

> Lisa: How do you judge where you are?
> Joan: Why do you judge where you are?
> Jim: Can you skip stages?
> Jean: How are these theories developed?
> Bob: Isn't Kohlberg saying higher stages are better?
> Ellen: What is it that makes one person keep developing and another stop?
> Jim: At Stage 6 a person obviously can't please everybody. What does he do, just go for the greatest number?
> Bob: What about the guy who reasons at Stage 6 but in everything he does goes back to Stage 2?
> Ellen: Would a person at Stage 6 change the greatest good of the greatest number to the greatest justice for the greatest number?

Validation for the concepts we were discussing sometimes came from the students themselves. I presented the idea that people hearing a higher-stage argument may see that this reasoning resolves the moral issue better than their way of looking at the situation. Ellen responded:

> Yeah. When we were discussing the thing about the lifeboat and who should live and somebody said something about the greatest good of the greatest number. I was thinking maybe that sounded right and then someone asked you what you thought. You said, "No," you don't go along with that. Then I thought about that some more. I guess what you said made more sense to me than what I thought. It said what I'd been thinking but in better words.

One potential difficulty when teaching about the Kohlberg theory is that students will become excessively concerned about their own stage of moral reasoning. That did not occur when I taught this material. Students expressed some interest in determining what stage of reasoning they used, but they did not become obsessed by the idea. They were less concerned than many teachers and other adults who learn about the theory.

Students also could use these stages to categorize other people, although this also has not been a problem in my experience. Students occasionally used stage identifications in a joking way but not to label other students. This may be because of the level of trust and the positive relationships among the students. By this point in the course students were also aware of the complexity of moral issues and were less willing to categorize other people's thinking.

Discussing Kohlberg's research also was important since I believed I should present to the students the underlying theory and assumptions of the course. The students examined the theory critically although they were limited in doing so by their lack of knowledge of developmental psychology and of other theories of moral development. They had read about and discussed briefly learning theory, psycholanalytic, rational analysis, and other approaches to moral development. Several students took issue with particular aspects of Kohlberg's theory, but they agreed that overall it made sense to them. When the class became involved in Phase 4, leading moral discussions with elementary school children, we reexamined specific aspects of the Kohlberg theory that were related to the adolescents' practice teaching.

In the second part of Phase 3 we discussed various aspects of moral philosophy. Students examined their own moral philosophies, that is, their own ways of making moral decisions, in light of various theories and ideas of philosophers. Readings from Beck, Sullivan, and Taylor (1972), and Hospers (1961) were used. I also simplified and rewrote material from Frankena (1963) and Rawls (1971) and created outlines of the major issues in the reading for use in class.

We began our dicussions by examining the sources of traditional moral roles, for example, parent authority, the law of the land, conscience, custom and public opinion, reason, and revelation. In talking about parental authority as a source of moral rules, Jean argued:

Jean: What difference does it make what rules your parents give you so long as you take them?

Teacher: Because Adolph Eichmann's parents may have given him certain rules that might not be good moral rules.

Jean: Yeah, but still the kid doesn't know what he's doing.

Teacher: But I'm saying that a person can't rely on parental rules just because they are parental rules as being good moral guides.

Joan: Because all it takes is one parent to tell you to kill or something. Then the next parent will say it.

Teacher: What we're trying to do is to find some standard for making moral judgments. The idea of making judgments just on the basis of rules parents have given you may not be a satisfactory way. Different parents could give a lot of different rules and some of them might be better than others. You have to evaluate these parental rules by some standards.

This precipitated an extended discussion of moral relativism and how you decide what is "really" right. Is it what is socially accepted? How do you know it is not right to kill? Can we be sure that any moral standards we set are absolutely right? These were recurring issues for several students throughout our discussion of moral philosophy. I argued that there might be moral principles that exist in all societies; but these principles might be applied in different ways because of specific social considerations or the predominant level of moral development of the people in the society.

An assignment for the second class was to keep a weekly log of the moral issues the students or people whom they knew encountered. The aim was for the students to be more aware that they faced moral issues every day. I hoped they would consider more carefully the way they resolved moral dilemmas in their own lives and relate that knowledge to the discussions we had been having in class.

A number of these issues were raised during the next class by the students. George observed that people became selfish and aggressive when they drove a car. Lisa, who had graduated in January, was looking for a job and found that in order to qualify for many jobs she had to lie and say she was not planning to go to college in September. An interesting issue was presented by Joan.

Joan: My parents don't like me to be at another person's house when the parents aren't there. So I usually don't tell them. That's what I did this weekend. Those parents, they don't mind so long as there's always more than two people in the house. But there are lots of times when there are just two people.

Laurie: When you stay over or just in the daytime?

Joan: In daytime. One other person in the family has to be there.

Julie: Is your friend a boy or a girl?

Joan: A boy.

Bob: I don't understand.

Joan: I really don't think it's a moral question because it's so habitual. It was sort of like it was their own little idiosyncrasy, not anything that was important at all (laughter). If they didn't know they wouldn't have to worry about it.

Teacher: Yeah. A lot of things we do are like that. We don't think of it as being an issue of morality or of lying or breaking promises or whatever.

Mike: Have you ever asked them why they say that?

Ellen: She's a girl and he's a boy. I don't think they have to respond more than that.

Joan: No, it's more than that. It's because they don't like anybody at my house when my parents aren't home. If you come home and my parents aren't home you stay out in the backyard. Like my girlfriend. I used to go over to her house and say "Are your parents home?" "No." "Well, I guess not." I was in junior high school!

My father has this thing. He doesn't like me to be at a house where the parents aren't home. It drives me crazy. So that's his own problem, not mine.

Mike: I think it makes a lot of difference what the parents, why they say that. My parents say you can't have anyone over to the house of the other sex (laughter). So I ask them why. And it's not that they don't trust me. It's because . . . .

Julie: They don't want the neighbors talking.

Mike: Yeah! And we have across the street (confusion of comments and laughter).

Joan: The neighbors will never know.

Mike: Oh, you don't know Mrs. Smith across the street! She's got a telescope or something (laughter).

Joan: I go over to this guy's house and I'm not allowed in the house. I'm sitting on the front step. Now maybe the neighbors had a laugh about it but it seemed so stupid. I think basically the reason why I lie to my parents is because I know if I told them things they'd be hurt. Most of the time the easiest thing to do is to go my own way and (laughing) not let them know I'm going that way.

In later classes various ethical theories, for example, teleological and deonto-logical theories, Kantian theory, hedonism, utilitarianism, and Frankena's (1963) synthesis, were analyzed. Questions were raised and answered about the theories and we applied them to moral decision situations and tried to evaluate them. The students had also been asked to think carefully about their personal moral philosophy. Lisa responded to a question about how she made moral judgments.

Lisa: The only thing — I tell you I'm really confused because I, since this class, I've had to consider an awful lot more than I ever would. And so I'm confused as to what is really right and what is really wrong. I feel like in a sense that I know so little about what is right and what's wrong that I can't really say that Hitler was even bad. Or that we all have a right to own our lives. I don't know.

Teacher: One thing, we are making a distinction between whether Hitler was bad or whether he was wrong. These are two separate moral questions.

Lisa: I don't really know whether he was wrong. Just because I don't want to say anything definite. I'm afraid somebody could prove me in a different way. If I was to be selfish, if I was to really think to myself and be selfish about the whole thing I'd say Hitler was wrong. I would say that we all have a right to our own lives. As a matter of fact, last week when you asked about how we would consider, how we would judge things morally right or wrong, the first thing that occurred to me was whatever pleases myself, whatever I thought was good for myself. That's how I decided what was right or wrong. Then I thought about it a little while and

I thought, "Gee, I wouldn't feel very good about myself unless other people felt good about it, too." And then I could keep going on and on and on, just keep enlarging on it really. And then I just really didn't know how to go about judging things.

Teacher: In other words you were judging on an egoistic basis, what was good for you?

Lisa: Yeah, and then I just decided that wasn't right either but I couldn't find anything better.

Rich: And then you went beyond to larger and larger numbers of people beyond yourself?

Lisa: Right. So I'm going to stay up in the air.

Teacher: You may find the idea of justice which we've been talking about and will talk about next time helpful.

Lisa: Myabe we should talk about this some more then. I'm doing a lot of thinking.

PHASE 4: ADOLESCENTS AS MORAL EDUCATORS

Phase 4 was planned as a practicum in which the high school students would lead moral discussions with elementary school students under my supervision. This "practicum," however, was expanded to two separate projects. One was leading moral discussions. The other was the creation of a Board of Appeals for disciplinary and justice questions within the high school. The general aim of Phase 4 was to have students take the knowledge and skills they had gained in the earlier phases of the course and apply them to situations and problems outside the class.

Creating a Board of Appeals

The idea for a Board of Appeals grew out of a class discussion that occurred near the end of Phase 3. We were talking about actual moral issues the students faced in their own lives and I raised the question of how just or unjust the high school the students attended was. Each student could cite instances where he or she felt that the school had acted unjustly. What followed was a discussion of whether anything significant could be done by students to make the school more just. Mike observed that the majority, being seniors, would not personally benefit from any change they produced. Several people pointed out areas where they felt students had had an impact on the school. I mentioned that the State Department of Education had recently issued a Student Bill of Rights. How these rights might be enforced in a particular school, including the idea of a court, was explored by the class. The class was pessimistic about how effective such a court would be. Bob expressed this point of view when he argued that there was more bad than good in the school and one would have to overhaul the whole justice structure of the school, not simply create a court.

In order to counter this pessimism, I stressed the potential impact I believed this sort of organization might have. I supported the belief that students had the power to accomplish something within their school environment. Some students began to see the benefits that could be produced by such a court of appeals.

Bob: One of the things that I'm worried about is that most students don't have much of a concept so far as justice is concerned in the general sense of the word.

Teacher: One of the things the court of appeals might do is create an atmosphere in which people can begin to develop a sense of fairness or justice. The fact of living in an authoritarian system teaches a lot about authority and obeying and behaving, but it doesn't teach you much about being fair or just.

Bob: It'd be interesting to see how a lot of students would handle it. I think it would be a good experience for students who were judges or part of the board. I think in the beginning it would be hard for most students because they don't think in those terms. And also I think many students might have trouble getting over prejudices one way or another. As a student in an authoritarian environment you don't have to be very just in your treatment of a lot of people around you.

Rich: A lot of schools have done things like this and in all of the reports I've read they've noted a change in the students. They're a little less apathetic.

Bob: Well, shall we make one? Should we do that for a class project?

Jim: Yeah!

Joan: I think we should.

John: I'd be willing to work on it.

Lisa: So what are we going to do now? What is it we have to do?

Teacher: I guess we'd have to write up a proposal first and we have to have a good justification for it.

Jim: We can get a justification for it. We know what's just and unjust and we have to work on it now.

A major portion of the next four classes was used to work out the details of the Board of Appeals. The composition of the board, its selection, the extent of its powers, and so on, all had to be determined and worked into a comprehensive proposal to be submitted to the Student Faculty Administration Board (SFA). This board had been created several years previously as a governing structure for the school. Student, faculty, and administration representatives established school policy subject to veto by the principal. The students' task was to create a proposal and convince the SFA to pass it.

An important step was to create a justification for this new body. The students compiled a series of arguments that could be used when they presented the proposal.

Teacher: How do we justify something like this?

Bob: The whole concept of trial by peers is very important.

Lisa: Another reason why I justified it is that it kind of broadens our civil rights. We were talking about the fact that being in school we kind of lack some civil rights that we would have normally. This is one step toward it.

Teacher: And toward the recognition of students as having rights?

Lisa: Yeah. Another reason is that all people will have a right to be heard. Someone just doesn't assign discipline without the other side being heard.

Teacher: How can we convince people that this is a necessary thing?

Lisa: Give examples of "laws" or rules that need to be thought about.

Bob: Is this something you have to justify? Is it something you have to say why it would be a good thing? I suppose there's a problem with standing inertia, but couldn't you just say it's a good thing to have in case it's ever needed?

Teacher: I guess whenever you propose a new sort of body you have to have some reasons, like when they wrote the Constitution they put forward some justifications and reasons for it.

Joan: I don't know if this is a reason for it, but it would sort of bring home the idea that there is such a thing as fairness in administration bodies. You don't just have to follow along after you've done something and someone says that's wrong and you know it isn't. It might also evoke a little thinking about whether or not it's fair, like whether or not what you're doing is fair.

Teacher: Are you saying it might bring to the front the question of fairness? The administration and everyone will have to consider more often if they're being fair in what they do.

Bob: It's so much easier to be arbitrary, especially with small cases.

All important and contested aspects of the proposal were decided by majority vote of all members of the class when consensus could not be reached. The students attempted to create the fairest procedures possible while still keeping the proposal politically feasible. The issue of whether the school principal should have the power to disallow a decision of the Appeals Board was hotly disputed. At first some students did not want the principal to have this power; but after talking with members of SFA they realized that the proposal would not pass without that provision. The students were able to compromise in order to get the Appeals Board adopted. They had also concluded that it would be difficult for the principal arbitrarily to go against decisions of the board.

After the proposal was completed, the students lobbied with members of SFA. They argued the need for an appeals mechanism. The proposal was taken up at an SFA meeting attended by a number of the students and myself. The students presented cogent arguments in favor of the proposal and answered questions. After some minor changes the members of the SFA voted unanimously in favor of the proposal, including the school principal who was a member of the board.

Leading Moral Discussions with Elementary School Students

The original "practicum" that I planned for this course involved the high school students leading moral discussions with elementary school children. This occurred in tandem with the formation of the Board of Appeals. The students worked with fifth- and sixth-grade students because children at this age are starting to make the transition from preconventional to conventional moral reasoning. Partly on the basis of Grimes' (1974) work, it was thought that children, at this "critical point" in their development, benefit from moral discussions. Also, students of this age are better able to sustain extended discussions than younger children.

Two elementary school principals were approached by several of the class members and myself. The principals and teachers were receptive to what the students and I proposed. Six sixth-grade classes were made available to us for 45-60 minutes once a week.

Almost all students indicated a desire to participate in the teaching. They taught in pairs so they could give each other support. Faced with a whole class, the high school students often divided the class into two groups of 10-12 students each. This presented a problem since it did not allow them to give each other much feedback on what was occurring in the class.

The students were supervised by me whenever they led discussions. The elementary school teachers usually listened to the discussions but did not provide supervision. I talked with the students immediately after each class about what had occurred. Tape recordings were also made of the class discussions. Additional supervision was provided during the regular class meetings of the moral development seminar. Students could reflect there on their experiences and plan strategies for future teaching.

The curriculum materials the students used in their teaching were a series of filmstrips produced by Guidance Associates, *First Things: Values.* These moral dilemmas were especially designed for use with elementary school children by Robert Selman and Lawrence Kohlberg. They included separate dilemmas of 10-12 minutes each and dealt with issues such as keeping promises, fairness, telling the truth, breaking rules, and so on. Had there been time, the elementary students would have created their own moral dilemmas for discussion.

We developed lists of possible discussion questions and teaching strategies for the students to use. Each of the Guidance Associates dilemmas was discussed by the high school students in detail in class. We tried to identify the central moral issue, arguments that might be effective with elementary students, typical Stage 2 and 3 responses to the dilemma, probe questions, and so on.

The first two classes of this phase were devoted to planning the logistics of the teaching (who, when, where, and so on), a review of Kohlberg's stages of moral reasoning, and discussion of the teacher training filmstrip for the Guidance Associates curriculum. We stopped the filmstrip at various points to discuss what was occurring:

> Teacher: The little girl said, "It's not nice to lie because you might get in trouble." What stage reasoning might that be?
> Bob: Stage 2? I'm not really sure.
> Lisa: Stage 1!
> Mike: Stage 1.
> Teacher: Why do you think it's Stage 1?
> Lisa: Parental punishment.
> George: Being wrong because you get punished.

We examined each of the dilemma filmstrips and discussed how it might be used with elementary school students. One filmstrip concerns a young girl, Holly, who is the best tree climber in her neighborhood. After she falls from a tree her father makes her promise that she will not climb any more trees. Shortly after that her friend's kitten climbs to the top of a tree and cannot get down. The friend is sure his parents will give the kitten away if they find out it is causing more trouble. Only Holly can climb to the top of the tree and get the kitten. She has to decide whether to keep her promise to her father or try to help her friend by climbing the tree.

I encouraged the students to decide how they would use this particular filmstrip and what responses the children might make to it. I also asked the students to determine what stage certain arguments were and how they might respond to particular arguments. Students were "rehearsing" what they would do in actual discussion.

> Teacher: What if a child said, "Of course she should climb the tree. After all it's her friend and her friend's cat and she should help her friend." How would you respond to that?
> Joan: You wouldn't say "Stage 3!"
> Rich: And the kid looks at you, "Are you weird?"
> Julie: Yeah, because if it's so that her friend will help her sometime it's Stage 2.
> Rich: What if it wasn't her friend?
> Teacher: That's important. You have to get at why they should help their friends. Suppose they say it's because you may need your friends' help sometime?
> Bob: That's Stage 2 reasoning.
> Teacher: How do you respond to that at a higher stage? What would be a Stage 3 response?
> Bob: How would your father feel if you fell out of the tree?
> Teacher: Trying to get the child to put themselves in the place of the father? An important aspect of Stage 3 is being able to put yourself in the place of someone else. So that's an important thing to try

to get them to do. You could ask them how they think the father would feel about that, either breaking the promise or about her getting hurt or whatever. That gets the child to think about someone else's point of view.

Joan: What do you do if they say, "Well, her father will never find out."

Teacher: You could say, "Suppose that her father found out some way. How do you think the father would feel?" And then how would she feel about that?

Bob: You want to come back with an argument against what they're saying at a stage higher rather than confirming what they're saying. Isn't that it?

Mike and John were the first to begin leading discussions with sixth graders. The following excerpts of dialogue from the discussion they led demonstrated that they were effective in stimulating thinking and discussion. The class saw the "Cheetah" dilemma. In this cartoon story Sam Wilson tells his son that they are going to get a new car but he has to do something first. The son is going to meet him near the car dealer's showroom. While waiting for his son to arrive, Sam sees that some men are robbing a nearby bank that is closed. Sam changes into his other identity, Cheetah, superhero and one of the Cat People, a group dedicated to fighting crime. Sam/Cheetah climbs up to the second floor of the bank and captures the crooks. He ties them up and leaves them for the police. He changes to his regular clothing and climbs back down a drain pipe. His son sees him climbing down and asks him what he was doing in the bank where the robbers were caught. Sam must decide whether to tell his son about his secret identity or abide by the rules of the Cat People and his oath to them never to tell.

John: How many of you people think he should have told his son who he was? Should he or shouldn't he tell his son that he's Cheetah?

Student: No, he shouldn't.

John: He shouldn't? Why not?

Student: He was pledged to secrecy.

Mike: Why is it important for him to keep that promise?

Student: Because it's a promise.

Mike: If he told everyone, what would happen?

Student: He'd get kicked out of the Cat People.

Student: He'd be disgraced.

Student: All the crooks would find out like who he was and kill his wife.

Student: They'd force him to tell who the rest of the Cat People were.

Mike: Nobody? What is his son going to think of him?

Student: He's a crook.

Mike: If you were a father would you want your son to think that? You wouldn't want to think that of your father, would you?

Student: He could have just said he was kidnapped.

Mike: He'd be lying to his son. Is that right?

Mike: But he could tell the truth to his son.

John: Which one would be worse, then?

Mike: Do you think it would be worse for his son to think he was a robber, or do you think it would be worse if he told him and possibly his son told everyone and he got kicked out of the Cat People?

Student: Getting kicked out of the Cat People.

Mike: Why do you think that would be worse?

Student: I don't know. They might kill him or something.

John: What would you do if you were Sam? If you were Cheetah what would you do?

John and Mike asked good probe questions and attempted to get at the reasoning behind the children's arguments. The elementary students were reluctant to give reasons why, and Mike and John moved on to new questions. In supervising them, I pointed out this pattern. In later classes they pursued questions in more depth and with more patience.

The adolescents encountered many of the same problems that beginning teachers experience, for example, getting students to interact with one another and not the teacher all the time, maintaining discipline, asking specific questions, listening to and understanding children, and so on. Since they were also leading moral discussions, they had an additional set of skills to learn – how to recognize stage arguments, how to make arguments one stage above a child's, how to probe for moral reasoning, how to keep the children from avoiding the moral issue. By analyzing their teaching in retrospect they were able to understand how these things should be done. It was another thing to do it in the "heat of battle," but almost all of them were quite competent as leaders of moral discussions.

The high school students became very adept at recognizing the stage reasoning characteristic of the sixth graders. They also were reasonably able to formulate Stage 2 and 3 responses and were excellent at getting students to give reasons supporting their arguments. Their chief difficulty was in keeping the discussion focused on a specific question until it was explored in a reasonable depth. They tended to move quickly from question to question within a dilemma. In part, this was because they had difficulty thinking of analogies to pose to the students that would focus on the same question but without seeming to be "the same old thing." Overall, the adolescents proved to be quite effective as moral educators.

EVALUATION

The students who participated in this moral reasoning course were compared to two other groups in the same school. The first of these (Group B) was a class taking a one-semester course in psychology. This group was as comparable to the experimental group as possible, given the limitation of using intact classroom groups. Students who signed up for psychology were assigned randomly to classes by computer. A second group (C) of juniors and seniors taking a full-year course in science allowed me to compare the development of the experimental group to another group of students who worked together as a class for the full year. All three groups were pre- and posttested with the Kohlberg Moral Judgment Interview (1973) and the Loevinger Sentence Completion Test (1970).

The data from the Kohlberg measure indicated that the experimental group moved from a mean Moral Maturity Score of 301 on the pretest to a posttest mean of 345, an advance of 44 points, or almost a half stage. Comparison Groups B and C advanced 9 and 5 points, respectively. The analysis of covariance demonstrated that there was a significant difference between the experimental and control groups (F = 9.64, p < .001). Thus the moral reasoning scores of the group of students who took the moral development course advanced significantly during the year while the scores of those in the other two groups did not. The difference between the three groups is represented graphically in Figure 9.1.

There was an upward movement on the Kohlberg measure for all the students in the experimental group. The gain for these adolescents ranged from a low of 25 points to a high of 72 points. Such developmental change in every subject has not been found in other studies. Every student seemed to benefit from the intervention to a greater or lesser extent. The consistency of the change suggested that the curriculum provided a powerful stimulus to development. The pattern of stage change was also in accord with developmental theory. In each case the change was to the next higher stage adjacent to the person's pretest stage. Despite fairly intensive experience with and knowledge of the Kohlberg theory there was no evidence that the students attempted to create arguments beyond their developmental level, for example, Stage 6.

I also argued that this curriculum when taught to high school students should significantly stimulate their ego development. The hypothesis was upheld by the data on the Loevinger measure (F = 47.30, p < .001). The pretest mean for the group taking the moral reasoning course was near the conformist or I-3 level and moved to the conscientious or I-4 level on the posttest, a mean change of almost a full stage (see Figure 9.2). A change of this magnitude has been found in few studies. No gain was found in either of the comparison groups.

Why did this substantial change in moral reasoning and ego development occur among the experimental group members? The most obvious answer is that the curriculum provided substantial stimulation to their development. A more specific and more difficult question asks what aspects of the students' experience in the course account for the changes observed? No definitive answers can be given to this question until subsequent research assesses the relative effectiveness of each phase of this curriculum, but my experience suggests some tentative answers.

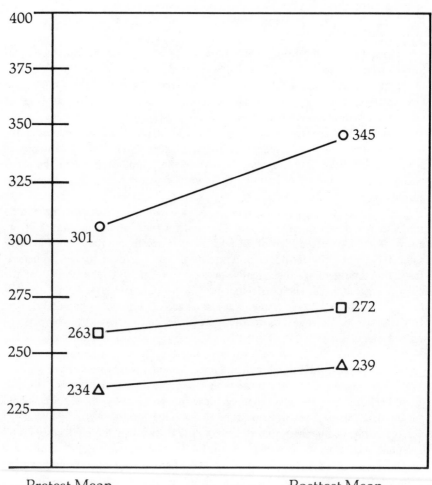

FIGURE 9.1

Group Pretest and Posttest Means for
Kohlberg Moral Judgment Interview

Pretest Mean   Posttest Mean

O = Group A
□ = Group B
△ = Group C

Source: Compiled by the author.

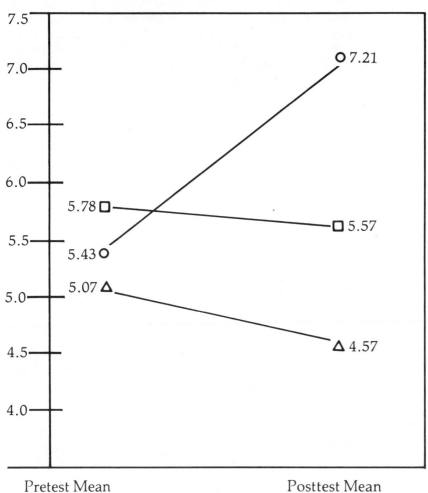

FIGURE 9.2

**Group Pretest and Posttest Means for
Loevinger Sentence Completion Test**

Pretest Mean   Posttest Mean

O = Group A
□ = Group B
△ = Group C

Source: Compiled by the author.

The curriculum provided a means for the students to consider moral issues, think carefully about their own reasoning, and interact with the more complex arguments of other people. The difficulty students had initially in identifying ethical issues in their own lives suggested that these things were not often given conscious, concentrated periods of thought. As Joan said about lying to her parents, "It's so habitual I don't even think about it."

Schools typically have provided little opportunity for the discussion of moral issues. This curriculum, however, encourages the adolescents to think carefully about moral questions. The range of levels of reasoning among the students in the experimental group (Stages 2 to 4) also let the adolescents interact with a variety of stage arguments, including those at a stage higher than their own. This increased the likelihood of individuals experiencing internal conflict and restructuring their ways of thinking.

Creating a Board of Appeals and being moral educators were especially important for the students' moral and ego development. The adolescents had the experience of being responsible, respected, competent people with significant social roles. They acted as well as thought. They became "teachers" and had to deal with all of the role conflict that engendered. This experience of social service also caused them to see themselves and others from new perspectives. In creating the Board of Appeals at their own initiative they further asserted themselves as responsible members of a social institution, working to revise the rules of the system and make it more just. I believe the creation of the Board of Appeals by the students was fully as important a confirmation of the effect of the curriculum as was the gain in Moral Maturity Scores.

Possibly two brief case studies will illustrate the interrelation between the curriculum and the development of individual students. Joan was one of those who advanced the most in Moral Maturity Score, from 342 to 400. Similarly she advanced from I-3/4 to I-4/5 on the Loevinger measure. She was also one of the most active participants in class discussions. The reader will recall that she was the student who in one of the early moral discussions said she was not going to give her opinion because it kept changing from the beginning of the discussion to the end. She then proceeded to give her opinion and participated actively in the whole class. Her involvement in each of the phases was exceptionally high. Joan also proved to be one of the best leaders of discussions in the practicum phase. Predictably, she was a prime mover in the creation of the Board of Appeals. She volunteered the next year to orient the people chosen to serve on the board.

In contrast, Julie was one of those who advanced least in Moral Maturity Score, 242 to 272, and she did not change from a Loevinger pretest score of I-3. She participated marginally in class discussions. She did not lead moral discussions in the elementary school and her participation in creating the Appeals Board was limited to discussing the aspects of the proposal we talked about in class. It was interesting, however, that her voluntary class participation was enhanced when we were considering the board. This project seemed to stimulate greater involvement by everyone.

The conclusion seems clear. Those who participated most actively in discussions and took part in the practicum showed more development on both measures. This was consistently true for the members of the experimental group. Development was stimulated both by thinking about moral issues and by social/moral action. Everyone who advanced more than a half stage on the Loevinger ego development measure led moral discussions and worked actively for the Board of Appeals. While this conclusion clearly rests on correlation, my opinion as the teacher is that the curriculum I have described can have a significant influence on the development of adolescents.

10
THE SOCIAL BEHAVIOR OF STUDENTS AT DIFFERENT STAGES OF DEVELOPMENT

Mark Masterson

In the last decade considerable educational research has been done with students in schools and colleges using developmental theories, for example, Kohlberg's stages of moral reasoning and Loevinger's ego stages (see chapters 2 and 7). This research has tried both to measure and to stimulate development, as defined by these theories. Many of these studies have succeeded in producing significant developmental change in the stages of moral reasoning or conceptions of the self. Higher levels of reasoning and personal integration have been reached by students in various experimental courses; in effect development has been induced. Yet these studies have largely ignored the relationship between the stages of development and behavior. This chapter will report a study of the relationship between ego and moral stages and social behavior. The rationale for this research was developed from three major sources: developmental theory, empirical research, and clinical applications.

DEVELOPMENTAL THEORY

Finding a positive correlation between behavior and developmental levels would fortify the validity of the theoretical idea of moral and ego stages. The construct validity of the developmental theories — the relationship between the tests and the respective theories — would be significantly enhanced if such correlations were in fact established. Conversely, assuming the measures are valid and no relationship is found between behavior and these developmental stages, such results would undermine the validity of each of these theories.

More concretely, if persons at the earlier developmental stages, "precon-ventional" in Kohlberg's terms or "delta" in Loevinger's, are observed to act similarly to persons at the higher stages, it will be difficult not to reevaluate critically both the theories and measures of ego and moral development. In fairness, Kohlberg has said his is a theory of moral judgment, not action. Similarly, Loevinger's theory does not assume nor predict any relationship between ego development and overt behavior. "But there may be patterns of behavior — 'helping behavior,' responsibility-taking, 'conformity' — which are congruent with and predictable from the individual's ego level." Part of the difficulty in Loevinger's ego stages is due to her unwillingness to define what she is measuring. Her discussion of each stage is limited to descriptive comments regarding perceptions, conceptual complexity, types of value judgments, and self-awareness. Yet if ego stage is an organization both of thought and feeling, then it is not illogical that a delta person would in some situations act differ-ently from an autonomous person. If the developmental notion of stage has any meaning at all, it lies in the individual's understanding of the social behaviors that are available to him.

As a concrete example, a person who is at preconventional level of moral reasoning cannot take a "group perspective." Someone at a higher stage *can* focus on the wishes or needs of the group. Such differences in perspective among individuals ought to affect an individual's relationships with peers, parents, and teachers. Preferences for leadership, teaching styles, and even kinds of therapy may well be related to developmental level. At least to the extent that a stage limits a person's perceptions of a social situation, people at different stages ought to demonstrate some distinctive social behavior. In any specific situation, a person at one stage may act similarly to a person at any other stage; however, over time, if stage theories have any construct and/or discriminant validity, social behaviors ought to vary. In summary, I am suggesting that stage theory implies a belief that behavior will follow. Less technically, there ought to be relationships between disparate stages of moral development and social behaviors.

EMPIRICAL RESEARCH

The theoretical connection of behavior with developmental stages is in fact supported by research. Krebs and Kohlberg (1975) found strong correlations between moral stage and the likelihood of cheating in both college students and sixth-grade children. Kohlberg further reports that in the follow-up inter-views with Milgram's (1963) subjects, those at higher stages of moral reasoning were less likely to administer shock than those at lower stages. A study by Hahn, Smith, and Block (1968) on the original Berkeley student protesters found different reasons for sitting-in by moral stage. Further, higher-stage subjects acted more ethically. In McNamee's (1972) study, students at higher stages of moral reasoning were more apt to disobey the directions of the experi-menter and to aid a student in need.

Persons at the conventional levels of morality are more apt to conform than those subjects at either preconventional or postconventional levels (Salzstein, Diamond, and Belenky 1972). Of this group of studies none is better than a thesis by Donivant (1975), who found with a large sample of students that moral judgment significantly predicted resistance to the temptation to cheat even after the effects of sex, socioeconomic status, Scholastic Aptitude Test scores, and ego strength had been partialed out. In general, where moral judgment has been used to predict moral action the results have been in the expected direction.

Loevinger's students and coworkers do not seem to share her reluctance to study the relationship of ego stages and behavior. Their research suggests that in fact there is some predictive validity to the theory. Blasi (1971) found that ego level had a significant effect on the students' degree of responsibility; he also reports that different types of behavior seemed correlated with ego level. His conclusion was that ego stages have a meaning that goes beyond the verbal data. Carl Hoppe (1972) found that as ego level approached the con-formist stage from delta, conforming behavior actually increased; as ego stage passed the conformist level toward the conscientious stage, net conformist behavior correspondingly decreased. Another study by Frank and Quinlan (1976) showed that delinquents are at lower ego developmental stages than nondelinquent adolescents. More delinquents are at I-2 than normal adolescents; and they reported classic delinquent behaviors: street fighting, homosexuality, and running away from home. Thus despite Loevinger's caution, the literature does suggest some relationship between ego stage and behavior.

As noted, the developmental theories are being used as the rationale for education to stimulate students' growth (Kohlberg and Mayer 1972). Educators so doing are ethically obliged to study the possible effects, beyond the purely cognitive, of these developmental programs. How persuasive is the argument for promoting more complex thinking if such advances have no discernible effect on social or moral behavior? Aren't we left with "all talk and no action"? In addition, if there are learning styles, types of leadership, or social behaviors that are stage related, such information would be valuable to educators. If stage-related behaviors do exist, teachers, counselors, and administrators could respond more appropriately to students.

There seems ample reason, then, to investigate the relationship of these devvelopmental stages to behavior. However, the problem of predicting behavior generates several critical questions: What behavior? Or behaviors? What measure-ment instruments? Clearly there is no single correct answer; Mischell (1969) categorizes a dozen methods. Perhaps the best way of responding to these questions is to return to the developmental theories themselves to determine which behaviors would most strengthen the predictive (and consequently the logical) validity of the stages.

The following guidelines for research were developed from my analysis of the theories:

Utilizing a body of research knowledge, such as social psychology, is better than a totally unresearched area, for example, natural observations.

As a corollary, using a proven instrument obviates the problem not only of finding correlations, but taking on the added burden of instrument reliability and discriminant validity.

The instrument ought to be broad enough to provide a perspective on several behaviors, no one behavior is likely to be stage-specific, and yet not so broad as to make the results ambiguous.

An instrument sensitive to group interactions speaks better to critical issues regarding social behavior since a strong component of these developmental theories is interpersonal relations.

Since no single behavior is expected to be stage-specific, "yes/no" statistical measures will be less adequate; an instrument amenable to expressing curvilinear relationships, rather than merely linear, is preferable.

As will be demonstrated, Robert Freed Bales' theory and measure of interpersonal behavior best approximate these guidelines.

BALES' THEORY AND MEASURE

Bales (1950, 1956, 1958) began studying social groups and creating a series of character types or, as he calls them, "Types of Group Roles" with "Value Directions." They are abstractions of the social roles people play and are based on his observations and inferences with groups over a quarter of a century. The following types are defined in terms of how group members perceive and evaluate each other. Given space limitations, it is difficult to adequately summarize Bales' (1970) discussions of group roles and value directions. Nonetheless, an outline of the three main group "types" follows. Bales' first set of polarities contrasts the "Upward" person to the "Downward" person.

> A *Type U* person (Upward) is egocentric, active, talkative, powerful; he assumes that his goals are the same as the group's. He ignores or blots out negative reactions to himself, and by dint of his interaction occupies a central role in the power structure of the group because he tends to combine with others to convert drives to action (p. 193).
>
> A *Type D* person (Downward) on the contrary is self-effacing, completely unassertive, passive, and powerless; he requests nothing for himself and accepts things as they are, but without enthusiasm. He shows little of himself and is generally focused on the "world within" (p. 377).

Bales' second distinction was between the "Postive" and "Negative" person.

A *Type P* person (Positive) is friendly, sociable, and informal; he seems interested in group members as individual persons. He likes to be liked and rates others positively; he accentuates the positive to win affection (p. 258).

A *Type N* person (Negative) on the other hand, is unfriendly and disagreeable; he is self-centered, isolated, detached, unsocial, negativistic, and defensively secluded. Any contact with others is a threat to this privacy, autonomy, and freedom of movement; he is more reactive than active (p. 289).

Bales' last set of types contrasts the "Forward" person with the "Backward" person:

A *Type F* person (Forward) is described as task and value oriented; he is concerned with the work of the group, conservatively defined. He tries to preserve the best in group beliefs; he exerts his influence by working to increase the motivating and binding power of value consensus. He tends to think of the group as a task force (p. 273).

A *Type B* person (Backward) stands at the opposite pole; he is heretical and disbelieving. He refuses to admit the validity of nearly all conservative group beliefs and values and is generally unable to strive for anything in the far future. He is threatened by the hold values of the social system have over his motives and behavior. He tends to move the group away from goal attainment, to disassociate group distribution of rewards and resources from conformity to values and norms (p. 305).

These character types can be combined in a variety of ways, resulting in 23 distinct group roles including Type A (Average), which occupies a centrist position in relation to all the possibilities. One cannot help but be struck with the similarity between Bales' role abstractions and various ego and moral stages. For example, compare Bales' Type P with either Kohlberg's Stage 3 or Loevinger's conventional stage I-3; each of the three abstract types is oriented toward social acceptability and belonging. Further, Bales' Type N person so closely resembles Loevinger's delta that the two abstract types could be interchanged with little loss to either theory. From logical perspective alone, there is much cause to link the two previously separate areas of research.

Further, the Bales measure describes how people interact socially — in the case of this research, classroom behavior seen by students at different developmental stages. Developmental theories are structural theories; as such they provide a unifying scheme for a person's specific ideas and sometimes seemingly idiosyncratic thinking. Bales' theory and measure provide a similar pattern for specific, idiosyncratic social behaviors. The Bales measure analyzes the pattern and not the subject matter of a group's interaction in the same fashion that the developmental stages are concerned with the structure of thought rather than its content.

The intent of this study was to describe the pattern of social behaviors characteristic of high school students at different developmental levels. A strength of this study is its concern with "whole" organized social behaviors, for example, a student's friendliness or hostility toward others. Furthermore, the study was not limited to the viewpoint of any one individual but includes perspectives of teachers, classmates, and the persons observed. While the psychological distinction between perception and behavior is indeed complex, the methodology of this study provided an acceptable level of validity and reliability for the results.

THE RESEARCH METHODOLOGY

The Sample

The adolescents studied were largely juniors and seniors in the Brookline school system. This system serves a population, both urban and suburban, that ranges widely across socioeconomic levels and subcultures. The quality of the faculty is exceptionally high. Six faculty members — two from the high school Guidance Department, three from the Social Studies Department, and one eighth-grade social studies teacher — agreed to participate with their classes in this research. These teachers described their teaching as encouraging student participation and interaction; the nature of the subject matter for each course also encouraged discussion.

Finding persons at higher developmental stages (a Moral Maturity Score of 400+; ego stage of I-4+) is a problem in any developmental study; but finding several persons at very high stages interacting in any one group may be more the stuff of fiction than natural selection. Successful effort was made, however, to garner some higher-stage students by selecting a sample group from a local college class composed of both young and older adults. All together, there were eight classes in this study; half were taught by men and half by women. Although the subjects taught were social sciences, each class studied a different subject matter. The total number of subjects in this research was 120. Two groups, A and E, were predominantly female; consequently there were 75 females and 45 males in the total sample.

Research Procedures

This study was conducted in 1976-77. During the second week of the semester, I explained to each class that they would be participating in a research project, described the three measures that students would be required to complete, handed out a parent consent form, and answered any questions that arose. The fact that anonymity was guaranteed by a computer code system and that no individual's test results would be shared with anyone connected with the school was emphasized. Within the next three weeks, Kohlberg's Moral Maturity Measure and Loevinger's Sentence Completion Test were administered to each group. The Bales measure of interpersonal behavior was administered six to eight weeks into the semester. This point in the Massachusetts school calendar is midway between February and Easter vacation. Pilot studies had shown this period to be one of initial group solidarity, that is, group roles were formed and operating.

Data Processes

When the Kohlberg and Loevinger measures were completed, they were scored blind by certified scorers. The Bales measure (N - 120) generated 2,000 forms with 26 questions each, and therefore about 50,000 items of data. A series of computer programs was then run to produce the raw data for the Bales types. Consequently the variables under consideration in this research were: ego stage (Total Protocol Rating); moral reasoning stage (Moral Maturity Measure); behavior ratings (Bales' Adjective Checklist): self-ratings and ideal self-ratings, group ratings of each member, teacher ratings of each student, students' ratings of each teacher, students' ratings of ideal teachers; sex; age; IQ (school records); and mark in the particular course, for example, B-.

Clinical Observations

A clinical approach, consistent with the research, was also utilized. After the three instruments were completed for all the classes, an open-ended interview with each teacher was tape recorded. Inquiries were made into the seating arrangements selected by the students, groups and subgroups within the class, especially active and inactive participants, students with a sense of humor, and both positive and negative leaders. Other than these general issues, the teachers were encouraged to make whatever observations characterized their class.

Behavior Patterns

In comparison with the studies cited earlier, this research did *not* study specific kinds of behavior, for example, cheating (Krebs and Kohlberg 1975; Donivant 1975), helping (Cox 1974; McNamee 1972), obedience (Milgram 1963), or conformity (Hoppe 1972; Salzstein, Diamond, and Belenky 1972). Rather, the aim was to analyze the patterns of social behavior in class characteristic of students at different developmental stages. The design required the students to complete both the developmental measures and then, using the Bales checklist, to provide perceptions of the social behavior of all the group members. The next step was to compare the patterns of social behavior at each developmental stage. Four views of classroom social behavior were considered: teachers' perceptions of students' behavior, students' perceptions of teachers' behavior, students' perceptions of each other's behavior, and students' perceptions of their own personal behavior.

The teacher, by virtue of classroom role and experience in dealing with adolescents, presumably has more discriminating perceptions of the individual student than the students have of themselves. Also the teacher was assumed to be at a higher stage on both the developmental measures than the average student in the group.

The other view of behavior considered in this research was that of the students. Students will be at a range of developmental stages, consequently their views of their own behavior and that of the teacher's may vary. Therefore, this study compared, by developmental stage, the students' observations of their behavior, of that of their classmates, and of their teachers.

THE RESULTS

This study generated an enormous amount of raw data, necessitating over 400 statistical tests. Several graphs and over 40 tables were used just to present the complete statistical results (see Masterson 1979). The task of the following discussion is to create, from all of this information, a meaningful mosaic. Consistent with this metaphor, the strength of this research is not any one significant or insignificant finding, nor the amount of variance explained or unexplained by any one correlation. Rather, it is that these myriad findings can be pieced together into a comprehensible whole.

One of the questions confronting this study was whether it dealt with perception or actual social behavior. Significantly, no two viewpoints on behavior were antithetical to each other, that is, there were no negative correlations. Had the teachers perceived a given developmental stage demonstrating one pattern of behavior and classmates another, the validity of the entire study might have been in question. In fact the teachers' and the classmates' perspectives of themselves and the teachers' perspective of them. The results of this study suggest general agreement on patterns of social behavior demonstrated by different developmental levels regardless of who observes the behavior: the teacher, the student himself, or his classmates.

A second question was whether social behaviors in class were a function of actual developmental stages, or a students' developmental level relative to that of others in his group. The answer varies. When the behavior patterns of the "pure" or absolute ego stages and the relative levels are compared, there is no difference in the results. For example, students at low ego stages as well as the lowest relative ego stages tend to be (N) unfriendly and (B) unwilling to support the norms of the group.

My own judgment, based both on the statistical and the clinical results, is that a student's absolute ego stage is more determinative of his social behavior than his relative distance from the average ego stage of other students in the class.

Conversely, when the behavior of both the absolute and the relative moral stages are compared, the relative moral stages produce twice as many statistically significant F-ratios. While the results are the same, for example, those students with the lowest absolute and relative moral stages are seen as least (P) friendly by their teachers, the fact of the analysis is that students' relative distance from the average moral stage in any given group may be a more significant determinant of social behavior than students' actual moral stages.

The results of these analyses also suggest that ego stages are better predictors of social behavior patterns in class than are the moral stages. When each aspect of behavior in class was considered separately, both developmental theories produced an equal number of significant F-ratios. Although the difference in the strength of the correlations was small, ego stages correlated better with the behaviors than did the moral stages. When the behavior dimensions were taken together from the perspective of teachers, ego stages had a significant multiple R of .38. For the moral stages the multiple correlation was not significant. Similarly, as seen by classmates, ego stages had a multiple R of .40 and again the multiple R of the moral stages was not significant. When the three dimensions of behavior were taken together across various perspectives, ego stages better predicted patterns of classroom social behavior.

The next three sections of this chapter, those discussing the preconventional, conventional, and postconventional developmental levels, respectively, are a mosaic of the results. Each section integrates statistical data from various perspectives and clinical observations into a discernible pattern of classroom social behavior associated with the particular developmental levels. The reader should bear in mind that all the linkages described in these sections are supported by the data of this research, not theoretical speculations.

Students at Preconventional Developmental Levels

Moral Stage II

The statistical results demonstrated that students at moral Stage II were viewed by their teachers as more (N) hostile than students at Stage III, but not less (P) friendly than Stage IV students. Both teachers and classmates perceived those whose moral reasoning was at Stage II as (B) least willing to support the norms of the classroom. In addition, classmates perceived these students to be somewhat (U) dominant. When the Moral Maturity Scores were considered relatively, students with the lowest scores were again seen as most (N) hostile by teachers and least (B) willing to support the norms of the group by both teachers and classmates. In summary, students at Stage II of moral reasoning with the lowest relative MMS scores in the groups evinced patterns of social behavior Bales

(1970, p. 297) called role type NB

> seems to base his self-picture on the power to be different and cynically defiant of conventional values
>
> rejects not only conformity, but the proponents of conformity
>
> seems particularly sensitive to the threat of domination
>
> is against both people and assigned group tasks
>
> is defined primarily by a contrary reaction to what is expected for social conformity in task-oriented groups that receive their tasks from the larger society
>
> appears in many ways as a member of another culture; his ideas and beliefs seem to clash deliberately . . . with the conventional norms of the group
>
> evinces moderately high rates of dramatizing, joking, showing tension, and laughing
>
> most likely to address his rejection of social conformity to the autocratic authority
>
> may voice as well as agree with sentiments calling for rejection of social success, failure and withdrawal, and individualistic isolation
>
> tends to be the delinquent personality in the group context, "tough" and impervious to attempts at social control
>
> tends to break down all attempts at consensus upon which task activity could be based
>
> moves the group away from satisfaction with interpersonal relations as well as from goal attainment
>
> is likely to be a "bad example"
>
> on occasion when negative feeling is generally high in the group, and task progress difficult, he may exert a considerable influence through a contagious spread of his tendencies toward deviance.

This pattern of behavior is consistent with the observations of the teachers, for example, "skipping classes," "discipline problems," "needs one-to-one, teacher-student attention," and "aggressive," characterizing Stage II students. The correlation between academic grades and MMS scores was $r = .32$, indicating that Stage II students received somewhat lower grades than higher-stage students. In theory, these students have little or no capacity for shared perspective, that is, in reasoning about moral issues they are unable to assume the "third-person," objective view of the group or of themselves. In fact the data comparing Stage II students' perceptions of their own behavior and that of their classmates supports this. Stage II students' perceptions of their own behavior did not correlate with their classmates' views, that is, Stage II students were least able to predict how others saw them. Further, Stage II students may perceive their teachers to be (D) submissive. Lastly, students at Stage II and students with the lowest relative MMS scores also preferred teachers to be more (D) submissive and (N) less friendly than did higher-stage students. Students at moral Stage II seem to be less interested in positive personal relations with their teachers and are more concerned with who dominates whom.

Ego Stage 2 and Delta

The statistical analysis demonstrated that both teachers and classmates described the behavior of ego Stage 2 and delta students as (N) unfriendly and (B) least likely to support the norms of the class. Basically the students at preconventional ego stage demonstrated similar behavior to students at preconventional moral stages; however, lower ego-stage students demonstrated some (U) dominant behavior in addition to the NB role of moral Stage II students. Ego stages 2 and delta tended to be role type UNB. The UNB person, in addition to those behaviors characteristic of role type NB,

> seems identified with the power to defy authority and rise above and outside the law
>
> is the outlaw and apparently is provocatively aware of it
>
> tends to overtalk to the group as a whole and to underrespond to each individual
>
> is distinguished by low involvement in group problem-solving, preparation for the task, and eliciting problem-solving attempts
>
> frequently disagrees and seems unfriendly, dramatizes and jokes often
>
> is a potential leader, or at least collaborator, in movements toward social change
>
> may be an essential ingredient to revolution, but if successful is inherently unstable and typically unable to survive his own triumph
>
> may be adventurous, callous, active, and dominant (Bales 1970, p. 238).

The teachers' informal observations of the lower ego stages were very much in concert with role type UNB, for example, "not good students, failing, discipline problems; isolates, can't take group perspective; boys tend to be vocal leaders, aggressive, prone to violence, hostile," and so on. The correlation between grades received in their academic courses and ego stages was 4 = .38; lower stages tended to receive the poorest grades. Finally, in comparison to the higher ego stages, students at the lower stages had the least accurate notion of how they were perceived by others.

Students at Conventional Developmental Levels

Moral Stage III

Students at Stage III of moral reasoning did not evince as clear-cut a pattern of behavior as those at Stage II. However, the statistical results suggest that they are seen by teachers as more (P) friendly and positive than students at Stage II and perhaps also more so than students at Stage IV. In addition Stage III students prefer teachers who are more (P) friendly and informal than the ideal teachers of either Stage II or Stage IV students. These behaviors and behavior preferences support the theoretical notion that persons at Stage III of moral reasoning orient themselves toward positive interpersonal relationships and trust, that is, Bales' role type P.

Ego Stage 3

Although it had been predicted that students at Stage 3 of ego development would be seen as PF by their teachers, in fact teachers saw no clear patterns of behavior evinced by Stage 3 students. From the perspective of their classmates there is some evidence that students at ego Stage 3 are more (P) friendly than students at other stages. While not always reaching statistical significance, the data are in the expected direction. Ego Stage 3 students seem to be associated with role type P. The type P person

aims to elicit positive reactions from others

tends to overlook or deny negative traits in others and himself

is seen by group members as least individualistic, hence as highly identified with the group

accentuates the positive to elicit love and affection

tends to agree with information and suggestion from others

tends to receive more from each individual than he addresses to that individual, which is a general indication that he is supported

values work and forward movement of the group, but does not want to have to accept a hierarchy as a means to it, or as a result of it

values emotional supportiveness and warmth

most characteristic actions are seeming friendly and asking for opinions

asks for information and opinions of others and consequently is unlikely to arouse disagreement, laughing or showing tension, or unfriendly behavior from others

is a potential representative of his peers

tends to move the group toward satisfaction with interpersonal relations (Bales 1970, p. 258).

Moral Stage IV

In this research, the highest MMS category was 320 plus. These were students with some Stage IV reasoning as well as students with predominately Stage IV reasoning. Since there were very few students "solidly" at Stage IV (that is, an MMS score of 400), to some degree these results are an extrapolation beyond the data. Consequently they should be conservatively interpreted as only an indication of behavior patterns characteristic of Stage IV persons. Teachers and students tended to perceive these Stage IV students as most (F) task oriented and likely to support the norms of the group. Teachers saw students with the highest relative MMS scores in any group to be the most (U) dominant. These Stage IV students had strong correlations between their self-perceptions and how they were seen by their classmates. Thus, in comparison to their lower-moral-stage classmates, they were best able to take an objective view of themselves as seen by others. Lastly, these highest-moral-stage students tended to have the best academic grades in the courses; and there is some evidence that Stage IV students may see their teachers as more (P) friendly and informal than lower-stage students. These results are very much in line with the teachers' clinical observation: "very bright, generally verbal, often subgroup spokespersons, not popular."

Postconventional Ego Stages

Both teachers and classmates perceived the behavior of students at the post-conventional ego stages (I-3/4 and I-4) to be (PF) friendly and task oriented. These students and those with the relatively highest ego scores in any group tended to see themselves as (F) task oriented. Both their teachers and classmates also perceived students with the relatively highest ego scores in the group to demonstrate more (F) task-oriented behavior than relatively lower ego stages. There is a slight tendency for higher-stage students to perceive their teachers as (B) unwilling to support the norms of the group. Teachers and classmates perceive the higher ego stages as somewhat (D) submissive. These students tend to get the highest grades. In comparison to the preconventional students, those at postconventional ego stages, regardless of who is commenting, demonstrate the behavior pattern of role type PF. The PF person

> sees the good in others rather than the bad and tends to raise their status
> is most likely of all types to feel and express admiration
> provides much agreement to the group and consequently has somewhat of a strategic location through which ideas of the group must pass to gain acceptance
> tends to believe in the familial ideal of unconditional love and speaks for egalitarianism, trust in the goodness of others
> tends to solicit opinions, suggestions, and information
> most marked tendency is to agree and consequently elicits much opinion from others
> is strongly cooperative, task oriented but usually free of status conflicts or other obstructions
> likely to be conscientious, conservative, and high on role-playing ability
> has the power to idealize and can provide a group with the power to overcome internal hostility, deviance, and passivity, and harness its resources of liking and affection in the service of task achievement
> can perform the rare and improbable feat of simultaneously moving the group towards satisfaction with interpersonal relations and satisfaction with goal attainment (Bales 1970, p. 265).

Although the number of ego Stage 4 students is small, there is a tendency for Stage 4 students to be less (P) friendly and informal than students at ego Stages 3 and 3/4. The students at ego Stage 4 demonstrated behaviors characteristic of role type F. The type F person

- does not appear to have a critical place in the interaction network; does not address much to the group and is not frequently addressed
- chooses to exert his influence by working to increase the motivating and binding power of value consensus
- is conservative in religious, economic, social, and political attitudes; tends to resist changes that disturb traditional beliefs and political arrangements
- does not identify with mankind in general, nor trust people in general, nor regard himself as the source of authority
- orients towards God or the local representative of God as the source of authority, this interpreter of God represents the F person's own social class, ethnic group, and economic position
- views the group as a task force, working instrumentally toward the goals given by a local organization of society, which is accepted as the more ultimate source of authority
- is markedly high on giving opinions and receiving agreement
- cooperates closely with the PF member in enunciating, building, and applying the conservative norms of the group which provide approval from external authority and rewards through successful accomplishments of assigned tasks
- tends to be a strong, serious, cooperative current of task-oriented efforts and endorsements
- is straightforward in his beliefs, tends to express what he believes; social norms have a reality and an objective existence for him
- is fair-minded, impartial, as well as impersonal
- believes in conditional love, "justice under the law"
- tends to demonstrate single-minded, persistent, undeviating devotion to the received tasks of the group (Bales 1970, p. 273).

Again the clinical observations of teachers are consistent with Bales' role type F: "bright, intellectual, often opinionated; can be cutting, sarcastic; intellectual leaders, but aloof, social isolates, sometimes abrasive, obnoxious."

CONCLUSION

Having studied the preceding stage descriptions and the behavior patterns associated with them by this research, the logic of a developmental stage relationship to social behavior is clearer. This is not to say that the relationship is simple, nor unrelated to other factors such as intelligence or socioeconomic level. But it can be said with confidence that a student's developmental stage is clearly related to his mode of social behavior in a classroom.

The fact that stages of moral and personal growth are associated with social behavior in school is significant. While neither moral or ego development theory has argued that higher-stage thinking affects behavior, there is widespread practical interest in a possible connection. The results of this research significantly enhance the practical persuasiveness of these developmental theories for teachers and educators. While the intent was to investigate the relationship of developmental stages (structures of thought) to social behavior, it was not by chance that the study was conducted in public school classrooms. We can now say to teachers that the maturity of the adolescent's thinking does affect how he behaves toward others. Further, if development in the way the student thinks and feels is promoted by education, qualitatively different and more mature school behavior seemingly will follow.

JUNIOR HIGH SCHOOL CURRICULA

11
THE MORAL EDUCATION
OF EARLY ADOLESCENTS

Diana Pritchard Paolitto

If we had to choose the period of our lives that we would wish *not* to repeat, nearly all of us would be likely to agree on early adolescence. Being a "twitch," in Edward Martin's (1971) words, in the never-never land between childhood and adolescence is stressful both to experience and to behold. The moral educator who ventures to design curriculum for these young adolescents needs to be particularly resourceful in developing materials that mesh with their frequently graceless and disjointed strides in development.

This particular effort to construct a moral education curriculum began with two related notions about early adolescent development: that it is a period of marked transition: psychosocially, intellectually, and morally; and that it is a stage unto itself, characterized differently from adolescence proper (Blos 1962, 1970). Because previous moral education curricula, which served as an inspiration for this study, were designed for high school adolescents, careful reading of the literature on early adolescents as well as close observation of junior high school classes were necessary first steps.

CHARACTERISTICS OF EARLY ADOLESCENT DEVELOPMENT

With the onset of puberty, early adolescents do not suddenly resolve the developmental tasks of late childhood. Nor does puberty necessarily occur

The author wishes to thank Muriel Ladenburg for her valuable editorial suggestions.

at a predictable time, although 9 and 16 are the usual outer limits of this bio-logical change (Blos 1970). There is no agreement on how best to organize schooling for early adolescents. The "junior high school" (grades seven to nine) and "middle school" (grades six to eight) concepts reflect a slim age difference but clearly attempt to mediate childhood and adolescence with an *inbetween-ness* that is recognized by a separate facility with different curricula. While a "K through eight" concept of schooling makes the physical and symbolic statement that the years 11-13 still belong to childhood, even the more tradi-tional systems introduce structural and curricular changes around sixth and seventh grade (for example, changing classes, choosing electives, taking a foreign language) to provide an educational experience that is different from what came before.

For the practical purposes of targeting a more clearly defined group, this curriculum was designed to address the development of junior high school youngsters from ages 12 to 14. Although Lawrence Kohlberg's theory of moral reasoning was obviously key to this first research to measure the effects of a moral education curriculum specifically designed for early adolescents, the works of three other developmentalists — Erik Erikson, Jean Piaget, and Robert Selman — were crucial. Their theories of psychosocial, cognitive, and perspective-taking development with respect to this particular population were essential to both the design of the curriculum and its methods of evaluation.

For Erikson early adolescence is a time of transition between the final resolution of the latency conflict between industry and inferiority and the beginnings of an extended period of identity formation. This part of his theory implies that it would be developmentally useful for the individual to become personally involved in activities that fulfill the sense of "industry" (having the psychosocial meaning of mastery, competence, self-confidence) and at the same time open up opportunities to explore his or her identity. At this juncture outward activity merges with inward reflection. Young adolescents attempt to find out who they are by *doing*, by "trying out" different aspects of that sense of self on themselves and their environment of people and objects. While the feeling of "crisis" over one's sexuality, ideological commitments, actual voca-tional choices, and economic and social independence from the family described by Erikson (1968) is characteristic of the high school or college adolescent, for early adolescents it is an experience yet to come. Personal identity at this age is still in a delicate state of formation rather than a tumultuous state of erupting confusion.

This shifting between outward and inward that characterizes the psycho-social development is accompanied by a parallel change in intellectual capacities. Piaget (1972) presents early adolescence as the time when the individual begins to develop formal, or abstract, thinking, which follows the concrete reasoning of middle childhood. Piaget sees this new capacity as a *transition* leading to the stage of formal operations. While not yet ready to perform "operations upon operations," reasoning about reasoning, deductive-hypothesis testing, the emerging adolescent for the first time is capable of epistemological questioning that, with the growing capacity to focus on the self, is likely to lead to a state of cognitive doubt.

The realization that many of the discussions and issues that engage the minds of these youngsters are at base moral ones calls for a thorough theoretical grounding for a curriculum that is intended to foster the moral development of young adolescents. Kohlberg and his colleagues have found that this point, between the ages of 10 and 13, marks the first critical period of transition in moral thinking from preconventional to conventional moral reasoning (Kohlberg and Turiel 1971). Kohlberg's longitudinal studies suggest that children who do not achieve conventional moral thinking patterns by age 13 will not achieve postconventional thought in adulthood (Kohlberg 1969). This first "open" period of transition from childhood into early adolescent moral thought is therefore a preparation for continued stage development during adolescence itself, as well as during adulthood.

The major change in thinking that occurs in this movement from preconventional to conventional moral reasoning is the development of "reciprocal role-taking ability." According to Kohlberg, role-taking is an awareness on the part of the individual that others may be like him or her, but that they have different ways of viewing the world. Role-taking also includes the ability to examine one's own behavior and pattern of seeing the world from the viewpoint of others. If individuals cannot perceive that other people often have a point of view different from their own, they will not "see" any moral conflict when problems involving other people's rights confront them.

With the onset of abstract reasoning the young adolescent for the first time becomes capable of cognitively "walking in the other person's shoes" mutually and simultaneously, as in the New Testament interpretation of the Golden Rule. Selman (1971b) and Byrne (1973) have further refined Kohlberg's notion of the importance of cognitive role-taking in the development of moral judgment by delineating stages by which the young person develops the abilities of social role-taking.

These stages proceed first from an egocentric view of the world in early childhood, toward an understanding of others when in a two-person relationship. Then in early adolescence individuals become capable of taking an observer's or third-party perspective on the interaction among themselves and others. In adolescence and adulthood perspective-taking develops toward a more abstract understanding of social groups and institutions as well as of deeper personality motivation. Selman and colleagues have also demonstrated that development in the cognitive ability to take the perspective of another precedes the corresponding development in moral reasoning (Selman 1971a).

From a theoretical standpoint, therefore, it would seem obvious that a focus on role-taking, both in terms of measuring its development and in providing opportunities for its stimulation, would be crucial to a curriculum in moral education for young adolescents. Kohlberg (1973) himself distinguished the characteristics of role-taking experiences needed to foster stage movement for children and young adolescents as different from those necessary to do the same during late adolescence and young adulthood. He contrasts "personal" role-taking, or committed action, as necessary to the movement to postconventional reasoning for this latter group, with the largely "vicarious symbolic" role-taking experiences needed by the younger adolescent for movement to conventional moral reasoning. That is, role-taking opportunities for early adolescents need to be *indirect*. They should for the most part be experiences that stimulate individuals to a more complex, differentiated form of thought. However, given the natural direction to which such thinking leads developmentally, it would seem important at this time also to expose emerging adolescents to those very social groups or institutions to which, in their later development, they are likely to be faced when making an actual moral commitment.

Given this theoretical backdrop, then, with particular focus on the importance of role-taking opportunities for early adolescents, three research questions emerged: Does a curriculum offering cognitive role-taking experiences stimulate the moral reasoning of early adolescents? Does such a curriculum also facilitate the development of early adolescents' role-taking ability? Which types of role-taking activities are most effective in a moral education curriculum for the junior high adolescent?

THE PROGRAM

The one-semester role-taking curriculum was randomly assigned to one of the three eighth-grade health education classes in an elementary school of over 400 children in Brookline, Massachusetts. One of the remaining two classes was also randomly chosen as the comparison group for the research. Both of these classes were taught by the author for one semester as part of the full-year health education course required of all eighth graders in the city's school system. Students were assigned to each class on a heterogeneous, or "nontracked" basis. The population of the school itself is ethnically diverse and includes significant numbers of low-income, single-parent families.

These arrangements proved to serve a practical as well as a research advantage to the purposes of this study. This same curriculum, however, could be adapted easily to a social studies or language arts classroom. This latter arrangement appears to be preferable for the way in which it would integrate moral education more fully into the school's core curriculum.

The 16-week class met twice a week for 40 minutes each session. In addition, there were two field trips into the local community during the last part of the course. The curriculum was divided into three major "phases," modeled after Mosher and Sullivan's (1974) curriculum. Within the context of moral dilemmas, role-taking experiences were construed as those that moved from personal and hypothetical situations toward the broader perspective of the school and neighborhood community.

The emphasis was on understanding the perspective of adults whose immediate life experiences were already familiar to the students. As Kohlberg (1973) suggests, this approach is preferable to exposing young adolescents to social and institutional perspectives represented by people whose roles are more abstract and removed from their lives.

Phase One: Understanding Moral Dilemmas

This part of the course (seven class sessions), was designed to help students understand the process of moral reasoning and role-taking in the context of two types of moral dilemmas: "daily" conflicts and "life-and-death" situations. It seemed that both extremes, the readily familiar and the captivatingly unusual, would be engaging and concrete enough for eighth graders to grasp the essence of moral dilemmas. In addition, responding to the dilemmas that arose within the classroom emerged as an important means of integrating the many facets of moral decision making. The kind of life and death dilemmas that appealed could be found in the film segment from the feature-length film *Abandon Ship,* entitled "The Right to Live: Who Decides?" (Learning Corporation of America). A "daily" dilemma chosen for small-group discussion was "Accidental Injury" from Blatt, Colby, and Speicher (1974). This was a case where a student pulled a chair from underneath another student as a prank, which resulted in a serious back injury.

Young adolescents are reluctant to reveal their own feelings and experiences until a trusting, secure classroom atmosphere has developed. The usual moral discussion format, either with the class as a whole or in small groups, was applied here, and a log to record personal dilemmas was assigned at the outset. It was especially useful to employ a variety of discussion and written formats with an interesting range of dilemmas that would tend to engage and not intimidate the students. Creative and sensitive planning at this stage was crucial for facilitating a cooperative group setting, or "moral atmosphere," and for cementing interest in the class. For only when this has been achieved and the youngsters are attuned to the cognitive developmental approach to moral education can they successfully begin the work of Phase Two.

Phase Two: Communicating Moral Dilemmas

The second part of the course (seven class sessions) was intended to increase interaction between the students and their initiative of moral dilemmas. The teacher as "presenter" in Phase One modeled the identification of moral issues and the moral discussion format. The more students begin to take over this role, the more the process of development can be set in motion. The two major ways of accomplishing these goals in this curriculum were role plays, in which students take the perspectives of characters in dilemmas that the teacher introduces, and student-designed dilemmas with open-ended probe questions for class discussion.

For the role plays three "daily" dilemmas from Blatt, Colby, and Speicher (1974) most likely to occur within the life experience of these students were selected: "Mrs. Hernandez — Property Damage Case," "The Used Car," and "Drunken Driving." Each small role-play group was instructed to act out the dilemma in such a way as to communicate the dilemma, clarify the reasons on both sides of the conflict, and to decide on a solution. Each group independent of the teacher and the other groups decided to involve the class in making a decision about the dilemma — in one case, as a jury; in another, as participants in a moral discussion led entirely by the role players themselves.

The second major activity of Phase Two, the writing of dilemmas by the students, was intended as practice preparation for the third part of the course, in which students would discuss real moral dilemmas with adults from the school and the community at large. Each student was to work with a partner on writing one dilemma and probe questions, around which they would focus an interview with someone of their choice from their own school. The students chose people with whom they felt "safe": the principal, librarian, other students, or, in most cases, a former teacher. The class as a whole discussed the effectiveness of the dilemmas and probe questions, and each pair of students wrote up its interview discussions. A few sample dilemmas follow:

For a Student: Your teacher has given you a spelling test. Beside you, you saw your best friend taking the vocabulary words out of her pocket. The teacher did not know she was cheating.

1. Should the student talk to her best friend and ask her why she cheated? Why?
2. Should the girl cheat, whether it was a good reason or not?
3. Should the student tell on her best friend? Why?
4. Should she make believe she didn't see her best friend? Or should she bring herself to tell on her best friend? What would be a good reason for telling on her? What would be a good reason for *not* telling on her?
5. If the teacher does find out, what should she do?

For a Teacher: The Halloween pumpkin was on top of the light in a teacher's classroom. Sam went up to push it over to get it down from there, and John was supposed to catch it. John missed the pumpkin and it fell. It broke all over the floor.

1. Who should be blamed in this case for the pumpkin breaking? Why?
2. Is anyone more at fault that the others?
3. Who should have to clean it up? Why?

For a Principal: Three girls are caught on school property smoking during lunch. A teacher finds them and reports them to the office. Two of these girls have been caught smoking on school property before. The other wasn't smoking with the other girls but is known to smoke off school property with friends.

1. Should all three girls be considered in the same manner? Why?
2. What should a fair punishment be? Why is that fair?
3. Should the principal consider their smoking habits in other situations in making his decision? Why? Should he involve the girls' parents? Why?
4. Should the principal tell the girls' teachers? Why?
5. Would it make a difference if this incident was the first time they were caught smoking on school grounds? Why? Would his decision be any different in that case?

Phase Three: Learning about the Moral Dilemmas of People in the Community

Phase Three (12 weeks) was the most experimental and the most important part of the role-taking curriculum. It was also the most interesting for the teacher and a majority of the students. Phases One and Two had focused the elements from previous moral education programs known to be developmentally effective and pedagogically interesting to students.

The basic moral discussion among students was extended to include people who assumed various community roles. These experiences were intended to stretch the students' perspectives through interaction with viewpoints that would include a cooperative outlook and group-oriented perspective, both in moral reasoning and role-taking. That is, the choice of moral issues on which to focus and the reasoning to highlight were aimed at a Kohlberg Stage 3 level. Toward this end two groups of people were chosen: immediate school personnel, and representatives of more distant community roles in the human and legal services familiar to early adolescents.

In both categories the students brainstormed the roles that most interested them, and the teacher chose the specific people for the class to talk to. The decision as to whom was chosen was a crucial factor in determining effective interaction. Adults for the most part are used to coming to a school to "talk at" students about some topic, and in these situations it is necessary to select adults who are able to maintain a *dialogue*. Even with a half-hour to an hour's preparation, including a simplified explanation of the cognitive developmental approach and the modeling of the moral discussion format with the person, true discussions with students were not always attainable. It would seem that adults often become as tense and insecure around adolescents as youngsters do around them.

The school personnel responded to dilemmas designed specifically for them by the students. Among the most interesting and important discussions for both students and adults took place with the cafeteria workers and the custodian. The dilemmas that follow give evidence of the adolescents' pressing interest in the moral problems they shared intimately everyday with these often-forgotten school personnel.

For Cafeteria Workers: One table of girls constantly leaves trays on the table. Because of this the cafeteria workers say that everyone who eats that period can't have ice cream until those trays and a few other scattered trays start getting cleared on a regular basis. Unfortunately, the girls at that table don't buy ice cream anyway, so they don't care.

1. Should everyone get deprived of ice cream because of a few people? Why or why not?
2. What should they do now that they know the ice cream punishment isn't working? For instance, should they punish each individual who doesn't clean his or her tray, individually? Why would the solution you choose be a good one?
3. Is it important to find out just who clears their trays or not? Why? How should they go about finding out?
4. Would the consequences of the decision to deprive everyone of ice cream be any different if the kids who left their trays did like ice cream? Why or why not?
5. Should the principal get involved? Why or why not?

Two general questions:
1. Why in general should people clear their trays?
2. What do you think of people who leave their trays on the tables?

For the Custodian: The custodian gave a boy a key to the teachers' room to buy a Coke, but when the custodian got the key back, he found that there was some money missing from the teachers' room.

1. What should the custodian do? Why?
2. Who is responsible for the money being taken — the boy, the custodian, or the teacher who left it there? Why?
3. What is the importance of trust in this situation? What does trust mean to you?
4. What does the boy think the custodian is thinking? What is the custodian thinking?

In the second part of Phase Three several community people came to the class to discuss examples of real moral dilemmas involving themselves and young people they knew. From a long list of possible roles chosen by students, those that represented different types of community institutions were selected, and the most promising representatives contacted. These were a waitress, juvenile lawyer, nun, pediatrician, and fireman.

Once more, the teacher spent preclass time with each adult, modeling the cognitive developmental approach and trying to select those dilemmas most likely to elicit Stage 3 issues. Evaluation material revealed that the adults who were most effective with early adolescents were able to sustain a personal, nondefensive dialogue with students and to challenge their perspective, one step immediately beyond their own thinking. In most cases, this meant talking to the students from a Stage 3 orientation.

The discussion with the pediatrician demonstrated these points. He was a "natural" moral discussion leader in his questioning, his responsive manner of dialogue, and his choice of dilemmas. An excerpt from that discussion follows. The dilemma the physician presented was whether he should tell one of his twelve-year-old patients with a progressive brain tumor that he was going to die, when the boy directly asked him.

Doctor: Does he have a right to know?

Ramon: Yeah, I said "Yes."

Teacher: Why?

Ramon: Because, like if it was me, I'd want to know.

Teacher: Why? Why would you want to know? Why would that make a difference?

Ramon: Because like, I just, I don't — like that kid last night [referring to the film *Death Be Not Proud,* coincidentally on television the night before], he knew, he knew that he was going to, that they was lying to him and he might, like just get mad at them, that they weren't on his side.

Patty: I'd want to know if I was going to die, but I wouldn't want to tell someone else they were going to die.

Sarah: I don't think you can say whether you *should* definitely tell them or you *shouldn't* definitely tell them. It depends on the person and the situation. If it won't serve any good reason or useful purpose at all, and if you don't think it will, then I don't think you should tell them. You should look at it more individually than, say, "Oh, you should *always* tell."

Angela: Yeah, but if you told, he might feel sorry for himself. And then he'd sit around. But it depends on the person. Some people will just forget all about it and go about their life.

Doctor: O.K., let me raise the question then of who should decide?

Sarah: People who know him.

Ramon: His parents.

Angela: The parents.

Patty: The kid should decide.

(Others give their opinion)

Ramon: (Disgustedly) How could the kid decide? Are you going to go up to him and say, "Am I going to tell you that you're going to die or not?!!" (Laughter)

Patty: I'd want to know.

Sarah: I think the parents and doctor. 'Cause if the parents know the kid, they know better than the doctor.

Angela: (To Patty) You just said you wouldn't want to. You keep going back and forth changing your mind.

(Doctor explains that the "rule" used to be to tell the parents everything and tell the child nothing. Then he gives the psychiatrists' solution):

Doctor: "Let's tell the kids everything, and let's work with them, let's prepare them for death. It's unfair, immoral almost to let somebody die without letting them get prepared."

Several: What do you mean? Get them prepared? How? How could you prepare them?

(Lots of voices discussing it)

Doctor: Talk about what it's going to be like, instead of lying there just thinking about it. If you can talk to someone about it, someone who's talked to a lot of other people about dying, someone who can go over the whole business of dying.

(Silence, students watching him intensely)

(Doctor and teacher explain the right to know about death as an experience of life and the "right" of the family to know so they too can prepare for it. The doctor then poses the question: "If your best friend had leukemia and your parents told you that your friend did not know, should you tell him?")

Angela: No, definitely not.

Sarah: No, I personally wouldn't because it would be hard to sit there and not tell him.

Angela: First of all, he didn't ask me to. It's not up to *us* to tell him long how long his life span's going to be.

Doctor: But you're one of the most important people in his life.

Angela: If someone's going to tell him it ought to be his parents.

(Silence)

Peter: (With emotion) . . . I wouldn't even see him!

Ramon: I wouldn't see him either, I'd be afraid I'd tell him.

(Several argue loudly)

Doctor: You'd have trouble facing it.

Maria: It would bother me. I'd just stand there and start to cry if I saw him. Maybe you can't hold it in any longer.

Doctor: (Warmly) Yeah, you might cry if you're with him, and he might see you crying. Yeah, that's hard.

(Discussion continues)

THE IMPACT OF THE COURSE

The results of a pretest/posttest statistical comparison showed that the group participating in the role-taking curriculum developed significantly ($p < .01$) in their moral reasoning on the Kohlberg Moral Judgement Interview compared to the other health education class taught at the same time by the same teacher. The students' role-taking ability as measured by the Byrne (1973) Role-taking Tasks, however, showed no significant change in scores. This highly experimental instrument presented validity and reliability problems. When considering the effects of a curriculum such as this it would seem wise to give more attention to the notion of so-called horizontal development, or *decalage,* in Piaget's terms. That is, does the intervention help to foster the expansion of an early adolescent's current mode of taking the perspective of others into *new* content areas? To date we have only rudimentary means of measuring this important developmental process. The analysis of tape recordings of discussions as the course progressed, for example, reflects several changes related to this type of development. Both in moral judgment and role-taking, the students took the initiative in analyzing new problems. They also learned to differentiate elements of their thinking from black-and-white statements to include shades of grey. Finally, and equally exciting, they began to notice differences in each others' thinking and in the group as a whole as time went on, and to help elicit and clarify those thoughts with one another.

Another area of impact of growing importance is the translation of growth in moral reasoning into behavior. One of the most important outcomes of this research was the number of "unobtrusive measures" of more "moral behavior." These were instances where egocentric (primarily Stage 2) concerns gave way to more cooperative and altruistic (or Stage 3) considerations when it came to the students' own moral decisions. Such evidence was documented outside the classroom as well as during class discussions. The most dramatic example occurred when a group of boys from the class approached the principal on behalf of a fellow classmate "in trouble" to try to reach a reasonable solution to the problem together. The principal told me such initiative had never been taken in his eight years as head of the school. This is the essence of moral education. It involves starting in motion a process of thinking, an entire way of viewing the world, that can thrive of its own accord when formal education has ended.

12
FACING HISTORY AND OURSELVES: HOLOCAUST AND HUMAN BEHAVIOR

Margot Stern Strom

A RATIONALE FOR TEACHING THE HOLOCAUST

A principal of a school gives the following letter to his teachers at the beginning of the school year:

Dear Teacher:
I am a survivor of a concentration camp. My eyes saw what no man should witness.
Gas chambers built by learned engineers. Children poisoned by educated physicians. Infants killed by trained nurses. Women and babies shot and burned by high school and college graduates.
So I am suspicious of education. My request is: help your students become human. Your efforts must never produce learned monsters, skilled psychopaths, educated Eichmanns. Reading, writing and arithmetic are important only if they serve to make our children more human (Ginnott 1972, epilogue).

Compelling as this letter is, a rationale for including curriculum on the Holocaust in the schools is essential. Some teachers avoid teaching about genocide because they fear it is too emotional, controversial, ethnic, and painful. Others contend it is blasphemy to draw lessons from this event and "maybe bad history is best forgotten." Many teachers, victims of the silence on this history in their own education, perpetuate that silence. Studies show that the Holocaust has been almost totally ignored or inadequately taught in both secondary schools and colleges (Friedlander 1973; Pate 1978; Raskies 1975).

Even after intensive training, teachers fear teaching about the Holocaust:

> The unit was much more difficult emotionally and I felt that my school and the people who worked in my school had a lot of fears about how the kids would react and the parents would react and I had some of those fears myself so that I was apprehensive (Strom and Parsons 1979).

The Holocaust is easily mistaught even by competent teachers who have made careful plans and who are sensitive to the importance of the issues and to the students' reactions. It is possible to teach about the Nazi Holocaust in a way that encourages glorification of power, identification with adventure, or that increases anti-Semitism and stereotyping. And it is possible to present materials that are not developmentally appropriate so that students "tune out" or become paralyzed by the content. Recently the New York *Times* carried a story about the head of the American Nazi party who describes how he first became interested in the Nazi movement.

> I can remember the day that I became a National Socialist, he said, back in 1952, when I was 7 years old. There was a film on television called "The Twisted Cross." It was made by the Anti-Defamation League of the B'nai B'rith so it was anti-Nazi. But, there was a lot of source material and when they would show a close up of Adolf Hitler's face, I still remember my feeling that there was a man who was saying something; whatever it was, he was deeply committed to it. He was feeling it deeply. And when they showed the crowd, they were deeply moved as if they had just had an awakening to something, something very important. It was like Niagara Falls, and it was something that transcended language and everything elso. I've loved Hitler ever since (Strom and Parsons 1976, p. 11).

Certainly the intent of the film was not to produce Hitler admirers!

Why take the risk then? Why ask teachers and students to struggle with this history? Terrence DesPres, the author of *The Survivors — An Anatomy of Life in the Death Camps,* captures the reactions of his students who learned about the Holocaust.

> And for all their shock and depression and yes, also their tears, what emerges finally are things so clearly good and life enhancing, that the danger we run and the damage we share in meditation on the Holocaust seem not too high a price to pay (Strom and Parsons 1976, p. ii).

Another answer to the question "Why teach this history?" becomes the simple "We must!"

As a humanist and as a teacher of history, I feel compelled to bring to the attention of my students those events and ideas which have nobled and uplifted the human spirit as well as those which readily serve to illustrate man's inhumanity to man.... The knowledge and understanding of what any given generation has about morality is enhanced by the endeavors of those who won't allow humanity to forget the lessons of history (Strom 1980).

The Nazi Holocaust, the most thoroughly documented example of human behavior in extreme situations, is a major historical event the teaching of which can help educate students and teachers to the meaning of human dignity, morality, law, and citizenship. Because the universal questions of morality and the lessons to be learned from a history of totalitarianism, racism, and dehumanization are not unique to the Holocaust, comparisons and parallels must be made to past and contemporary events and choices.

As it is our aim to study man and society we cannot escape searching for parallels ... comparisons are essential if we are to learn the lessons posed by the Holocaust ... we have seen that the impulse to exterminate is old and pervasive; we only have to read the newspapers to know that it still exists. In intent and performance Nazi genocide was not unique; in technological efficiency it was sui generis; for the first time a modern industrial state implemented a calculated policy of extermination. Of course, no single historical event duplicates the Nazi deed, but many share different aspects of the process that led to the death camps (Friedlander 1979, p. 531).

We look to the history of the Holocaust as ... "an event whose various aspects — political, ideological, administrative, technological, sociological, moral, and so forth — symbolize the problems and dilemmas of the contemporary world" (p. 522).

Holocaust teaching is education for tolerance — tolerance for Jews and non-Jews, against intolerance toward racial or religious or political or national groups.

AN OVERVIEW OF THE CURRICULUM

Facing History and Ourselves: Holocaust and Human Behavior is a curriculum developed for junior high and high school students that has been implemented in Brookline.

In the 13 chapters of this unit both the readings and the pedagogy engage students in reasoning about racism and prejudice and are selected to produce conflict about issues of human behavior and history.

The eight- to ten-week unit builds on the concepts of conflict and conflict resolution, power, fairness and justice, leadership, decision making, and obedience. As students examine these concepts in history they learn how power is abused and they are challenged to think about what they consider good and evil in their daily lives.

In the introductory lessons, students investigate the individual as a decision maker in society with readings like *The Bear That Wasn't* by Frank Tashlin and in films such as *Love to Kill.* After reading *The Boy of Old Prague* by Ish-Kishor, they discuss prejudice, stereotyping, learned behavior, rumor, and scapegoating in its historical and present-day contexts. Later, students study German history from World War I to World War II in order to place Hitler's "Grand Plan" and the Holocaust in its historical perspective. They ask questions about how Hitler rose to power, why the unlikely happened, and how such excesses can be prevented from happening again.

Students compare their education with that planned for Hitler's youth with selected readings from Erika Mann's *School for Barbarians* and Gregor Ziemer's *Education for Death: The Making of a Nazi.* After reading letters, diaries, and testimony of persons involved in this history, students try to clarify the reasoning given by those who obeyed Hitler and by those who resisted. The film *The Milgram Experiment: A Study in Obedience* helps students clarify questions about obedience and conformity.

The concepts of stereotyping, discrimination, prejudice, and injustice take on new meaning for the students as they see the film *The Warsaw Ghetto.* Some students read excerpts from *The Holocaust* by Bea Stadtler for further information on the Warsaw Ghetto. Exposure to the experiences in the concentration camps raises questions about human behavior in extreme situations. Students examine the experience of victims and victimizers through readings from Victor Frankl's *Experiences in a Concentration Camp* and Milton Meltzer's *Lest We Forget.* Visitors to classes — survivors of concentration camps, refugees, children raised as Nazi youth — personalize issues as they share their experiences.

The issue of resistance, a complicated topic for Holocaust study, is approached through discussion of movies like *The Hangman,* which relates to the study of behavior, obedience, fear, group behavior, and choices. Students write about another film, *Joseph Schultz,* based on an actual case of a German soldier who refused to obey an order to kill a group of hostages in World War II. Selected readings and additional films provide discussion of individual and group responses to the Nazi Grand Plan. Students learn about the responses of nations, those that collaborated, some that resisted, and some that stood as bystanders, and later students feel compelled to make judgments. In the chapter on Nuremberg the dilemmas about individual responsibility and obedience take on new meanings. Finally, students are encouraged to examine contemporary issues and recognize that the history they have learned has important relevance and lessons for today and the future.

TRAINING TEACHERS FOR THE HOLOCAUST CURRICULUM

The original interdisciplinary training model included an art teacher, librarian, multicultural teacher, and guidance counselor who, after training, gave workshops for their respective departments. The idea was to build support for teaching the Holocaust by identifying others besides the classroom teacher who could help make this curriculum experience successful. Later, the social studies teachers in eight Brookline schools were trained in workshops and were able to bring the new curriculum into a supportive setting. The teams of support staff were encouraged both to plan with the teacher and to visit the classroom. In addition, we gave workshops for parent-teacher organizations, principals, and administrators in the eight schools.

One teacher described how this model for support worked for her:

> [My principal] was incredible. First of all, he was visible. I would mention to him, as I mentioned to other teachers, when a film was coming up that might upset kids. I could ask him to come in for a session. He would come in and out. He also sought out and got a speaker for us. We met every Tuesday as a group of teachers (all teaching the unit) with the guidance counselors. Sometimes the librarian joined us. The principal was there, arranged for the room, the logistics — he legitimized it (Strom and Parsons 1979).

Before the Holocaust curriculum is begun, the teacher and the students discuss the type of classroom atmosphere that best supports candid responses to the sensitive issues of race and personal behavior the unit stimulates. Free discussion and provocative content must be supported by a classroom atmosphere that encourages a learning process where students confront conflict, identify reasoning, and struggle for meaning.

The following teachers have been asked whether there are special requirements and teaching methodology needed to make the Holocaust unit effective.

Teacher 1
As a teacher you feel a responsibility; this curriculum makes you feel there shouldn't be any of those kids who don't respond or keep it in — who stonewall you. Somehow if they stonewall the Puritans, so what? It is more important that they don't stonewall [this unit. However,] this is far more threatening than anything and there's far more chance they will stonewall it [and] prejudice is of different sorts. For some, prejudice is really this harboring of intense hatred and for most people prejudice is just there because [we] live in a racist society. For those people this unit was about stuff they had no idea about — they didn't know it existed. It made them think and they really came through it beautifully.

Teacher 2
The unit certainly contributes to classroom atmosphere because it tugs at a lot of gut issues. Before this we were talking about how a bill becomes law; there's not a lot of emotion involved in that. Knowing that the kids were struggling with gut issues rather than with just pure

head issues brought a closeness and a warmth to it. And the kids felt closer to me knowing that I was also struggling, knowing that I cried when I saw *Love to Kill*. It made me more human. I would hope that I establish that kind of atmosphere at any other time (Strom and Parsons 1979).

PREPARING STUDENTS FOR THE HOLOCAUST CURRICULUM

Materials and methods that raise highly engaging dilemmas for the students are presented in the initial lessons of the unit. They are designed to introduce skills that provide a necessary foundation for discussion of the more sophisticated and complex moral issues raised in the unit.

The concept of the individual in society is introduced and students clarify those aspects of society such as family, religion, political group, school, grade, friends, race, nation, and values that contribute to their "individual identity."

What types of decisions does an individual make in order to maintain his or her identity in a society? For example, does the individual recognize a decision-making situation? Does the individual avoid or attempt to solve conflicts? Does he or she obey or disobey laws or sets of values? To whom does the individual choose to be responsible, obedient, or loyal — to him- or herself, to the group, to the family, to the nation, to humanity? Do society's labels (for example, leader, coward, patriot) influence the types of decisions an individual makes? For example, if a person is labeled by his or her friends as a "bully," does the person choose to disobey rules and live up to that label as an aggressor? Why or why not?

These lessons encourage students to initiate questions, clarify the issues of a conflict situation, define "dilemmas," struggle with the vocabulary of conflict (that is, consequences, motivation), draw analogies to past lessons and everyday situations, and respond to the reasoning of their peers. In addition to defining the content of a conflict situation, then, students are introduced to a process for decision making.

To help clarify decision making and explore the consequences of individual decisions in a society, class discussions and lessons focus on the dilemmas individuals face in situations where their actions might defy societal norms or the law. Students speculate on the consequences of those actions to the individuals and to others.

How students made meaning of their experiences with these initial materials and activities is found in these excerpts from their reactions:

Student 1
Most important of all though, is the fact that one of the biggest impressions social studies has made on me is that now, I can honestly say, I can take both sides of a dilemma and judge them accordingly. This has helped me in both social studies and in other things also.

Student 2

The more I learn the more questions which are impossible to answer I come up with. Questions such as is there something that every person is born with which tells them that killing another person is wrong? If so, we are capable of being untrained from this instinct. I know for sure that we are capable of being trained to consider one person, or one group of people as beasts or worms with no feelings (Strom and Parsons 1979).

Students begin to realize the power of the individual to choose. In this quotation from the *Ascent of Man,* part of the teacher materials, Jacob Bronowski captures the critical concept of "choice," which the methodology, content, and teacher of the curriculum attempt to translate with the student.

Man is the only creature not locked into his environment. His imagination, his reason, his emotional subtlety and toughness make it possible for him not to accept the environment, but to change it. And that series of inventions by which man from age to age has remade his environment is a different kind of evolution not biological but cultural evolution (Bronowski 1973, Introduction).

The following list of questions generated in one eighth-grade class was used as points of reference throughout the unit: What is an idea? How can one judge whether an idea is good or bad? Why are bad ideas more powerful than good ideas? How can we help our culture survive? Who said people are ascending? Progressing? Why would anyone want to conquer the world? How do people who abuse power get power? Is power always a negative thing? What is a holocaust?

Students have investigated the themes of power, prejudice, scapegoating, bureaucracy, obedience, loyalty, decision making, and survival as they developed the notion of the individual in society and as a decision maker in hypothetical situations. I want to turn now to a detailed description of two chapters in the unit. My purpose is to illustrate how the materials, the teaching, and the students' activities interact in the classroom practice. The interested reader is referred to the curriculum "package" for the comparable materials of the other 11 chapters (Strom and Parsons 1979).

A CASE STUDY OF THE HOLOCAUST CURRICULUM

Anti-Semitism

In the chapter "A Case Study in Prejudice and Discrimination: Anti-Semitism" students are asked to analyze the "why" of individual and group behavior in a particular historical context. Here, before students study the composition of Hitler's Grand Plan, the curriculum examines some of the rumors, suspicions, and fears that have perpetuated anti-Semitism; it is in this chapter that students attempt to make meaning of the question, "How could this happen?" Students apply and practice the model for looking at situations of choice they used in the initial lessons.

They are encouraged to think about how societies or groups maintain an identity. Students learn that one way a society can develop its identity is to distinguish itself from others, either by stating what it represents and advocates or by defining those characteristics that distinguish it from other groups. If a society likes what it is, then what it is not can be construed as "bad," a way of thinking that inevitably leads to prejudice and discrimination.

The point at which prejudice toward a person because of his group membership is translated into hostile actions against the particular group is an important distinction made in these lessons. In *Semite and Jew,* Jean Paul Sartre (1948, p. 121) describes the person who choses to "lose one's individuality":

> Through hatred, the anti-Semite seeks out the protective community of men of faith, who reinforce each other through a collective uniformity of behavior. . . . The phrase, "I hate the Jews" is one that is uttered in chorus; in pronouncing it one attaches himself to a tradition and to a community of the mediocre. . . .
>
> This type of person is fearful of changing his or her opinions and therefore searches for simple answers in order to "distinguish between good and evil." An anti-Semite does not want to "think," instead he or she wants only to find a simple explanation. The question, "What is evil?" is simple for the anti-Semite. "Jews are evil, therefore let us eliminate them. To eliminate an evil is to perform a good."

Speculating about prejudice and discrimination toward others compells students to "think" about their own attitudes and behavior. The capacity to perceive others as individuals deserving of respect is the beginning of a developing capacity in the student to understand a notion of reversable roles and therefore to think in terms of reciprocity.

The comment of one student reveals her reflection on the identity of others, the Jewish people. She expresses pride in her attempts to struggle with her prejudice.

> Then when we started the Holocaust how much you prepared us and worked us up to this unit was well done. I'm glad this unit was taught to us, especially to me. At the beginning I have to admit I was prejudiced against Jews and was glad they were killed. I know this is awful especially if that is your religion. Then you and the class discussions proved to me I was wrong! Jewish is just like me and other people.
>
> I learned so much this year that I am proud of myself, especially when I was prejudiced against the Jewish people. I was going to tell you sooner, but I was afraid you would not consider me a person. It's over now.

Another student, struggling with the knowledge that her belief system and that of her parents was vulnerable to the facts of history, felt that the title of the course had new meaning for her; she was "facing history" for herself for the first time. She said to her teacher, "My mother said what you are teaching isn't true. I don't know what to believe." For others awareness comes in a different construction.

Today we talked about prejudice and stereotypes people put on each other. It was funny to notice in our class that most of the stereotypes didn't fit.

Today we talked about anti-Semitism and it was pretty interesting to hear other people's opinions about it. I never know what other people thought about Americans being fat lazy slobs (Strom and Parsons 1979).

It is in lessons like these that the teacher is reminded of the crucial role of the classroom environment where students can practice cooperation and decision making as an individual in a communal setting of trust. How students actually behave toward one another becomes the content of class discussions. The comments of two teachers illustrate how this happens.

Teacher 1
I walked into my class to find written on the chalk board, "Hitler rules — Hitler is #1." Under this in another handwriting was: "Whoever wrote this is a sucker." The students saw me read the board and they waited for my reaction. I Could Ignore It, Erase It and Go On, I Could Find Out Who Did It, or I Could Talk About It. Because the course belongs to the students, I said, we would discuss it in class . . . I felt good about what was discussed and the next day I walked in to see a swastika again. Then, I started class as usual. One kid, the scapegoated kid in our class, came up and on his own erased the board. This is a student who can't read or write — the other kids in the class said he was courageous.

Teacher 2
I feel for the teachers it's very important that the expectations of actual behavioral change that takes place over 8 to 10 weeks not be unrealistic, that kids not be expected to make a great leap from 13-14 year old child to mature adult. If one sets oneself up to expect that, you'll feel you failed with the unit because the kids are still acting like kids.

[One of my boys, who was Turkish] really was upset over the Armenian [Genocide] talk. Then the kids really talked about that. One of the other boys confronted him and said, "But you call me Armenian when you're mad at me." They were much more open with one another, much more candid.

Another time, a couple of boys witnessed a fight and their friends
were both the victim and the victimizer. Nobody said anything. I went
to the kids afterwards and said, "Now I know you two saw what
happened. You have to decide, because one of your friends is going to
miss out on the 8th grade camping trip and you can go and tell the
principal what happened, or you can keep quiet about it. You have to
decide that. This is the time for *individual* decisions. This is exactly
what we've been talking about." And they did then go and talk with
the principal. The curriculum gives you a handle for then relating
what's going on that you know the kids have been exposed to and you
can start talking about it — like decision making and personal responsibility — they have a basis to work from when you're discussing. It's a
shared vocabulary. I notice the principal uses it now too. He was very
active in this. You have something to refer back to that was a common
kind of thing. It's a reference point (Strom and Parsons 1979).

Many junior high school (and high school) students, whose thinking is still
predominantly concrete, yearn for the simple explanations, the one reason for
a person's action. Instead they hear a variety of voices — some who speak about
motivation in terms of power or loyalty to a group, and others who talk about
conformity, obedience, power, and loyalty. Confronting so many explanations
is very difficult. A teacher describes how he tried to challenge those students
who sought only the simple answers.

I got the feeling that people were going to walk out of the room saying
well, if we could just do away with stereotyping them — if it weren't
for stereotyping them the Holocaust wouldn't have come about.
Somehow it didn't seem like an adequate thought for people to begin
to develop. So I decided I wanted to fight that somehow. It wasn't that
kind of thing that created the Holocaust — that's ridiculous, because if
that was the case we'd have Holocausts every day in Brookline. Somehow that seemed much too simple an answer to a complex problem. So
I decided to raise the issue with both of my classes. In one class, one
girl really picked up on it and became kind of the leader of the group
that day although she had not been notably outspoken earlier in the
course and really made a very strong case for why stereotyping is good.
How it would be very difficult to grow up and form values and make
decisions about right and wrong if you didn't stereotype. Some people
in the class agreed (others didn't). I put the concept of human values
on the board and said, "Now what kind of thing is it that might be
worse then stereotyping, that might dig deeper than stereotyping, that
might set the stage for an environment in which the Holocaust could
occur?" What we came up with was the notion of dehumanizing people.
I asked them to do an exercise in which they free associated words that
kind of dug at them as repugnant. We had to define repugnant. They
came up with some things like racism and prejudice and gifted. They
talked about how "gifted" is too general. It seems to designate certain

individuals as innately superior, rather than saying the person is a wonderful painter or outstanding math student.

The point was to show that there's stereotyping, and then there's building up inside of people a kind of gut level reaction that some people are below the level at which we can deal, worse than bad. They'd have to be pushed. The issue of stereotyping versus dehumanizing was a big moment (Strom and Parsons 1979).

When students confront the conflict that arises in their reasoning, they ask questions about law. The content of their questions is about social justice and why did the event happen? How could it happen? They draw analogies to their daily experience where appropriate and think about their own reasoning and action and behavior. Finally, this study compels students and adults to think about judgment, in moral and legal terms. What would I do? What should I do?

In the following excerpts the writers trace their first impulse "to think about thinking" to their study of the Holocaust. This is a particularly critical skill for the teacher to encourage. In the first excerpt an eighth-grade student remembers back to the time he was a seventh grader as he listened to the eighth-grade class next door viewing a film on the Holocaust. He describes the change in this "thinking."

What was the Holocaust? I didn't think about it much then, but I knew camps, where they were all killed. That there was a man named Adolf Hitler, who was a leader of Germany and finally there was no reason for these killings. I know the U.S., Great Britain and Russia and France were trying to stop the Germans from taking over Europe. There was one thing I wasn't sure about, that was, did the good guys try to stop Germany from killing all these people?

Oh, I couldn't wait to see all those movies with all these armies blowing up cities and shooting at each other. For some reason, I loved watching war movies. I didn't mind watching all those innocent people die in battle. I couldn't wait to see pictures and learn about different planes, tanks and battleships.

Yep, that's what I thought I was going to learn during eighth-grade Social Studies. Well, I was wrong, but I won't regret it either, because what I did learn will probably change the way I think, and look on life for the rest of my life.

I hope you can see that the Holocaust really did change the way I think, and will think.

I've learned a lot of points that I can refer to when I use my thinking process.

1. You've got to believe that nearly anything can happen, after all, the Holocaust might not have happened if this wasn't true.

2. That you have to think about how your decision about the kind of government you want, isn't always the one you should have.

3. When you look at a person, you've got to completely understand him/her, and even make up things they might do. This is hard, maybe even impossible.

4. You should remember your conscience when you have to make decisions.

5. Finally, remember that human life is valuable, and that you always lose something when you don't try to save it (Strom and Parsons 1979).

And in this next excerpt Hannah Arendt traces her impulse to think about thinking from the time she watched Adolph Eichmann at his trial. She accuses Eichmann of thoughtlessness, the Socratic evil. How, she reasons, could a man who thought, who considered the meaning of his actions, have done Eichmann's work? Thinking, she said, is the urgent work of a species that bears responsibilities for its own survival. She implores us to think with her, to do philosophy, by criticism or agreement, to carry on thinking, the authority by which we survive in human form.

> Could the activity of thinking as such, the habit of examining whatever happens to come to pass or to attract attention regardless of results and specific content, could this activity be among the conditions that make men abstain from evil-doing or even actually "condition" them against it? (Bernstein 1978, pp. 1-2).

These lessons elicit abstract thinking: thinking about thinking and considering multiple causes or what Piaget called Formal Operations. The students have become comfortable with questions instead of answers.

In the following reflection a student described what she thinks are the critical changes in her "thinking" brought about by her confrontation with another person's perspective.

> Looking back at the past year, and my development in all facets, I must say I learned a lot. If not facts, how to think and to approach thinking in a more advanced way. The discussions were very enhancing, and I met, for the first time a collection of different people from various back-grounds, who had differing opinions and intelligences. . . .
>
> To tell the truth, when the whole project on the Holocaust began, I was disenchanted, when after my expectations of stories, statistics and the like, I got "dilemmas," "values" and all of those criteria. Now when I think of myself and what I was expecting from this course, I feel gruesome.
>
> At the beginning I was aloof (wasn't I), and underestimated what others might know, that is, after I found out they didn't really know about the Holocaust. I even had to sever relations with various people because of this project, but I really don't regret it. It changed my way of approaching the thinking system; if not my thinking and thoughts themselves.
>
> When I look at other kids in the class, the one who developed thinking best, to my opinion, was X, because whenever she says

something it makes more sense, it is to the point, and interesting at a level many kids couldn't have thought of independently, and I'm saying this as one of them. X applies what she has learned as well as her common sense. Y also has very interesting standpoints, and has a lot stored in, but I think her development is more natural, she is sort of born with it. . . (Strom and Parsons 1979).

Victims of Tyranny

The chapter "Victims of Tyranny," the history of the systematic murder of a race, taxes the belief system of adults and students because the Holocaust, finally, is a history of death and extermination on an unprecedented scale. How then do teachers help students make meaning of expulsions, resettlements, ghettos, transports, labor camps, factory camps, and the origins of the "final solution" that resulted in the "crematoriums"?

To this point in the unit, the students have used a vocabulary of decision making and justice to investigate human behavior in situations of *choice* that stimulated conflict and promoted growth in their reasoning about moral issues. But now the actual history demands a departure from this model of reasoning based on the language of morality. The values, standards, and vocabulary of the normal world are insufficient tools with which to examine the experience in the extermination camps where the rules of law and morality and the choices available for human decisions were not permitted. Lawrence Langer suggests we have no "vocabulary of annihilation" with which to know events where victims were presented with an existence of "choiceless choice," where crucial decisions did not reflect opinions between life and death, right and wrong, but between one form of abnormal response and another.

Langer uses the following excerpt to convey meaning to the concept of "choiceless choice."

Two days after Christmas, a Jewish child was born on our block (that is, in the prisoner barracks). How happy I was when I saw this tiny baby — it was a boy, and the mother had been told that he would be taken care of. Three hours later, I saw a small package wrapped in cheese cloth lying on a wooden bench. Suddenly it moved. A Jewish girl employed as a clerk came over, carrying a pan of cold water. She whispered to me, "Hush! Quiet! Go away!" But I remained, for I could not understand what she had in mind. She picked up the little package — it was a baby, of course — and it started to cry with a thin little voice. She took the infant and submerged its little body in the cold water. My heart beat wildly in agitation. I wanted to shout "Murderess!" but I had to keep quiet and could not tell anyone. The baby swallowed and gurgled, its little voice chittering like a small bird, until its breath became shorter and shorter. The woman held its head in the water. After about eight minutes the breathing stopped. The woman picked it up, wrapped it up again and put it with the other corpses.

Then she said to me, "We have to save the mother; otherwise she would have gone to the gas chamber." This girl had learned well from the SS and had become a murderess herself.

Langer explains:

How is one to pass judgment on such an episode (which may be extreme, but is not uncharacteristic of Auschwitz, where saving one life frequently meant surrendering another)? How are we to relate to it to the "inner freedom" which many commentators on the death camp experience celebrate as the last dignity available to the victim or survivor? Does the moral choice have any meaning here? The drama involves the helpless infant, whose fate is entirely in someone else's hands (and the fate of the infant Oedipus only reminds us how far in Auschwitz life has drifted from the moral order, and even the moral ironies, of art): The absent mother, who may or may not have approved of the action; the "agent" of death, who coolly sacrifices one life to preserve another, as a deed of naked necessity, without appeal, not of moral choice: and the author, sole witness to a crime that is simultaneously an act of kindness and perhaps of literal secular salvation to the mother. Vocabulary limps through this situation that allows no heroic response, no acceptable gesture of protest, no mode of action to permit any of the participants, including the absent mother to retain a core of human dignity. The situation itself forbids it together with the "law" stating that mothers who refuse to surrender their newborn infants to death must accompany them to the gas chamber.

One student bent her knees to her chest, wrapped her arms around her knees and peered out at me for a long silent time. Finally, she raised her head high and said: "Mrs. Strom, I think these pictures are going right through me — I can't understand or believe what I see" (Strom and Parsons 1979).

In class, we talked about how we have no vocabulary for these horrors and atrocities. These following students reflect on how they attempted to make meaning of what they were seeing and thinking:

I think for once the enormity of the things that went on really hit me. I imagined all those people who had families and little problems of life just being killed.

I was frustrated that I myself could not believe or accept that what I was seeing really happened.

It was awful. Those were people and other people did that to them. How? No matter what kind of teaching they had, training or whatever. Didn't they ever stop to think that the people in the Warsaw Ghetto were people?

For history you need good and bad things all the time. Why? I am not sure, but I think it is because without the good things, you couldn't tell the bad things, and without the bad things you also couldn't tell the good things.

During the year we saw a film called *The Warsaw Ghetto.* Some people in the class were affected very much by this film. I was not affected at all. At first I felt guilty but then I thought that I shouldn't feel guilty because there's nothing I could have done about it. I must admit though it did leave a mark on me. I think you should show this film as long as you teach the Holocaust. I think that it is very important for me to realize not to feel guilty about my opinion about the movie. I thank you for helping me see this (Strom and Parsons 1979).

In one class two students argued over whether concentration camps should be left up as a museum, a memorial. "No, they must be torn down, destroyed," said one girl. "We have to see," responded her classmate. "If my mother had been there I would want to know what she had been through." "Not me," said the first student. "I don't want to know, anyway, if we leave them up they'll remind and teach others how easy it is to do the same horrible thing over again and I'm afraid of that" (Strom and Parsons 1979).

The complex social and psychological phenomena of the survivors' experience is difficult to understand. But knowledge of their experience and reflection of the meanings we make for contemporary society will yield important lessons about the dimensions of humanity.

Eyewitnesses and survivors spoke to the classes. A teacher remembers the visitor:

I remember especially one class as a survivor of Auschwitz [was] speaking, his eyes filled up and his voice choked and he said he was unable to go on. There was a five minute lull and during the entire time, not a single one of the fifty kids smiled, or smirked or glanced sideways at a pal or made a wisecrack. There was total silence, total respect. . . .

A student responds to the visitor:

When the lady came in to tell us about her life during the Holocaust and watching her cry because it was so bad, I could tell everyone felt bad, even myself. As I watched and turned my face to the others, I could see the expression on everyone's face. I could pull out guilt, revenge, sadness, unhappiness — everyone was sitting there so quietly you could hear a pin drop.

A student asked a survivor who spoke about his life in a concentration camp, about his liberation and his love for America. "Do you know something about freedom that we don't know?" another asked, "How old are you?" Mr. Bonovika replied. "I was born in 1945." When the meaning of that date came clear — you could have heard the silence in that room" (Strom and Parsons 1979).

Survivors of genocide speak about an appreciation of life and freedom. Isabella Leitner remembers these words her mother told her as they rode to the extermination camp in a cattle car:

Stay alive, my darlings — all six of you. Out there, when it's all over, a world is waiting for you to give it all I gave you. Despite what you see here — and you are all young and impressionable — believe me, there is humanity out there, there is dignity. I will not share it with you, but it's there. And when this is over, you must add to it, because sometimes it is a little short, a little skimpy. With your lives, you can create other lives and nourish them. You can nourish your children's souls and minds, and teach them that man is capable of infinite glory. You must believe me. I cannot leave you with what you see here. I must leave you with what I see. My body is nearly dead, but my vision is throbbing with life — even here, I want you to live for the very life that is yours. And wherever I'll be, in some mysterious way, my love will overcome my death, and will keep you alive. I love you.

And that frail woman of love died a few days later. (Strom and Parsons 1979)

Resistance is taught as a response to a situation. Without making the critical distinction between a choice and choiceless situation the tendency among students of all ages is to measure the victims' actions against normal standards of moral action and behavior where there was a choice. When students ask why didn't the Jews resist or when they say, "I would have fought or run away," their tendency is to define resistance with a very narrow interpretation. For many, resistance conjures up a picture of a "violent" act — a person with a weapon in hand. But when students read about those who described resistance with a vocabulary of hope, loyalty, and defiance they are hearing resistance described in a different voice. These additional perspectives make reasoning about resistance more complex and the students' attempt to "understand" more difficult.

Throughout the curriculum both the teachers and the students yearn to read about those acts of courage in the name of humanity that give legitimacy to their belief that human nature triumphs in the name of "good." The acts of resistance and obedience among German citizens and soldiers — the church leaders who stood up for their nieghbors, the survivor who remembers times of hope and speaks of freedom, the average citizen whose conscience wouldn't let him act in any other way but to aid the victims, the nations that made a stand against actions of the occupying nations — are powerful reminders of hope in an otherwise dark history. Many teachers are tempted to end the study of the unit with the story of the Danish rescue of their Jewish neighbors. But we remind teachers that although there were courageous examples of disobedience and resistance among individuals, institutions, and nations, the reality is more one of compliance, collaboration, and obedience in the name of evil. We look to the Danish experience to try to understand why one society behaved so courageously. What in their history and tradition, in their environment, in their education prepared them to resist evil? These answers help us make the necessary connections to our individual lives and responsibilities in a democracy.

EVALUATION

Throughout this chapter, both teachers and children have been quoted at length on their understanding of the Holocaust. For the author, their voices are the most persuasive evidence of the effect of the curriculum and teaching. In addition, much formal, systematic data has been collected. Chapter 5 reported some of that data.

The following description from Marcus Lieberman (1979), the principal external evaluator, further summarizes important findings.

> During the first year of the project, the two authors taught the unit in their own schools. Since there was evidence from standardized test score data that there were ability (as measured in reading achievement) differences between the two schools, a control class from each was chosen in which another unit from the eighth grade curriculum was taught.
>
> Both experimental and control classes were pre- and post-tested in four domains: knowledge and understanding of concepts and vocabulary; interpersonal awareness (Selman 1974); moral reasoning (Kohlberg 1969) and ego development (Loevinger 1966).
>
> A word about "history" as a threat to the internal validity of this evaluation design (Campbell and Stanley 1963) is in order. The television series on the Holocaust was aired some weeks after the unit ended in the schools and after the post-tests were administered. In addition, record breaking snowstorms in January and February, 1978 in Boston caused suspension of classes for more than a week, but the effects were judged to be minimal.
>
> The results of the social studies concepts, skills and vocabulary test showed the experimental group growing more in attaining these goals than the control group, especially in describing decisions made by individuals as members of a society. Large numbers of students in the unit classes were able to give adequate definitions or examples of vocabulary words, though there were some interesting confusions, such as Aryans and Armenians (terms probably never mentioned in the same class) and many students identified Nazis as soldiers, rather than members of a political party.
>
> Two of the developmental measures allowed both quantitative and qualitative analysis. Both interpersonal awareness and moral reasoning have continuous counterparts to their stage determination. In these scales, 100 corresponds to a pure Stage One response, 150 corresponds

to a transitional stage between Stages One and Two, etc.

Students in the program classes grew more on both measures than did students in the control classes. An analysis of covariance with post-test score as the dependent variable and reading level and pre-test score as covariates was performed once the assumptions had been shown to hold for this data. The program group grew statistically significantly more in interpersonal awareness, mostly from Stage Two to a transitional state between Stage Two and Three, while the growth in moral reasoning over the control group could have been attributed to chance.

To respond to the concerns of developmental psychologists that continuous measures and aggregate scores such as the mean offer little information that is useful to them, two qualitative analyses were performed which used proportions of subjects at each state on both groups on both testings as the data. Then, by comparing cumulative distributions with the well known but seldom employed Kolmogorov-Smirnov non-parametric two sample test, the same hypotheses may be tested using procedures which maintain the integrity of the data. This analysis was performed on the global state scores of each of the three developmental measures but only interpersonal awareness retained the significant difference favoring the program group.

Significant growth over that of the control group is evidenced in several issues within interpersonal awareness. Rule Orientation, Decision-Making/Organization, Leadership, Jealousy/Exclusion, Conflict Resolution, Termination and Gobal Score all showed more subjects in the experimental group reasoning at a more complex level, than in the control group.

A second analysis was performed to determine the proportion of subjects in both groups who showed a new stage of reasoning on the post-test not present in the pre-test. Here, too, there were several issues in interpersonal awareness where growth in the experimental groups exceeds the control group students.

Finally, an analysis of papers describing students' experiences in the unit, written after the unit ended, revealed much evidence of an understanding of more than one perspective on a dilemma, the ability to put oneself in another's position, an ability to draw analogies in school life to the content in the unit, changes of attitudes toward minority groups, reduction of stereotyping, increased interest in personal histories of parents and grandparents, awareness of cultural differences, and a willingness to express ideas in class without fear of ridicule. These themes were present in several students' papers and showed a sophistication not displayed in the other instruments.

ELEMENTARY SCHOOL
CURRICULA

13

MORAL EDUCATION IN THE ELEMENTARY SCHOOL: UNCONVENTIONAL METHODS FOR CONVENTIONAL GOALS

David Stuhr

Louise Rundle

The authors have been associated with developmental moral education in the elementary school for a number of years and it is our intention to step back and critically examine this effort. We begin with a review of the moral stages relevant to elementary educators and their educational implications and continue with a review of efforts to develop curriculum. Included in this review of curriculum development are specific discussions of the merits and difficulties of training teachers and parents. Finally, we turn our attention to the elementary school as an institution and in so doing attempt to anticipate what the future innovations in moral education at the elementary level may be. It is our considered opinion that as we enter a new decade the time is right for an examination of the course of developmental education. The 1970s were a time of enthusiastic beginnings. The 1980s probably will be a time of slowed progress dominated by the difficult task of incorporating developmental moral education into the mainstream of public education.

MORAL STAGES AS EDUCATIONAL GOALS

Elementary educators are involved in the task of providing the conditions that facilitate childrens' development from Kohlberg's Stage 1 of moral reasoning to Stage 3. In general the task is to help students move from a preconventional to a conventional or emerging conventional level of development in moral understanding.

Stage 1 with its punishment and obedience orientation and Stage 2 with its naive instrumentalism compose the preconventional level. (For a fuller description of Kohlberg's moral stages, see Chapter 2.) In both of these stages, actions are evaluated with the use of one criterion: Will they avoid punishment or lead to rewards? Certainly Stage 2 is more sophisticated and reflects a child's growing awareness that he has control over his own destiny, but Stage 2 thinking primarily calculates the outcome for the individual. Concern for others is not readily apparent in this level of reasoning.

Stage 3, the apparent highest level of moral reasoning attainable by children under 12 years of age, is the first stage of "conventional" moral reasoning. Here we see the beginning of concern in youngsters for a good image. Stage 3 thinking is preoccupied with gaining the approval of other people by being "nice." In many ways Stage 3 thinking is the dominant mentality of traditional, "good" elementary schools. In a "good" elementary school, students are nice to one another. Students are deferential to all adults. Teachers are deferential to principals. Everyone is pleasant and happy. If the assumptions of Stage 3 thinking and Stage 3 school environments are not questioned and challenged, and if the subtle social discriminations go unnoticed, then the outcome can be a superficial comfort. Although Stage 3 is the obvious goal of moral education in the elementary school, the educator must avoid the trap of creating the conditions that lionize Stage 3. Beck, Sullivan, and Taylor (1972, p. 34) illustrate the danger.

> In one of the schools in which we worked, we inquired of the whereabouts of a student in one of our biweekly classes, we were told that the teacher asked him to leave the class "because he was a wise guy and a Stage 2." It is important to be constantly sensitive to the fact that the assessment instruments that we devise and the labels we use can easily be made tools of victimization by ourselves and teachers with whom we work.

ELEMENTARY EDUCATION AS PREPARATION

Elementary educators have never had the advantage of producing finished products. While it is true that a developmental educator never truly produces a finished product, only elementary educators are in a position to know what experiences students will encounter upon leaving them. Secondary educators can and do act as if their students will never again experience structured moral education. The elementary educators' lot is to provide the basics and to leave the refinements to secondary schooling. Traditionally, elementary moral educators have conceived their task to be teaching students to recognize a moral dilemma when they encounter one, to understand that a moral dilemma is perceived and understood by different people in different ways, and to learn that moral questions can best be answered by group discussion leading to more comprehensive resolutions. All of these teaching goals can be accomplished by involving students in the discussion of vicarious ethical dilemmas. New developments in secondary education have brought into question whether such indirect experience is sufficient preparation.

Other contributors to this book describe curricula that consolidate conventional moral reasoning and prepare students for higher stages of reasoning. The latest innovations are placing students in democratic schools in which they have greatly expanded roles in school decisions. Students are expected to engage in decisions about who can be included in their school, what rules of social conduct should be employed, and what we do with rule breakers. The elementary educator must now begin to ponder the question: How do we prepare students for the opportunity and responsibility to participate in this degree of self-governance? We will address these questions, following a discussion of moral education research and a thorough description of some of our most recent work.

CURRICULUM DEVELOPMENT IN MORAL EDUCATION IN THE 1970s

The first curriculum development of the past decade in moral education for elementary school children was based on a traditional teaching model. In this model, the child was taught moral reasoning skills through specified instructional techniques and materials in a formal class. The goal was to improve the child's ability to reason on moral issues. Kohlberg Moral Judgment interviews were used to measure growth in the child's reasoning ability. Early studies showed that this adaptation of the traditional teaching model could be successful in raising the moral reasoning ability of elementary school children.

Blatt (1968) was a pioneer in moral education with young children. He taught a small group of sixth-grade children in a church school to improve their ability to make moral judgments. He presented the children with hypothetical dilemmas, encouraged them to discuss the issues of the dilemmas, and challenged the adequacy of their thinking. He predicted they would incorporate a higher stage of reasoning as a result. Blatt's experimental students improved in their reasoning ability by two-thirds of a stage when measured on the Kohlberg Scale.

Grimes (1974) added two things to Blatt's research. She taught fifth- and sixth-grade students in a public school and she included mothers in one of her classes. Grimes' curriculum presented hypothetical moral dilemmas in case studies, filmstrips, and through the use of morality plays for group discussion. Her results were striking. All of the students but one began at Kohlberg's Stage 2. By the end of the one-semester class, the reverse was true. All but two students in the mother-child class were testing at Stage 3. The average gain was one-half stage. Grimes also taught a small experimental class of children without their mothers as participants. This group of children improved their reasoning one-third of a stage. Children in the control group, however, changed not at all.

Selman developed a filmstrip curriculum to improve role-taking and moral reasoning skills. The filmstrips presented hypothetical moral dilemmas in story form, accompanied by teacher guides. Selman taught this curriculum of film-strips and guided role plays and discussion to second-grade children. He measured their moral development through his own dilemmas, created for the young child. He found that this curriculum produced a significant change in the children's reasoning abilities, a change from a Stage 1 to a Stage 2 orientation (Lieberman and Selman 1975).

Blatt, Grimes, and Selman employed a traditional teaching model. They developed curriculum and taught classes in moral reasoning to elementary school children. Hypothetical dilemmas were used as the content for discussion. The curricula were designed to be taught in discrete periods of time during the school day. All three curricula succeeded in raising the moral reasoning of children.

Following these early studies, moral educators began to question the suffi-ciency of the traditional model. Grimes speculated about the appropriateness of hypothetical dilemmas. In reflecting on her study, she stressed the need for dilemmas to be real and vital to the children. Selman examined the potential role of the classroom teacher as moral educator. He found that, following his study, the children continued to increase in reasoning ability. He concluded that such gains would not have been possible without the support of the teachers after the study. The teachers had been using the techniques of the intervention and applying them to everyday experiences in the classroom.

Kohlberg (1976) examined the power of the classroom as a moral environ-ment. He suggested that classroom management may be a part of an unstudied or hidden curriculum in moral development. His examination of classroom structure and management led to the Cluster School Project, an experiment in school democracy. Early findings from the project suggested that, as a result of their participation in a democratic environment, high school students were demonstrating improved skills in their ability to reason on moral issues and, in addition, improved *behavior* toward one another (Wasserman 1976). The cumu-lative effect of this development activity was to suggest ways in which the traditional model of moral education could be adapted to encompass the whole of the classroom experience.

A CURRICULUM IN CLASSROOM DEMOCRACY

Rundle's (1977) study capitalized on this earlier work in moral education. We used the traditional techniques of moral dilemma discussion as described by Blatt and Kohlberg (1971). However, following Grimes' suggestion, the everyday classroom experiences of the children were the content for discussion. Role plays and games were used to clarify moral issues. Capitalizing on the Selman and Kohlberg findings, we considered the classroom teacher to be functioning as a moral educator in both the formal and "hidden" curricula. Ways were explored in which the classroom, its structure, activities, and interactions could be used and shaped to promote the child's moral development. Our task was to develop a curriculum for an elementary classroom that would provide a variety of developmentally appropriate experiences to promote the growth of the children.

Planning for the Curriculum

Mosher (1975) described the planning process in curriculum development and emphasized the importance of the critical first step: to examine who the client is and what one can encourage the client to do and learn. In this study, our client was a fifth-grade classroom. Our goal was the improvement of the children's ability to reason on moral issues and to behave cooperatively within the group. We intended to accomplish these goals through practice in classroom democracy.

Classroom democracy was defined by our considerations of the Model Outline for the Cluster School Project (Kohlberg, Wasserman, and Richardson 1975). We gave equal weight to creating conditions in which the children perceived their environment as fair and just and to social contract making in which the children must participate in group decisions on moral issues and collective action to resolve them. Having defined our task, we began a two-year planning process. The process was a cyclical one of observation, thinking, and classroom experimentation. This planning process allowed us to apply moral development and school democracy theory to practice, and as a result of practice, to translate theory to a classroom with a particular teacher and a particular group of children.

The classroom chosen for study was one of three fifth-grade, self-contained classes in an elementary school. We studied the classroom, its structure and system, and how the teacher shaped the classroom environment with her personal and professional style. The teacher's interactions with the students and her style of teaching and discipline were closely observed; so, too, were the children's behavior and group norms. What we saw and heard was related to the theory and research findings of moral development.

Educating the classroom teacher was an important factor in the planning process. We trained her in the theory and practice of moral education. She learned to listen to the children and to recognize the moral structures implicit in their thinking. Problems in the childrens' classroom behavior and their management were discussed. The teacher shared her successes and frustrations. We explored the natural dilemmas arising in her classroom and, together, discussed ways of framing these dilemmas to underscore their inherent moral issues. Finally, we supervised her work during the weeks of the study as she functioned as a moral educator.

Through a process of observation and study, through training, consultation, and supervision, we and the teacher began to understand ways in which democracy could be effectively translated to the fifth-grade classroom.

Teaching the Curriculum

The program ran for 12 weeks. The instruction time was one hour per week. During these formal sessions the classroom teacher was a participant or small-group leader. The complete curriculum is described in Rundle (1977).

In the four introductory classes, hypothetical dilemmas were used to teach the children how to identify a moral issue and to participate in an informal moral discussion. The Selman filmstrips introduced role-playing skills.

The children next became involved in an examination and resolution of natural moral dilemmas of the classroom. Classroom issues needed to be identified as proper for discussion and solution, whether their origin lay in teacher-student interactions, peer relations, or in the relationship of the group to other members of the school.

A "That's No Fair" list was introduced. The children identified classroom situations in which they had said: "That's no fair." During one session, for example, the students listed talking back to the teacher, having candy for snacks, talking in class, and tipping children's chairs. Topics for group discussion and resolution were chosen from this list. As the curriculum progressed, a formal list became less important because the content for discussion grew naturally out of each session.

The children acquired the skills to identify and discuss the natural moral issues in their classroom living. They then took on the responsibility of resolving them. Interestingly, children do expect moral reasoning to lead to concrete action. We stated that a decision must be made on the basis of "what's fair for everyone." The children began to perceive the curriculum as having a group-task focus. The task was to discuss and resolve classroom issues on the basis of what was fair and just for everyone. Small groups discussed the issues. The final decision was by consensus.

Hypothetical dilemmas, structured exercises, and games were used throughout the curriculum to introduce new skills, to address new concepts, and to stimulate the children's awareness of basic issues in their relationships. The assumption was that new skills and concepts would be best learned through a formal teaching session and then more effectively applied by the children to their life together.

The classroom teacher carried on Rundle's work between the formal class sessions. Dilemmas were discussed as they arose, role plays helped to clarify the conflicts, and resolution of everyday situations was achieved through consensus. The impact of the teacher's role as moral educator was a major one.

Results

The children who participated in the experimental class improved one-half a stage in moral reasoning, achieving a solid Stage 2 on the Kohlberg scale. In addition, they were able to demonstrate an improved ability to cooperate with others. Cooperation was defined as the group's ability to work together to complete a task. The Bridge Building Simulation Game was designed to measure group behaviors as the children planned and accomplished the bridge building task. These findings were reflected in their thoughts following the study. In individual interviews, students gave the following responses to interviewer questions.

Q. What's important about your friendships in the classroom?
A. "You can trust people [here]."
A. "[We] think about being considerate."
Q. What's important about the teacher?
A. "[She's there] to help us, to get to know us, to understand as best [she] can."
A. "[She] takes on the responsibility to be fair and good for everyone."
Q. What responsibilities do students have in the classroom?
A. "Well, if they aren't happy with the way the classroom was being run, . . . they might try to work some way out."

These children were ready for participation in school democracy. The oft-voiced concern that children in fifth grade may be too young to participate or to assume social responsibility in this way was refuted by what they did; but their readiness did not happen unaided or overnight. They had learned to identify their own feelings and thoughts on issues that affected them. They were able to state their positions on these issues in an open forum. The students had learned to accept the decision of the group as definitive and to behave in accordance with the prosocial norms of the classroom. When the school principal requested that representatives from the class work with him on a brochure describing the school rules to parents and students, they were delighted. The children were ready to articulate their learnings in classroom democracy to others in the school.

ISSUES IN PROMOTING MORAL DEVELOPMENT IN THE ELEMENTARY SCHOOL CLASSROOM

We have shown that a comprehensive curriculum in classroom democracy can be effective in the fifth-grade classroom. As sixth-grade students, this class began to generalize their experience to the formulation and explanation of school rules and policies. Our study thus provides one model for moral development curricula in the upper elementary grades. What we did is not, however, to be followed without careful thought. Our curriculum was developed for *a particular class*. It is not meant to be transposed to dissimilar settings. Through observation and consultation we defined the particular learning experiences that this class needed to participate democratically.

Further work is necessary to design suitable programs for children with varying experiences and at other stages of cognitive and socioemotional development. In this section we offer guidelines for this work. We describe a framework for observing the classroom and suggestions in teacher training and supervision of the teacher in the elementary classroom who has the children's moral development as a goal.

Considerations of Teacher Authority and Student Responsibility

One of the characteristics of a democratic group is that its powers are widely and equally distributed. All members have a voice, a vote, a "say" in how things are to be done. Student participation in social contract making demands shared authority and shared responsibility for classroom management.

In a democratic classroom, the teacher must, by this definition, give authority away to the students. How the teacher defines her authority, how she gives her authority away, and against what criteria are critical matters in a democratic classroom. The authority of the teacher is defined through her teaching style, her way of interacting with students, and by the children's own developmental perspective. A student's ability to assume responsibility depends not only on how much he is given by the teacher but also his developmental stage as reflected in his perceptions and behaviors. The point is that appropriate grants of authority and responsibility are both interrelated and will vary according to grade level.

Thus, the nature of teacher authority in the kindergarten classroom may be quite different from the appropriate kind of teacher authority in fifth grade. The amount and nature of a child's ability to participate in democratic decision making in second grade will not be the same as that of a child in sixth grade. Inappropriate use of authority or inappropriate grants of autonomy or prosocial responsibility will create confusion and regression. It is important if the classroom is to promote growth in students' capacities to participate, decide, and be socially responsible to monitor the balance between teacher authority and student autonomy.

In this section we describe the impact of students' development on their perception of teacher authority and student responsibility. We comment on ways in which children's classroom behaviors reflect these developmental changes. Finally, out of our experience, we offer examples of classroom environments that did and did not reflect an appropriate balance between authority and responsibility.

The Children's Perceptions

We will describe some changes in the children's perceptions of authority/ responsibility in the classroom based on our interviews with them. The results of these interviews have been summarized and divided into two groups: the early stages of moral development (grades K-2) and the later stages of moral development (grades 3-6). The reader should keep in mind that moral development may not be as neat and tidy as these groupings seem to imply.

In the early stages of moral development (Stages 1 and 2) the teacher is perceived as the unqualified authority. Recognition of the class as a group may not be evident. The group derives its identity from the teacher (for example, Mrs. Miller's class). The students may perceive rules as being ordained by some distant vague power (the principal) or by the teacher. Breaking rules automatically leads to punishment, and he who transgresses is bad. Rewards, like punishment, are distributed by the teacher. One who is rewarded is a good person.

In the later stages of moral development (Stages 2 and 3), student responses reveal a gradual shift. The teacher is still seen as the authority, but her authority is qualified by her perceived relationship with the students. The teacher's authority may be understood as benevolent, as being used for the good of the student. The teacher is seen to be concerned and helping. Children begin to recognize that their interactions with the teacher, and with each other, are guided by prosocial norms. They perceive rules as protecting the safety and desires of the group. Maintenance of the rules is seen to be a cooperative group effort. Punishment may be necessary if rules are broken for a good reason. Rewards come to those who conform to the group norms.

The Children's Activity

In the early stages of development, individual activity is predominant. Children in the classroom may work as a total group, in small groups, or in pairs, but each child tends to work alone. Trading activity may govern the child's interactions with a classmate ("I'll let you use the truck, if you give me the car").

In the higher stages of development, sharing and cooperation are observed. Children learn to work together to accomplish a group task. Their behavior demonstrates a growing independence from authority and an increasing ability to take the responsibility for group behaviors.

Implications for Curriculum Development

We have stated that the classroom environment must reflect an appropriate balance between levels of teacher authority and student responsibility. Our experience suggests that this is a critical factor that must be addressed in the course of education in democracy. For example, the reported study by Rundle was conducted in 1976 in a classroom where the teacher was perceived as a benevolent authority. The children felt that she was concerned about them. Prosocial norms for group behavior were already emerging. The children were

246 / *Moral Education*

demonstrating a growing ability to work together on group projects. The curriculum in democracy provided a good fit for this classroom environment. It reinforced the prosocial norms by defining them as criteria for acceptable (that is, good) behavior. It allowed the teacher to examine her changing role of authority in the classroom and encouraged her to become a participant in the democratic process. It empowered the entire group to work on their life together as a common task and, by voting, to resolve the everyday dilemmas of classroom life.

The same curriculum in fifth-grade classroom democracy, however, failed in 1975. The curriculum that produced change in 1976 produced no observable change one year earlier. That study was done in a classroom that was not self-contained. The children were taught by five or six teachers each day according to subject matter. The teachers varied in their expressions of authority. The children perceived one as authoritarian, the rest as permissive. There was no emerging group concept and cliques were the norm. Rules were poorly defined and inconsistently enforced. The inappropriate level of the children's autonomy and the confused definition of teacher authority did not provide an environment where the curriculum in classroom democracy could succeed.

Classroom democracy demands an environment where children feel secure, where the teacher is trusted, and where caring for others is a value. *Then* the challenge is to move ahead. Conflicts can be identified, discussed, and decisions made. With work, growth can result. Children in a classroom environment that is not in balance on issues of authority/autonomy, however, may not be ready to assume the responsibilities of self-management. When asked to do so, they may react with helplessness and rage. Careful analysis of the classroom is required before beginning education for democratic participation.

Teacher Training

The authors drew from a cognitive-developmental theory when we designed a curriculum in classroom democracy. We believed that developing more adequate ways of thinking can interact with developing more adequate ways of behaving. Promoting moral reasoning was a central focus of our classroom research.

To help children grow in moral reasoning, a teacher must understand its developmental characteristics and an array of pedagogical techniques. For example, she must learn to help a child identify his reasons. She should be able to recognize the structure of thinking underlying those reasons and offer an appropriate response to encourage growth. A teacher who can reason at one stage above that of the child helps improve the child's reasoning ability. A teacher who reasons below, or too far above, the level of the child's present understanding will not succeed in effecting change. Training *is* necessary to either raise the level of the teacher's reasoning or to teach her to lower it, so that she is successful in being understood by her students.

Consultation and supervision with the teacher proved useful in our work. These sessions allowed her the opportunity to step back and look around the classroom. She examined her responses to issues of authority and autonomy, her rules and how she justified and conveyed them to the children, and her participation in discussions of the moral dilemmas of the class. When a teacher is knee deep in moral development, an objective view from a knowledgeable consultant, supervisor, or peer provides support and encouragement.

Teachers who work in self-contained classrooms, in our experience, have a golden opportunity to promote the moral reasoning of their students. Moral dilemmas arise naturally out of the life of their classrooms. By utilizing the everyday dilemmas of the classroom as content for discussion, and by helping children to decide and to act on their solutions, the teacher can have a powerful effect on the moral development of her students.

We have found that it is critical that teachers be trained as moral educators to implement successful programs in classroom democracy. It remains unclear whether all teachers with varying styles can profit from training as moral educators. We encourage further research that examines the interaction of style and training on the moral development of children.

BROADENING THE PERSPECTIVE

The moral educator easily can begin to employ tunnel vision and to focus attention only on students and teachers. However, students and teachers do not live in a vacuum; they are influenced by peers, parents, and the school system itself. We conclude our comments on elementary moral education with some thoughts on the need to include parents and other school personnel for program development to be fully effective.

Parental Involvement

Our work can be faulted because it ignored the influence of parents on their children's moral growth. Elementary educators have traditionally supported parental involvement in education. While this position often receives more lip service than it does action, the idea that parents should join with professional educators in the educational process is as American as apple pie. Moral education has often been argued to be the responsibility of the family and the church, but within the context of moral education nationally, the involvement of parents has been largely ignored.

If preparation to fully participate in decision making for an ever enlarging group is to be one of the primary aims of the moral education of young children, then the involvement of parents and family seems inevitable. The parents of children who are learning to participate in the governance of the classroom will likely become aware of their youngsters' interest in addressing group decisions.

Will parents be ready to respond to such requests? The answer is likely to be "no" unless parents have been prepared and understand the value of such experiences. Even with such preparation, alterations of parenting style are difficult to achieve. Parents who have been raised in parent-controlled families have little understanding and often little motivation for allowing children to participate in family decisions. Such suggestions are perceived as a repudiation of family and tradition and order. Only when parents begin to grasp the notion of development and the goals of group responsibility are they willing to experiment.

The only research that incorporates parents with their elementary-aged children was that done by Grimes (1974). As described earlier, one of the experimental moral education classes she taught included the mothers of the children. Their inclusion was important to the course outcome. The students in this group experienced significantly more growth than did the students in the student-only group. It has been speculated that the mothers extended the treatment into family life and that their presence motivated the students to more fully participate in Grimes' curriculum.

Grimes' work was completed several years ago. It offered much promise, yet no additional joining of elementary children and their parents in a moral education curriculum, to our knowledge, has been attempted. It now seems clear that studies are needed that combine the opportunities for classroom decision making with family decision making. Chapters 19 and 20 in this book by Stanley and Azrak suggest the impact of such a common cause. In moving children from a perspective where their own interests are paramount to a perspective of concern for the norms of the group, the need for the participation of the family seems apparent. The family is the first group of concern for a growing youngster, and the opportunity to more fully learn about the concerns and needs of family members seems an obvious next step in learning to develop group feelings and less egocentric perspectives.

School Implications

For developmental education to be adopted in elementary schools, many changes would be required. They would be much more than cosmetic and transitory modifications. Rather they would be philosophical, organizational, structural, and procedural changes of a basic nature. Developmental education, in our opinion, forces the schools to adopt carefully conceived democratic education as a way of life. Secondarily, it requires educators to accept pedagogic inquiry as an integral part of instruction. As Sarason (1971) has pointed out, the constitution of the classroom is typically designed by teachers *for*, not with, children. And Schaefer (1967) has described why schools are not centers of inquiry. So there are miles to go before we sleep.

Relative to school democracy, we have argued for elementary students to be appropriately involved in decision making in the classroom, but such subversive activities cannot be contained for long by the four walls of the classroom.

Some students will assert their right to participate in schoolwide decisions. Also one can question whether it is possible for elementary educators to participate in democratic instruction while being treated as inferiors by administrators. Sarason has described teachers' consternation when they realize that they typically exclude children from authority and decision making in the same way they feel excluded by their superiors. The emergence of teachers' unions, negotiations, and master contracts as common elements of school life are appropriate precursors for democratic education. Teachers have demanded and obtained a voice in the governance of schools. Until they had done so it was very unlikely that they were going to give students greater opportunity for decision making.

All of these changes have created pressures for administrators and school board members to adjust. What is needed is a comprehensive understanding of democracy, human development, and the way in which education relates to both. This is asking much of people who for the most part have been educated traditionally and like most of us resist fundamental change. The success of developmental education is very much linked with the ability of educators to comprehend and successfully apply its principles. So we may be hoist by our own petard: a conception of human rights, potential, and the educational means to their realization beyond the grasp of many teachers, public officials, and schools. Yet, in the same breath, the elementary school may be able to offer a suitable place for this work to grow because of its fundamental commitment to students. This has been and will continue to be the strength of elementary education.

Developmental education has a basic premise that the extent of growth is unknown and the opportunity to seek truth, and for intelligence to operate freely, is vital for development to occur in people or their institutions. This clearly implies that educators must engage in inquiry simultaneously with their students. Educators will continually need to search for the best means to promote development. This search will set the stage for development to occur in the classroom, the school, and the family. Knowledge is there to be discovered and development occurs as a result of the search. That is the journey and the promise and you are invited to join.

14
MORAL DEVELOPMENT IN ELEMENTARY SCHOOL CLASSROOMS

Roger Aubrey

The only method of moral training effective with youth is that which discards formal precepts, and by restraint of actual vice, or practice of the desired virtue, engrafts it insensibly on the daily conduct. The habit of right acting is thus unconsciously acquired, but not till a much later period is the mind disposed to survey critically this action and pass judgment upon its propriety. The maturity of the mind is an indication of the proper season for moralizing (Kiddle and Schem 1877, p. 598).

Historically much of what passed for moral guidance in American elementary schools fell into two categories. First was the time-honored attempt to indoctrinate a sense of right and wrong in children by the use of stories, examples, teacher advocacy, discussions, exercises, and curricular materials. Second was the actual imposition of standards of behavior as agreed upon and enforced by school personnel (for example, being strapped for talking back to a teacher).

The adage that "the more things change, the more they remain the same" is readily apparent in most approaches to moral guidance in today's elementary schools. What is sought and expected by school personnel are two demonstrations of morality in children. One is the ability to pick out and repeat from various problems and materials those conclusions deemed appropriate by the adult caretakers. The other is behavior evidencing moral character as best typified by adherence to the codes and norms of school society.

Readers of this book are well aware that a third demonstration of morality is also available to educators. Its manifestation lies in the moral reasoning of students and is readily accessible to the trained observer. This chapter will highlight the salient features of a program designed to educate teachers in stimulating this aspect of the moral development of the children in their classroom.

CLASSROOM MANAGEMENT AND MORALITY

Responsibility for citizenship and character development has long been a charge for the elementary schools. At its best, this has led teachers to conscientiously select materials and experiences intended to promote those qualities exemplifying adult virtues. Some teachers even modeled fairness, respect, thoughtfulness. At its worst, this responsibility has resulted in forms of socialization and indoctrination designed to bring about a thoughtless and submissive adjustment to the status quo. What both approaches have in common is a mistaken notion that more highly advanced and adult-like forms of reasoning and behavior can be acquired by young children.

Among the motives that prompt teachers to engage in activities intended to strengthen the moral character of students, classroom control is high on the list. The linkage of morality with the maintenance of the teacher's own preferred norms of classroom behavior is not new to education. Lortie (1975, p. 113) is representative of many investigators who have discovered that

> connecting compliance with classroom norms to future citizenship authenticates the teacher's control efforts. Thus discipline becomes more than mere forbidding and ordering; the dross of classroom management is transformed into the gold of dependable citizenship. Whereas some critics of school cry "oppression" at the teacher dominance of classrooms, these respondents see it as preparing citizens for the Republic.

WHAT'S IN IT FOR ME?

The introduction of programs, methods, and materials to stimulate moral development in children can be successful only if they are fully accepted by teachers. In turn, this acceptance must be much more than mere acquiescence. Teachers need to make a commitment to these efforts and they must be willing to shift previous objectives to accomodate these new purposes.

Teachers have various reasons to be receptive to programs aimed at moral guidance. However, in my work with them I have found that there are at least six compelling motives (or combinations thereof) that initially attract teachers:

> To please administrators and school officials.
> To acquire and improve classroom management techniques.
> Guilt for not previously having done anything in this area.
> Keen interest in this area but ignorance of programs, methods, and materials.
> Desire to improve efforts already begun by acquiring additional training and new approaches.
> Excitement and curiosity in a new challenge.

Please Administration

In all school systems, a certain proportion of teachers will jump on any bandwagon encouraged by the local school administration. Doubtless, this is not where one would like to recruit the majority of teachers for a program in moral education. Nonetheless, from the ranks of such a group I have frequently encountered many fine and dedicated teachers who eventually overcame their initial intimidation by the school administration. Once this had been accomplished, and they had been given an opportunity to decide for themselves if they wished to embark on a planned effort at moral education, those deciding in the affirmative were just as effective in their efforts as any other teachers.

Improved Management

Teachers who conscientiously wish to improve their classroom management practices or "discipline" are often drawn to new approaches. Invariably some of these teachers will be extremely interested in efforts geared toward the stimulation of moral development in children. Just as invariably, some of them will be highly disappointed by programs and approaches that purport to improve behavior by first attempting to improve the adequacy of children's moral reasoning. Those reared on a diet of social learning theory and a one-dimensional view of behaviorism especially will be disappointed by approaches that view internal behavior (moral reasoning) as the crucial factor in determining external behavior. On the other hand, those teachers who have found earlier techniques wanting may be quite willing to try something new. The major concern of all teachers interested in classroom management techniques is efficacy and immediacy. In working with teachers motivated by these factors, it is well to keep this uppermost because cognitive restructuring does not lend itself to overnight results. As a consequence, they may need a disproportionate amount of encouragement in implementing classroom programs in this area.

Guilt

Guilt occasionally serves as a stimulant in motivating teachers to become interested in moral guidance. They may feel that they have neglected or underprized this aspect of education due to their overemphasis on the academic and basic skill areas. Although semimotivated to broaden their curricular objectives to include moral guidance, these teachers will need reassurance from time to time. In particular, the dilemma facing them comes down to one of priorities between academic versus social competencies in children. The most logical and practical means of reconciling this dilemma is to assist these teachers in incorporating moral guidance into their existing academic programs (more on this later).

Ignorance

Ignorance is hardly a spur to action. On the other hand, it is not uncommon to find clusters of teachers with a keen interest in character development and little knowledge of how to approach this concern in a classroom. These teachers are usually avid and energetic learners and require little special attention. In fact, they often are the pacers who extend their own colleagues and enliven any group.

Improvement

Many teachers interested in citizenship and moral development have existing programs in this area. Some of these curricula are commercially prepared while others have been developed by individual teachers. Like their counterparts who lack information about alternative programs and approaches, these teachers are generally highly motivated. However, it is well to keep in mind that they have made a commitment and are currently implementing alternative approaches. They will need to be convinced that anything novel is "better than" their current program.

New Challenge

Many of today's teachers are bored and understimulated. Sarason (1972, pp. 123-24) captures this mood and its explanation in noting that "the assumption that teachers can create and maintain those conditions that make school learning and school living stimulating for children, without those same conditions existing for teachers, has no warrant in the history of man." This observation seems especially applicable to creative and ambitious elementary teachers who pride themselves on "teaching the whole child." For many of them, a "return to the basics," or a strictly three Rs curriculum, is not the *sine qua non* of schooling. Instead, these teachers seek excitement and challenge for both themselves and their students in approaches expanding their current horizons. I suspect there are a great many more teachers with this need than one would imagine, especially in outstanding school systems. And they are a very important resource to programs in moral education.

DEALING WITH DISSONANCE

Whatever their motives, an assemblage of teachers interested in approaches to the moral development of children is a demanding group. Not only are their motives different, their belief systems are also dissimilar. As a consequence, the starting point in introducing approaches to the moral development of children is the moral development of the teacher.

The Kohlberg theory of moral development has been amply covered in other sections of this book. Suffice it to say that if this theory and approach to education is to undergird an elementary school program, it must be thoroughly understood and accepted by participating teachers. A starting point is to allow teachers to experience the theory as it complements and clashes with their own ethical beliefs.

A number of successful means have been employed to introduce elementary teachers to the Kohlberg scheme. Practically all have one common theme: an experience of dissonance on the part of the teacher forcing that individual to compare and contrast his own ethical system with that of Kohlberg. Needless to say, when this experience occurs in a group context, it also compels the individual to consider the belief systems held by his counterparts as well.

Festinger's (1962) theory of cognitive dissonance contains a number of propositions that are helpful in dealing with elementary teachers being introduced to Kohlberg. One of these propositions states that "if two elements are dissonant with one another, the magnitude of the dissonance will be a function of the importance of the elements" (p. 16). This proposition is useful in explaining why some teachers react quite dramatically when first encountering Kohlberg's theory. To the casual observer this reaction may signal undue tension and conflict. However, to those knowledgeable of Kohlberg and Festinger, it is a sign that a strongly held view of the teacher is being challenged by new and equally powerful views and requires time for serious deliberation.

Another proposition of Festinger provides a guideline for understanding the behavior of teachers in this situation of dissonance. It states that "the presence of dissonance gives rise to pressures to reduce or eliminate the dissonance. The strength of the pressures to reduce the dissonance is a function of the magnitude of the dissonance" (p. 18). In working with groups of teachers interested in moral development, this proposition is a caution against allowing premature closure of discussion before all parties truly have had their say. It also explains why teachers in groups will frequently spend more time seeking support from others for previously held positions than in understanding newly introduced material.

A final proposition by Festinger speaks to how tension and conflict can be handled in a group setting. According to this proposition, "the effectiveness of efforts to reduce dissonance will depend upon the resistance to change of the cognitive elements involved in the dissonance and on the availability of information which will provide, or of other persons who will supply, new cognitive elements" (p. 265). In brief, this position stresses the importance of supplying teachers with adequate resources during their initial period of exposure to moral development theory. These resources include both knowledgeable group leaders as well as supporting materials.

HOW DO WE DO IT?

Once interested teachers have had an opportunity to experience and understand Kohlberg's theory, they will want to know how applications can be made to the classroom. If the exposure to Kohlberg has been experience in discussing a number of dilemmas, the linkage to the classroom should be apparent. On the other hand, if the presentation of the theory has been purely didactic, teachers will require further training.

I have found that a combination of didactic and simulation materials is the best vehicle for introducing teachers to Kohlberg. One resource designed for this purpose is a six-hour teacher workshop produced by Guidance Associates (1976) with the aid of Kohlberg and Robert Selman. However, many other means are available for accomplishing this end such as a number of film clips from movie and television presentations as well as written dilemmas. What seems important in this aspect is not the "slickness" of the media so much as the believability and intrinsic interest of the dilemma being presented. It is the retrospective thinking of the teachers after they have actually taken a position and discussed the dilemma that provides the real springboard for learning in these group meetings.

As readers of this book are well aware, individuals reason predominately at one stage of thought and use contiguous stages as secondary thinking patterns. The attempt to stimulate moral development in children, to deliberately facilitate stage transition, means that teachers need to be aware of stage differences and, even more important, of hypothetical or real moral dilemmas that will arouse cognitive conflict in their students. Research has shown that the vast majority of elementary students reason at a preconventional level. As a consequence, teachers may well select dilemma and conflict situations consistently portraying this level. However, teachers also need to keep in mind that some children will be able to comprehend and appreciate conventional arguments well before others do so (in fact, their parents and the world around them prefer to deal with them on this level). It is therefore important for teachers to have a keen grasp of the position of each of their students as well as how to juxtapose students in small group discussions for maximum stimulation of all. This will frequently require the teacher to mix and sit with small groups in order that the teacher provide higher-stage arguments for children at more advanced levels with no peers for stimulation.

The "nuts and bolts" of how to conduct and lead elementary students in moral discussions can be found in a number of kits produced by Guidance Associates (1972, 1976) under the supervision of Kohlberg, Selman, Byrne, Lickona, and colleagues. All of these materials include audio cassettes, filmstrips, and booklets field-tested by teachers in elementary classrooms. They provide an excellent means of helping the inexperienced teacher launch a classroom program of moral guidance based on Kohlberg's theory. However, even the best-prepared materials have limitations. The real crux in programs of moral guidance in elementary schools is the ability of teachers to select, design, and lead moral discussions between their students.

WHAT'S THE RIGHT ANSWER?

Elementary teachers I have worked with in programs of moral education seem to fall into three distinct categories in terms of anticipated outcomes. I suspect their perspectives mirror their own education and training in pedagogy as well as the teaching models they chose to emulate. The recognition of these three styles can be extremely helpful in both analyzing their leadership behavior as well as in conducting in-service workshops.

The first and more traditional stance is that of the teacher expert/authority. In effect, teachers of this posture "teach" even the Kohlberg approach in much the same way as traditional subject matter. As an example, I conducted a series of workshops on Kohlberg for the entire teaching staff of one school. I later did a number of classroom demonstrations using filmstrip dilemmas as well as actual moral dilemmas arising from school situations. In later follow-up visits to classrooms, I observed one teacher doing a dilemma discussion in which her class was evenly split as to whether a child should break a promise to her father in order to help a friend. At the conclusion of the discussion, the class was still evenly divided. The teacher then addressed the class and said, "All right, let's take a final vote to see what Holly really should have done in this case."

This type of teacher seeks closure when none is apparent and the reduction of dissonance when it is most beneficial. She also assumes that there really is a correct way of eventually resolving difficult ethical situations and that this should be part of the classroom program (in this instance by a group vote or consensus). The message to students conveyed by this teacher is one that says, "Even the most difficult of moral choices can be solved by appealing to a majority of the group." Over a period of time this approach will result in students looking to their peers whenever a moral discussion arises. They will hesitate to take positions until they perceive where their peers are leaning and then will join the winning team.

The second type of teaching style is one reminiscent of the discovery method in certain academic disciplines. This teacher does not fall into the trap of allowing group consensus to determine what is ethically correct in a given situation. Instead, she will allow all students to actively take an individualistic position throughout any moral discussion.

What characterizes the discovery-method teacher also is the subtle and persuasive message to the students that there really is a "right" answer in determining the outcome of any given moral conflict. Just as the academic discovery method forces children to consider many alternatives before arriving at a solution to the problem at hand, this teacher will lead children through an array of questions and probes. Eventually, some children will arrive at higher-stage positions on various ethical conflicts and they will be rewarded by having "discovered" the answer. In time, their peers may pick up on this game and argue identical positions. The astute observer will then note a class tendency toward unanimity over time. Like the traditionalist, the discovery teacher is not content to allow children to seek, defend, and retain their own ethical positions. Instead, both teachers fall prey to the belief that the role of the teacher is to know the right answer and to be sure these answers or means of ethical resolution are passed on to their students.

The third teacher position is one of compatibility with the Kohlberg approach. This type of teacher is not uncomfortable if the class is evenly or unevenly divided on a moral dilemma. She is fully aware that students are at different stages or in periods of transitions and expects a divergency of opinions on any true dilemma. Knowing that she cannot expect a singular "right answer" from each and every student, this teacher encourages diversity and does not allow intimidation or peer pressure to dissuade children from spontaneous thought. Finally, she does not allow her feelings to influence the positions of her students.

HOW DO WE GET THEM TO LISTEN AND DISCUSS AND NOT TO FIGHT?

The implementation of a program in moral education is predicated on the ability of children to listen to and discuss hypothetical and real moral dilemmas. Obviously, there is a major assumption here that is belied by evidence in the vast majority of American elementary school classrooms. Children, especially young ones in the lower age ranges, simply are not endowed (nor systematically helped via schooling) with listening and discussion skills of the order required in implementing programs of moral guidance. Further, children often are not able to separate discussions of ethical issues from their sum feelings of personal worth. Until these concerns are addressed, programs of moral guidance will be ineffective at best, and at worst, detrimental to the well-being of their students.

There are a number of ways teachers can ensure that listening and discussion skills are adequate and can avoid undue personal hurt. Some teachers require little assistance in this area because of activities they have already incorporated in their daily or weekly schedule. Other teachers, by virtue of the presence of older children or those exposed to previous programs, will also have few difficulties. However, the majority of teachers will require some form of training and appropriate materials.

Listening and discussion skills require time and practice. The acquisition of these abilities also calls for a sensitive teacher who can discern between the parroting of other individuals' words and the attempt to actually grasp the position of another. I have found it especially helpful to introduce groups of teachers to the work of Selman and Byrne (1972, 1974) and Selman and Kohlberg (Guidance Associates 1974) in the area of perspective-taking. By understanding the various stages involved in perspective-taking, teachers are sensitized to both the concept and competency underlying this theory. In turn, this alerts teachers to a key variable associated with stage movement in moral growth.

Another way teachers can impart listening and discussion skills to students is through the use of classroom guidance programs. Such programs as Developing Understanding of Self and Others (Dinkmeyer 1973), Human Development Program (Bessell 1972), Focus on Self-Development (Science Research Associates 1973), A Teaching Program in Human Behavior and Mental Health (Ojemann 1967) are but a few of many attempts to introduce humanistic education programs into elementary classrooms. Whereas the goals of many of these programs differ considerably, all stress listening, communication, and tolerance for others as prime objectives. In conjunction with efforts aimed at moral guidance, they provide highly useful, complementary activities.

EVALUATING AND USING MATERIALS EFFECTIVELY

A combination of humanistic and moral education programs is an excellent starting point for elementary teachers desirous of furthering the moral development of their students. In addition to the skill-building these programs provide, they also give the inexperienced teacher a structured approach. This is especially helpful to the diffident and harassed elementary teacher who otherwise might be overwhelmed by yet another planning activity.

Although a number of excellent humanistic and moral education programs are available, they are in competition with many curricula of questionable caliber. I have found the criteria listed in Table 14.1 of considerable help in evaluating such materials. Few programs will meet all criteria; nonetheless, it is reasonable to assume that the producers of these curricula should be able to speak to all criteria.

If the programs initially utilized by teachers meet the majority of the criteria listed (following in-service efforts), there will be sufficient structure

TABLE 14.1
Criteria in Reviewing Programs of Moral Guidance and Humanistic Education

Ethical	Structural	Evaluation
Does not violate student's right to privacy and confidentiality.	Design, materials, and experiences in the program have intrinsic interest for students.	Has been field-tested on population(s) designed to influence before being released to public.
Does not intrude on rights of parents/family to privacy and confidentiality.	Conceptual and reading level congruous with age or grade level of students exposed to program.	Evaluation component built in or included with program.
Goals of program are compatible and harmonious with stated aims of school and community.	Contains a clear scope and sequence of learning experiences progressively leading to specific and definable objectives.	Lends itself to verification by already existing assessment and/or measurement instruments.
	Has a logical starting point that takes into account existing group dynamics in class or group.	Feedback from students and teachers in some systematic manner an integral part of program for self-correction.
	Includes an early entry point for each student to participate in the program.	
	Can be implemented by teacher/counselor without extensive training and/or contains a well-devised training component.	
	Program is based on established theory in the behavioral sciences.	

Source: Compiled by the author.

to launch the programs. However, this is but a starting point. What is essential is that teachers develop two interrelated abilities that permit them to function independently of curriculum guides and commercial programs.

The first ability teachers need to function autonomously is that of recognizing and constructing dilemma situations from the real-life experiences of their students. These dilemmas might arise from school-related situations or be associated with play groups or family or community matters. Such commonplace incidents as friends allowing some students to cut into lines while excluding others make for excellent discussions. Similarly, school and playgroup games invariably bring about questions of rules and fairness. What is required on the part of the teacher is both the recognition of potential moral dilemma discussions and the ability to construct the dilemma so it is actually perceived by the students as a dilemma.

The second ability required of teachers is really an enhancement of their existing discussion skills. Time and exposure in leading preplanned dilemma discussions should give teachers confidence in leading spontaneous and teacher-planned dilemmas. Even more important, experience in leading moral dilemma discussions should enable teachers "on the spot" to conceptualize scripts to stimulate their students. This ability to conceive of a plan of action (or script) and implement it concurrently is no small pedagogical art and requires practice and patience. For those serious in their endeavors at character development, it will prove an invaluable tool in other teaching activities as well.

WHAT ABOUT PARENTS?

Everyone talks about the need for schools to strengthen the moral fiber of society. However, when a teacher, principal, or school system decides to embark on a deliberate program of moral development, the public clamor quickly turns to a concern about indoctrination. Suddenly, the hue and cry for citizenship education is forgotten and old fears predominate. In point of fact, moral education stands next to sex education as one of the most espoused but also most controversial efforts by the school.

Parents, in particular, may be obstacles to the school implementing programs of moral development. Some of their concerns will be quite rational and valid and need answering by persons directly involved in the program. Other questions posed by parents may seem biased, inaccurate, or irrational. Irrespective of perceived legitimacy, all of these concerns require thoughtful and sensitive responses. One does not need to persuade parents to the position of Kohlberg, Rawls, or any other theorist so much as to convince them that these programs are a worthwhile effort in this direction and will not turn their children away from the values of the home.

Successful efforts to deal with parents regarding programs of moral education seem to have three components. First is communication with the parents before the curricula are actually implemented. Nothing can kill a program quicker than the discovery by the parents of these activities with no previous information. It therefore behooves school people to make these programs known by flyers, newspaper coverage, parent-teacher organizations, or annual open-houses.

A second essential component is the active participation of teachers. It is the parents' confidence in the teacher that is really at the heart of their concern. These parents will wish access to the teacher and an explanation of just what these curricula contain and intend to accomplish. This is why across-the-board efforts to implement programs of moral development are inadvisable. At some point teachers will be called upon to explain and defend their work and only the committed will be up to the task.

The third element in any successful program goes hand in hand with teacher participation. This is allowing the parents to view the actual materials being used in the program. I go even further and actually demonstrate to parents the various materials or invite them into classrooms when discussions are conducted.

Careful attention to these three components will go a long way in avoiding parental uproar. In fact, it will probably create a support group for these efforts. Teachers and administrators should be prepared, however, for a few parents who will remain unconvinced regardless of all the school might do. They will have to be dealt with individually, and the school and its faculty will have to take a position or abandon the program. This is a moral dilemma that each school and faculty must determine for themselves. My own view is that the rights of a few parents can be guaranteed without prejudice to the general good.

HOW DO WE KNOW ANYTHING IS HAPPENING?

Teachers are usually very good judges of the behavior of their students, even though their confidence is shaken from time to time by the results of standardized tests. I have therefore relied very heavily on teacher observation to validate outcomes of moral education programs. For those interested in more objective and psychometric means of assessing moral development and related areas, a number of instruments are available (Carroll 1974; Flavell 1968; Gordon 1968; Johnson and Kalafat 1969; Rest 1974; Selman and Byrne 1972, 1974; Shure and Spivack 1972).

It would seem accurate to predict that teachers will be vocal in desiring tangible evidence that their efforts in moral education programs have resulted in changes in their students' behavior. This is a reasonable expectation in terms of the time and energy required to implement these programs. It is also understandable from the perspective of the self-interest of the teacher. If this has been a high priority of the teacher and if the teacher must justify this priority to parents and colleagues, the teacher needs some concrete proof that change has occurred.

It is a serious mistake to use a single index of change when assessing moral education programs. In particular, looking solely at stage gains dooms most efforts in advance. This is so because there is a limit to stage advancement in elementary-school aged children imposed by cognitive factors until the preconditions demanded of "formal operations" or abstract reasoning have been attained, most children will show slow movement on measures of stage advancement.

Multiple indexes of behavior change seem the best means of avoiding the pitfalls of singular assessment of stage advancement. These indexes might look at such variables as children's self-concept, perspective-taking and role-taking, social awareness, locus of control, and so on. However, from the point of view of the teacher, these variables may still seem rather esoteric and distant.

There are other student behaviors teachers can utilize in validating their investment of time and energy in moral education. These include an increased ability of their students to sustain attention over long periods of time. Related to sustained attention would be improvement in listening as evidenced by the ability to comprehend what has been presented. A correlate to attention and listening is that of communication skills. If these programs have had a positive effect, students should also be better able to communicate to others both the content and meaning of what has been presented. Also, do children give more reasons? "Better" reasons?

Teachers might also take a careful look at the tolerance levels of their students. Have these programs influenced their students by tangible evidence that individual differences are more respected than in the past? Are divergent views on controversial issues accepted and considered with equal consideration? Do students feel free to take unpopular positions?

The creative teacher will discover a number of behaviors that test makers ignore. They should be encouraged to use this evidence for without it the flow of their enthusiasm and confidence will dwindle. In the final analysis, it is within the crucible of the classroom that moral development will have an opportunity to flourish. This environment must therefore at all times be supportive to teachers as well as children.

JUST COMMUNITY AND SCHOOL DEMOCRACY RESEARCH

15
AN ALTERNATIVE HIGH SCHOOL BASED ON KOHLBERG'S JUST COMMUNITY APPROACH TO EDUCATION

Elsa Wasserman

In 1970, in the Cambridge, Massachusetts, school system, there was a serious racial conflict and a student strike in the high school. Many consultants were called in to give the staff the kinds of skills thought necessary to put the high school back together again. Somehow, the school never quite regained the atmosphere that supported the original rules and policies that had kept the school going relatively well until the late 1960s. A mood of student and teacher unrest and dissatisfaction prevailed. Some teachers felt there had been a serious breakdown in the discipline of the students and many students agreed. A larger number of students felt that the teachers were disinterested in them as "persons."

As a result, several alternative high school programs were begun that fostered closer student-teacher relationships and provided a context for student participation in decision making. One of these, the Cluster School, was formed by a group of parents, students, and teachers. It was to be based on Lawrence Kohlberg's concept of a "Just Community School." The school was organized and implemented in ways that aimed at supporting the concept of school democracy, one person—one vote, in a weekly community meeting.

In Chapter 2 of this book, Kohlberg has given a most explicit rationale for school programs that promote direct democracy and a sense of community among staff, students, parents, and administrators. This chapter will provide the reader with a description of the Cluster School in practice: how it began, research about the just community and moral development, the structure of the Cluster School, an assessment of the ability of the school to provide the conditions for moral growth, and some reflections of the first graduates.

STARTING THE SCHOOL

The opportunity to establish this school came in June 1974 when a group of parents, teachers, and students asked permission to open a new alternative school within Cambridge High and Latin School. The Cambridge School Committee approved a summer planning workshop. One resource person was the author, who had been chosen as workshop coordinator. Another resource person was Harvard's Lawrence Kohlberg, who had been invited to help by some of the parents and encouraged to accept the invitation by the superintendent of schools.

By the end of the summer the workshop group had spelled out the enrollment, staffing, curriculum, governance, and space needs of the new school, which they decided to call the "Cluster School," the name "Cluster" derived from a proposed career education plan for a "cluster" organization for the Cambridge Secondary Schools. The group also committed itself to implement Kohlberg's "Just Community" approach to education (this would be the first attempt to do so). The approach integrates social studies and English curricula with a program of moral discussions and participatory democracy.

The students in the summer workshop were most enthusiastic about the possibilities of creating a school where they could have equal say with staff about how the school was to run. Some of the teachers and most of the parents, however, had serious doubts as to whether or not high school students were capable of sharing decision making.

Both the students and the staff volunteered to participate in the program. The students initially were selected from volunteers by random lottery stratified by neighborhood, race, year in school, and sex to reflect the larger high school population. (The heterogeneous mix of backgrounds and ages produced a variety of responses at Stages 2, 3, and 4 of the Kohlberg scale to moral dilemmas that came up in community meetings and classroom discussions. More basic, it resulted in a Cluster School membership demographically and democratically representative of the larger school and community.) The enrollment in the school varied from 50-72 students in grades 9-12. The year the school had 72 students, there was agreement that this number was near the upper limit for effective small group interaction and direct participation in the governance structure.

The Cluster staff were regular Cambridge High School teachers who volunteered to work in the program. They were committed to working for a democratic school and willingly spent many extra hours attending weekly evening staff development meetings, advising students, meeting with parents, and working on retreats and other community-building activities. The school tried to maintain a 10-1 student-staff ratio, including one counselor. Initially, all the staff members were assigned to the school on a part-time basis, retaining half of their original teaching assignments in the other two Cambridge high schools. Subsequently, four staff members became full-time Cluster teachers and the remainder continued their dual responsibilities with the larger high school.

All students participated in the Cluster School core curriculum in English and social studies. Students from ninth to twelfth grade enrolled in the same classes. This core curriculum centered on moral discussions, on role-taking and communication, and on relating the governance structure of the school to that of the wider society. The first year the staff taught courses with which they had some experience and made a conscious effort to use books and materials that lent themselves to moral discussions and the analysis of a variety of organizational structures.

During the summer of 1975, the staff and several students met to plan the curriculum for the second year. The consensus was that the school required a developmental curriculum to both complement and supplement the theoretical framework of the school and to accommodate the wide variety of learning styles. Interestingly, emphasis on reading and writing skills was requested by the students.

The second-year curriculum for the fall was built around the theme of communities and how they are governed. Related readings and trips were planned to prisons, courts, schools, social clubs, monasteries, and so on. The spring semester curriculum was a large project entitled "Law in a Free Society," based on the materials developed by Charles Quigly and the California Bar Association. It incorporated Kohlberg moral dilemmas.

The third-year curriculum took the place of U.S. history and focused on the individual and society, a recurring theme in community meetings. "This year's core was a combination of recent American history and problems in democracy. The focus was on the Quest for Justice in American History in terms of race, sex, and nationality" (Kohlberg and Higgins 1978, p. 5). The Cluster School also offered a small number of elective courses in creative writing, Shakespeare, black history, physical education, and so on, as deemed necessary by staff and students or as offered by student teachers.

Since Cambridge High and Latin School is old and crowded, the Cluster School started out with very poor accomodations in the basement level of the building. The Cluster School then graduated to two offices and four classrooms on the second floor. This change in physical space came slowly, a little improvement each year. Like other Cambridge students, members of the Cluster School took advantage of the wide range of curricular offerings available in a large comprehensive urban high school, including traditional college preparatory courses, business and vocational education, work-study plans, and career internships. Cluster students also participated in the extracurricular activities, including varsity sports, dramatics, band, wilderness programs, and the larger school government. Hence, they were not cut off from the wider school, as students are in so many alternative schools.

The Cluster School community worked to define and maintain the degree of autonomy it needed to function as a just community within the larger high school. There was strong support from the superintendent of schools, the headmaster, and some key administrators. A cooperative relationship was established with other administrators in the school who traditionally handled disciplinary, curriculum, and guidance functions. State laws and basic school rules could not be voted out, but often enforcement and specific definition of these rules were handled by the community democratically. Trust and respect developed as the Cluster School continued to evolve its governance structure and handled difficult discipline problems.

The administrative model developed by the staff was consistent with the just community approach. Each month a new spokesperson was selected to represent the Cluster School in all meetings within the system that required an "administrator." Finally, the rotation was one staff member per semester. No major decisions or commitments were made without first consulting the community. Thus, the conventional administrative pyramid was replaced by a flexible structure that permitted the authentic sharing of authority, power, and responsibility.

THE JUST COMMUNITY SCHOOL AND RESEARCH ON THE CONDITIONS NECESSARY FOR MORAL DEVELOPMENT

Many alternative schools strive to establish a democratic governance, but the literature indicates that few have achieved a vital participatory democracy. We believe that the failure to link democracy to developmental theory is partly responsible for the return to more teacher-dominated decision making in these schools.

Kohlberg's research and his experience with participatory democracy in correctional institutions and kibbutzim suggested reasons why we might succeed where others failed. First, participatory democracy sometimes had failed because it was not perceived as a central educational goal but as one of several important and sometimes conflicting school goals. Democracy as moral education provided that central commitment. Second, democracy in alternative schools often failed because it bored the students. Students preferred to let teachers make decisions about staff, courses, and schedules rather than to attend lengthy, complicated meetings. Kohlberg's research, however, suggested that school democracy should focus on issues of morality and fairness. Issues concerning drug use, theft, disruptive behavior, class cutting, and grading were rarely boring if handled as issues of fairness. Third, democracy sometimes failed because of the extreme difficulty of making policy in a large student and staff meeting. Experience suggested that the community needed to be small enough so that all members could have direct access to participation in community meetings. In preparation for these community meetings, students and staff discussed issues in small groups (upper limit of 15) in order to foster stage change and to prepare proposals for the community meetings that would reflect the best thinking of each small group.

Kohlberg's theory stipulates direct and indirect conditions for moral growth in schools. Direct conditions include the quality of discussion and interaction in classes, committee and community meetings, and other group contexts. Indirect conditions refer to the general moral atmosphere of the school. Moral development takes place because the school provides a number of contexts where the students have the opportunity to express their views, listen to one another, and make group decisions. These contexts include the advising groups and meetings of small groups, the discipline committee, and the community as a whole. In each context, the effort is to stimulate moral growth through the following means:

Exposure to Cognitive Moral Conflict: In all these contexts, students and staff alike discuss real-life moral issues: How should they deal with a student who has broken the rule forbidding the use of drugs in the school, or what should they do about a student who has stolen money from another member of the community? Students and staff members present their views and try to work out a resolution.

Role Taking: Staff and students consider the feelings and points of view of other people involved in an issue. They consistently try to put themselves in the person's position as a way of increasing their own understanding of the problem under discussion.

Consideration of Fairness and Morality: The group discusses issues it confronts in terms of fairness to the individual(s) involved and to the community. The students also talk about basic human rights and their relationship to pragmatic or legalistic bases for decisions.

Exposure to the Next Higher Stage of Moral Reasoning: One of the particular tasks of staff members is to guide discussions so that the students have opportunities to consider higher-stage reasons as the basis for a decision. They encourage students who think at contiguous stages to discuss issues with each other, and they use the Socratic method of questioning to introduce one-stage-higher arguments if those do not emerge spontaneously from the students themselves.

Active Participation in Group Decision Making: The members of the school make and enforce their own rules. The staff makes an effort to stimulate a concern for the fairness of the rules and to develop a sense of responsibility that is essential when students and staff have the power to sanction.

The indirect conditions of moral growth are represented by the school's moral atmosphere or hidden curriculum. The collective expectations, norms, values, and community spirit make up the moral atmosphere. Objective assessment of the moral atmosphere is based on a moral atmosphere interview and an analysis of statements of individuals in the context of community meetings (Power 1978).

THE STRUCTURE OF THE JUST COMMUNITY SCHOOL

The school's organization and procedures were derived from theory and from the collective experiences of the community as its members strove to build and maintain a just school. School structure was built on community meetings, small group sessions, advisor groups, the discipline committee, and the staff-student-consultant meetings. In this participatory democracy the community meeting was the central form of government; it was here that final agreement was reached as to the policies and rules for the school. Its function was to promote the controlled conflict and open exchange of opinions about fairness that were essential to the moral development of the individuals in the community.

We opened our school with no rules of our own but with an agreement to abide by the rules of the larger school. Our students quickly saw that if we did not make our own rules and our own procedures for handling them, we were no better off than we were in the traditional high school. As issues arose (as students created disturbances in classes or were caught with drugs by school officials, and so on) we established rules, consequences, and decision-making procedures in our community meetings. The   long-run result was a social contract established jointly by staff members and students. Each staff member and student has one vote in rule making and in the resolution of conflicts through discussions of fairness.

The meeting of the school as a whole established rules and disciplinary procedures for disruptive behavior, class-cutting, unexcused absence from school, drug use, theft, and grading. In addition, there was extensive discussion and decision making on appeals of disciplinary decisions and on broader policy issues: race relations in the school, student recruitment and enrollment, and the content and design of curriculum.

Central issues and the agenda for each weekly community meeting were carefully thought through in advance by staff and some students in a weekly meeting with the consultants. Issues coming before the community meeting were usually discussed in small groups the day before the meeting.

At the community meeting, a representative from each small group presented the group's position on a particular issue and a general discussion followed that usually involved a comparison of various proposals. At this time, members of the small groups were called upon to defend their positions.

The first community meetings, chaired by staff, were often chaotic. Accordingly, a group of students and one consultant decided to create a democracy class whose purpose was to train students to chair community meetings and to help develop fair and efficient procedures. This group helped to develop a procedure in which a student or a pair of students chaired the meeting. The chair recognized students or staff in the order in which they raised their hand. Still, much disorder arose when the issue was "hot" and everyone wanted to speak at once. The most difficult problem was to determine when to call for votes. A premature call cut off important discussion and led to a poor decision, while lengthy discussions were boring and frustrating to students and staff.

On major substantive motions a straw vote was taken to clarify whether there was agreement or a need for further discussion. Finally, a "real vote" was taken on the motion with all approved amendments. If the proposal passed, the result was a policy or rule for the community.

The small groups (upper limit of 15) were like a small-scale community meeting. They preceded the community meetings so that the issues and argument around a specific problem could be clarified. The small groups allowed for greater personal involvement in moral discussions, more role-taking, and more exposure to higher-stage reasoning. In addition, they led to more widely discussed and carefully thought out decisions in the community meeting. The small-group meetings were essential for the creation of a viable governance structure and for an increased sense of community.

Advisor groups also played a vital role. Each student had a faculty advisor. Teachers, as advisors, assumed some general guidance and counseling functions with supervision from a counselor. Students were taught peer counseling skills. The function of the advisor group was that of a support group where students could discuss problems of a personal or academic nature. It differed from the small group in that personal concerns were emphasized over community concerns. In one advisor group a student spoke of feeling hurt about what she perceived to be unfair and unequal treatment at home. The group helped her clarify her perceptions of the conflict, gave her their ideas on how they perceived the situation, and offered her advice on how she might best present her feelings to her parents.

The discipline committee was formed to help in the enforcement of the school rules for both students and staff. The committee was composed of one student representative from each advising group. These representatives were randomly selected and rotated each term. Participation was required by all students — similar to jury duty. One staff member also served on the committee. The function of the discipline committee was to assess the fairness of the prescribed penalties in individual cases.

Decisions of the discipline committee could be appealed in the community meeting. Many of our more fruitful community meetings dealt with appeals that resulted in reconsideration of rules based on substantive issues of fairness.

The staff, interested students, and the consultants (Kohlberg and an associate) met one evening each week. At these meetings they reviewed the preceeding community meeting, analyzed the current functioning of the school from a theoretical point of view, suggested new ways to meet problems that had arisen, developed the skills of staff members, planned the coming community meeting, and clarified the staff's understanding about the moral issues that came before the community. Since the staff had no opportunity to study Kohlberg's research or to develop skills during the summer when the school was being planned, these staff meetings played an indispensable role in the school. Initially the learning process was experimental. Discussions of the theory were most useful as the staff had concrete examples from their experiences in the school.

Subsequently, all staff members attended Kohlberg's course in Moral Development and Moral Education at Harvard University.

THE CLUSTER SCHOOL IN OPERATION

The theory, structures, and practices discussed in the preceding sections were illuminated by the real-life situations that regularly confronted the community. There was no "how to" manual for the day-to-day operation of the Cluster School.

The early community meetings reflected the difficulties the students and the staff encountered as they tried to develop a successful democratic community. The staff members tended to dominate discussions and to present reasoning that reflected their own concerns. Many students, not used to participating equally with staff, tested the one person-one vote system. The first community meeting ended with a vote (reversed at the next meeting) that everyone could leave before the close of school if they did not like the courses offered. This incident led to the use of the straw vote as part of the decision-making process.

After several months, however, the school had developed a viable democracy. The conditions for moral growth (considerations of fairness, concern for the community, role-taking, and active participation in and a sense of responsibility for group decisions) were directly observable in most community meetings. There was a greater awareness of the concern for the feelings of community members who were diverse ethnically, academically, and in life style.

The just community approach was based upon the premise that people should be involved in the decisions that affect their lives and should be empowered through experiences to be full participants in the school society. The program of the school emphasized the creation of a "constitution" or "social contract" that was shared by everyone in the community. This process involved the students in taking responsibility for developing and enforcing the rules, understanding others' points of view, and developing reciprocity in human relationships.

The aim of the Cluster School was to stimulate moral reasoning and moral action by providing the conditions necessary for development through the six stages defined by Kohlberg.

The major rules were developed during the first six months of the school, but the students and teachers could not have predicted in advance what rules would be needed in order to develop a functioning community. The most important learning for the school at this time centered around the fact that until an event took place, either a violation of the traditional school rules or an event that violated the community spirit we were trying to build, no rules were made. Issues discussed in the abstract, that is, stealing, drug use, or class cutting, did not summon up enough feelings of urgency from the community to create the energy to develop a rule. It was only when the community felt threatened from the outside, as when a student was caught smoking dope by the head-master, or from within by a specific event, such as stealing from a community member, that discussions became focused and concrete.

Initially, making rules was hampered by the unwillingness of the students to commit themselves to an agreement. They did not want to make a rule that might get them in trouble later on. Many of the students were reasoning with Stage 2 concerns that the school survive as a vehicle to serve their own interests. It was only later that some students realized that without agreements about behavior there would be no community.

As rules for behavior were established, the community voted that no rule was to be retroactive. This provision meant that, in practice, first offenders received no punishment. In the total rule-making process, first offenders served the community by bringing an issue to collective attention so that a discussion could be focused on a real situation. The consequence of being the focus for community discussion was considered severe enough!

Generally, students found it easier to make rules than to enforce them. The enforcement of rules meant that students had to be responsible for their own and others' behavior. The fact that some students might know of rule violators who were not brought before the community or discipline committee created an enormous block to voting a discipline for a student who had been apprehended.

One of the most frustrating examples of the difficulty of rule enforcement was the issue of class-cutting. The original rule governing class attendance stated that the penalty for more than ten cuts per semester was expulsion. Although this penalty proved to be too severe and was later modified, the community struggled constantly with the fairness of voting expulsion for a student caught cutting when other students' cuts had gone unreported.

The fact of possible expulsion did serve the function of raising community consciousness and the feelings of collectivity in the community; but the level of frustration was high for students who realized they could not always enforce their own rules.

The fair and consistent enforcement of rules was a necessary component for building and maintaining a sense of community. All decisions of the discipline committee and community meeting could be appealed. Some of the school's most productive meetings were appeals. Each case presented its own unique problems: the family background of the student, his/her previous school performance, the time of year the offense occurred, and the future plans of the student all differed from case to case. As the community gained experience in hearing and voting on appeals, they became more efficient in their use of community meeting time. Longer and more frequent meetings did not insure more just decisions; in fact, quite the opposite may have been true.

ASSESSING THE CONDITIONS FOR MORAL GROWTH

Kohlberg in Chapter 2 in this book elaborates on the types of issues addressed in Cluster community meetings. Race relations in the school, expulsion, admissions, drug use, requirements for being a participating member of the Cluster community, stealing, and other moral issues were discussed on a regular basis.

As stated earlier, Kohlberg stipulates five direct conditions for moral growth to occur. These are considerations of fairness and morality, exposure to cognitive moral conflict, role-taking, active participation in and concern for group decision-making about moral issues, and exposure to the next higher stage of moral reasoning. A systematic method was devised for categorizing and comparing statements made by students and staff in community meetings in terms of these criteria (Power 1977).

For this comparison, seven community meetings were selected: three from year one and four from year two. In both years, admission policies and enforcement issues regarding stealing and class cutting were discussed in community meetings. The nature of the conditions for moral growth changed and developed from the first to the second year in these meetings. Some of the conditions could be assured by the staff, that is, considerations of fairness and morality, exposure to cognitive moral conflict and (exposure) to the next higher stage of moral reasoning. On the other hand, active participation in, and concern for, group decision-making about moral issues and role-taking were the conditions that most depended on the student. Since the students were in the majority and since students are oftentimes the most powerful voice in moral issues that affect them and their peers, it was necessary for students to be actively involved to have the outcome of community meetings reflect a higher-stage morality.

The example that comes immediately to mind is the issue of stealing in the Cluster School. Since stealing was generally accepted at school, the fact that the staff wanted to make a stealing rule when some items were taken from an intern during the first year of the school made little or no impression on Cluster students. The overall feeling on the part of the students was that people were stolen from because it was their fault. After all, if people didn't leave their possessions around, no one could take them. Nine months later, at a meeting involving another stealing incident, a student was able to step back and question this reasoning: "I think there are a lot of crimes in this society and it is really funny ... like the people who are the victims get punished more than the people who do the crime. ..." A Cluster student had been relieved of $9.00 and since neither her class nor the discipline committee had been able to help resolve the theft, the community was discussing a motion that everyone should put in $.15 so that the community member could have her money returned. This time the most persuasive reasoning in the community was given by a student who was voicing Stage 3 concerns:

> If you have friends over to your house and they come in your house and they rip you off and a couple of friends say you got money in there, let's take it, and they take it and you find out and say you can't trust your friends, before long you are not going to want your friends

coming over to your house, so I think if people start ripping each other off in this community, nobody is going to want to be in this community, and sooner or later you are not going to have a community, and everybody is going to end up in Rindge or Latin and they will be messing up their own school and everything.

This statement was greeted by applause and shouts of "Right On!" The student who had stolen the money did admit it to the community at the following meeting and it was arranged for her to make restitution.

In this meeting the presence of the conditions for moral growth were well documented. The issue of whether or not to restitute a student for her stolen money was certainly a consideration of fairness and morality. Cognitive conflict was present in the juxtaposition of the Stage 2 and 3 arguments. In fact, even though the community voted for the restitution, there were still some students struggling with their Stage 2 concerns of why should they pay when it was obviously the victim's fault. It was clear that the Stage 3 argument of community and trust was more appealing since the final vote was almost unanimous.

The crucial statement included a request for the other students to examine their own feelings had they been the victim. The importance of role-taking as a condition for moral growth cannot be overstated. In each instance where there was hostility and anger toward an individual and/or his views, role-taking statements were the key to a new flow of discussion.

The ability to feel and also to communicate another's point of view, whether the individual agrees or disagrees, was by no means common among the students and staff. Creating opportunities for role-taking experiences was a crucial task in the building and maintenance of a just school. (One very powerful way to do this is to give adolescents systematic experience in counseling one another.) The increased presence of role-taking responses was also an indication of improving communication and meeting skills that in a circular way helped to strengthen the other conditions.

The consideration of moral issues in the community meetings showed a gradual shift from preconventional to conventional thinking. Concurrent with this was the growth of community consciousness in the individual thinking of the students and the staff. This heightened consciousness also was evidenced by statements in the public meetings. The community meeting process, then, reflected a development of moral concerns and a higher expression of these concerns through the introduction of student-centered issues that produced significant cognitive conflict. In addition, the community process showed the development of a sense of the school as a moral community. There was increased reference by students to the point of view of the school as a whole and an effort to speak for and represent that community point of view. In sum, these changes can be seen as the progress of the school toward providing the conditions for moral growth.

What can we say, then, about the role of the Cluster School in preparing students to take leadership roles and/or roles of participation in society?

Kohlberg states that the

> primary problem of disadvantaged street youth is that they have no
> sense of power and participation in the wider organized society, in the
> secondary institutions of high school, or work, of government. Their
> world is a the world of Stage 2 instrumental exchange or of Stage 3
> informal loyalty or caring. The Stage 4 world of organized society is
> not a world they can understand or identify with since they and their
> families have no roles of power and participation in that world (Chapter
> 2 of this book).

My view is that the Cluster School and the wider school practices that have been
developed from it do in effect give students the experience they need to be
effective members of the community beyond the school.

Several graduates were asked to reflect on their Cluster experience. Here is
one student's perception of belonging to his own political system:

> First of all, you are inside something and watching how it works, like
> democracy, people relating to each other. It is a lot different when you
> are in America and watching a political system, but you are really not
> seeing it, but once you get in there and start talking and saying I want
> this and I want that, it makes it a lot different and you can understand
> a lot better what power is and how you control it and how you can
> use it.

Another student commented about learning to be responsible:

> All of us at that time came from very traditional grammar schools
> where we were forced to take this course and you had to do this. . . .
> And now we had to vote . . . And the idea that we were the authori-
> tarians, we had to give ourselves authority, so it wasn't as if we really
> looked up to someone to try to do the right thing.

One of the reasons often given for racial problems is that people don't know
each other and they are afraid of those who are different. Here are some observations of Cluster School graduates about the experience of being in a racially,
ethnically diverse school:

> It made me change my way of looking at people, because I didn't like
> half the people in the school anyways, but then toward the end of the
> year, year after year, I understood them more, and it kind of helped me
> out more because now I don't jump at people anymore. I try to under-
> stand them before I say the wrong thing to them.

> Like if you live in a project like I do, you don't relate to someone who
> lives in Brattle Street. And you learn how to do that, you find out that

people are basically the same. . . .

> I wouldn't put it [Cluster School] in a neighborhood where there is one type of people, all middle class or something like that, or all white, but where you get a diversity of people.

And a view of Cluster that helps explain the wider society:

> Whenever we make a rule we never think emotionally that it could be one of us, or one of our good friends. It is always THEM. And always in the Cluster School, THEY did this, and THEY did that, and we have to get rid of THEM and then Cluster School will be great. . . .

LOOKING AHEAD

During the third year of the Cluster School, the superintendent of schools in Cambridge decided to adopt some schoolwide programs based on successful Cluster School practices. The governance structure of the larger high school was the vehicle for building in contexts for students to have a voice in the decision making in the school. We knew that we could not adopt the small community meeting approach in a school with over 3,000 students, but we did know that students would voluntarily attend meetings to discuss issues of fairness. Our first endeavor, then, was to develop a schoolwide procedure for students and staff to have a forum for discussing school rules, staff-student and student-student conflicts, and policies. This effort was well received and the Fairness Committee is now in its third year. It is called a community approach for resolving school grievances.

Another practice we transferred from the Cluster School was the teacher/advisor program with the focus being "the building of community with students and staff." We have found that with careful training teachers who volunteer to be advisors assist the traditional counseling functions in some very important ways. They meet with students on a weekly basis and in one-to-one sessions as requested to do so. In 1979 over 200 students volunteered to have advisors, an indication that students do want and need adult support and guidance. Additionally, teacher/advisors perform another crucial role for many students, one that we didn't think about at the outset — that is, the role of mentor, best described by Daniel Levinson (1978) in his book *The Seasons of a Man's Life*. A mentor is a teacher, advisor, sponsor, counselor, "guru-someone older" who acts in ways that state, "I believe in you." While this is not a study to describe mentoring, I have become convinced that finding a mentor or similar role-model is the critical difference for many students in terms of succeeding in school versus just barely pulling through or not getting by at all. When teachers take on the role of moral educator, they are more likely to assume a mentor role.

The third program we created was a Student Service Center, which is staffed by a paid group of students trained in both peer counseling and advocacy skills. This project is partly funded by a grant from the Massachusetts Committee on Criminal Justice.

These three projects plus a recently activated student government have given the high school a new perspective on dealing with important student issues. We are very aware that teachers have needs, too, and there is time and space for teachers to work cooperatively together and with students to insure the best thinking about the hard issues the school must address if it is to help students grow and develop into complete people.

Now, five years since the start of the Cluster School, the Cambridge Rindge and Latin High School, in my judgment, is a unique secondary school environment, characterized by a respect and caring for persons and a determination to make the governance structure one in which students can experience the roles necessary for full participation in a democracy. The Cluster School has also undergone a profound change. The program now has 40 students and is called K-100 in the course catalog. The course description invites students to learn how to be school and community leaders by participating in a social studies and governance curriculum that not only looks at its own rules, but those of the larger school as well. K-100 students will do internships on both high school governance committees and in the wider Cambridge community. Reports from the staff and students are hopeful that this new focus will not only help K-100 students but will also continue to serve as a model for the high school at large in helping it to resolve issues of fairness.

It is clear to me that the final word cannot be written about the effect of the Cluster School experience on the students who helped to build and maintain that community. We plan a follow-up study of students in several years. The effects the Cluster School has had on the high school are very clear. These include the Fairness Committee, Teacher/Advisor Program, and Student Service Center, all viable programs that increase the likelihood of educating students for a just society.

16
A DEMOCRATIC HIGH SCHOOL: COMING OF AGE

Ralph Mosher

The initial experiences of one alternative high school with school democracy have been described at length in Mosher (1978). The bittersweet character of those beginnings is reflected in the title of the case study: "A Democratic High School: Damn It, Your Feet Are Always in the Water." Presumably one of the points of history is to help us avoid the mistakes of the past. The reader interested in the genesis of the coming of age described in this chapter should review the very real initial difficulties we encountered in establishing and sustaining school democracy. Space limitations restrict me to a precis of some of the potholes we hit and the changes they led to in my thinking.

I as the principal consultant had begun in 1975 clear neither about the meaning of a "just community" or democracy in a school nor how to go about their practical implementation at the School-Within-A-School (SWS), Brookline's alternative program. Nor was anyone else able to tell me. I slowly put together bits and pieces of the necessary understanding, which any cognitive developmentalist could have told me. I spent my time going back and forth from *Robert's Rules of Order* (1973) to Kohlberg's writings on the just community school to Dewey's *Democracy and Education* (1968a) to "town meetings" at SWS in a cram course. The extensive and personally influential synthesis of Dewey's ideas of school democracy (Mosher 1978) was not written until 1977, two years into my association with the school. I could not have done it sooner. Dewey, as much as anyone, would understand. Experience is a master teacher.

In any event, my honest uncertainty in the beginning limited my ability to assist the faculty and students of SWS to become democratic or just. Indeed, it made me feel like the Wizard of Oz at the moment of truth with Dorothy, the Cowardly Lion, the Scarecrow, and the Tin Woodsman. The point is not simply personal or idiosyncratic. Reimer and Power, in the next chapter, describe it as "the unresolved dilemma of communal democratic education. As soon as educators move from teaching about the values of democratic and communal living to trying to realize those values in a social world, they become involved in developing new patterns of action for which there are few available models in either the students' or the educators' experience."

One consequence of such on-the-job training, however, was the crystallization of school democracy as my key concept and objective for SWS. What had begun as a moral education project to parallel Kohlberg's "just community school" in Cambridge but in a different setting — suburban Brookline, with different, that is, white, middle-class students — became progressively the exploration of a different idea: school democracy. Justice was Kohlberg's essential aim, mine was human development. Perhaps we were exploring the same ideas at different stages. I have never professed to be at what Kohlberg then identified as Stage 6. My own odyssey has had to do with understanding and acting at Stage 5. Beyond my understanding of democracy as much more than a procedural form of justice and my correlative stage of moral development was a feeling that the ideology and practices of school democracy were a more comprehensible framework for general education than was the "just school."

I felt so for several reasons. One was that the nature of a Stage 6 just community or school was elusive to me. Nor did reading Kohlberg or Rawls help very much. Further, if we were dealing with stages of moral, social, and political thought, Stages 5 or 4 were understandable to far more educators, parents, and adolescents than was Stage 6. One thing I had learned was "that groups of students and teachers will create qualitatively different democratic schools or just communities depending on the predominant stage of [the students'] moral and ego development" (Mosher 1978, p. 106). Similarly, political and social democracy might find substantial school and public support as an aim in educational practice. Indeed, the American public school has some precedents for experiments in being democratic.

Also, I was uncomfortable in construing school democracy as having its primary effects on the moral reasoning of adolescents and the "moral atmosphere" of the institution. These were the criteria in studies of the Cambridge Cluster School and SWS by Harvard's Center for Moral Education (see Chapter 17). Common sense told me that as we changed school processes as radically and systematically as we were trying to do, there would be consequences at least for young people's political and social, as well as their moral, development. For me the issue was a little like building a new house and then judging it primarily by how the heating or air conditioning system works.

Kohlberg's just community school clearly was intended to be a, or the most, sophisticated form of moral education. My position was that we needed education (of which democratic schools might be the most sophisticated form) to stimulate the all around development of students. School democracy seemed a possible way of organizing education to accomplish *multiple* developmental effects. Its provisions for student participation in school governance, in creating the school's programs, and its sense of community meant a "hidden curriculum" more likely to promote general growth than did traditional education. Or, at least, that seemed a promising possibility.

That SWS, as a school and faculty, had an ideological history and objectives of its own was another political reality. Moral education was by no means its only or highest priority. My supposition is that it will be rare to find schools or teachers willing to make morality or citizenship (or anything other than academics, for that matter) their number-one priority. Newmann has found this to be true of an imaginative high school program in community studies, for example. Certainly there were able faculty members at SWS skeptical of what they characterized as "the creeping moral developmentalism" of the Cambridge Cluster School (see Chapter 15). That rather cutting phrase bespoke, I think, a concern with reductionism (that is, that moral development and moral education were all that really mattered to Kohlberg or me). The language of school democracy did fit more felicitously with SWS's own general goals for its students. They were (Mosher 1978, p. 87): "(1) Taking as much responsibility for their own education as possible; (2) Sharing in the governance of SWS; (3) Contributing to the building of the SWS community." Increasingly, both I and the staff talked that language, out of expediency and as a common meeting ground.

Finally, the rich diversity of the more than 100 individuals who made up SWS, coupled with their adolescent ego centrism, were a salutary antidote to any singular or prescriptive views I might have as to what was most worthy in their lives (morality, for example). Adolescents and their institutions are complex and fluid. They are, in one continuous breath, banal: "You seem like a pretty interesting person"; poignant: "But my mother is divorced and I'm the only person she has. We're really close and if I go away to college . . ."; opportunistic: "Can you write me a letter of reference because you taught at Harvard, didn't you?" Most apparent of all is their rich stream of consciousness, of living in the here and now. And their existence is anything but one dimensional.

On any given day adolescents at SWS can be far more concerned about their after-school job, their dance class, what labor in childbirth is really like, or their cold than they are about morality or their school's governance. Self-government was not a compelling interest to the majority, or a norm in the school, in the first years. When moral issues occur in their individual or school life they deal with them. Typically they do so with intensity and seriousness. Often they sound like good liberals who intend to talk and never to act. Rarely, however, do they duck entirely. The excited use of newly emerged abstract thinking, the play of ideas in discussion is an important part of this. Anyone concerned with promoting complexity of thought will celebrate it, but morality does not preoccupy or happen in the "natural" lives of these adolescents with the pre-processed or total quality of formal classroom moral discussions. That, frankly, is the abstract ritual of the moral educator. Nor does morality begin to span the rich play of their individual or collective lives. Close encounters of this kind with SWS adolescents made it very clear to me that to be concerned only with their understanding and practice of justice *is* reductionistic and dehumanizing — bad psychology and bad education.

Thus it was that I began my third year of collaboration with SWS increasingly aware that we were nurturing a halting process of adolescents' participation in governance and social cooperation in school. It, in turn, was refracted onto several interrelated strands of their growth: that is, political, social, moral, and ego. I was determined to describe this multiple interaction, at least clinically, to any who might listen, including the most singular of my colleagues in moral education. Nor did I confuse this practice of democratic education with the whole loaf. My basic vision was Dewey's. The democratic school in its curriculum, teaching, governance, and social character has, as its central purpose, the all-around development of each student.

PART ONE: COMING OF AGE AS A DEMOCRATIC HIGH SCHOOL

Year Three: 1977-78

The cautious tone of the earlier analysis of the years 1975-77 in the School-Within-A-School will not predominate in the narrative of Year Three. Yet, at the same time, none of what has been said about the real difficulties in establishing and sustaining school democracy in SWS is subject to retraction.

So how do we explain the very substantial progress in both understanding and acting on democratic practices that occurred in SWS during 1977-78? Suggestions that the year was one of coming of age as a democratic school, that in the spring semester the school may have approached an optimal level of democratic functioning may be seen as simply romantic or hyperbolic. Conversely, the claim of progress may be more credible because of candor about the problems of years one and two. In any event, a description of the processes consolidating school democracy is in order first. Two kinds of "evidence" will be used: the impressions of consultants and staff (obviously subject to bias) and preliminary data from research on the political, social, and moral development of SWS students.

Democracy in school commonly is understood to mean student self-government; that students and staff share many decisions about policy, grading, teaching methods, discipline, extracurricular activities, and so on. The basis on which power is dispersed (equally: one person—one vote) or the extent to which the teachers and the school relinquish their authority to students (concerning the curriculum or their provisional authority over subject matter), for example, are moot questions. But a fundamental characteristic of a democratic group is that power and decision making about issues affecting the common life and purposes of the polity are dispersed widely and equitably among the members. That process of self-governance clearly progressed (and dramatically so) in SWS during 1977-78. Attendance at the weekly town meeting had been voted as mandatory at the end of the previous year, after lengthy and anguished debate.

During 1977-78 attendance at town meeting remained high; averaging 50 of the 70 students whose schedules permitted them to attend. Some of the most productive meetings came in the last quarter, when "senior slump" and spring fever ordinarily extract a heavy toll of student commitment.

The seriousness and centrality to the life of the school of the town meeting issues was also apparent. The concerns expressed in prior years that some of the issues being discussed were "Mickey Mouse" (that is, trivial) or that students were simulating debate were rarely heard. Drug and alcohol rules for retreats and due process of student offenders; the rights of students to know the "who" and "why" of visitors to SWS; whether all members of SWS should make restitution of stolen property; the multiple obligations as well as the rights of students who are members of SWS; the criteria and guarantees of due process for students suspended from SWS; the appointment of a new coordinator/counselor and a social studies teacher were demonstrably vital issues to the school. The staff knew it, the students knew it, and a marked level of seriousness pervaded the town meetings. There was no faking of democracy during this year.

Vigor and seriousness also characterized the functioning of at least three committees whose processes were critical to the school. The agenda committee, chosen by lot, was charged with planning the weekly town meetings. A staff member ordinarily sat with the agenda committee as did Mosher. Three of four agenda committees (a new one was selected every academic quarter) grew markedly in their ability to solicit and analyze the issues affecting the community, in parliamentary skill, in chairing town meetings, and in a commitment to the common good.

Two hiring committees, composed of 20 volunteers and on which students outnumbered faculty three to one, worked long and systematically through the spring semester in interviewing prospective candidates for the positions of coordinator/counselor and social studies teacher. In no sense were their nominations stage-managed by the faculty or by the school's administration. The committees (and through them, the community) selected the new faculty members. The superintendent of schools remarked to me, quite independently, "They chose the new coordinator." Interestingly, a suggestion that students have a major role in the future in evaluating teachers followed. The argument was that if students were to hire faculty they should also evaluate (and presumably have the right to fire) them. While not officially voted on as policy, a substantial student role in staff evaluation did evolve in year four. The more general point is that vigorous standing and select committees had the effect of dispersing power and participation more widely among the members of the school.

Another characteristic of a democratic group is that it lives together in a way that promotes the interests and the claims of the greatest number of its members. Where it cannot accomodate the wishes of all or of significant minorities it goes the extra mile in according its "dissidents" due process, a full and fair hearing and certain inalienable rights and respect. It is here, of course, in cooperating on behalf of common purposes and thereby learning to understand that others hold different views than one's own and why they do so, that contrary opinions can have merit, and that other people have a right to those views and their satisfaction, that Dewey said the real educational power of democracy lay. Kohlberg analogously would argue that this is the moral developmental core of social democracy.

In previous years, as described elsewhere, SWS had seemed to be divided into cliques, including an elitist group of higher-stage students who behaved as though they owned the school and a larger group of students who because of individualism, preconventionalism, or simple immaturity were marginal to the school and its efforts to create common purposes. In another sense, this was the group that was always slightly off-stage, noisily milling about, united more by negativism to convention or authority than by any capacity to contribute to the school community.

The school's prior way of dealing with this group of students had been to moralize at them (but since they were rarely present at town meetings such pieties feel on absent ears); to throw them a bone (for example, to invite a musician friend of one of the "dissident" leaders to recite poetry and perform music at town meeting); to excuse them (as "doing their thing"); and, in a sense, to stereotype and exclude them, while concurrently anguishing in town meetings over their nonparticipation. Ultimately it was the somewhat desperate realization that SWS could not build a future, much less sustain a present, against the dead weight of so many nonparticipants that forced adoption in 1976-77 of the policy of mandatory attendance at town meeting.

In 1977-78 these "marginal," "self-centered," or "free-spirited" students joined the school. Several critical happenings gave evidence of this. A first, early in the year, involved apparent incidents of drug usage, pilfering of food, and sex during an SWS overnight retreat. The coordinator confronted the community with the alleged incidents and asked for a policy for subsequent school functions. A policy of no drugs, no alcohol, no "blatant" sex was proposed. One student, apparently a spokesman for many others, said he did not agree with this policy, would not abide by it, and what did the community intend to do about him. An extended debate followed, in which the case for rules and their equitable application was extensively argued pro and con. The upshot was a no drugs, no alcohol, no blatant sex rule, with violators to be reported and brought before an ad hoc committee of two students and one faculty member for adjudication. In short, a norm and due process for violators were established. The rights of members to dissent, not to attend retreats, also were recognized.

No great enthusiasm for the new policy was evident on the part of the students concerned about the norms and good government of the school, much less on the part of the preconventional kids. As one of the leaders of the latter group said to me: "I think the coordinator is full of crap on this sex stuff." But significantly, the dissenting kids spoke their piece to the community and the staff, had their days in town meeting, were listened to, and influenced school policy. What had been a hidden curriculum of dissent was surfaced and respected, if not agreed with, in the community's governance. It is in issues in one sense as trivial and in another as vital as this that normative thought and behavior are formed, that dissent is translated into influence, that people, politically and psychologically, join and construct a group.

Significantly, at the end of the year the same student was a vigorous spokesman for the "revolutionary cadre," which was successful in having town meeting effect a very comprehensive statement of the rights/obligations of members in SWS. The issue was to determine the essential responsibilities of membership in the school (which were decided to include taking and attending two courses per year in SWS, attending town meeting, serving on one major committee or making an analogous contribution to the school, "hanging out" at SWS, and so on). The related matter was to decide on due process for students suspended for failing to live up to those obligations (peer review by a committee of two students chosen by lot plus the coordinator with appeal to Town Meeting).

No claim is made that all of the formerly marginal students moved as vigorously as their spokesman to the making of norms and the qualitative definition of the obligations of membership in the community. (Their apparent growth in contribution to building SWS as a community undoubtedly reached back to the previous year just as it was reflected in, but not caused by, the incidents described.) However, immigrants often are especially resolute in support of the conventional definitions of being a citizen, that is, they are honestly more "patriotic" than Americans. Perhaps this is because they see such norms with a fresh, unjaded eye.

Another facet in the dispersion of power to the students was adroit education for such responsibility by the faculty and particularly the coordinator. Power was not romantically given away, with the students left to sink or swim. Those interested in the promotion of democracy, to paraphrase Disraeli, must educate their masters. The week-by-week consultation with the Agenda Committees; the evolution of the Revolutionary Cadre from a social studies class; Abby Erdmann's sophisticated efforts to make her English classes democratic; the coordinator's skillful throwing down of the Stage 4 authority gauntlet on the matter of suspending chronically absent SWS students ("Until the community instructs me otherwise I intend to suspend these students and put them at the end of the waiting list for admission") — all were illustrative of teaching students to be more responsible and competent democrats. And this seems a central educational task in the slow, often lurching construction of democracy in the understanding of adolescents and the practices of their school.

Year Four: 1978-79

Gaul, according to Caeser, was divided into three parts. Either because of my comparative limitations as an observer, which seems likely, or the greater complexity of a modern adolescent society, the year 1978-79 at the School-Within-A-School had at least four parts. The purpose of this commentary will be to characterize the year in the school and to give the flavor of some of its most interesting public events.

Phase One: A Long Indian Summer

Because of its size, 100 students and five teachers (two of whom divide one full-time position in English), individuals do make a difference to SWS. Their presence and absence is felt. Similarly, the school's character is affected visibly each year by the ebb and flow of seniors leaving and sophomores arriving. Some of the vitality and the unpredictability of the school has directly to do with the fact that it must socialize anew a significant proportion (one-third or more) of its membership each year. Assimilating immigrants, to say nothing of educating them to citizenship, is nowhere a task quickly accomplished. In SWS the processes and obligations of membership are much more complex than in a regular high school. The expectation that students will participate, be responsible for many aspects of their education, and for the building of SWS as a community is central. The progress of individual students and the school as a whole toward these goals is all the more remarkable because of their complexity, the turn-over of students, and the fact that the school engages all students for only part of their time.

There *was* some flavor of Ellis Island for me in the first town meeting of the 1978-79 school year. Two veteran staff members (Mike Frantz, the social studies teacher and a founding father of the school, and Ann DiStefano, an especially vigorous and influential coordinator/counselor) and an outstanding group of seniors were gone. Two new faculty members (including the coordinator, Ellen Kaplovitz) and many new students were present. Perhaps a personal anecdote may be excused. I was introduced as the Danforth consultant. The students responded with a burst of applause. (The fact that subsequently they applauded virtually every visitor during the year in no way dulled my special sense of welcome.) I was moved to say genuinely to the group: "That was one of the nicest things that has happened to me in months." At which one of the students, sitting on a filing cabinet to my right, said instantaneously: "Poor old Ralph!"

The first town meeting was, then, a moving affirmation of my acceptance and membership in the community. It also reminded me that I was beginning my fourth, and perhaps final, year of association as a consultant to the school. For me, SWS wasn't Ellis Island. In fact, I had been in SWS longer than any of its students. In Bob Dylan's words I was aware that "the times, they are a' changing." And I felt real apprehension about the transition in leadership in the school.

The concern was that with the departure of two senior faculty, including a dynamic coordinator, there would be a slump in energy and direction in the school. If anything, the reverse happened. The students and continuing faculty worked even harder to carry the school's governance and policy making. The new coordinator respected the school's democratic traditions. Town meetings in the fall were of an unusually high caliber, commensurate in energy and procedural norms to those in the spring semester of 1978, when the school, in many ways, came of age as a participatory democracy. Indeed, the vigor of the fall was conclusive evidence of the degree to which participation in building the school had been shared and accepted by the students in the previous year. A democratic institution is more stable in a period of transition of formal leadership, because of the norm that its maintenance is everybody's business. Student morale was high, good feelings prevailed; a sense of an intact, secure, and valued community was tangible. Visitors remarked on a palpable *esprit de corps*.

An extract from a *Boston Globe* article (Robb 1978, p. 39) communicates the sense of school at this point. The particular town meeting had to do with establishing rules for an all school overnight "retreat":

SWS kids are at Stage three and four already and they, too, generally advance one stage before they leave the school. That means that the SWS community as a whole should create a Stage-four atmosphere ... and it certainly did the day I attended the school's town meeting. It was amazing. Everyone voted on all issues. And the issues were rules — for the school's weekend retreat coming up in two weeks. And they voted eagerly right down a short list: "no alcohol, no drugs, no cigarettes in shelters" — they really wanted to vote for those rules, and they really wanted to obey them. You could feel their sense that these rules somehow measured and expressed how they wanted to have a good time as a group. The theoretical word for Stages three and four is "conventional," . . .and you could see why. These kids were embracing conventional prohibitions that another group might call sissy or Mickey Mouse. They were choosing to be straight-arrow; they wanted obligations and they wanted to fulfill them.

For want of better imagination this phase in SWS's year will be termed Indian Summer. It was characterized by a feeling of mellowness and ripeness — that SWS was a good place to be. Its momentum was to persist into the late fall.

Phase Two: A Time to Hibernate

Some of the good spirit and optimism of the fall derived from a well-placed sense of security that SWS had a very good thing going, that it had achieved a high level of effect and common purpose in the spring of 1978. That sense may also have contributed to some complacency or conservatism on the part of the students. "Why change a good thing?" is an understandable position.

A 57-year-old housewife from Maine, asked by a reporter why she had travelled all night by bus to participate in an antinuclear power march in Washington, said; "If democracy is to work, you have to work at it." That simple truism has to be learned again and again by any group trying to be democratic. And it is hard, often-frustrating work sustaining a democratic group, particularly its every-day minutiae. The temptation to rest one's oars, to leave it to others, to blame peers for collective failures can be very great. Teenagers are no more immune to such frailties than their parents.

With the first snows, a new season in the school's internal cycle also became apparent. The annual issue of a waiting list for admission to the school resurfaced. The coordinator's projection was that more students would apply to SWS than could be admitted. A flurry of student proposals to deal with the problem was advanced. SWS should be increased to 125 (or more) students; anyone wanting to join should be permitted to do so; SWS should ask for more classroom space, teachers, and an increased budget. The most seriously argued proposal was to reduce SWS to 75 students, all of whom would be held rigorously accountable to the obligations of membership as established by the town meeting in 1978 (that is, to take two classes per year in SWS; mandatory attendance at town meeting; service on any standing committee for which a student is selected by lot; "hanging out" at SWS). Proposals to make attendance at town meeting voluntary and to change the criteria of eligibility for the waiting list also were vigorously debated.

The community labored mightily and brought forth the status quo ante bellum. SWS would remain at 100 students and 4.5 staff; town meeting would continue to be mandatory; the only preference on the waiting list would be "first come, first admitted" and "dire need" students. The debate of these proposals was serious, protracted, and frustrating to the community. It is unclear how important these issues were to the sophomores or juniors or how much the apparent inability to move on them contributed to a subsequent period of student and community "apathy."

The predominant tone and outcome of these debates was conservative. The school was not to grow or change very much. The seniors, whose views prevailed, saw to it that the school's capital was conserved. Stage 4, among other things, is a rule- and institution-maintaining perspective. From another point of view, the sophomores and juniors were socialized into many of the school's norms (for example, equality of access to SWS was reiterated as was the commitment of the community and every member in it to internal self-government). The academic and constitutional inheritance of the school began to pass to new executors, even if the portfolio of investments was little changed. Marvin Berkowitz, an observer, characterized this period as one in which SWS was "on an even keel but with not much forward motion being accomplished." In New England one wonders if people and their institutions are not peculiarly subject to the seasons. In SWS a particularly beneficent fall had yielded to a protracted winter, a time of discontent, of lowered spirits and energy, of hibernation.

Phase Three: "If Winter Comes, Can Spring Be Far Behind?"

With the beginning of the third quarter, a marked resurgence was evident in SWS. A new and particularly energetic agenda committee was selected by lot. Abby Erdmann returned as faculty advisor to that committee. Faculty and student impatience with apathy, with the unfinished business before the house, surfaced. The agenda committee was mandated to energize both town meeting and the school's standing committees (for example, the teacher evaluation and the AWOL committees), to ascertain what needed doing and to get things accomplished. Further, the agenda committee pressed for a reexamination of the purposes of SWS plus renewed commitments to those purposes. "Apathy," "participation," and "community" were code words in the vigorous discussions that followed.

The trigger to what was to be the most interesting and significant town meeting debates of the year was a flagrant case of student irresponsibility. Mark, one of SWS's few genuinely alienated adolescents (those whom the student body as a whole categorize as in "dire need") had been selected by lot to serve on the new agenda committee. He attended one of the weekly planning meetings and then simply failed to show up. The agenda committee brought the issue to town meeting. Two proposals were forthcoming. The first was to have volunteers, only, constitute the committee. This proposal was decisively rejected, only two students voting for it.

The second proposal was that the first time a student is selected to any standing committee, he or she must serve. The only exception would be in the case of a direct academic conflict. Any student refusing is subject to a formal peer review (this was to prove a critical amendment) and/or expulsion from SWS. If a student is selected a second time in any given school year, he or she may refuse (that is, in this circumstance, committee membership is voluntary). The same policy was to apply to any student who failed town meeting (that is, had nonexcused absences from more than one-third of the town meetings for any one quarter). A peer review would then be automatic. Students failing town meeting would receive a second chance in the following quarter. If failure persisted through two consecutive quarters, the student was to be expelled. The first part of the proposal, that reasserting the requirement to serve on standing committees, was approved overwhelmingly. The sanctions, including expulsion for refusal to serve on standing committees or for nonattendance at town meeting, passed by a vote of 35-23, with perhaps ten abstentions.

The arguments for pro and con sanctions this severe were perhaps more interesting than the vote per se. Those arguing for the proposals said that attendance at town meeting and serving on standing committees was *a*, if not *the*, basic commitment to SWS; two hours of obligation per week to the community was a nominal expectation of members; the school could not function without a sense of obligation on the part of the students; frustration at people like Mark who goof off was justified; to neither have nor insist on one standard was as unfair to those people who didn't want to serve on the agenda committee (yet do so out of a sense of obligation) as it was to those who desperately wanted to serve yet could not because their names weren't called.

The arguments against expulsion were that the policy, in effect, would make failure of standing committees and town meeting more important than failure of an academic course (for which expulsion would not ensue), and that SWS was creating a dictatorship of rules. Stated more positively, this view was that people should attend town meetings and standing committees out of a sense of moral responsibility rather than fear of sanctions. If not, how was SWS an alternative to the "downstairs" high school in its discipline? Finally, it was argued that students should be entitled to a second chance. (This due process argument was the basis for an amendment that, as noted, was critical to eventual passage of these proposals.)

One interpretation of these debates was as a further reaffirmation of SWS's social contract as a self-governing community. In a personal community like SWS, public espousal, habit, and unwritten consensus are at least as characteristic and binding of the membership as is formal rule-making. At times, however, good intentions or moral responsibility break down and Stage 4 norms, with a vengeance, become necessary. Indeed, I found myself arguing in support of the due process amendment for offenders. One of the tasks of educators in such a school is to press more complex arguments to which the Stage 4 students may respond. I did not, however, argue the issue of the rights of individuals to refuse to participate on the grounds of individual freedom or civil disobedience. All things in due time. Mark was not Thoreau. Rather, he was smoking dope with his friends outside school and the kids in SWS knew it.

The town meeting discussions that followed on how to build an enhanced sense of community in SWS were some of the most searching I had observed in my four years in the school. I say that about their process, even if the immediate outcome of the discussion did not conform to a pure Deweyan, or my ideal, view of the school as a social community. The issue was what kind of community SWS was to be. To recapitulate, the students had made it decisively clear that they would continue to be self-governing. All members were to attend town meeting and participate, if chosen, on the school's standing committees. Power and decision making in the school were to be shared and individuals and committees were to be held accountable for its exercise. A hard-won norm was reaffirmed with a new group of students and new leadership. A historian might remark these discussions as representing a four-year high-water mark in the school's evolution of self-government.

Second, there has been no doubt in recent years that SWS is an academic community (and tending to become more so). Many good students are attracted to the school because of the reputation of its teachers as lively, stimulating, and accessible. At least until 1978-79, the size of its classes permitted a more informal, personal style of interaction between teacher and student, and in learning itself, to be characteristic. The general point is that teaching and learning are more personal and individualized than is the case in the typical high school. The teachers know the students as individuals and spend much time on assessment and planning with them. In this sense the school has always conformed to another Deweyan criterion of a democratic education. However, the academic intent or curriculum of the school, faculty, and a majority of its students have never been other than very open and acknowledged.

In terms, then, of its curriculum, SWS is not an alternative school. Both the students and their parents show a prototypical suburban concern about admission to the best colleges. So there is a widely shared norm that studies, academics, or "doing well" come first. Commitments to town meeting, standing committees, to the yearbook or newsletter, to the hiring committee, to school retreats a week away, are measured against academic requirements in SWS and the "downstairs" school. Energy and commitments within SWS are hydraulic to the commitments and demands of Brookline High School, jobs, and extracurricular activities. What goes up in SWS must go down elsewhere.

It was against this backdrop that the debate on the extent to which SWS would intensify its efforts to be a social community, where people shared a number of common purposes and activities and in that way came to know and care for one another, was played out. The issue itself generated a great deal of momentum. Proposals came fast and furiously: from a kite-flying festival, to a school fair and car wash, to a week away on retreat in New Hampshire, to an overnight in June. Several of these ideas were quickly adopted.

The most ambitious proposal was that one block of each school day be reserved for community buiding. The requirement for each student to take two SWS courses was, at the same time, to be reduced to one course. The "F block" proposal was introduced by Abby Erdmann:

> One day we would have town meeting. We would have a second component which might be an academic component, that we would all read a book together . . . [F block] would also include a personal group which I think throughout the year has been a theme here, like how can we be supportive to each other . . . having peer groups where you could be with each other. The other thing would be some kind of community service, where you all would get time to do things like a newsletter or the yearbook, where the committees could meet but other things could also happen, things that people do not have time for. . . . The second thing is that we would have no trouble getting credit for this whole component.

This proposal tapped a wellspring of action and reaction. Additional town meetings were called for Thursdays during this period and were well attended. The arguments in favor fundamentally were that this was a structured, organized way for SWS to get together; that students were being asked to sacrifice only two "largely wasted" F blocks to make greater community; that community results when a group of people have common purposes and when they cooperate to realize those purposes. The counterarguments were these: a sense of community can't be imposed or forced on people; SWS gym was to be preempted; students who want "school stuff" (academics) would leave SWS; SWS is a community but not a commune or a family; there would be a reduction of SWS English and math classes; no waivers were provided for.

The initial sentiment and straw votes were strongly in favor of the F block proposal. As the debate progressed over several weeks a cautious reaction set in. Ultimately, the proposal fell short of an unprecedented 75 percent majority vote stipulated by Erdmann. Her purpose in so doing was to require a clear, self-imposed moral commitment to intensified community and to participation in the F block program on the part of all SWS students.

One interpretation is that some students considered the notion of community being advanced as utopian or asking too much. As noted, they lived demanding lives, in SWS, Brookline High School, and in the larger community. They were reluctant to prejudice a good education in a good school for a want some of them understood to be a Stage 3 conception of family. They argued, persuasively, that SWS was an academic community and a committed self-governing polis. It was not a commune and limits had to be drawn. Significantly, however, the F block proposal was to resurface in modified form at the year's end and be passed. Of that, more shortly.

One point about the role of consultants in such democratic schools is pertinent. I hold the Deweyan view that a democratic school will be one in which students have common purposes toward which they cooperate, in the process learning to know and, hopefully, respect one another. I believed the F block proposal would promote social cooperation, cohesion, and a consideration of the common good in SWS. I said so several times in the course of the public debate and in my participation with the agenda committee. Had I spoken more often, lobbied more actively, been an advocate in Kohlberg's way, it is conceivable the F block proposal might have passed. I chose not to do that. To have intervened more actively, I believe, would have confirmed Piaget's rather cynical observation about "the American question, or how do we accelerate development." To pressure a democratic school to move too quickly or blindly in a direction which in Dewey's or my theory would benefit them is premature. Ends do not justify overzealous means. I am reminded of the saying attributed to Thoreau: "If I knew a man was coming to my house with the conscious intention of doing me good, I would flee for my life."

Democratic groups must decide their own destinies within certain broad principles. Consultants, especially those who believe they know the shape of that destiny, need to permit the pooled intelligence and experience of the democratic group to operate and grow, even to make "mistakes." Dewey (1968b, p. 59) said: "[A] faith in human intelligence and in the power of pooled and cooperative experience [is necessary]. It is not belief that those things are complete but that if given a show, they will grow and be able to generate progressively the knowledge and wisdom needed to guide collective action." My experience in SWS's slow but incremental approach to binding its members to governance of the school was helpful to me in understanding the community's analogous approach to defining what kind of social group it was to be. And significantly, the school in late May unanimously passed a proposal establishing peer advisory groups for all students during F4 blocks for 1979-80. As a teacher put it: "The next step is better than the one before; the higher good must be in moving forward."

PART TWO: STAGE 5, EVEN IF YOU CAN GET THERE, ISN'T ENOUGH

The Good News

This section will summarize, in general, what we have learned from a modest effort during the four years, 1975-79, about developing democracy in one alternative school.

1. These high school students can learn to govern themselves. They can establish their own Robert's Rules of Order, make reasoned arguments and proposals, deliberate and legislate school policy on a variety of complex, sensitive issues. These have ranged from student evaluation (that is, grading policy); moral development research at the school; the appointment of new staff members and a school coordinator; the evaluation of faculty; the voting of mandatory town meetings; the rights and obligations of membership in SWS; the criteria and due process for suspending students from SWS, and so on. Nor do the students finesse or avoid difficult issues. Indeed the only derelictions with which I could charge the community after four years as a participant observer are that a state law requiring a minute of silent meditation each day and my pleas for an affirmative action program on behalf of increased black or working class membership have been ignored. The equally important bullet of insisting that membership in SWS entails obligations as well as rights was, as noted, in Part I, firmly bitten in 1978. It continues to produce indigestion, however, as I would expect it to in any adolescent society.

After four years of observing the weekly town meetings and assisting the agenda committees, it would be hard for me to say that these students govern themselves any less responsibly or democratically than do teachers, school committees, town meetings, or university faculties I have known. That may sound cynical, or like damning with faint praise. It is not intended to be so at all.

These students practice self-government with more good humor, forgiveness of their own frailties (as one student, rather generously, said to me: "I'm only 15, you're 45") and lightheartedness than their elders. That may have something to do with the fact that I observe little covetousness or abuse of authority on their part. I think that comes more with the territory of Stage 4 thinking. For whatever reasons, bemusement with personal power and its exercise is not apparent. School democracy lodges authority in the community; Stage 3 adolescents are affected by a relational ethic, that is, the niceness of the person gives her influence. In summary, the progress in SWS's governance procedures has been toward both a greater seriousness and efficiency in conducting the school's business.

The disinterest of many, indeed the majority of, SWS students over the first two years in school democracy experienced as self-government has been described in a prior article (Mosher 1978). Mandatory participation in town meeting, voted by the community in 1977, did have the effect of getting students to attend. What people do they tend to become and even value; norms do affect behavior and vice versa. The fact that a series of real and compelling issues impinged on SWS beginning in 1977-78 undoubtedly helped keep these students in town meeting. Both attendance and participation have remained high since then. Probably 75 percent of the students are consistently enfranchised. The general point is that self-government in SWS has grown progressively stronger, both as an ideology and a practice. I believe this is because the students have participated (in the case of the seniors, over several years), they see the school's governance as open and fair, and they realize that important decisions about the school are made and effected in the process. Without sounding mystical, I also believe democracy "works" because its core ideas and practices contain great wisdom and generativity for the expression and equilibration of human interaction. Powerful ideas, after all, are worth vitalizing. Once rooted, self-government acquires a certain sturdiness and life force of its own.

It is also clear that if the faculty and students do not work at school democracy, it will wither. Participation means giving time and energy to other students and to building the school. It asks for unselfishness at a time in life when there is much self-centeredness; when one's social horizon is typically a circle of close friends. Nor are there guarantees that anyone will applaud. The risk and potential embarassment of standing out from the crowd, by leading, judging, or holding peers accountable is clearly felt. Apathy calls. It really *is* easier to leave matters to George, or the teachers. Further, SWS students live an important part of their life in Brookline High School. There, they are made dependent upon adults: for grades, for college references, for passes. Sarason (1971) has said that the constitution of Brookline and every other high school is written by teachers for teachers, the notion that students can or should participate in governance is alien; norms and policies aren't made to be changed. The point of SWS's experience is that school democracy can operate despite these many impediments, but only if students and faculty work at it. Their feet *are* always in the water.

2. I think it is valid to say that those students who participate in school democracy learn important parliamentary skills: chairing meetings, generating agendas and proposals, speaking to the point, taking other students' views into account, and so on, which should generalize to participation in college or community politics. There is evidence that this happens. Eva Travers (1980) of Swarthmore College studied Brookline High School students in 1970 and again in 1979. She was interested in the students' beliefs about their schooling, their government, and how much they participate in politics or social action. Her 190-item questionnaire was administered to 250 juniors (one-half the class of 1970) at Brookline High School; 28 of those students were members of SWS. Her findings imply much about the larger high school, SWS, and the class of 1980. In summary, the SWS students think more critically about school than any other group at Brookline High. They have a high degree of intrinsic motivation to learn; they do not accept as a given that school prepares them well for their future; they recognize inequality of educational opportunity around them; they seek more influence in decision making about their curriculum, disciplinary rules, grading, and so on. In all of these attitudes toward school they are significantly different from the average student at Brookline High.

Second, SWS students are moderately more critical of government and the political system than are other students at Brookline High. Comparatively speaking, they are already thinking citizens. Third, and perhaps most importantly, SWS students participate to a degree unusual for Brookline High School students in political and social action in the community. At the political level that tends to translate to support for local candidates for city government, for example, campaigning, wearing a button, going to political meetings. The past governor of Massachusetts, a resident of Brookline and a graduate of Brookline High School, received similar active support at the state level. But there is no general political action at the state or federal level.

The forms of social action by SWS students vary: from environmental issues such as save the whales to antinuclear and antidraft protests, to Zionism. Incredibly enough, most of the political and social participation in the whole high school (circa 2,300 students) comes from SWS (100 students). Membership in SWS is much more likely to predict participation than are the student's academic track or socioeconomic status. In 1970 those factors, in order, predicted a students' degree of participation. On the other hand, there is no evidence that SWS students are affecting others (for example, high-ability-track students) to go and do likewise. Nor are the 1979 students as consistent in what they believe and act on as was "the new left" of a decade ago. In this sense, they are less ideological. However, the fact that SWS students think more critically about their education, want a voice and a vote in deciding its forms, are more concerned about local government and politics, and participate far more actively in the larger society is no small validation of the school's impact on the students' civic and social education.

3. Further, there is preliminary evidence that children and adolescents who participate in democratic (that is, self-governing) classrooms or alternative schools show significant gains in their measured moral reasoning (see Table 16.1). Such gains range from a one-sixth to a one-third stage increase in moral reasoning per year, which parallels or exceeds the amount of gain achieved in most moral education courses within the existing curriculum. Much more comprehensive longitudinal data now being analyzed on students at SWS, the Cluster School in Cambridge, and the Civic Education classes in Pittsburgh will clarify these highly preliminary, but promising, data as to the effects of a more democratic or just environment on moral reasoning (see Chapters 5 and 20). The data will be available for groups of adolescents very different in social class, race, and section of the country. An extension of development and research in Brookline into the effects of democratic classrooms on younger children similarly will help to clarify Rundle's pioneering study with fifth-grade students (see Chapters 16 and 21).

One thing that has become clear to me is that the sustained experience of school democracy affects several aspects of adolescents' development. It has already been suggested that they learn political skills and increased consideration of the rights of others (that is, morality). Their ability to put themselves in another's shoes and to cooperate for common purposes probably is enhanced. Selman (1977, p. 3) following Mead has suggested that this understanding of how our social perspective relates to that of other people is "the core of human intelligence." Finally, I suspect a sense of individual efficacy or competence, that a person can say and do things to make a difference, can be enhanced. For example, many students selected for the agenda committee are shy and anxious about chairing town meetings. Nor is it surprising that they vary in their competence in the complex role of the chair. But four of five of them do grow in that role. Their enhanced self-esteem and sense of competence as a result is very tangible. Longitudinal data on ego development of SWS students now being analyzed will provide a broader answer. The general point is that participation in school democracy is refracted onto several interrelated strands of human development: moral, social, ego, political. Our present research on that effect, which essentially has been to measure gains in moral reasoning, is far too narrow.

4. The issue of whether development in the students' thinking about right and wrong, their education, themselves, or politics has consequences for their behavior, in school or out of it, is obviously important. The Travers (1980) data say that participating in governing SWS, deciding the nature of their education there, and building it as a small society goes with far more political and social action in the larger community than is true for any other students at Brookline High School. Such participation at both levels of their society (Newmann calls them "micro" and "macro") in time may further stimulate the students' moral and social thought. "Them that has, gits."

Masterson's data (Chapter 10) indicate that a student's stages of moral and ego development are related to how he will behave toward classmates and

TABLE 16.1
SWS – One-Year Change Data, 1977-78
  (n = 10)

		1977		1978			
Grade	Year in SWS	Stage Score	MMS	Stage Score	MMS	Change	MMS
10	1st (new)	3(2)	280	3(4)	325	+ 1/2	+ 45
10	1st	3	300	3(4)	345	+ 1/3	+ 45
11	1st	3	300	4(3)	367	+ 2/3	+ 67
11	2nd	3(2)	262	3(4)	336	+ 1/2	+ 74
11	1st (new)	4(3)	379	3(4)	333	− 1/3	− 46
11	2nd	4(3)	350	4(3)	369	0	+ 19
11	1st	3	300	4(3)	371	+ 2/3	+ 71
11	2nd	3	300	3(4)	320	+ 1/3	+ 20
11	1st (new)	3(4)	323	4	383	+ 1/2	+ 55
11	2nd	4	413	4	381	0	− 32
			x = 321		x = 353	+ 1/3 stage	+ 32 MMS

Stage	3(2)	3	3(4)	4(3)	4
3(2)					
3					
3(4)					
4(3)					
4					

Notes: All of the seven students beginning with predominance of Stage 3 moral reasoning Stages 3(2), 3, 3(4) moved toward Stage 4 reasoning, gaining between 1/3 to 2/3 of stage.

The students beginning with predominance of Stage 4 moral reasoning did not show any positive change over the year's time, suggesting that Stage 4 may be a ceiling for development in SWS.

Source: Compiled by the author.

teachers and who will influence whom in classrooms. Reimer and Clark (Chapter 17) report that norms against stealing and cutting classes progressively worked at the Cluster School. Norms for racial and social integration and against drug usage declined, however, in their effect on students' behavior. This paralleled an average increase of one-fifth of a moral stage per year among the Cluster students.

Of this very complex relationship of growth in moral thinking and behavior there is clinical evidence from SWS too. I have described how a no drugs, no alcohol, no blatant sex rule was adopted following the SWS fall retreat in 1977. (This was done in response to marijuana smoking, sex, and alleged petty thievery of food from another group at the same camp. The latter incident had led to SWS being blacklisted by the director of the retreat center.) In year four, 1978-79, the same rule was adopted for all SWS functions, with more group support than had ever been voiced previously. A Boston *Globe* reporter's description of the seriousness of that particular town meeting has been quoted previously. Even more impressive to me was the fact that absolutely *no* violations of those rules occurred during a 20-hour retreat. Some 90 of the 100 students in the school attended the overnight. Having been present myself until 2 A.M., I can vouch for the fact that a community-developed Stage 3-4 norm had clear situational consequences for the social behavior of 100 adolescents.

What is implied in the school democracy projects is that altered student behavior is associated with greater intellectual maturity. Common sense would suggest this should be so. Candee (1978) argues that higher stages of development permit greater participation. Obviously an enormous amount of research remains to be done to identify, describe, and validate these tentative interactions of school democracy and adolescent growth.

5. Let me conclude the good news with some personal reflections on the SWS adolescents I have known over the past five years. I do not confuse 500 kids, mostly white and middle class, in Brookline, Massachusetts, with the world of American adolescence. I am the father of adolescent children. I even have had the tenacity to edit a major text on adolescence. I am not romantic about teenagers, but I strongly believe the world is in good hands with these kids. Their minds are sharp, they study hard, they think critically about their education and society, they pursue a rich range of avocations, given half a chance they try to be responsible, their instincts are decent. Drug abuse isn't in, ivy is. So what is the problem? Haven't they created a school that does something constructive about character, caring, and self as well as tending to academics?

Adult analysis and prescriptions for the young abound. Kohlberg and many others see these students as disaffected and privatistic. Travers' (1980) data say that SWS kids are not but that Brookline High School students, in general, are. Another view is that self-centeredness is a trademark of adolescence. Often it is exasperating to parents or teachers. A period of moody preoccupation comes with the territory. To begin to sort out the many possibilities of one's future and to become one's self is still, I think, the central task of American adolescents. It is one that both exhilarates and causes them to break out in a cold sweat. But that self cannot mature without a society and participation in it is what Dewey, Kohlberg, Newmann, and others caution against. Whether that society oppresses or enhances human development is of the essence.

Others write about poor black and white adolescents as the new barbarians, prone to violence, racism, sexism. Such adolescents attend Brookline High School. The recent stabbing death of an Iranian college student by a teenage gang convulsed the community. Friere (1970) may have the most to say about how their fuller humanity is oppressed. My concern for the SWS adolescents is with a far more benign channeling. Admission to Harvard College is the ultimate ideal and achievement held up to them by the home and school. It is not so much that they sell their souls to Ivy League admissions officers, aided and abetted in this by their counselors and parents. It is the Good Housekeeping seal of approval on what kind of individual they should be: competitive and achieving good grades; the right college, the right job-vocationalism; the right friends/spouse-social exclusiveness, into which they are so unrelentingly socialized. Thus I am particularly glad of Travers' finding that SWS students think critically about their schooling and want to participate in formulating its conditions.

Add to these aspirations good citizen of sound moral character. Kohlberg says in Chapter 2: "Our Cluster [School] approach . . . comes close to the indoctrinative in its use of teacher advocacy. Its goal is . . . a solid attainment of the fourth-stage commitment of being a good member of a community or a good citizen." Reimer and Clark (Chapter 17) state: "The move to [democratic] alternative schools is motivated by a desire simultaneously to stimulate individuals to think and act more justly and to create institutions that run more justly." So psychologists (and here I am included) raise their voices with those of parents and teachers in the advocacy of conventional virtues. Does our ideology of what ought to be oppress what is or might be? Do we risk repeating what Erikson (1959, p. 91) cautioned against a generation ago? "Youth after youth, bewildered by some assumed role, a role forced on him by the inexorable standardization of American adolescence, runs away in one form or another: leaving schools and jobs, staying out all night, or withdrawing into bizarre and inaccessible moods."

Purpel (1979, pp. 30-31), in a review of my recent book on adolescence, said:

> One general question has to do with the distinction between socialization and growth, and to what degree . . . this book blurs the distinction. Certainly, there is a tone of preservationism in this book — indeed, one can say that the curriculum is directed at finding ways of preserving many institutions currently under attack — democracy, the schools, the curriculum, and at least by inference, capitalism. I keep having the fear that we confuse maturity with the acceptance of the status quo and confuse growth with progress. We need to seriously examine the ideological goals and consequences of the developmental metaphor, particularly on whether or not the so-called inevitable momentum

towards "maturity" turns out to be a useful construct for the forces of stability and order. Conversely, what is the personal and social meaning of resistance to growth? What about the losses that seem to be part of the trade-off in the rush to "maturity" — e.g. the loss of idealism, optimism, creativity and spontaneity?

Maxine Greene (1978, p. 6) has written:

> It seems evident to me that an assumption of a human essence and a linking of that essence to an arbitrary notion of perfection subsumes all human beings under an abstraction. Moreover, it fixes and freezes the ends of human life. I prefer to acknowledge that human nature cannot be defined. It is protean and cannot be captured by any category.

A developmentalist begs to differ. Human nature does not easily change its form or principles. If there are any facts/"truths" to developmental psychology, one is that a person cannot become autonomous without first being conventional. Adolescence typically is a period of passage into convention rather than out of it. It is a time when youths join the human race. Cliques, friends, gangs, teams are the small societies adolescents can understand and form. Greene would have them know "that the extremes of wealth and poverty that seem so 'natural,' the school bureaucracies, the work patterns, the rush hours, the movie lines all constitute a constructed social reality." The developmentalist argues that they recognize this by first constructing and experiencing smaller everyday societies. The transcendence of everydayness, the emancipation from convention for which she argues is a later developmental epoch. Perhaps its threshold is young adult experience, responsibility — and sociomoral choice. Nonetheless, I welcome the radical critique that the developmentalists' commitment to the full range and variability of human potential is rhetorical until we devote equal effort to an education for postconventional thought and action.

My basic point in this section is that I believe SWS students *are* relatively mature compared to most adolescents. While still conventional, they are on their way to personal and moral autonomy. They think for themselves, want to formulate the conditions of their schooling, and, to some degree, the larger society. Permitted to participate rationally, they do. My experience, however, is that they are not ready to understand one another with the skill of a Carl Rogers, create schools just enough to satisfy Kohlberg, or democratic enough to satisfy me nor to transcend their everydayness. But we can trust the next generation of these ideals to them. The entire chapter has been an argument that we assure adolescents progressive opportunities and freedom to do so.

The educational issue is how best to support them. I think it is crucial that we not indenture or indoctrinate adolescents in either our dreams or our science. Their task is an authentic next generation. Peters (1973, p. 100) strikes me as being very wise in his view as to how adults should try to assist:

surely in any way that helps them to learn rules which does not stunt their capacity to develop a more autonomous attitude to them. When children are at or near the autonomous stage obviously discussion, persuasion, learning "for themselves" in practical situations with adults and peers, taking part in group activities ... all help to stimulate development, to encourage seeing the other person's point of view, and so on.

I will echo Peters' remark even more strongly. To pressure adolescents by any authority other than reason or example to adopt "wise" definitions of how they should be good citizens of good character, good democrats, good humanists respects neither their integrity, their right freely to decide who they will be, nor their developing competence to do so. Ends do not justify overzealous, judgmental means. I believe the latter can produce only caricatures of justice, community, or development. Reimer and Power in Chapter 17 argue that to build community requires a process of inquiry leading to new patterns of group action. Let me mention one other equally vital ingredient of an education for development. It is agape or compassion. If we, as adults, are not compassionate when kids fall short, if we do not understand that people will make mistakes, then we deceive ourselves and our personal example consumes our theory.

Epilogue

I have two points to make in conclusion. The first has to do with generating knowledge. I don't know whether the ultimate promise of school democracy (however defined) outweighs its problems. In the fifth year of our research, I am persuaded that school democracy, where it can be established, is a powerful participatory social and learning process for both children and adolescents. It may prove to stimulate growth in our children commensurate with the effort it entails. It may prove to be yet another splendid fable brought low, but significant development in either individuals or institutions is not accomplished easily; and I know that we need much more educational research before the answers become clear. I am unaware of any way to generate that knowledge except by more hard thinking and hard practice. If such findings come first from unrealistically funded and supported experimental studies that may have to be so. Should cancer research stop because it is enormously costly and of uncertain outcome? Should it surprise anyone when a particular experiment in school democracy fails? The importance of research and development on democracy and its implications for education is incontrovertible. Our glass is sufficiently "half-full," in contrast to "half-empty," to warrant vigorous continuing study.

The last point is, for me, the most important of all. A democratic education is one whose aim is the full development of every individual's potential. Its psychology and its education must lead to whole people. It is unfortunate that that term has become clichéd. Rationality, character, ego, social contribution, the aesthetic, a sound body, emotion, work, and soul are integral parts of human being and potential: a ninefold helix that is everyone's birthright. For a variety of reasons including a sufficiency or insufficiency of psychological theory about one or another of these interrelated strands of development, a division of labor or the inability to keep a multivariable model of human growth in mind, we may choose to practice a reductionism in either our psychological research or our educational development. I can see no moral justification for limiting our conception of, or educational provision for, human and social potential. We need to persist in the effort to create the educational, social, and governance conditions within and without our schools to support the full development of every person. Institutionally, that requires social democracy. Nor can we deny equal access to such an education, once it is practicable. That is the ultimate meaning of a democratic education.

17
EDUCATING FOR DEMOCRATIC COMMUNITY: SOME UNRESOLVED DILEMMAS

Joseph Reimer
Clark Power

As developmental moral education moves from classrooms to alternative democratic schools (Kohlberg Chapter 2; Mosher Chapter 16; Wasserman, Chapter 15), the task of moral educators grows more complex. Having observed for the past three years the operations of the Cluster School in Cambridge and the School-Within-A-School in Brookline as part of a study on democratic schooling sponsored by the Ford Foundation, we can echo Mosher's (1978, p. 69) sentiments that "translating powerful political, educational and psychological theory about development into human or institutional behavior is hard, often frustrating work." On the basis of observational and interview data we have collected, we will explore in this chapter some of the rewards and difficulties of running these democratic schools. In particular we will focus on some of the unresolved dilemmas involved in building democratic communities.

THE MOVE TO DEMOCRATIC SCHOOLS

Why did developmental moral education move in the direction of alternative democratic schools? Rereading Kohlberg's (1971, p. 82) earlier works on moral education leads to one outstanding rationale:

> Moral discussion classes are limited, not because they do not focus on moral behavior, but because they have only a limited relation to the "real life" of the school and the child.... Education for justice requires making schools more just and encouraging students to take an

active role in making the school more just.... Ultimately ... a complete approach to moral education means full student participation in a school in which justice is a living matter.

While classroom programs may be powerful stimulants of individual development, they leave the structure of the school experience essentially unchanged. The focus remains single classes. Kohlberg's concern has been to affect development not only on an individual but also on a social and institutional level. The move to alternative schools is motivated by a desire to simultaneously stimulate individuals to think and act more justly and to create institutions that run more justly. This goal is in keeping with John Dewey's (1968, p. 69) statement that "the course of education is one of development, focussing indeed in the growth of students, but to be conceived ... as part of the larger development of society."

From the perspective of moral development theory, the move represents a slight shift in focus. While classroom programs in moral education rely primarily on the principles of stimulating development through the creation of cognitive conflict and the promotion of social role-taking (Kohlberg and Turiel 1971), alternative school programs rely primarily on the principle of matching individuals' reasoning and action to the structure of a particular social world.

A theory of "match" in morality should account for the effects of inputs of moral judgment and moral action at particular stages. In its broadest sense, the match problem is the problem of the fit of the individual's ideology to his world. Stage 2 "fits" a slum or jail world, Stage 4 fits the traditional army world, Stage 5 fits the academic and bureaucratic worlds. In this regard, the changes of "world" characterizing adult socialization may require the same types of theoretical analyses as those of childhood (Kohlberg 1969, p. 404).

Kohlberg is not implying that every participant in a given social world reasons at the same stage of development but, following Piaget (1967), that cognitive operations develop to adapt an individual to his or her environment. While individuals in prisons, for example, may have the capacity to reason at higher stages, the prison environment calls for the regular usage of lower-stage reasoning that "fits" that world (Scharf 1973). Conversely, individuals reasoning at preconventional levels may enter a social world that calls for conventional thinking. If that conventional world can successfully draw individuals into its social operations, it may, as Reimer (1977) showed about a kibbutz school in Israel, call forth the construction of higher-stage reasoning to adapt the individuals to that environment. The task of moral educators from this perspective is to create a real-life social world that operates at a high stage of moral functioning. Students participating in that world would be motivated to construct more adequate modes of reasoning and action to "fit" that environment.

Creating a morally appealing "world" for adolescents in schools is indeed a difficult task. If Coleman's findings (1961) about adolescents are still valid, their social focus is primarily on the nonacademic aspects of the school experience. What shapes their values and attitudes is not what goes on in classes, but in the halls, on the playing fields, at parties, and behind the wheels of their automobiles. A "world" needs to encompass and influence these concerns. The move toward alternative schools reflects the recognition that to have an impact on individual adolescents, educators have to help restructure the adolescent society.

THE JUST COMMUNITY APPROACH

Kohlberg believes this alternative "world" should be characterized by "full student participation in a school in which justice is a living matter." It is not to be a utopia set up by adults for adolescents, but a shared democratic process of community building. Democracy is the *sine qua non* of the just society, for democratic process best promotes just relations: equal participation and respect for individual rights. Democratic process alone, however, is insufficient, for a group can democratically arrive at unjust decisions. They can, for example, democratically decide to exclude from membership all individuals of a given ethnic group. While the process is just, the results are unjust. Less dramatically, democratic decision making can simply be amoral if all that is ever discussed are administrative details. Kohlberg's concern is to make justice "a living matter." His design calls for using a just (that is, democratic) procedure to discuss moral issues and arrive at just decisions.

These schools are also to promote communal relations among members. They are to be "just communities." While "community" may simply designate a small society, Power (1979) argues that "community" should properly refer to an ideal of a society whose social relations are primarily regulated by norms of trust, intimacy, participation, and collective responsibility. As translated into the world of adolescents, the stress on community calls for developing more caring and open relations and an attitude of responsibility for the welfare of the group as a whole.

Our observation of the Cluster School and SWS indicate that both the students and the teachers have been much concerned with communal issues. It would probably be accurate to claim that while democracy and justice are attributes of the schools, for the adolescents involved the main benefits have been communal. These schools operate as social worlds — as the anchor of the adolescents' life in the larger school. Here is where the students feel comfortable, and because they feel comfortable, they can perform best socially and academically. Their comfort extends to their relations with their teachers, which because of the democratic atmosphere are characterized by a greater degree of relaxation and openness. However, if community is a great benefit, it is also a great problem. For as we will see, the desire to create a community leads to conflicts that are not easily resolved. Kohlberg has coined the phrase "just community" to reflect a dual concern for the ideals of justice and community; but putting these ideals into practice remains a formidable task.

THE MORAL ATMOSPHERE OF THE DEMOCRATIC SCHOOL

> The unit of effectiveness of education, insofar as it has social value, is not the individual but the group. An individual's moral values are primarily important for society as they contribute to a moral social climate, and not as they induce particular pieces of behavior. (Kohlberg 1971, p. 82).

An individual's social world — in this case, the alternative school — can function as both the means and the end of promoting moral development. As the means, this world involves the individual in social activities and relations that would call for the use of the best of his or her modes of judgment and action. As the end, the "world" would become the object of the individual's action. His moral actions would be directed toward creating a better community.

In our research we have attempted to study whether this dialectical process has gone on in these schools. Taking the school as a means we have asked whether participation in its democratic process has elicited the highest of the students' stages of moral reasoning or stimulated the construction of new stages. Taking the school as an end we have asked whether the members have acted so as to expand its social structure and contribute to its moral climate or atmosphere. In this chapter, we will concentrate on the second question of creating a moral atmosphere.

To illustrate we will take a town meeting at SWS where the subject of discussion was whether to admit more student applicants into the school or limit the membership to the existing number. The meeting took place at the beginning of the school year and a large number of new students had already come in; but there were a few more seeking admission. The students in favor of admitting argued that these applicants were qualified to enter and the current members did not have the right to exclude otherwise worthy applicants from the benefits of the program. Those opposed argued that SWS was already suffering from a lack of intimacy due to its expanded size, and to admit more students would only aggravate the existing problem. After an expanded debate a vote was taken and the majority decided against admitting more.

As researchers we took note that the members were not treating this as a simply procedural or administrative issue but as a moral issue. Of particular interest is the argument for greater intimacy. While the level of moral reasoning underlying this argument is no higher than the level of reasoning underlying the opposing argument, the thrust of this argument is to create a particular atmosphere in the school. Its proponents were implicitly committing themselves to the goal of building a more intimate community within SWS. As the year went on a small number of them would remember this decision and would call the others to task to work toward this goal. They had a vision (however vague) of how SWS should be and acted to make that vision real.

Our research has been concerned with the process by which goals such as this one are formulated, publicly articulated, and adopted by the students of these schools as expectations for members' behavior (Power and Reimer 1978; Power 1979). More specifically, we have noted that issues such as intimacy among group members have an identifiable history or evolution within these schools. One can find or infer a time when the issue was not yet an expressed group concern. When a school is being formed, order is a first priority and the possibility of intimacy seems remote. As order is created, some members may begin to express a concern for establishing friendlier relations or building a sense of community in the school. Their expression could be called a proposal in the sense that they are proposing that greater intimacy would be a worthwhile goal to pursue.

If others agree, the goal may emerge as a shared ideal: "It would be great if we could have a school like that." Slowly more concrete proposals for establishing friendlier relations are heard: "Let's go on a retreat so we can get to know each other better." These are accepted by the group and first steps are taken "to get to know one another better." If these succeed, the group experiences "a high" and expresses feelings of "how wonderful it is to be a close group." But the "high" proves premature and fades with the passage of time. The goal is recalled as "how we once were, but aren't any longer." Some members make a renewed effort to get the goal back on track and make it a more durable expectation within the group. If that effort succeeds, the group is likely to take specific steps to institutionalize the goal as part of its experience: "Let's have small group meetings every Thursday where people can get together just to talk." If the institutionalization continues, the goal becomes established as a "collective norm" in the sense that every member feels that to be part of this school one has to act in this way. If one acts in a contrary way, others are likely to disapprove of those actions.

We have called these steps along the way the "phases of the collective norm." With each step taken or new phase evolved, we can see the school's moral atmosphere coming into being. The members are acting on some shared sense of "what would be best for the community"; they are taking the community as their end and are using the democratic process to bring that idea of community into existence. A "community" and a "moral atmosphere" are only as real as the members make them. They exist in the shared perceptions of the members, but their social reality can be felt in how they guide the members' actions within the group. They appear as qualitative characteristics of group, akin to the group's sense of identity and moral purpose. Our research has attempted to chart their coming into being as characteristics of these two schools (see Table 17.1).

TABLE 17.1
Phases of the Collective Norm

Phase 0:   No collective norm exists or is proposed.

COLLECTIVE NORM PROPOSAL

Phase 1:   Individuals propose collective norms for group acceptance.

COLLECTIVE NORM ACCEPTANCE

Phase 2:   Collective norm is accepted as a group ideal but not agreed to.
           It is not an expectation for behavior.

   a.   some group members accept ideal
   b.   most group members accept ideal

Phase 3:   Collective norm is accepted and agreed to but it is not (yet) an
           expectation for behavior.

   a.   some group members agree to collective norm
   b.   most group members agree to collective norm

COLLECTIVE NORM EXPECTATION

Phase 4:   Collective norm is accepted and expected (naive expectation).

   a.   some group members expect the collective norm to be
        followed
   b.   most group members expect the collective norm to be
        followed

Phase 5:   Collective norm is expected but not followed (disappointed
           expectation).

   a.   some group members are disappointed
   b.   most group members are disappointed

COLLECTIVE NORM ENFORCEMENT

Phase 6:   Collective norm is expected and upheld through expected per-
           suading of deviant to follow norm.

   a.   some group members persuade
   b.   most group members persuade

TABLE 17.1, continued

Phase 7: Collective norm is expected and upheld through expected reporting of deviant to the group.

    a.   some group members report
    b.   most group members report

Source: Compiled by the authors.

Our methodology relies on analyzing data from three sources: the democratic town meetings, interviews with the members on their perceptions of the social life of the schools, and observations we made of social behavior within the schools. Having previously (Power and Reimer 1978) described our methodology at greater length, we will here report on our analysis of community meetings and interviews with students at the Cluster School. We will describe, using our phase system, how the students perceived over a four-year period (1974-75 through 1977-78) the evolution of specific norms within their school.

A word on the relation between "norms" and "moral atmosphere." In our attempt to make concrete what we mean by a school's moral atmosphere, we reason that what gives a group (or a social world) its particular moral characteristics are the specific expectations that the members have of one another for how to behave in the group. We refer to these expectations as "norms" and infer their existence from what members say is expected behavior in the group. Norms, then, are our unit of analysis for describing the group's moral atmosphere. However, norms refer to specific areas of behavior and to specific issues within a group. We do not yet have an algorithm by which we can average or otherwise synthesize our analysis of discrete norms to come up with an overall moral atmosphere of the school. Nevertheless, we believe that when the evolution of a set of norms within the school is presented, one can get an adequate idea of how the moral atmosphere of that school has developed.

Broadly speaking, there are two types of norms whose phase evolution we have traced: norms of order (discipline) and norms of community (attachment). The former deal with the rules of appropriate school behavior, such as not cutting classes, not stealing property, and not using drugs or alcohol. The latter deal with ideal forms of relationship, such as caring for others (intimacy), being trustworthy, participating in the program (commitment), and taking responsibility for the collective's welfare. The evolution of the former allows for the smooth organizational functioning of the school; the evolution of the latter allows for a sense of community to emerge in the school. They both evolve through the democratic process — through discussions of how the school should be run and how the members should act in relation to one another and the group as a whole.

THE EVOLUTION OF NORMS IN THE CLUSTER SCHOOL

Four norms stand out as issues of consistent concern during the first four years of the Cluster School.* They are integration, property, drugs, and attendance. Integration refers to the expectation that students of different ethnic and, particularly, racial backgrounds would mix and be friendly with one another rather than remaining in exclusive cliques. Property refers to the expectation that individuals would respect the property of others and trust others to respect their property. Drugs refers to the expectation that members would not use drugs (that is, marijuana) or alcohol while in school or at school functions. Attendance refers to the expectation that members would not skip classes without legitimate excuse.

It is important to note that when Cluster began, there were no preexisting normative agreements about these issues. Often students joined this democratic school thinking that here they would have greater freedom to miss classes and use drugs. They did not expect that being a member would carry any special expectations about making friends with peers of different backgrounds, and they seemed to expect that stealing would go on here as it did in the rest of the high school. It was only gradually through intensive discussions at community meetings that any normative expectations developed within the group about these issues (Wasserman 1977).

Reviewing the meetings from the first two years of Cluster, we were particularly struck by one in the middle of the second year that dealt with the problem of stealing (Power and Reimer 1978). There previously had been a number of meetings at which stealing was discussed and at which rules against stealing were formulated. However, this was the first time that the group as a whole agreed to take responsibility for the problem. They agreed to either get the person who stole to admit the crime and pay back the stolen money or to themselves restitute the money to the victim. Having assumed the responsibility, they carried it out effectively and the person who stole was reported and reprimanded. More importantly, we noted that thereafter there were few incidents of stealing, and when some did occur in the fourth year, the community continued to assume responsibility and to deal with the problem as a group issue. We thought this was an impressive record (given the initial frequency of thefts) and inferred that a strong norm of property had developed in the school.

Similar developments occurred around the issue of attending classes. There were frequent discussions during the first two years about excess cutting, and rules against it were passed and some students were publicly warned against their flagrant violation of the rule. However, there was little serious effort on the part of the group to stop cutting behavior. During the third year, a new attitude evolved. Students initiated discussions about how they were not learning enough in classes and wanted to improve the quality of learning in school. In that context, they got serious about a "no-cut rule." Reports from the students

---

*The data for this section and the next are taken from Power (1979).

indicated that the collective effort to improve learning resulted in a marked reduction of the number of people cutting classes.

Integration arose as a communal issue during the second year when an opportunity arose to admit more students to Cluster. The minority of black students requested that the vacancies be filled with other blacks so that they could feel more comfortable in the community. After some intense debate, the community decided to act to more fully integrate the school. During the third year's discussions about improving the quality of learning, the question of students' choosing classes by race was discussed. Members recognized the problem, and some voluntarily chose to move to racially integrated classes. Discussion continued during the fourth year about the tendency of students to remain in segregated subgroups between classes and during free time, but these discussions did not lead to positive actions being taken.

Given these observations we hypothesized that the data from the annual interviews with the students about their perceptions of school life would corroborate our sense that strong norms about property and attendance had developed in Cluster. We were less certain about a norm of integration for the meetings devoted to discussing this issue yielded less clear results. We suspected that the norms of drugs would be the weakest.

The results of our analysis of student interviews can be seen in Table 17.2. As anticipated, the phase of "property" rose dramatically and significantly between the first and second year and remained stable thereafter. Similarly, the phase of "attendance" rose dramatically and significantly between the second and third year and remained stable thereafter. The phase of "integration" also rose slightly but not significantly between the third and fourth year, but remained lower than the first two norms. The phase of "drugs," however, declined from the second through the third and fourth years.

The results leave us with a mixed picture of Cluster's moral atmosphere. On two issues the school developed a strong norm for behavior, but on two other central issues no such strong sense of expectation developed. This can be seen even more clearly in Table 17.3 when we compare what students in their interviews reported as the actual behavior they perceived in relation to the norms of attendance and drugs. While there is a significant decrease in the percentage of students reported to have cut classes during the third and fourth years, there is a parallel increase during those years in the percentage of students reported to have been using drugs in school. Thus the same students are simultaneously increasing their adherence to one norm while decreasing their adherence to the second norm. These results call for further explanation that we think can illuminate some of the complexities involved in the running of these democratic schools.

THE DRUG ISSUE

There is probably no other issue that divided the adolescent society of the 1970s from its teachers as much as the use of drugs, and particularly the

TABLE 17.2
The Modal Phase Scores

Collective Norms	Year	Modal Phase Score
Integration	I	—
	II	2 (4)
	III	2 (4)
	IV	4 (2)
Property	I	0
	II	4
	III	—
	IV	4
Drugs	I	3 (4)
	II	4 (0,3,5)
	III	3 (2)
	IV	0 (1)
Attendance	I	3
	II	3 (2)
	III	4 (6,7)
	IV	4 (7)

Test of Differences between Phase Distributions of Perceived Phase

Collective Norm	Years Contrasted	n_1/n_2	Maximum Difference (percent)
Integration	II - III	6/10	3.3
	III - IV	10/13	26.0
	II - IV	6/13	20.0
Property	I - II	5/8	100.0[b]
	II - IV	8/9	11.0
	I - IV	5/9	88.0[a]
Drugs	I - II	6/4	25.0
	II - III	4/10	40.0
	III - IV	10/11	34.0
	I - II	6/10	34.0
	II - IV	4/11	41.0
	I - IV	6/11	54.0
Attendance	I - II	14/16	10.0
	II - III	6/18	100.0[c]
	I - III	14/18	100.0[c]
	III - IV	18/7	30.0
	I - IV	14/7	71.0
	II - IV	6/7	71.0

[a] $p < .05$ [b] $p < .01$ [c] $p < .001$

Source: Compiled by the authors.

312

TABLE 17.3
Relationship of Modal Phases to Reported Norm Violation*

Norm	Year		n	Percent of Students Reporting Violation
Rule following	I	3 (4)	6	67
(drugs)	II	4 (0,3,5)	10	70
	III	3 (2)	21	90
	IV	0 (1)	10	100
Participation	I	3	14	86
(attendance)	II	3 (2)	10	70
	III	4 (6,7)	21	19
	IV	4 (7)	7	29

Note: x^2 test on differences between Years I-II, I-IV, and II-III on participation (attendance) norm, all significant $p < .05$; no significant differences between years on rule following (drugs) norm.

Source: Compiled by the authors.

smoking of marijuana. We found the division not only at Cluster, but also at SWS and the Murray Road Alternative School in Newton, Massachusetts, and we suspect it exists in almost all schools. It is not a clear-cut division, for not only are there adolescents in each of these schools who oppose the smoking of marijuana, but there are also teachers whose opposition is not to the use of drugs per se but to their improper use during school. Nevertheless, the battle over "pot" seems a constant feature of contemporary high school life.

Our interest in this issue derives from the way it affects not only questions of order, but also questions of community. For smoking "pot" differs from cutting classes and stealing property in that we found little debate over whether it is right or wrong to cut or steal, but much debate over the pros and cons of using marijuana. Cutting and stealing are part of life in high schools and can sometimes be accepted as inevitable; but no one argues for their virtue or potential contribution to the social relations of the school. However, that is what one hears about pot. Some of its adolescent users argue that it contributes to the school's sense of community because it both allows people to relax and serves as a means to bring together people who would not ordinarily mix. Thus while their teachers and some of their peers argue that drugs cause divisions among smokers and nonsmokers and serve as an escape from social participation, the smokers claim they can best participate in and create a sense of community by a moderate use of drugs.

The battle over pot extended throughout the first four years of Cluster, coming to a head usually at the time of retreats (organized trips away from school used specifically for community building). The first retreat during the first year was preceded by a meeting at which a discussion about drugs led to a deep division of opinion between the marijuana users and nonusers. It was only when the faculty threatened to cancel the retreat that a rule against drugs on the retreat was adopted. However, no sooner did the retreat begin than there were reported violations of the rule. The faculty called a meeting on the spot, but although there followed a good discussion about community, there was little commitment to get tough on drug use.

After a number of drug-related incidents, including a student's being caught smoking by the headmaster of the high school, a working agreement about drugs did evolve. It became clear to almost everyone that the open use of drugs — which after all broke the rules of the state and the larger school — would generally endanger Cluster's existence and particularly put the teachers in the nasty position of having to enforce the law against the students. Thus a rule against drugs in school was adopted and those students who flagrantly violated it were punished. However, many students implicitly interpreted the rule to mean that they were obligated to be discreet about, rather than cease, using drugs. While this implicit understanding helped to avoid open conflict, we can see from Table 17.2 that no strong normative expectations evolved and from Table 17.3 that at least two-thirds of the students interviewed reported that drug use continued.

This working agreement, which became known as the "be cool rule," was not much discussed until the retreat at the end of the third year. At a meeting before the retreat, one teacher challenged the "be cool rule," saying it was only a pragmatic gesture to satisfy legal requirements and was not a true commitment to stop using drugs. Many students acknowledged that but defended their practices in the terms of community-building that we discussed above. With combined faculty and student pressure, everyone promised to be straight. However, it was subsequently reported that while a majority left their marijuana at home, a minority of students brought theirs and smoked with greater discretion.

When it came time at the end of the fourth year to plan the retreat, the faculty grew more adamant about wanting assurances that there would be no use of drugs. Reluctant assurances were given, but the teacher who the previous year had challenged the students stated frankly that he did not believe them and would refuse to attend the retreat.

The retreat took place without that teacher but was a disaster. Students made little attempt to hide their use of drugs and alcohol, and a number, in the words of one, "got totally wasted." The staff called a meeting and the students promised greater discretion. When it became known that two white students had drawn up a list of students who had broken the agreement by using drugs, some of the black students got very angry and confronted the two. A fight ensued, after which there was an unprecedented degree of tension between the white and black students. The staff felt powerless to act. Sensing that there was no community to draw upon, they thought it futile to call another meeting. Although upon returning home many of the students expressed shock and genuine regret for what had happened, and wanted, even desperately, to make amends, the events on the retreat had torn at the school's social fabric. Thereafter it proved increasingly difficult to sustain a strong sense of community in Cluster.

INTEGRATION AND COMMUNITY BUILDING

Neither the issue of drugs nor the fourth-year retreat can be understood in isolation. They point beyond themselves to more fundamental questions: Why were agreements made that were not honored? Why were the staff not able to deal more effectively with the events? How meaningful is it to speak of an evolving community and moral atmosphere if the values they represent can be so suddenly overturned?

These are hard questions to answer, especially since we as observers were caught as off guard by the events of that retreat as were the participants. We knew there was disagreement in the community over drugs and that, as we will see, the drug issue was related to the problem of integrating the school, but we thought that through democratic discussion these disagreements could be worked out. The events on the retreat left us wondering what had gone wrong that we had not forseen. Our attempt to answer this question has led us to revise some of our assumptions about moral atmosphere and to take a second look at Kohlberg's just community approach. We have been helped in doing so by Harvard Professor Chris Argyris who, from the perspective of his theory of action (Argyris and Schon 1974), has called our attention to aspects of educational intervention to which we had not previously given sufficient consideration.

Why were the agreements made about refraining from drug use on the retreat not honored by the students? Drugs, as we observed earlier, represent a different type of problem than do stealing property and cutting classes. The latter are classical issues of discipline: most individuals know they are wrong but are tempted to do them and need to be stopped by either internal or external pressures. At Cluster, through a good deal of discussion, there developed a near consensus among members that these activities could no longer be tolerated, and the group applied pressure against their continued happening. With drugs, however, there was no general agreement that it was wrong to use them and the only pressure the group applied was on those who did not act discreetly. Perhaps most importantly, what made it hard for students to give up drugs was that smoking marijuana played an important prosocial function within Cluster's adolescent community.

Cluster had two salient characteristics which for the purpose of this discussion distinguished it from the other two alternative schools — SWS and Murray Road — in which we did observations. First, Cluster had a more heterogeneous population that included black, white working, and white middle class students. Second, Cluster's staff put more of an emphasis on building a deliberate and inclusive community in the school. SWS and Murray Road had mostly white middle class students, and although they set greater intimacy as a goal, they did not stress the overcoming of subgroup affiliations as strongly as Cluster did. What strikes us as far from coincidental was that it was during the same year that Cluster had the most intensive discussions about the need for social integration that the drug problem finally got out of hand.

Kohlberg (Chapter 2) describes the strategy that the Cluster staff used at a community meeting in December of the fourth year to deal with the problem of a lack of integration in the school.

> In the fourth year . . . the school was more than one-third black. But many of the black kids were still practicing black separatists, over-crowding the classes of one black staff member. In this meeting that teacher confronts the school with the black-white division in the community. While staff join in to urge the need to agree to a norm of integration . . . they do not see themselves as adults indoctrinating black students and whites with their liberal trip. They see themselves as advocates of true community in a racially divided community.

One series of interchange from the community meeting to which Kohlberg refers is significant for our discussion.

> White student: There are two groups . . . if there was a way for all the groups to get together and interact, that would be much better. Some people said that we should have had a retreat by now; we should have. You can't meet these people; they go to different classes, they are a different group.
> Black student: That's true; the only time people get together in a group is on a retreat when we are high.
> Consultant: I don't think that we can say we can't work on it at a community meeting and go off on a retreat and get high. We've got to work it through to some extent here.
> Teacher: I can see why getting high on a retreat makes it a lot easier to relate to some other people in the community. But I am also being pulled the other way in saying we have to learn to confront one another's innermost thoughts and communicate without the help of a drink or a reefer. There ought to be other ways of doing that during the school day.

The students are not resisting the staff's advocated position of the importance of integration. They acknowledge that a problem of two groups exists but are unsure of what to do about it. The one strategy they can forsee is to go on retreat and get high with one another. Reinforcing that perception, one white girl told us in her interview that year about another girl who did not use drugs:

> She doesn't get to know many of the black kids very well because she doesn't smoke "grass" and most of them do. She doesn't go out

and party with them, so they think, "I am not going to get to know her or I can't relate to her."

Rather than dismiss these statements as excuses offered to justify adolescent drug use, we take them as testimony of the social situation in which the students found themselves. They were being urged by the faculty to find ways of building an integrated community; but the black and white students had not grown up in the same neighborhood, come from the same social class, or attended the same elementary schools. They did not have a common mode of interaction, and their personal histories led them to go separate ways and form different groups. The main occasion when they did feel free to mix was in partying when the social barriers could recede, partially through the use of drugs. Retreats were viewed as a type of partying for they allowed for free mixing, partially through the use of drugs.

The staff's response at the community meeting to the students' statements is somewhat ambivalent. They do not deny that drug usage can bring people together on retreat, but suggest "there ought to be ways of doing that during the school day." They acknowledge the students' view that "getting high on a retreat makes it a lot easier to relate to some other people," but advocate a position of having "to learn to confront one another's innermost thoughts . . . without the help of a drink or a reefer." Having advocated their position, though, they do little to advance the discussion beyond the impasse at which it stands. Specifically, they neither concretely spell out what are some alternative ways to build community nor inquire of the students why they cannot envision alternatives to drug use.

What we are suggesting is that the staff's sole reliance on a strategy of advocacy backfired. When it came time several months later to plan for the retreat, little had changed as a result of this earlier discussion. The students apparently took the planning as a sign that all would proceed as usual, including the "be cool rule" about drugs. The staff, however, insisted that this retreat would have to be different and the "be cool rule" would not be in effect. When the students balked, they were accused of being dishonest for not intending to uphold the ban on drugs. That put the students in a double bind. They were supposed to be building community on retreat but were being told they could not do so in the one way they knew how. They were supposed to be honest with the staff but were being blamed for having been honest about the "be cool rule." When adolescents are put in binds like this, they often lose control, act out, and break agreements made. That is indeed what happened on this retreat.

ADVOCACY WITH INQUIRY

Our intention is not to shift blame onto the staff but to analyze why they did not act more effectively in this situation. We began this chapter with the observation that the move to democratic education makes the task of the moral educator more complex. Now we can see why. While these teachers continued to appeal to the students' better judgment — to what they *ought* to do for the sake of the community, that appeal and advocacy only functioned as the application of pressure to the point of explosion. The teachers acted in accordance with the just community approach as outlined by Kohlberg (Chapter 2) but did not get the just results they anticipated.

What we are suggesting is that the events on the retreat revealed a flaw in the design of the just community approach. While not disputing that as members of the community the staff should have been putting forth their views of how the community should act, we believe that by leaving the discussion at that level of normative discourse, they were not engaging in a true dialogue with the students. The democratic process provided the students with the opportunity to express their hesitations over achieving integration, but the staff's preoccupation with advocating "true community" did not leave them sufficiently open to considering the implications of those hesitations for the community's achieving its goal of integration.

By itself advocacy does not lead to an open consideration of how a group can best achieve its espoused goals. Therefore, advocacy needs to be coupled with inquiry. If the just community approach at Cluster called for increasing social integration while decreasing student reliance on drug use, the staff might best have served that goal by initiating a joint inquiry with the students as to why they could envision no alternative ways of advancing integration. A process of inquiry allows a group to discuss why they are having problems achieving their goals and, given those problems, what can be done to solve them. While immediate solutions may not be found, the members can at least become aware of the complexity of the tasks they are undertaking.

What a process of inquiry may have specifically avoided at Cluster was the trap into which the community fell by unreflectively going ahead with the planning of the yearly retreat. The espoused goal of having a retreat was to bring the community closer together. The meeting in December had raised problems about achieving an integrated community that had not been sufficiently addressed or resolved. Had the just community approach included a process of inquiry, the members would have realized early on that unless the retreat were carefully planned so as to be different from past retreats, it would have only led to a repeat of past failures. By not realizing that and allowing the planning to proceed as usual, the staff unwittingly placed themselves in a position where at the last meeting before the retreat the only options left to them were to either try to put the brakes on drug use or to not attend the retreat. Neither option proved effective, for the students had already come to expect the retreat would be run as usual. Unfortunately, the sole reliance on advocacy did not leave the staff with the flexible options they needed to deal with the issues before the problems had reached the point of crisis.

THE UNRESOLVED COMMUNAL DILEMMA

We would not conclude from what has been presented that Cluster did not develop a real sense of community or evolve an identifiable moral atmosphere. Real progress was made in regard not only to the norms of property and attendance but also to the norm of integration. A large majority of white students agreed to admit into the school an increasing proportion of black students, and initially segregated Cluster classes were voluntarily integrated. However, as we have tried to demonstrate, the approach that worked successfully in achieving these goals ran into serious problems in trying to achieve a more extensive form of social integration and community building. These problems can be traced to the limitations in the strategies employed by the just community approach and the failure to see fully enough the complexities of what we will call the unresolved communal dilemma.

Community, especially democratic community, represents a social ideal. Few in our culture have grown up or been educated for living in community. We may have a vision of what the ideal should entail, but when we move to realize the vision in a particular social context, we discover that neither vision nor commitment alone can create community. For there are many existing social patterns that we bring with us to community building that stand in the way of our acting communally. In Cluster the patterns that most clearly stood in the way were the students' tendencies to affiliate by subgroup, to segregate along racial lines, and to use drugs as a means for mixing. Less obvious, but equally significant, were the patterns used by the faculty to convince the students to change their ways. Existing patterns are not easily altered, for their prevalence in the larger culture predisposes us to view them (that is, the ones that are part of our individual behavior patterns) as the natural way of acting in the social world.

This brings us to the unresolved dilemma of democratic communal education. As soon as educators move from teaching about values of democratic and communal living to trying to realize these values in a social world, they become involved in developing new patterns of action for which there are few available models in either the students' or the educators' experience. Thus unlike in most other educational endeavors — including classroom moral education, the task is not to teach what one already knows, but what awaits to be discovered. The dilemma is how can one teach others what one has yet to discover for oneself.

Our own conception of moral atmosphere has not yet done justice to the complexity of this dilemma. We have conceived of the task of democratic education in terms of evolving specific norms or expectations for behavior and have tested for the degree of adherence or commitment in the school to these norms, but our conception assumes that once expectations are developed, people will be able to act on the basis of those commitments. What has been lacking is an appreciation of how people can intend to act but find that they do not have the skill or the ability to do so; that community members can want to overcome social barriers and become more intimate but have no way of inquiring as to what is blocking that and what has to be done to remove these blocks.

The significance of the conception of a moral atmosphere lies in its focusing on the normative dimensions of democratic education. The conception implies the recognition that the move to democratic community needs to begin with and be informed by a normative vision of how people ought to live in society. Kohlberg's vision of a just society accordingly informed the philosophy of the Cluster School. However, there is a parallel need to take into account the dilemma of community: the realization that even though educators may share a vision of how the community ought to develop, they still need to discover how to put that vision into practice. For while a normative vision of a just community can and should lead to statements of advocacy — to statements of how members of the community ought to act, it would be a fallacy to believe that one can derive statements of how people *do* act from statements of how they *ought* to act. These represent separate processes (what Argyris and Schon (1974) refer to as "espoused theories of action" and "theories-in-use"). If they are run together, the results may be a frustrating situation in which the advocates of the vision cannot understand why others are agreeing to statements of what ought to be done but are not acting in accordance with those agreements. What needs to be added as a corrective to our normative model is a model of discovery: how people in groups can learn to act on the goals and expectations that they cognitively and emotionally endorse.

CONCLUSIONS

Democratic education aims to change many of the regular patterns of school experience. As a statement of goals we share the enthusiasm for making schools more democratic, more communal, and more just. As a statement of methodology we wish to stress that there are many small steps along the way to democratizing schools that we have yet to master. More immediately, these are steps we have yet to identify and old patterns of action of which we are unaware that may be undermining our best efforts.

From what we have learned from analyzing this chapter in Cluster's history we have identified some limitations in the strategy of advocating commitment to norms and have suggested that to build community requires a process of inquiry leading to the learning of new patterns of action. We believe that democratic education moves us significantly beyond the scope of other forms of developmental moral education; the task it involves is not only the promoting of development along an identified sequence of stages but also the designing of new programs of action that will be sufficiently complex to allow us and our students to live and grow together in democratic community.

18
DEMOCRACY IN THE ELEMENTARY SCHOOL

Thomas Lickona
Muffy Paradise

THE CASE FOR DEMOCRACY

> Elementary school for me was an environment that stifled develop-
> ment. I can remember many times when I'd be doing fine with a math
> lesson until a new concept was introduced that I didn't understand.
> I know there was no way I could clarify in my own mind what this new
> concept meant. The teacher just kept going, unaware of my frustration.
> The fear of telling her that I was lost kept me sitting quietly at my
> desk, feeling helpless and defeated. I never felt understood or cared
> about in the classroom.

Most of us could tell similar stories: a time when we were afraid of asking
a question; afraid of annoying the teacher; afraid of looking stupid before our
peers; wanting someone to know that we didn't understand, how frustrated we
were, how bad it felt when everybody else seemed to be "getting" what we
couldn't figure out. At such times, in the words of the young woman quoted
above, school stifled our development. It gave us less than we needed to learn
and grow. It put obstacles in the path of our becoming more capable and confident persons.

What do such experiences have to do with democracy in the elementary
school? In our judgment, everything. A democratic school environment, as we
see it, is one that tries to provide the conditions that best support the development of all students. It is an environment where students are actively encouraged
to speak up, to ask questions, to make their voices heard. It is an environment

that attempts in a dozen different ways to foster in children the feeling that they are important and respected, that somebody cares.

Is "democracy in the classroom" to be equated with helping children feel cared about and understood? Don't all good teachers try to do that? In what way does democratic education go beyond that? Does it mean letting students "run" the classroom and decide everything by majority vote? If it doesn't turn all decision making over to students, how does it enable them to participate responsibly in making decisions that affect the life of the classroom or school? Does it mean one thing with older children and something else with younger, less developed children? Does it work? Does it really help children become better people?

To such questions this chapter is addressed. It reports the work we have done over the last two years, along with Ralph Mosher, Joseph Reimer, Margot Strom, and two dozen teachers in our Democracy in the Schools Project in Brookline, Massachusetts. Funded by the Danforth Foundation and jointly carried out by Boston University and the Brookline Teachers' Center, this project set out to explore the question, "What does it mean to do democracy with children?"

Specifically, our task in this chapter is threefold: to clarify the many meanings of democracy in the elementary grades through examples taken directly from classrooms and schools; to let teachers describe in their own voices some of the "problems of democracy" they encounter, some of the questions they wrestle with when they travel down this road; and to point briefly to formal research on the effects of democracy with children.

What Is Democracy?

Before describing the details of democracy in the elementary school, let us quickly map the general terrain. Democracy, broadly considered, can be taken to mean three things: an *ethic* of mutual respect and cooperation among persons; a *faith* in what John Dewey called "the power of pooled and cooperative experience" (1968, p. 59), a faith that people do their best, grow their most when they participate in making and carrying out decisions that affect their lives; and a pervasive *process*, a "way of life" (Dewey 1968), whereby mutual respect and cooperative, participatory decision making are put into practice among people, be they a nation, a community, or a classroom of children.

Why Democracy with Children?

One could acknowledge that children should certainly respect and cooperate with each other but still ask, "Are they ready for participatory decision making?" Why do democracy with children? Why not wait, say, until junior high or high school?

An answer to that question comes unwittingly from a high school principal. He was decrying to a visitor the follies of a neighboring teacher education project that was training teachers to do democracy with first, second, and third graders. This idea of letting a first-grade child make a decision was, to this principal, preposterous. "Hell," he exclaimed, "I've got high school *seniors* who can't make a decision!"

The irony of his statement is obvious. People do not learn how to make decisions if they never make them. If high school seniors cannot make intelligent, rational decisions, it may be because schools never required them to do so, never demanded that they think through problems individually and in groups, consider alternatives, weigh consequences, and choose a best course of action. If, instead, students had to begin doing that as children, and had to do it over and over all the way up through the grades, they would be far more likely to be responsible decision makers by the time they collected their diploma.

To us, there are at least three good reasons for doing democracy with children: children *need* democracy to become all they are capable of being; they are *capable,* even as children, of handling the responsibilities of a democracy that is properly scaled to their world; and they have a *right* to be dealt with democratically, to receive the respect and understanding that was missed for the young woman quoted at the beginning of the chapter, and, in addition, to receive the growth-demanding challenge that real responsibility uniquely provides.

Having made the general case for democracy with children, we turn now to teachers for examples of democracy in action, for the concrete *forms* that democracy can assume. In working with teachers, we find this distinction — between democracy as a broad-gauged ethic, faith, and process, on the one hand, and the particular forms democracy can take in a school setting, on the other — to be an important one. Teachers who begin by thinking that democracy means that "the majority rules" are usually relieved and challenged to learn that there are many ways to create a democratic classroom.

Democracy and Valuing the Child's Point of View

The first and most fundamental step toward creating a classroom democracy is to value the viewpoint of the child. That means two things: finding out what a child's viewpoint is; and attempting to acknowledge or incorporate that point of view in some way.

A teacher of a second-grade class had set up a group reward, contingent upon the class' performance as a whole. A girl in the class objected: "It's not fair. I can work as hard as I can, I can help others, but no matter what *I* do, there might be kids who aren't going to do their work, and I'll lose the reward."

The teacher commented: "I had to stop and think. I had to agree with her. She was right, it really wasn't fair."

The child who protested the group reward clearly thought that the classroom was a place where she could speak her mind, and her teacher's response to her protest gave her additional reason for thinking so. Many children, however, perhaps the majority, are more like the child who suffered in silence during math lesson because she was afraid to tell her teacher she didn't understand. Even in a democratic classroom, some children may retain a fear of adult authority that inhibits them from speaking honestly. They need to be directly encouraged to express what they are thinking and feeling. A conversation with a fifth-grade girl offers a case in point.

Jennifer is a student in a team-taught classroom in Brookline, where both teachers have been participants in our Democracy in the Schools Project. The first author (TL) was visiting the classroom one day as the children were working on stories they had been assigned to write. The teachers who had devised the project asked Jennifer to take their guest aside and describe what the project involved. Jennifer explained that the fifth graders had each interviewed a kindergarten child "about where they lived, if they ever lived anywhere else, what they like to do after school, what their favorite animal is, whether they have brothers or sisters, and stuff like that." Then, Jennifer said, "you have to write a story, with that kid in it, that uses all the information from your interviews." The completed story was to be presented to the kindergartener for him or her to keep and learn to read. "But I'm stuck," Jennifer said. The following dialogue ensued:

> TL: Why are you stuck?
> Jennifer: The teachers have a way they want you to do this. First, you're supposed to write an outline. Then you have to write the first paragraph, then they're going to look at that, then you write a rough draft and they correct that, and then you turn in a final copy. I'm stuck on the outline. I *hate* making outlines. I just like to write the story.
> TL: Why don't you explain to your teacher that you work better without an outline and ask if you can skip that step?
> Jennifer: No, they would just say, "This is the way you're supposed to do it."
> TL: Why would they say that?
> Jennifer: Because teachers think that their way is best.
> TL: I see. Do you think teachers try to figure out what's best for kids? Do you think they have to *think* about it?
> Jennifer: They *try* to figure it out. But they can't, because they don't have a kid's mind. They were kids once, but it's been so long that they've lost a kid's mind.
> TL: Well, how can you help them understand a kid's mind?
> Jennifer: You can *tell* them, but, you see, you have to *have* a kid's mind in order to understand a kid's mind!
> TL: Do you really think so? Are you absolutely certain your teacher wouldn't understand you if you told her just what you told me?

I understand you.

Jennifer: But teachers wouldn't *listen* the way you did!

TL: Why not?

Jennifer: Because they just think they know the best way!

TL: Is there any other reason why you don't want to ask your teacher about this?

Jennifer: I don't want to get yelled at.

What can we learn about Jennifer's point of view from this dialogue? Behind her reluctance to tell her teacher about her problem was a fear of getting yelled at. Behind her fear of getting yelled at lay her belief that "teachers think they know the best way." And in back of that belief is her conviction that even if teachers try to understand kids, they can't because "they've lost a kid's mind."

This conversation, then, gives us a window on the complex perspective-taking process going on in Jennifer's 10-year-old mind. We see how she thinks about how teachers think about how children think. Clearly, Jennifer is not prone to let go of her point of view about such matters. She held to it tenaciously despite our efforts to introduce an alternative conception of the teacher as somebody who tries to "figure out" what is best for kids and who might very well change her mind about how to teach something if she thought "her way" was causing kids trouble.

What surprised us was that Jennifer thought as she did despite the fact that she had participated in class meetings for several weeks where the teacher had encouraged children to share freely their experiences and ideas (although not yet about matters of curriculum). What Jennifer's persisting inhibition says to us is that teachers need to make clear to children, *again and again,* that they want to know what is on their minds, that teachers don't have all the answers, that they need students' help in discovering the best way to help them learn. Even if teachers are sending that message, they cannot assume that all children are receiving it. Jennifer certainly did not.

At the close of our conversation with Jennifer, we urged her to muster the courage to tell her teacher about the problem she was having with the story outline. She said she would try, but we knew she would need tangible evidence that her teacher would in fact listen. So we tipped the teacher off regarding what Jennifer had told us, knowing that this teacher would take constructive action. She called a class meeting and said: "I'm wondering how things are going with the story assignment. . . . Are there any changes we could make that would help you with the writing?" Jennifer's hand went up.

People often think that democracy in the classroom means a wholesale overhauling of the teaching-learning enterprise. In one sense, it does, but it begins simply: with respect for the child as a person, someone who has a point of view and a right and a need to express it.

Democracy and Rules

"Rules imposed by external constraint," Piaget wrote in 1932, "remain external to the child's spirit. Rules due to mutual respect and cooperation, on the contrary, take root inside the child's mind" (1965, p. 362).

When children cooperate with a teacher to formulate the rules that will govern the classroom, they are able to develop an insight that lies at the heart of their continuing moral development: namely, the idea that rules have a social origin and a social purpose. They are made by people, for people. People make rules so they can live together and get along, so they can function in groups. All of this is to say that children must "construct" their understanding of moral laws, just as they construct their understanding of logical laws, from the raw data of their first-hand experience. They need to participate in creating the small society of the classroom. They have to learn morality by living morality.

"The sense of a common law," Piaget concluded from his studies, "is possessed by children of 9-12." It "shows clearly enough how capable is the child of discipline and democratic life when he is not, as at school, condemned to wage war against authority" (1965, p. 364).

Our experience indicates that Piaget is conservative in his estimate of when the child is capable of "discipline and democratic life." Teachers of kindergarten youngsters, for example, have reported a measure of success in involving them in making decisions about the rules and life of the classroom. This is not to say that it is easy. Young children, as Piaget and others have amply documented, can be very egocentric. They need support structures that summon their better side. And, as one kindergarten teacher in our Brookline Project attests, the struggle to call forth their higher capacities may be a long and trying one:

> At the beginning of the year, our class meetings were chaotic. Children were all over the place — squirming, rolling on the floor, spitting. Supervisors, student teachers, everybody who came in said they're not ready for this, it will never work. The kids had so many individual problems, they just couldn't seem to pull together. But we stayed with it all year, and now the meetings are exquisite. They last for as long as half an hour.*

As another kindergarten teacher commented, "It takes a lot of slow to grow."

How should teachers begin a discussion of rules in the classroom? In one Brookline elementary school, teachers opened the topic by posing these questions: What is a rule? Why do we have rules? Who makes rules? How do you

---

*Unless otherwise indicated, statements by teachers are taken from conversations in seminars held as part of the Democracy in the Schools Project. In those cases where we quote from a written report, we identify the teacher by name.

change them? What should happen if a person breaks a rule? Who should decide what happens? Should teachers and students have to follow the same rules?*

Younger children, the teachers found, were better at giving examples of rules than they were at defining them, but many children revealed a surprisingly sophisticated grasp of rules, and many classes went on to develop rules for their classroom. One fifth-grade group even drafted and prominently posted its own "Constitution" with a "Bill of Rights" and a "Bill of Responsibilities." Said one boy in this class to his teacher: "We like them [the rules] because they're *our* rules. They're probably the same rules you would have made up, but we like them better because they're ours."

Among the most important rules that any group can make are those that govern and make possible their democratic discussions. Without clear rules, consistently enforced, classroom meetings can easily degenerate into free-for-alls, with everyone trying to talk at once, students putting each other down, no one really listening to anyone else. To avoid such disasters, we have recommended that teachers begin their very first class meeting by calling children into a circle (so all can see each other) and posing this question: "What rules do we need to have good talking and good listening in our class meeting?"

In a rural school in upstate New York, a first-grade teacher began with an even more basic question: "What is a meeting?" Her children's responses:

Mark: You go to learn things and discuss stuff.
Joe: You can straighten things out at a meeting.
Kathy: You can go to decide things.
Erin: You go over rules at a meeting.

Erin's comment about rules led into a discussion of rules the children wanted for their own meeting. Together, these first graders and their teacher came up with this list:

1. Listen to the person who's talking. We will stop the meeting if someone is not listening.
2. Sit up straight in a circle.
3. Don't interrupt.
4. Raise your hand only when the speaker is finished talking (proposed by the teacher).
5. Stick to the subject.
6. Don't leave the meeting unless you're sick.†

---

*We thank Louise Thompson, assistant superintendent for curriculum and instruction in Brookline for these questions about rules. They were a "homework project" for teachers in Ms. Thompson's workshop on the Democratic Classroom, Heath School, Brookline, 1978.

†Taken from a report submitted by Kathy Kittle, a teacher participant in Project Change at the State University of New York at Cortland. For an account of other Project Change teachers' efforts to foster social and moral development, see Lickona (1977).

Just making rules, of course, does not guarantee that children will follow them. Children need to know what will happen if they break a rule. That, too, can be democratically decided. In one kindergarten class, for example, all agreed that a person disrupting class meeting would receive one reminder, given by the teacher or another child. If the person was disruptive again, he or she would have to leave the meeting and go to a quiet activity elsewhere. "After a few days of leaving the circle," the teacher says, "the disruptive members joined the group successfully."

Many elementary teachers find that visual cues are helpful to children: "Our Meeting Rules" posted where all can see them; a "Talk Ticket" held by the person who has the floor; a "sad face" held up by a child or the teacher as a nonverbal reminder when someone forgets a rule. Many teachers also report that children take the rules of discussion more seriously when they help with the task of conducting the meeting. One way to do this is to have a "VIP," a child who chooses the next speaker and who calls only on persons who are following the meeting rules. Other teachers find it effective to let the meeting "run itself." Each speaker calls on the next speaker, with the teacher stepping in only occasionally to summarize, pose a question or move the discussion toward a conclusion.

"The only true discipline," Piaget said, "is that which children themselves have willed and consented to" (1965, p. 364). The most persuasive testimony to the wisdom of that statement comes from children themselves. During a class meeting of third graders in central New York, the teacher asked, "How do you feel when you don't follow a rule?" A girl, Susan, replied: "Well, I liked helping to make the rules. But when you break a rule of your own, it feels . . . well, it feels very weird." "Why is that?" asked the teacher. "Because," Susan said, "it's like disobeying your *own self,* and that's just weird!"*

We could take this as one goal of classroom democracy: Children so thoroughly internalize the rule of respect for others that when they depart from it, they feel they are violating something in their own selves.

Democracy and Conflict

No matter how many rules a class agrees upon, conflicts will arise for which there is no available rule. Teachers may use their authority to solve such conflicts (for example, "David, you broke John's lunchbox, so you're going to have to buy him a new one"). Or they may take a democratic approach, requiring children to share responsibility for solving the problem. There are different ways to share the responsibility. A teacher may have a meeting with an individual child to work out a fair solution to the problem or a meeting with however many children are directly involved. Or the teacher may decide to put

---

*Our thanks to Debby Boyes for this story, taken from an unpublished paper submitted as part of a course on promoting cognitive and moral development, State University of New York at Cortland.

the issue before the whole group as a challenge to their powers of cooperative problem-solving.

Once the democratic process is established in a classroom, the children may insist upon bringing up certain conflicts before the group. One of the participants in our Brookline Project, an elementary school counselor, recounted one such instance with a group of sixth graders with whom she had been doing class meetings, with varying degrees of success, for several weeks:

> A boy and a girl had a fight. The kids as a group wanted to discuss it. The girl said *she* wanted to discuss it, too. She said she had been angry at everybody, and she wanted to hear what other kids thought of her behavior.
>
> The discussion quickly became a debate between the boys and the girls. The girls said they didn't like the way the boys treat people. It got very noisy at times — so loud you couldn't hear. I tried to quiet it down by telling kids they could speak in the order of hands raised.
>
> Some children said, "I don't like this discussion. People are saying angry things." Some showed a lot of sensitivity toward the girl who had been in the fight and had been feeling angry at everbody. They said to her, "I know how you feel." Even one boy who doesn't like this girl said he knew how she felt.
>
> On the whole, kids listened better than they ever had before. The discussion seemed to clear the air. One boy said, "This is the best class meeting we've had."

PROBLEMS OF DEMOCRACY

Group discussions of conflict where names are named are obviously potentially explosive situations. Do they exceed the limits of the social and emotional maturity of elementary school children? Do they too easily get out of hand?

Another Brookline teacher described a discussion that erupted among her fifth graders. In the course of a meeting, several children began attacking one girl. They said things such as, "I hate you!" "You're a baby!" and "You don't do anything right!"

"I usually let the kids run the meeting," this teacher says. "They call on each other to speak. But now they were yelling out and saying cruel things. The structure had fallen down. I intervened to stop the meeting."

A month later, this teacher reported an unexpected turn of events:

> My kids voted to abandon democracy. I had a practice, three times a week, of calling for a three-fourths commitment to our democracy. A girl had run out of the room. I said to the class, "What do we do with someone who breaks the rules?" I tried to discuss this with them, but I didn't have their attention. I called for a commitment vote, and got only 10 of 23. They said, "It's your job to discipline."

The teacher reflected on what may have caused their democracy to go sour:

> Every three weeks I asked them to write an essay on what democracy meant to them. At first, they talked about rules and regulations. Later they talked about the importance of being friendly. Then they said, "We're tired of this. We're tired of making judgments about our friends." So in voting out their democracy, they were essentially voting to give up on disciplining their friends.

We found that this teacher's experience was not unique. While most of the classroom democracies in our project did not go out of business, several did, at least temporarily. The counselor's sixth-grade group (which had discussed the fight between the boy and the girl) voted to end their class meetings. So did the fifth-grade class that started the year full of enthusiasm about their class constitution. The teacher of that group reports:

> In September they loved their democracy. In the beginning, you get six kids who want to talk on an issue, and the meeting is short. Half way through the year there are 18 kids who are comfortable speaking out, and you get 18 kids who want to talk on an issue. The meetings get longer, and kids start to say, "This is boring."
>
> Before Christmas vacation, the vote was only 9-8 to keep the democracy, with the rest abstaining. After vacation, we kept sliding downhill. We had a system whereby the class voted on whether to give a kid a check for misbehavior. One day a boy who broke a rule refused to accept the agreed-upon consequence of having to write the rule 24 times. "That's not going to help me behave better," he said.
>
> At that point, another boy said, "We've lost our rules." Then the class voted 20-2 to do away with their democracy. They said they wanted *me* to make the decisions about discipline problems.

These children, like those of the other fifth grade that ended its democracy, wanted to be relieved of the responsibility to passing judgment on their friends. However, their teacher saw the problem as deeper than that:

> I had a political democracy, not a social democracy. My kids were better in the fall at rules and decision making than Joy's [a fellow fifth-grade teacher]. Joy began by working on *social* democracy — building positive relations among the kids and a sense of community in the class. Now her democracy is still functioning, and ours is not.

Even the teacher who succeeded in creating a "social democracy," however, said that "something goes out of it in February and March. My question is, how can we revitalize our democracy? Consistency gets real boring after a while. You need surprises."

Lessons for Successful Democracy

What learnings can we distill from these teachers' experiences? We would offer these seven lessons.

1. *Democracy takes time.* The time that democracy takes looms large in the minds of our teachers. Writes one: "After rules and procedures have been set up, the follow-through is very important. It is also the most difficult. It is time-consuming for everybody in the class and sometimes frustrating for me." Other teachers formulate the time problem as a conflict between the demands of democracy and the crunch of the curriculum. Says one: "Where is the trade-off? What do you do when subjects start to disappear — when you haven't had math for two days?"

2. *A democratic classroom must teach children how to deal constructively with conflict.* We saw one instance where children spoke abusively to a classmate in group meeting. Children need to learn from day one that there is no place for such abuse in a democratic classroom. People there must be as safe from verbal attack as they are from physical attack. Children need to be taught, quite directly, how to express strong feelings, how to disagree, without putting another down. Some teachers teach their students how to make nonderogatory "I statements" rather than accusing "You statements."

Democracy, like the phoenix, may rise from the ashes. This teacher reported that a few weeks after his fifth graders "voted out their democracy," they voted it back in (Gordon 1975). One fifth-grade teacher in our project taught his students to say "I support . . ." when they wanted to agree with someone, "I challenge . . " when they wanted to disagree. Many teachers, knowing that an ounce of prevention is worth a pound of cure, minimize the likelihood of hostile conflict by building up a "group feeling" or "team spirit" within the class.

If emotions do begin to run high in a class meeting, a teacher can bring them down in a number of ways: having children paraphrase each other's feelings; asking them to write down what they think or feel; asking students to imagine themselves in the other guy's shoes; calling a "time out" (and resuming the discussion at a calmer time). In any event, the teacher has a clear responsibility, as the moral authority in charge of the classroom, to protect the rights of individuals and hold the group always accountable to an ethic of fairness to all.

3. *Democracy can be boring.* The far more common problem for teachers is not that democratic meetings erupt into confrontations but that they sag into tedium. Children, like most other people, have a limited tolerance for democratic decision making. They have other needs and values: efficiency, productivity, a change of pace, a good time. The number of cases in our project where children grew weary of their democracy suggests that democratic teachers would be wise to vary the agenda and format of class meetings and err in the direction of too few meetings rather than too many.

4. *Democracy can be burdensome for children.* Democracy obviously is not all fun and games. After the novelty wears off, it's a lot of hard work. Some of that work may be more than children are up to. One responsibility that appears to weigh especially heavily on them is that of holding court to mete out consequences to their rule-breaking peers. In more than one case, children squirmed under the yoke of "judging their friends." It may be more of a yoke than they are developmentally ready to bear. A teacher who wished to accommodate to this developmental limitation could involve children in setting rules and consequences (and perhaps in keeping track of their own behavior) but not impose upon them the more difficult task of trying and punishing offenders.

In the early grades, a child may also balk at accepting the responsibility of disciplining himself. A teacher of first- and second-grade children in the Brookline project confided that she had become "interested in – obsessed, really – with the problem of discipline in the classroom." What, she wondered, were her children capable of? She reported the following conversation that she overheard between one of her children and another adult:

Child: I don't like Miss Baker.
Adult: Why not?
Child: I don't like what she does when I do something wrong, like hitting.
Adult: What does she do?
Child: She asks me why I did it, what I could have done instead, and what I'm going to do the next time. I have to make a *plan*. It's too hard for me to make a plan! I want *her* to control my temper!

That gave this teacher pause. She decided to try another approach:

The next time he was wild – it was the end of the day – I sat him down in his seat. Boom! That was it. The temper ended.

That week I started taking more control of the class. Things settled down, went smoother. We got more things done; the children were more cooperative. I began asking myself, "Was what I had been asking of them – that they take responsibility for their own behavior – developmentally appropriate for these children? Could they handle it?"

That brings us full circle back to our story about the high school principal who bemoaned his seniors' inability to make decisions. Will students ever develop responsibility if they don't have responsibility? Is the second grader who wants his teacher to control his temper copping out? Should she let him put that responsibility on her? Or is he making an honest statement that as a young child he needs the firm hand of an adult? Questions like these lead us to still another conclusion about democratic education, namely, that

5. *Democracy is hard and complex work for the teacher.* If democracy is sometimes difficult for children, it is even more so for the teacher. As we have

already indicated, teachers constantly grapple with the complex problem of how much responsibility children can cope with. They worry about the issue of time. And they have many other questions as well. A sampler:

> I'm having trouble deciding how much freedom is best to give my kids. Should they set the neatness standard in the room, or should I? Who should determine the acceptable noise level? What if they decide upon a harsh punishment for a member of the group? Is there a tension between trying to have a fair classroom and trying to meet kids at their developmental level? If young children are at the stage where punishment is swift and strong, can I give them the freedom to carry out their justice system?*

> My nine-year-olds still name-call despite the fact that the rule against name-calling is the one we spent *most* of our time discussing. They don't seem to feel the rules at a gut level. How can I get them to?

> Should you ever make exceptions to rules for particular children? Does it matter if they have special problems or needs?

> How can I get carry-over? When we were in a circle, the kids were great. But when they got back to their desks, they shouted answers out. It was a case of who could be the loudest.

> When I'm there, my kids are well-behaved. But when a sub comes in, they seem to treat it as a time-out, a vacation from responsibility. Is that inevitable at this developmental level [fifth grade]? Can I realistically expect them to maintain the democracy that they and I have developed when I'm not around?

> Aren't we being authoritarian if we say to kids, "This is *my* classroom, and we're going to have a democracy"? Should they be the ones to decide whether the class will be run democratically? What if they don't want the responsibility of a democracy, but we don't want them to push all the power back on us?

6. *Democracy is an experiment.* Clearly, teachers who are serious about doing democracy in the classroom have to be willing to do a fair amount of flying by the seat of their pants. There is no sure-fire formula, no easy, six-step recipe. Democracy is very much an experimental process of trying something and watching what happens. If one thing doesn't work, try something else. Invite children to be partners in the experiment; ask them to help evaluate what works and suggest what else should be tried. Operate on the premise that nothing, save perhaps a sense of humor, works forever.

---

*This quote is taken from a Harvard University Summer Workshop paper by Laurie Turner, a primary school teacher in Cambridge, Massachusetts.

Take Dewey (1968, p. 47) at his word when he said that "the meaning of democracy must be continually explored afresh . . . discovered and rediscovered, remade and reorganized."

7. *A healthy democracy means social community as well as self-government.* Rules and voting, by themselves, do not a successful democracy make. The fifth-grade teacher whose democracy was alive and well while others declined and fell had worked hard to build up a network of positive social relations in her classroom. That network, that social bonding, was the glue that seemed to hold the group together over the long winter months. For children, at least, a sense of community — a spirit of friendship, a feeling of belonging — appears to be an essential part of the democratic process. Teachers who hope to promote cooperative, democratic decision making among their children would do well to provide lots of opportunities for students to get to know and like other members of the class. We know one teacher who prevents cliques and fosters friendship among her fifth graders by having, every Friday, a fish-bowl drawing in which each child pulls out a new seat for the coming week. Before long, everyone knows everyone else.

One straightforward way to create a strong sense of community is to make helping an important part of the classroom agenda. With a little imagination, a teacher can also make helping serve the cause of the academic curriculum. Many teachers do this through cooperative learning, whereby students work together in pairs or small groups on a common project or task.*

A third-grade teacher in our Brookline Project involved his children in identifying "Learning Monsters" — thoughts or feelings that get in the way of learning. The class kept a running list of Monsters they spotted over the course of the year (for example, the "I've-Got-To-Be-Right Monster," the "I'm-Worried-I-Might-Do-Better-Than-Somebody-Else Monster," and the "I'm-Afraid-of-Finishing-This-Work-Because-I-Don't-Think-I-Can-Do-the-Next-Level Monster"). The teacher explains: "We usually discuss a different monster each week. I ask, 'What should you do when you meet up with this Learning Monster?' We also deal with the social responsibility side of the problem: 'What can you do to help when you see somebody else struggling with a Learning Monster?' "†

Why are social cooperation and the sense of community it creates so important to a classroom democracy? There are probably many reasons. Groups in general tend to function better when the members know and like each other. When a spirit of cooperative community is missing, "democratic" meetings can become merely a forum for pressing and defending one's narrow self-interest. "Fairness" in such a classroom does not easily rise above a morality of looking out for Number 1. Through cooperative relationships, by contrast, children begin to feel connected to others, to develop a sense of membership in the class

---

*For an essay that elaborates the case for cooperative learning and illustrates a dozen teacher strategies for fostering cooperation in the classroom, see Lickona (1980).

†Taken from a report submitted by Malcolm Astley of Heath School, Brookline.

and a morality of concern for "the good of the group." The awareness dawns, slowly, that every individual has a responsibility to the group, just as the group has a responsibility to every individual.

Democracy and the Wider School

Democracy need not stop at the classroom door. In one Brookline school, a workshop conducted by the assistant superintendent, Louise Thompson, sparked a schoolwide effort to implement democratic principles. It began when the librarian asked, "How can I be democratic in the library?"

From this question, the Library Council was born. A child from every class in the school, kindergarten through eighth grade, sat on the council. Leadership was provided by the librarian and a classroom teacher. They describe their goals as follows:

1. To extend the concept of democracy to the total school and build a sense of community across grade levels.
2. To involve students in the formation of library policy and rules and increase student adherence to those rules.
3. To brainstorm with children problems and solutions concerning the library.
4. To make students aware of the ways in which the library may serve them.
5. To establish in students' minds the connection between adherence to library rules and the quality of service the library can provide.

The Library Council met six times for one-half hour every other Thursday. At first, the younger children were reticent. With encouragement from upper-grade children, however, the contributions of the younger members steadily increased. "Older children," the teachers noted, "paraphrased and clarified statements made by the younger children."

What were the outcomes of this unusual experiment? The teachers report several concrete results of the Council's deliberations:

A library orientation program will be instituted for the coming school year, with the library teacher going to each room and holding a class meeting on the policies and uses of the library.

Seventh- and eighth-grade students will have more time made available to them to spend in the library.

Students can now be heard encouraging their peers to return books on time.

A group of students will be formed in the fall to aid the librarian in book selection.

Signs made by Council participants, announcing the library hours, now hang in every classroom.

There were other changes, the teachers say — less tangible but equally important. In the hall one day, for example, an eighth-grade girl passed a second-grade girl and said, "Hi, see you in Library Council tomorrow!" The teachers commented, "The warmth of this exchange between two children who previously had no common bond makes such efforts in democracy worthwhile." They add that "children become more sympathetic to the concerns at each grade level. All age groups argued to have more library time for the seventh and eighth graders, and the upper-grade children volunteered to help the younger children find books." Perhaps the most telling measure of the council's success was the fact that "the children voted to resume the Library Council in September and make it an ongoing part of the life of Heath School."*

There are many opportunities for children to be democratically involved in the affairs of the wider school. What should be the rules and responsibilities in the corridors? In the cafeteria? On the playground? Is there enough to do over lunch hour? What can everyone do to help keep the school clean? To reduce vandalism? Creating a democratic community in the school as a whole certainly doesn't mean putting children in charge of the institution. It does mean asking children to contribute their ideas and efforts to make the school a better place to be and learn.

THE BENEFITS OF DEMOCRACY

We have pointed out that democratic education takes time, energy, and a lot of thinking on the part of both adults and children. What makes the commitment worth it? Are there palpable benefits for children's development? On the basis of our experience, we submit that there can be many, although growth will certainly vary from child to child and classroom to classroom.

In the area of *cognitive development,* democracy can help children grow in ability to define a problem and think of alternative solutions; ability to think logically about cause-and-effect relations (for example, about the consequences of their behavior and the behavior of others).

In the area of *ego development,* democracy can help children grow in understanding of their own feelings; the self-esteem that comes from being a valued member of a group; courage to speak their minds.

In the domain of *social development,* children may grow in awareness that different persons may have different points of view about a problem; ability to communicate their own viewpoint in a way that can be understood by others;

---

*From a report to the Democracy in the Schools Project submitted by teacher Joy Sacca of Heath School.

ability to listen to and understand the viewpoints of others; skills in initiating and maintaining positive relations (for example, friendships); skills in cooperating with others on a common task; ability to participate in group decision making; understanding of the difficulties of democratic group decision making.

In the sphere of *moral development,* children who participate in democratic classrooms and schools may grow in a sense of their own rights as persons; respect for the rights of others; ability to help make and maintain fair rules; understanding of why rules are necessary; understanding that democracy means considering the rights of individuals as well as the needs of the group; understanding that democracy means fulfilling responsibilities as well as having rights; ability to function as a member of a human community.

Our statements about the benefits of democracy for children are clinical impressions based on our own observations and intuitions and those of teachers. To date, formal "tests" are not available to catch all the important kinds of developmental gains that we have enumerated; but some studies have gathered hard data on the effects of democracy on at least some dimensions of children's development, and we would like to briefly summarize those.

Louise Rundle's 1977 dissertation described in detail by Louise Rundle and David Stuhr (Chapter 13), found a half-stage gain in moral reasoning in a class of fifth-graders who over a 12-week period resolved real classroom issues through small and large-group discussion.

Selman and Lieberman (1974), working with second graders, produced a half-stage advance in social reasoning (defined as the ability to consider the intentions of others). The intervention used discussion of hypothetical filmstrip dilemmas for five weeks, followed by five months of small-group discussion of actual classroom problems. (A control group showed no stage change.)

Kubelick (1977), working with eighty 8-10-year-olds, implemented a program that combined problem-solving class meetings, clubs, citizenship checklists, instruction in group dynamics, and a reasoning-centered social studies curriculum. After seven months, all age groups showed significant advance on Damon's (1977) positive justice levels. (So did a "comparison group" that provided children with a broadly similar democratic environment but used less deliberate methods of moral education.)

Jaquette and Selman (1980) carried out a program of "developmental peer therapy" with a class of eight 11-13-year-olds who were "emotionally disturbed but intellectually normal." Strategies included democratic class meetings about real interpersonal problems, a social awareness curriculum, and various cooperative activities. At the end of eight months, these children had gained nearly a half-stage in "reflective interpersonal awareness" — a developmental advance that a group of roughly comparable children not in the program took a full two years to make.

Enright (1980) collaborated with a first-grade teacher on the implementation of a "social-cognitive model for processing interpersonal problems." When interpersonal conflicts arose, the teacher asked the children directly involved to describe what they did, how it affected the other's feelings, what else they might have done, and what they would do next time in a similar situation. Teachers held children accountable for following through on their new problem-solving plan. At the end of 11 weeks, children in the experimental class were superior to controls on measures of social problem-solving (Shure and Spivack 1972), interpersonal understanding (Selman 1979), and reasoning about fairness (Damon 1977).

Cole and Farris (1979) report a broad-scale elementary school program that included not only democratic class meetings but a cross-class Student Advisory Council at both the primary and intermediate levels. The principal worked directly with both councils on resolving democratically various schoolwide issues. An "informal comparison study" of students in this school and those of another school in the same district showed the former to be more independent of adult help, more considerate of the rights of others, and less likely to use physical force to solve problems.

The evidence is not all in, but what we have in hand is promising.

PART III

PARENTS AS MORAL EDUCATORS

19
THE FAMILY AND
MORAL EDUCATION

Sheila Stanley

American society is experiencing deep problems. The Vietnam war, political corruption, increasing violence, epidemics of drug abuse, the decay of our cities, and the isolation of suburban life clearly reflect the extensive confusion that exists in our time. If society is in trouble, so is the American family. No longer supported by an extended network of relative and the community, the modern family struggles uneasily and often unsuccessfully to cope with the breakneck pace of change and the moral crises of contemporary society.

Rather than see the family as a reflection of something awry in our society, social analysts often blame it for what is wrong. Using the family as a scapegoat occurs because historically it has had the primary responsibility for the socialization of our children. As Ned Gaylin (1971, pp. 66-67) cogently points out, however, by focusing so intensely on the family, which admittedly is disorganized, we fail to explore the basic problem: the values and priorities of the society at large.

> When things go amiss, rather than condemn, should we not, instead, question whether the family is adjusting perhaps *too* well, whether it is performing its functions too efficiently in grooming its children for society, the values of which may be somewhat askew? The basic question being raised is whether the social sciences any longer can

From *Adolescents' Development and Education,* edited by Ralph L. Mosher. Berkeley: McCutchan Publishing Corp. Copyright 1979. Reprinted by permission of the publisher.

afford the luxury of taking a stance of "scientific neutrality," of social relativism with regard to the society of which they are a part, while examining the institutions of that society. The answer seems apparent that social science must face its responsibilities as change agent and advocate, and therefore it must be prepared to examine and evaluate the values of that society in which it operates.

Some social scientists, among them Urie Brofenbrenner, Philip Slater, and Alan Toffler, agree with Gaylin and have critically scrutinized contemporary American values and their consequences. They charge that America's obsession with efficiency and the profit motive seriously interferes with the development of democratic values such as cooperation and concern for others. Productivity is given top priority in American society, and this compulsive need to "make it" has led to alienation and isolation in a variety of forms. We are a people segregated by age, race, class, and ability. The elderly are isolated because they are "unproductive." Children have little contact with adults other than their own parents and are segregated in school from others of different ages and abilities. Families play hopscotch from one community to another, thus aggravating the lack of commitment of suburban life. Shopping centers, large impersonal high schools, reliance upon the automobile, and pressure to conform, which characterize suburbia, breed anonymity and loneliness. We have lost the spirit of the democratic community, substituting instead the unrealistic fantasies of TV, competition rather than cooperation, and a preoccupation with privacy.

The lack of the emotional support formerly provided by an extended family and a neighborhood places added stress upon the already overburdened nuclear family. When the family fails at the impossible task of meeting all our needs for belonging, we condemn it as "a faultily constructed piece of social engineering" (Skolnick and Skolnick 1971, p. 29). We do not recognize that conditions of life have changed and that the actual responsibility for child-rearing has shifted away from the family to other sectors of the society.

The family has lost much of its power and influence, partly because parents and children spend so little time together. And yet the family, as Brofenbrenner (1967) reminds us, still has the primary moral and legal responsibility for developing character in children. What can be done? It seems to me that we need to do two things: first, find ways to strengthen and support the family rather than gradually replace it with more education, more therapy, and more reliance upon television, the peer group, and drugs; second, provide family members with the skills to examine critically and to evaluate society's moral values and priorities.

The program described below grew out of my interest in family education and a conviction that the family plays a decisive role in the moral development of our young. Because of the moral crises of our times, finding ways to stimulate the development of moral thought and action in children is a crucial task. The study presented here demonstrates that parents can be helped in their role as primary moral educators of children.

THE FAMILY AS A MORAL EDUCATOR

Certain experiences have been found to enhance moral reasoning in children and adolescents. Among these are situations that encourage new ways of thinking about morality, such as role-taking opportunities, participation in groups perceived as fair or just, and exposure to cognitive conflict (to contradictions in one's own moral views and in their relation to the views of others). As one becomes increasingly aware that there are points of view and feelings other than his own, and as the capacity to look at his own behavior from these other perspectives develops, so too does his level of moral reasoning (Kohlberg and Turiel 1971).

The family is a crucial source of such role-taking opportunities for the growing child. But, as yet, there has been little research on strategies for moral education in the family. Research on learning theory provides some tentative support for the notion that parental styles influence the child's moral development (Hoffman 1963; Bandura and Walters 1963). To be more specific, the use of inductive discipline by parents appears to be correlated with more advanced moral reasoning and behavior than either the use of coercive power or threats of withdrawing love (Hoffman and Saltzstein 1967; Shoffeitt 1971). Inductive discipline refers to techniques that appeal to the child's rationality and responsibility, to his sense of right and wrong. By encouraging the child to consider carefully his obligations and the rights of others as well as his own, inductive discipline may furnish the child with important role-taking opportunities. In a similar vein, Holstein (1969) and Peck and Havighurst (1960) found that moral maturity in children is related to active participation in family discussions and decision making.

The project described here was based on the assumption that, if a child perceives his family as being fair, and if conflicts involving members of the family are resolved equitably, he will have experienced significant role-taking opportunities and discussion of the right, wrong, or fair thing to do. Further, these experiences should stimulate the moral development of the child. No one has yet attempted to teach families methods of inductive discipline and problem solving with the purpose of evaluating the consequences for the moral development of the children. This study did that.

The purpose was twofold: to investigate whether a course that taught families democratic methods of resolving conflicts and establishing rules would affect the moral atmosphere of the family itself; to investigate whether such a course would stimulate the moral reasoning of the adolescent participants. Following Rawls (1971) and Kohlberg, Scharf, and Hickey (1972, p. 4), the moral atmosphere or justice structure of the family was defined as "the principles which govern the assignment of rights and duties and define the proper distribution of the benefits and burdens of social cooperation."

THE COURSE

The course was taught in a high school of a small city on the East Coast. The participants were volunteer ninth- and tenth-grade students and their parents; only families in which husband, wife, and adolescent all agreed to participate in the project were accepted. The families were divided into three groups. The first group (A) consisted of ten parents and seven adolescents (five families). The second (B) had twelve parents (six families) with their six adolescents participating in the evaluation only. This group was included to assess whether or not it made a difference to include adolescents in the course. The third group (C) was a control that was assessed, but did not attend the experimental course. The participants in all groups were predominantly lower middle class with occupations of the parents ranging from skilled labor to nonmanagerial white-collar jobs. All families were white and either Protestant or Catholic.

The course met for two and one-half hours a week for ten weeks. Both groups were led by me and a high school counselor whom I had trained to teach the course during the previous semester.

The course was influenced by two models of parental education: the Adlerian approach to family education (Dreikurs et al. 1959) and Thomas Gordon's (1970) Parent Effectiveness Training. The Adlerian concept of the family meeting and Gordon's problem-solving method were, in particular, seen as potentially effective ways of helping families develop and live by more just rules and agreements. As will be seen, both are based on democratic procedures for resolving family conflicts.

The course had four phases. Although the phases could not be neatly separated from each other by sessions, blocks of time were allotted for each. The following is a description of the curriculum of the parent-adolescent group and the group that included only parents.

Phase One: Communication Skills

This phase involved discussions of how family members talked with one another, particularly about rules and conflicts; and the teaching and practicing of the skills of empathic listening and of confrontation.

Theoretical considerations, as well as my own experience in working with families, led me to include these communication skills in the course. To solve problems productively, parents and children must learn how to talk to each other in nonauthoritarian ways. The inclusion of listening and confrontation skills also fits with the developmental perspective of the course. Moral development theory states that, if individuals have the ability to take the role of the other and if they can understand another person and convey that understanding, they are more likely to consider other positions and reach an equitable decision when faced with a conflict. Dowell (1971) had found that learning to listen and respond empathically has a significant impact on the moral reasoning of adolescents. Furthermore, it is possible that effective confrontation skills may also enhance moral development. Clear, nondestructive statements about a person's behavior help that individual understand the effects of his behavior. Practicing this skill would give parents and teenagers experience in accepting responsibility for the welfare of others. In addition, being able to empathize with and understand the claims of another can be expected to result in greater fairness toward that person.

The first class began with personal introductions and discussion of the goals of the workshop. Next, parents as a group were asked to reflect upon their own adolescence and to share with each other what communication and discipline were like in their families of origin. This was a powerful experience for all. Almost without exception, these parents grew up in families characterized by economic hardship, lack of communication, and much tension.

> L: There was a lot of arguing in my family. My father was an alcoholic. My parents didn't listen to me. I was the youngest, and they were too tired to care.
>
> J: I was very bitter about my own adolescence. There was no communication in my family. I felt very hurt and angry at my father for ignoring me, so I left home at an early age.
>
> M: I was an only child. Instead of asking me, "Do you like this?" they said, "You *will* like this." I never dared to disagree. I had never gone shopping for my own clothes until after I was married.

Many of the adolescents were visably moved by what they had heard. Several said they had not realized what their parents had gone through. When they took their turn, the most emotionally charged responses were those concerning decision making. "I don't like how rules are made. My father makes most of them." "My mother orders me around and never listens to my side of things. It's not fair." This discussion led naturally into the last part of the class, which focused on rules and typical conflicts in families. The participants were asked to write down their family rules and how these were decided (an activity that will be described more thoroughly below).

The second class was devoted to the teaching of listening skills (Carkhuff 1971; Gordon 1970) through modeling by the leaders and the role playing of both imaginary and real problems. The participants began by learning to distinguish between words and feelings and to focus on the feelings being expressed. They practiced, first, identifying feelings and, then, reflecting them by using the forms "You feel _____" and "You feel _____ because _____," filling in the blanks with the appropriate responses. They practiced in groups of three and were instructed to continue practicing these skills at home for the duration of the workshop. This was the case with all of the subsequent skills they were taught. Several participants found empathic listening artificial and difficult at first. As the weeks went by, however, most of the group members began to comment favorably on the positive results of their improved listening ability.

The third class focused on effective confrontations, that is, on some of the skills needed when one person's behavior interferes with another's. Complaints included: "My tools were left out in the rain" and "My dad borrowed some money and didn't return it." Participants examined the consequences (usually negative) of their typical responses to another's disturbing behavior. They were then taught "I messages," which communicate the feeling experienced by the person who is upset. The form used, at least initially, is: "I feel [*feeling*] when [*description of behavior*] because [*effects upon me*]." For example, "I'm really annoyed when you don't return the car at the agreed upon time because now I'm late for my doctor's appointment."

Peterson (1969) found "I messages" to be effective because they are less apt to provoke resistance and because they make the other person accountable for modifying his behavior, thus helping him assume responsibility for his own actions. Furthermore, because "I messages" are honest, they are apt to influence the other person to send similar honest messages whenever he is upset. This may avoid the snowballing effect of mutual name calling and of assigning blame that so often happens in families. Finally, as mentioned earlier, being able to understand the claims and perspectives of another can result in more fairness toward that person. The focus on the "because _____" part of the "I message" is thus important. In attempting to determine why another person's behavior was upsetting, participants often brought up issues of fairness. "I get annoyed when you leave the kitchen in a mess because I've just cleaned it up, and it's unfair." "It makes me mad when you turn on the light after I've gone to sleep because that's not thinking of *my* rights."

Participants were given an "I message practice sheet" to complete at home. They were also urged to send "I messages" to each other during the week and to report the results to the group. Most tried this method of confrontation and were generally pleased with the results.

Even though the phase on communication skills was brief, it did encourage participants to put themselves in the place of others, to see the world through another person's perspective. It was intended to provide them with some of the skills necessary to resolve conflicts equitably — the focus of the third phase of the course.

Phase Two: The Family Meeting

This phase of the course centered on the discussion of family rules and the family meeting as a way of promoting more democracy in the family and providing participation, particularly for adolescents.

During the first class, both adolescents and parents were asked to write down the rules in their families and how they were decided. Then they were grouped by family and shared what each had written. This exercise was repeated at the last session to aid both participants and leaders in evaluating any changes in the process of decision making over the course of the workshop. In discussing this exercise, some fascinating observations were made. The parents believed, in general, that many of the rules were made by joint decision with their children. In these same families, however, the adolescents disagreed vehemently, maintaining that the decisions were handed down by parents, or, as one boy put it, "decided by God: parents, not kids, have the last word." Many parents who initially thought they were making joint decisions came to realize that one or both parents pushed through a decision without general agreement in the family. It became apparent that most families experienced much dissension in making decisions. Parents struggled to keep the upper hand, and adolescents resisted. The parents seemed to regard continuous family warfare as unpleasant but normal; it was considered a usual and expected condition. They did not like the ways conflicts were resolved, but saw no alternative.

As a possible solution to the friction common to all the families, we suggested a weekly family meeting (Dinkmeyer and McKay 1973). The fourth class focused on discussion of such a meeting. It was described as a regular opportunity for family members to communicate with each other, to share information, and to make plans and decisions around such issues as chores and use of the TV and family car. It would provide a way of dealing with recurring problems and conflicts away from the heat of the moment. It would be a move toward participatory democracy in which each individual has a full and equal role. We explained that there would be less need for punishment because people are more likely to carry out jointly made decisions.

We urged that the weekly meetings be held at regularly scheduled times so that they would avoid being seen as the parents' meeting — to be called only when a parent had a gripe. We also recommended that each meeting have a leader and that the leadership be rotated and include all children in school. Finally, it was stressed that the way decisions are made is critical to successful meetings. Decisions can only be binding if every member present agrees. If a unanimous decision is not reached, further problem solving will be necessary, perhaps at another time. Majority decisions lead to grievances by the minority and impede cooperation. We advised, therefore, against voting in the family meeting.

The reactions to the concept of the family meeting ran the gamut from enthusiasm to strong resistance.

> L (parent): [with a raised, trembling voice] The ultimate responsibility for the family is with the *parents*. I can't let a twelve-year-old tell me how to run my life.
>
> M (parent): I'm not sure young kids can come up with intelligent alternatives to conflicts. Parents know best.
>
> D (adolescent): You're not giving us much credit. We're not *that* ignorant. I want to do more on my own.

L (parent): Well, I really do wish they would do more on their own. They need to be reminded *all* the time. But I get the feeling I'd be losing my job if I let them help decide things.

B (parent): That's part of it, L. Letting go of some of the control isn't easy to do. It's hard for us mothers at first to think that anyone else could do what we do. But no one else will start assuming responsibility unless you let go of some.

D (parent): I agree. I used to make all the decisions for my girls. I finally realized they couldn't make any decisions for themselves. So I'm beginning to let up. Maybe these meetings would help us even more.

To demonstrate a family meeting and to provide an opportunity to practice, we asked for volunteers to role play a meeting in front of the group. Three adolescents volunteered, one to play mother, while two parents volunteered, one to play a child. They got into a discussion of chores prompted by complaints from the "son" that he always had to do the dishes, a job he detested. With a little coaching from the co-leader, the "family" struggled through to a fair decision concerning the division and rotation of chores.

The families were instructed to conduct weekly meetings at home for the remainder of the workshop. Tape recorders and tapes were distributed to each family, as was a book entitled *The Family Council,* by Dreikurs, Gould, and Corsini (1974). The first and last meetings were tape recorded, and the tapes were turned into the leaders for the purposes of supervision and assessment.

All participants were willing to tape record the meetings, although a few seemed anxious and reluctant at first. The initial meeting of the M family illustrates a typical first meeting. They discussed summer curfews and mutually agreed upon times for all four children. The mother was a calm, rational chairperson in contrast to the father who was provocative and dictatorial at times. For example, when one boy began hitting his younger brother, the father blurted out, "No hitting J, or I'll belt you!" Despite some difficulties, the four family members present at the workshop session expressed delight at their first attempt at a family meeting.

Part of the following classes was devoted to the continued examination of the participants' family meetings. It was apparent that it took a lot of courage for many of the parents to share their power with children who formerly had very little. The meetings focused on a wide variety of issues ranging from conflicts between individuals, to infractions of family rules, to negotiations of new privileges. Problems were increasingly perceived not only as management issues ("How do we get the job done?) but also as moral conflicts ("What is the fair way to resolve this for everyone involved?"). There was slow but gradual progress toward democratic participation in the meetings, as evidenced by the tapes as well as the verbal reports of participants.

Phase Three: A Democratic Approach to Conflict Resolution

This phase of the course was designed to provide the families additional help in solving conflicts equitably. My experience had been that, without such help, family meetings did not work very well. Consequently, the participants were taught a democratic approach to problem solving that is based primarily on the work of Gordon (1970). Before the approach was explained to them, we discussed typical methods used by participants to resolve conflicts. Families shared personal examples of the "authoritarian parent" and the "tyrannical child" as methods of resolving conflicts. Parents and adolescents alike expressed feelings of resentment and anger at these methods of solving problems as well as their ways of "getting even."

As an alternative, the leaders presented a democratic approach to conflict resolution. The six steps in this approach, as adapted from Gordon, were described to the group.

1) Defining the Problem: This is the most critical phase of effective problem solving. Each person defines his perception of the problem, letting the others know what is problematic to him and how it is making him feel. Each needs to listen to the other's perceptions and feelings of the problem. Several attempts at clarifying both one's own and the other's definition may be necessary, with the aim to come to an agreement that *this* is the problem which we are going to solve, with a solution that is mutually acceptable. This phase also includes trying to understand why the conflict exists, what the factors are that are maintaining the problem in its present state.

2) Brainstorming: Everyone involved raises possible solutions, strictly avoiding any evaluation of solutions at this time. As many solutions as possible are generated.

3) Evaluating: At this stage, each person must be honest about which solutions he really and truly does find acceptable, and which will not meet his needs. Children will frequently need to be encouraged to share their evaluations and will need to be listened to with honest respect for their feelings about the possible solution. New solutions may be generated at this point, building on the acceptable parts of several earlier solutions.

4) Deciding: If problem solving is to result in *all* feeling that their needs are met by the solution, the decision must be by consensus. As one solution begins to emerge as superior, it helps to clearly restate it, and check again whether it satisfies each person's need, or can be modified to do so.

5) Establishing Procedures: Having agreed on a solution, the details of who will do what and when need to be spelled out, so no misunderstanding occurs. Having each member state what he will do to carry out the solution is helpful.

6) Follow-up: It is easier to reach a decision and carry it out when some agreement about when and how its effectiveness will be evaluated is agreed upon. Not all solutions will work, and a return to problem solving is needed

when any party to the solution has further problems with it. Knowing that modifications can and will be made as new problems develop is an important part of the process, one which needs to be emphasized, and for which time must be set aside.

We explained to the group that this approach to problem solving could be used by two people at any time or by the entire family at family meetings. It was suggested as a means of making family meetings fairer. Because the participants had already begun to look for more equitable ways of resolving conflicts as a result of their experience with family meetings, there was less resistance to this method than I have found in my previous work with families. It should be noted that learning this method of problem solving was tied to the first two phases of the course. The first step toward solving problems democratically — defining the problem — relies heavily on listening and sending clear messages of confrontation, which is the focus of the first phase of the course.

In small groups the participants practiced resolving conflicts supplied by the leaders and, later, examples from their own lives. Sometimes positions were reversed, with the adolescent playing the parent and vice versa, in an attempt to enhance empathy. Over the next few weeks this approach to conflict resolution was incorporated into the family meetings. The more family members were able to trust each other to be considerate of their needs, the more comfortable they became with the method. Participants began reporting a decrease in the number of angry conflicts and unresolved battles at home, accompanied by an increased willingness to cooperate.

Phase Four: Dissension over Values

Although conflicts over values between parents and children had come up repeatedly throughout the workshop, they were the main subject of the last three classes. Friction in this area affected patterns of family communications, the rules that were made, and the way conflicts were resolved — in other words, the focus of the first three phases of the workshop. Consequently, it was critical that the course address the issue of values. Furthermore, as Kohlberg stated, "values clarification is a very useful component of moral education" (1972, p. 19). Discussions involving disagreements over values can help to stimulate moral thinking. If such discussions are sustained over a significant period of time and range of issues, they can provide cognitive conflict and opportunities for role taking, two of the most powerful ways of stimulating moral development.

As a beginning, each participant was asked to rank a list of values both for himself and for the other members of his family. Participants were then grouped by family and asked to share their perceptions of each other's values. In the resulting discussion, most parents were surprised (some of them horrified) to learn what values their children imagined were most important to them. For example, many of the adolescents believed that their parents placed the highest value on such traits as politeness, obedience, and cleanliness. The parents, however, ranked broad-mindedness, love, and forgiveness as being most important to them. What might be responsible for this discrepancy was discussed. This exercise led to much interaction at home with family members disagreeing over the relative importance of certain values.

This segment of the course also included discussions of ways of handling conflicting values in the family and of moral dilemmas involving individual family members. Among the conflicting values were boys' long hair, girls' short skirts, drugs, choice of friends, political beliefs, and church attendance. We pointed out that the six-step method of resolving conflict would not be applicable here because people are usually unwilling to negotiate behaviors based on firmly held personal beliefs. We shared with the group the following ways suggested by Gordon (1970) for parents to handle conflicting values: practice the desired behavior (if you value saving money, save money); encourage open discussions between parent and child concerning their differences and the reasons for them; and modify your own beliefs or personal tastes. The discussion that followed was emotionally charged. The notion that it may be risky or inadvisable to attempt to maintain control in the area of values came as a shock to some parents and a relief to others.

The group had a lively discussion of personal moral dilemmas. The following examples show the kinds of moral issues that were raised.

> B (adolescent): One day in class I discovered that a good friend of mine was cheating on his math test. I confronted him about it after class, and he just laughed. He says that everyone does it. Well, I haven't so far, but math is real hard for me. And I sure need higher grades if I'm going to get into college.
>
> K (parent): M's situation reminds me of the time I found out my boss was fudging on the business accounts. It didn't affect me directly, but it really bothered me. I had just gotten this job and was afraid of losing it. I just didn't know what to do.
>
> D (adolescent): My best friend, G, is having this huge fight with her parents. They told her she can't date M anymore. They're really in love, and her parents are worried that something will happen. Besides, they don't like him anyway — he's not from the right family. She's seriously thinking of running away with him. What really gets her is they don't say anything to her brother who is going with someone.

The leaders focused the debate on the moral issues and encouraged interaction between the participants. For example, in the last dilemma, we raised such questions as: Do G's parents have the right to forbid her from dating M? Should G obey or disobey her parents? Why do you think the parents are reacting differently to her brother's going steady, and is that fair? Should G run away from home or not? What should G's friend do in this situation? What kind of authority, if any, do parents have over their children's lives? We asked participants why they thought the way they did about moral issues, requiring them to examine their own thinking. The teenagers, in particular, were encouraged to put themselves in the place of participants in the dilemma and to examine the way they would react. Members of the group seemed to feel free to challenge each other's perspectives.

Several members had a heated discussion of drinking while under age. The daughter in the M family faced a double dilemma: whether or not to drink at parties and what to tell her parents. Her friends pressured her to "join in," and she personally felt she could handle the amount of liquor she would drink. She knew her parents were terrified of her drinking, however, because alcoholism had been and still was a serious problem in their own families.

> B (adolescent): I think you should do what you think is best for you. You can handle the liquor; besides, other kids make fun if you don't.
>
> M (adolescent): I think you should do what your parents say unless you can convince them to change their minds. After all, they expect you not to drink and you have to realize what they've been through.
>
> D (adolescent): I disagree. Kids are growing up faster today than ever before. Respecting oneself and one's own decisions is emphasized more than parents or others. Some kids are more mature.
>
> L (parent): This thing has gotten away from the fact that it's against the law to drink under eighteen. Where does respect start if not with respecting the law? It was nice that D asked permission of her parents to drink at the prom, but if she had full respect for the law she wouldn't need to ask.

It was difficult at times to keep the discussion focused on the moral issues involved. The levels of moral reasoning present in the adolescents seemed to range from Kohlberg's Stage 2 to Stage 4½. All in all, this class was one of the livelist of the entire workshop. Families were interested during this phase, as they were throughout the course, to continue at home this kind of open discussion about moral conflicts.

EVALUATION OF THE COURSE

Three effects of the course were evaluated: The parents' attitudes toward family decision making and child raising, the families' actual decision making, and the adolescents' moral reasoning.

According to an inventory developed by me, parents in both groups significantly increased their egalitarian attitudes toward family decision making. A modified version of the Parental Attitude Research Instrument indicated that parents in both of the experimental groups became less authoritarian in their child-raising attitudes, but the changes were significant for parents in the class for parents only.

The second effect — actual family decision making — was studied by the Ferreira and Winter Questionnaire for Unrevealed Differences. Families in both groups substantially improved their effectiveness in democratic decision making. In other words, there was a significant increase in their ability to make decisions based on considerations of the greatest good for the greatest number. An analysis of the tape recordings of the family meetings led to the same conclusion. By the end of the course, parents in both groups had measurably decreased the amount of time they spent talking in proportion to the total time of the meeting, thus allowing more participation by the children. Parents in both experimental groups showed a marked improvement in eliciting feelings and opinions from their children. Only among parents in the class for parents and adolescents was there a significant decrease in the number of authoritarian statements they made. At the same time, these parents increased their reflective and summarizing responses during family meetings. Journals kept by the participants throughout the course provided further support for these results. They revealed enhanced communication, greater effectiveness in solving problems, and increasingly egalitarian family relationships.

The third effect of the course was upon the moral development of the adolescent participants as measured by the Kohlberg moral judgment interview. The gain in levels of moral reasoning by the adolescents who participated with their parents in the course (Group A) was significant. This was not the case for those in Group B whose parents participated alone in the training. The Kohlberg measure was given a year later as a follow-up. The moral reasoning scores of Group A continued to rise while Group B showed no significant change (Stanley 1978).

The results of this study indicate that the course was effective in teaching families ways of becoming more just in their methods of establishing rules and resolving conflicts. Participants made real progress, as evidenced by significant changes in both attitudes and behavior, toward making contracts or agreements that involved equal consideration of all points of view.

Why did these changes occur? The most obvious answer is that the curriculum stimulated their learning. A more difficult question centers on which aspects of the course account for the changes. Careful reflection suggests some tentative answers.

Most families came to the workshop with some dissatisfaction with their previous methods of discipline and the quality of the family interaction, and yet they were skeptical that things could really be different. All but one family were willing to try a new approach. The experience of creating rules for the family and solving conflicts collectively gave the children the opportunity to be responsible, respected, and competent individuals with significant contributions to make. Once this process began to occur, most of the parents saw that the children were not going to abuse their increased power. This enabled the parents gradually to relinquish their tight control and to begin to share the decision making. The family meetings allowed the children to assert themselves as responsible members and both parents and children to work to revise the rules of the system to make it more just. Thus it would seem that the teaching of the family meeting and the model for conflict resolution were most crucial to change.

Not only is the content of the curriculum significant when one is considering the findings of this study, but its method is as well. The curriculum was experiential and interactive; furthermore, it dealt with the real problems of the participants. In contrast to many education programs for parents, which are basically lecture and discussion in format, this curriculum focused on the development of skills. The "supervised practicum" nature of the course seemed to be vital to the participants' growth. As Carkhuff (1971) has suggested, people learn best what they practice most. Many families learned from practicing at home and listening to the tape recordings of their family meetings as well as from practicing new skills during the workshop sessions.

A major finding was that the course significantly affected both experimental groups, but in different ways. The class that included both parents and adolescents was more effective in changing parental behavior while the class of parents alone had more of an impact on parental attitudes. The first group of parents were more successful than the second in modifying their ways of responding to their children. This group had opportunities to practice with their adolescents the family meetings and skills of conflict resolution under direct supervision. The second group had no such opportunity; interacting with other adults who were playing the roles of adolescents was apparently not the same as attempting to solve conflicts directly with one's own children. The actual parent-adolescent interaction and supervised practice of skills may have been essential to bring about certain changes in the family's behavior.

There are several possible explanations for the finding that only the second group of parents changed significantly in their authoritarian attitudes. First, there was more time for them to discuss concerns since their group was smaller in size. Second, these parents were perhaps more willing and able to look honestly and critically at their own attitudes and behavior because their children were not present in the workshop. Finally, the socioeconomic background of the two groups was different. Those in the second group were better educated and thus may have been quicker to answer the questionnaire in the socially desirable manner.

The results also indicated that the course affected the moral development of the adolescents who participated directly in it. Despite the short duration of the curriculum and its lack of direct focus on moral dilemmas, four of the seven adolescents in Group A had made substantial gains in their levels of moral reasoning by the end of the ten weeks. We hypothesized that if the families continued to practice what they had learned during the course, the adolescents would show further change by the time of follow-up testing. This is in fact what happened. In Group A, all but one subject (whose score remained the same) showed gains in their moral reasoning scores. All five of these families were still holding family meetings by the time of the follow-up whereas only two families in Group B continued to conduct regular meetings throughout the year. Thus, the family meeting and the increased use of democratic problem solving may have provided the children with open discussions of conflicts and a greater sharing in the family's decision-making process.

Several limitations of the study need to be mentioned. All participants were volunteers who opted for the experience and therefore may have been predisposed to change. In addition, the size of the sample and the lack of randomization hinder the degree to which the results of the study can be generalized. Also, since the experimenter was also one of the group leaders, there was no control over possible bias on the part of the experimenter. The ideal situation is for the investigator to train others to conduct the groups. Finally, the democratic model of conflict resolution may not be a culturally fair technique for resolving family problems.

20
PARENTS AS
MORAL EDUCATORS

Robert Azrak

This book summarizes much educational research done over the past several years based on Lawrence Kohlberg's theory of moral development. Of particular pertinence to this chapter were studies showing that parents can stimulate their children's moral reasoning development with a "traditional" curriculum of hypothetical moral dilemmas and related activities (Grimes 1974) and through discussion by the family of the moral issues in their everyday life together (Stanley 1976). I shall report a study where parents of early adolescents were trained to isolate the moral aspects of family discipline situations and to use these experiences to promote the moral development of the children.

The writings of Lawrence Kohlberg (see Chapter 2) and Peter Blos provided the theoretical perspectives for this research. Each writer emphasizes the importance of completing "tasks" that press peculiarly on young adolescents in order that they may cope effectively with subsequent developmental demands (Blos 1962, 1967, 1970, 1971; Kohlberg, 1969, 1973a, 1973b). Kohlberg, for example, says that the early adolescent is in transition between preconventional and conventional stages of moral reasoning, while Blos describes the struggles of budding adolescents to separate themselves from childhood ties. My objective was to teach parents about the developmental tasks affecting their children and discipline strategies to help their children negotiate these tasks.

Earlier research on discipline had investigated sex and class differences in the way parents dealt with their children's misbehaviors (Brofenbrenner 1958; Gecas and Nye 1974; Kohn 1959). These studies confirmed that parents do differ in their use of physical punishment, restrictions on the child's freedom of movement or activity, the use of isolation, appeals to reason, and attempts to help the child develop internal controls. Discipline began to be viewed on a continuum from "authoritarianism to egalitarianism." Further studies described the difficulties faced by the parents of adolescents when their discipline was either "too authoritarian" or "too egalitarian" (Bowerman and Kinch 1959; Brittam 1963; Elder 1962, 1963).

Research had also been done on the effects of a particular discipline approach on the child's development. Hoffman and Saltzstein (1967) measured the relative effects of what they called "power assertive" discipline, "love withdrawal" discipline, and "inductive reasoning" discipline on the moral development of early adolescents. They found that inductive discipline, where the parent focuses on the consequences of the child's action for others, correlated highest with indexes of moral development. Hoffman and Saltzstein concluded that inductive discipline can promote moral understanding in youngsters since children exposed to inductive discipline had learned conventional moral reasoning while the other two discipline approaches were associated in children with Kohlberg's preconventional moral reasoning stages.

I designed this curriculum with the belief that moral and emotional development in early adolescence presented a challenge to the way parents habitually handled several aspects of discipline. During a pilot test I learned that parents were confused by the "new" moral reasoning that their children used in discipline situations. A second aspect was that parents did not want to be "too strict" but questioned how much freedom they should allow their children. Also, the parents in the pilot study clearly experienced their children's need to separate from close family ties as a personal rejection. Additionally, I learned that the early adolescents who participated with their parents in the pilot study were increasingly motivated to discuss different moral viewpoints in discipline situations when their parents showed a capacity to attend to issues related to separation and independence.

The curriculum was influenced by my belief that parents wanted to understand how their children were changing and how these changes affected what they should do in discipline situations. During the first study I found that parents wanted to learn skills to resolve immediate discipline situations *and* techniques to promote the moral and emotional development of their children. I designed a multidimensional curriculum to address these topics.

What interested me was whether parents could be trained to use inductive discipline to stimulate the moral development of their adolescents. Could parents help their children reflect on the egocentric aspects of their motives and behavior? Could they teach their children a more advanced level of moral reasoning plus new ways of behaving morally? The assumption was that the early adolescents would exhibit advanced moral reasoning if their parents learned how to lead moral discussions, became less authoritarian in their attitudes toward child rearing, and learned to attend to the separation issues of early adolescence.

THE TECHNICAL ASPECTS OF THE STUDY

The parents and adolescents studied were from a suburb of Boston. The subjects were identified with the cooperation of junior high school principals, guidance departments, and parent associations. The subjects were assigned to either a treatment group or a control group on a "first come-first serve" basis. A careful effort was made to include "average" families (for example, students or families receiving psychological treatment were not included).

The treatment and control groups of parents and children did not differ in composition. Each group consisted of 19 parents (7 couples plus 5 mothers) and 18 adolescents (seventh-, eighth-, or ninth-grade students in public school). All participants were white and a large percentage of the parents were college graduates. The children of the parents in the experimental class did not attend the course with their parents but were observed for its effects. The data were collected within a three-week period prior to and following the course for the parents. Testing was done at the homes of the subjects.

As I stated in my introductory comments, the major purpose of this course was to teach parents ways to use discipline situations as experiences to promote the moral reasoning of their children. The development of moral reasoning was described in this study by scores on the Kohlberg Moral Judgment Interview (Kohlberg 1975). The interview was individually administered to each child in the treatment and control groups before and after the course to observe whether the course produced changes in moral reasoning. Following the posttesting of both groups the protocols were scored, double-blind, by a certified scorer.

The parent group was the major focus of the treatment since the children did not attend the weekly class sessions. The parents were expected to motivate their children to participate with them at home in structured homework assignments and also were expected to apply what they learned in class to everyday discipline situations.

The parents were observed for change on three variables, each highly related to the major purpose of the course. The first variable was parental attitude toward child rearing, described in this study by scores on the Parental Attitude Research Instrument (Cross and Kawash 1968). On this test parents are asked whether they agree or disagree with 45 questionnaire statements. The test measures the degree of authoritarianism in parents' attitudes toward child rearing. I believed this was an important area to affect for two reasons. I thought that a rigid, authoritarian attitude would make it difficult for parents to use inductive discipline and thereby promote conventional moral reasoning. Second, I thought that if parents adopted more egalitarian attitudes toward child rearing they would be better able to attend to the separation needs of their children. Parents in the treatment and control groups were administered the Attitude Research Instrument before and after the course.

Previous moral education studies involving parents and children stressed the importance of helping the parents with specific communication skills. My pilot study confirmed these findings. I wanted to teach the parents specific skills to lead discussions of hypothetical moral dilemmas and then show the parents how to use the same discussion skills to resolve discipline situations and to promote moral reasoning. I defined discussion leadership skills as the ability to *encourage* the child's participation in the discussion and the ability to differentiate or explore the various moral choices involved in the dilemma. The "Karl and Bob" dilemma from the original Kohlberg Interview (Kohlberg 1973b) was selected as the stimulus story for the task. Parents discussed this dilemma with their children before and after the course, tape recording each session. In scoring for their discussion skill, parents received one point for an "encouraging" response and one point for a "differentiating" response.

The third matter of central interest in this study was parental attention to the adolescent separation process. Blos has compared the adolescent separation process to the separation strivings of infants struggling to individuate and to perceive themselves as different from their mothers. Separation in adolescence means that the child becomes gradually less dependent on his or her family and learns to relate to his or her parents and other important adults in different ways. My intent was to teach parents that they had an important role in the separation process, and that the process was critical to their child's development and overall personal adjustment. I also believed that attention to the separation process, along with moral discussion skills and less authoritarian attitudes toward child rearing, were all needed by the parents to use inductive discipline effectively and to promote the moral reasoning of adolescents.

The parents' view of the separation process was measured by a modified version of the Disengagement Measure (Manthei 1972). The parents read a story about an adolescent and then answered a series of projective questions. Higher scores on this measure reflect greater parental awareness of disengagement, the separation process just beginning in their children.

THE COURSE FOR PARENTS

The experimental course was taught to the parents over a ten-week period. The parents were assigned to one of two class sections and met as a group, weekly, for one and one-half hour sessions. The classes met in a local church. The meeting room had a large couch and a number of comfortable chairs that were arranged in a circle to facilitate communication. I was the class instructor. The children of the parents in the course formally participated through homework assignments that their parents did with them.

Parents were taught to consistently apply the principles of induction (Hoffman and Saltzstein 1967) in everyday discipline encounters. Concurrently, parents gained an understanding of how children differ in their thinking about right and wrong at different stages of moral development.

By elaborating the stages of moral development where family members typically functioned, I expected to increase parents' understanding of how there are different ways of thinking about right and wrong. I believed knowledge of Kohlberg's theory would increase the parents' skill in using inductive discipline. Also, I believed the discipline situations would be powerful moral education experiences for the children. According to Hoffman and Saltzstein, inductive discipline involves reasoning with the child about right and wrong behavior and the consequences of the particular behavior for the child *and* for others.

The course was divided into three phases. They were not intended to be entirely separate units and often overlapped. However, in each phase particular content was taught.

Phase I: Introduction to Moral Development Theory

Phase I was devoted to introducing the course of study to parents and children. In the first session I discussed openly the parents' motivations for participating in the course. Previously, I had found that parents were usually apprehensive at the first meeting and it helped them to hear that others had similar concerns. For homework, I asked the parents to complete a "Hassle Survey" with their children. They were each given a sheet of paper that was divided into four columns. On the top of each column was one of four headings: "Contracts," "Property," "Punishment (rules)," "Parent-Child Relationship," representing four recurrent moral issues defined by Kohlberg (1973b). Parents were asked to have their children share their perceptions of everyday conflicts and to categorize them by one of the four topic headings. The "Hassle Survey" was the parents' initial introduction to Kohlberg's theory and it was the first invitation to the children to participate at home.

The major teaching emphasis of Sessions two and three was the two-part filmstrip, *How Moral Am I?* (Tree House, Inc., 1973), which describes Kohlberg's theory of moral development. The group was directed to focus on the stage differences between their own moral reasoning and that of their children. These differences became clearer as they engaged their youngsters in the homework assignments.

A major task I had as teacher during Phase I was helping the parents examine the resistance they faced when they invited their youngsters to discuss moral dilemmas. The resistance was expressed in several different ways. Some parents became angry at me, some joked about the relevancy of Kohlberg's theory, some lost the weekly homework assignment. Parents were taught to examine such resistance as a result of the way they related (or failed to relate) to their youngster. For example, for one father this meant understanding the hypocrisy in ordering his 15-year-old son to turn off the television set to discuss a hypothetical moral dilemma about a character who needs to choose between alternatives!

Phase II: Typical Discipline Issues

During the next four classes, the moral issues of contracts, property, punishment, and parent-child relationship were discussed in detail to show how differently people perceive "What is Right?" To relate the class to home experiences, parents took the responsibility of initiating the discussion by describing an actual discipline situation. For example, one father had contracted the following with his daughter: "If you do the chores, I will give you your allowance and your mother will provide car transportation on weekends." Family problems occurred with this contract because on some weekends their daughter did not need extra money or transportation. The parents were directed to examine the situation for its moral conflicts and implications for encouraging moral development. We talked about effective ways of making contracts with children in the context of Kohlberg's theory. In this situation the group advised the parents to renegotiate the contract on Stage 3 terms. There was to be a new basis for the contract. Instead of "give and take" the parents would emphasize the need for everyone to do their share of household tasks.

The focus was shifting gradually from moral development theory to home discipline issues. There was increased parent interest in exploring attitudes toward child rearing, specifically issues of authority. Understanding the disengagement process also became more important. By now parents were beginning to feel comfortable expressing their ideas in the group. The direction of the course was clearer to them. I was also receiving reports from the parents of improved relationships with their children.

I began every class with a short activity designed to encourage discussion of these issues. For example, all participants were asked to state a "vividly remembered discipline situation from their youth." This kind of probe usually elicited negative past experiences and motivated the parents to examine their own practices. One parent recalled that his father used "embarassment" as his typical discipline technique and admitted to the group that when he was very angry he was prone to relate to his son in this manner. In addition to helping the parents to examine their own practices, these activities motivated them to learn alternative ways of relating to their children.

Phase III: Promoting Moral Development through Discipline

The focus of Phase III was direct application in the family of what had been learned. The parents were taught to confront the "morality" implicit in their children's misbehavior and to explain the effects of that behavior on others. They were directed to apply discussion leadership skills in the family's discussion of the moral aspects of everyday discipline situations. I asked the parents to review the "Hassle Survey" with their children. Further, I encouraged them to perceive each incident where they had to intervene with discipline as an opportunity to promote moral development.

In class the parents discussed discipline situations that occurred during the previous week. It was clear that discipline issues were the focus both for new understanding and practice between the parents and their children. However, it was also evident that the parents had difficulty consistently applying these new procedures. The change in the course from hypothetical dilemmas to real situations resurrected resistances from parents and children similar to the kind of resistance I noted earlier. During this phase of the course I was assigning homework that challenged the way the parents and children interacted during an already uncomfortable interpersonal encounter, the discipline situation.

There were specific activities during Sessions eight to ten to help parents and children handle this aspect of the course. For a homework assignment, both adults and children individually completed an adaption of Hoffman and Saltz-stein's (1967) measure of the way parents disciplined their children. They then compared their responses. Many parents were shocked to discover that their youngsters perceived their discipline to be predominately the assertion of power or the withdrawal of love. This led to discussion in class of the factors that inhibit parent-child communication and ways to make discipline a "positive" learning experience for the child.

The parents reported that this kind of homework activity was especially useful in helping their children perceive that they were conscientiously trying to make changes in their discipline style.

I also focused on the topic of adolescent separation during this phase of the course. I did not assign specific homework activities on the topic; however, when children perceived their parents as more egalitarian and as acknowledging the separation process, the parents reported less resistance to discipline and more interest in higher-stage moral reasons for behaving.

RESULTS OF THE STUDY

One hypothesis of the study was that the moral reasoning of adolescents would be promoted following their parents' participation in a course that focused on moral development theory and its implications for parental discipline. That effect was found.

The second aim of the course was to teach parents to adopt more egalitarian attitudes toward child rearing. That did not occur.

Third, I predicted that as a result of participation in the course significant changes would be observed in parents' ability to lead family discussions. That effect was found.

Finally, it was anticipated that parents who took the course would develop a deeper understanding of the child's need to disengage from them and the family. This, too, was borne out by the data.

DISCUSSION OF THE RESULTS

The significant effects of the course on the adolescents' moral reasoning are in substantial agreement with earlier parent-child moral education research (Grimes 1974; Stanley 1976). The average moral reasoning score of the experimental group advanced 17 points, nearly one-fifth of a stage and 11 of the 18 subjects evidenced stage movement. Several children attained a score of 300 on the posttest, indicating the use of Stage 3 moral reasoning.

It is important to note that the experimental course had several components. Only future research can determine the distinct effects of each aspect. My opinion is that all parts of the course contributed positively to the observed results. Further, it seems unlikely that any one phase of the course could have produced the significant changes in moral reasoning with the present experimental design.

The present discussion will examine the results from two points of departure. First, the parents explored attitudes toward child rearing, learned discussion leadership skills, and were taught to understand the process of adolescent separation. I will speculate about how these learnings contributed to the parent's success in promoting adolescent moral reasoning. Second, a course expectation was that all parent participants would complete weekly homework assignments with their children. I will discuss why I believe that these assignments were very important to the observed changes in adolescent moral reasoning.

Early in the course I perceived from the parents' comments that the most predictable and pervasive element of their discipline style was inconsistency! Many of them at times used an authoritarian style and other times tried an egalitarian approach. The techniques of "power assertion," "withdrawal of love," and "inductive discipline" were also applied randomly. A further complication was the parents' use of moral reasoning anywhere from Stage 1 to Stage 5 during a typical discipline confrontation.

Thus I emphasized Kohlberg's developmental perspective and fostered the attitude that there was an appropriate style of discipline to parallel each of the moral reasoning stages. I frequently reminded the parents that their children were in a period of transition from Stage 2 to Stage 3 and that they would need to adopt a flexible approach to accommodate these two very different modes of moral reasoning.

I believe that this part of the course was an extremely important factor to the parents' success in promoting their adolescents' moral reasoning. The parents sought and obtained a stable and consistent "modus operandi" to use in discipline situations. They received confirmation from me and from other group members that a blend of authoritarianism and egalitarianism was an appropriate way to interact with adolescents. The process of inductive discipline has a purpose. The act of discipline was perceived less as an aversive interaction and more as an opportunity to promote moral reasoning.

As noted, I did not find significant change in the parents' attitudes toward greater egalitarianism. The parents pretested high in this regard as compared to the parents in the Stanley (1976) study. Since I taught them to adopt a "middle ground" regarding authoritarianism-egalitarianism, it is not surprising the class as a whole did not make a significant change in attitude.

As already noted, in many of the families communication about discipline was inconsistent. The study of discussion skills helped the parents direct their attention to specific tasks of communication. For example, the parents learned that they first had to encourage their children's participation before they could explore different perspectives on right and wrong in an effective, growth-producing manner.

The parents' increased ability to lead discussions contributed to the change in the adolescent's moral reasoning in another way. The family discussions of both hypothetical dilemmas and "real life" conflicts became a forum for the exchange of ideas crucial to moral stage change (Rest, Turiel, and Kohlberg 1969; Turiel 1966, 1974). Parents helped their children think about the differences between Stage 2 and Stage 3 ways of perceiving right and wrong. The parents also reinforced Stage 3 reasoning as more socially acceptable in general and as more favorable to family group functioning.

A further aim was to make the parents aware that disengagement, a natural developmental phenomenon, was occurring. The parents were helped to realize that as a child separated, both the parent and child experienced a personal loss. The parents acknowledged that this was emotionally difficult for them and learned how their personal reactions could influence their children's behavior. By recalling their own adolescent years, the parents were able to conceptualize how the separation process must now be for their children.

Like the work on discipline style and discussion skills, learning about disengagement gave the parents another developmentally appropriate way to interact with their children. The parents began to understand their children's ambivalence about leaving the relative stability of home for the exciting but unpredictable peer culture. This offered the parents an opportunity to react to their child in a controlled and consistent manner and to balance the thought confusion, mixed feelings, and extreme moods that their children were experiencing.

The parents' attention to the disengagement process facilitated their children's transitions from Stage 2 to Stage 3 morality. The parents learned that they could actively promote both the disengagement process and moral reasoning by providing an atmosphere of trust and predictability whenever they observed separation strivings in their children. The children could now "test their wings," assured that the same social nest would be there when they needed to return. Additionally, I instructed the parents to utilize these "test flights" as opportunities to promote moral reasoning. For example, a discussion about going out with the gang on Saturday night instead of accompanying the family to the movies could be used to facilitate the separation process and also to negotiate a Stage 3 contract about what time the child should be home.

Let me conclude with the importance of "homework." Beginning with the "Hassle Survey," the homework tasks consistently were designed to help the parents and children categorize important thoughts related to family conflicts and the experience of discipline. I proceeded in this way because without this direction parents and children tend to react globally and very emotionally to discussions about discipline. It would have been an impossible task to have them focus on the moral issues of contracts, the parent-child relationship, property, and punishment rules without a structured and sequential program of assignments.

The task design was important to the gains in adolescent moral reasoning from a theoretical standpoint. The transition from Stage 2 to Stage 3 in early adolescence represents a major conceptual undertaking for children at a time when physiological changes force them to contend with strong feelings and confusing thoughts. The curriculum helped the children establish cognitive control over thoughts and feelings irrelevant to the discipline issue and to focus on, for example, the rule that was transgressed or the contract that was ignored. I am convinced that this aspect of the curriculum design was decisive to the success of the course.

The parents' reaction to a cognitively oriented curriculum is an important consideration for future workers in parent education. Many of them initially were disappointed when they discovered that they could not come to the class each week and "discharge tension." The parents who did the most complaining about not being permitted to use the entire class to vent feelings were the ones who had the most difficulty thinking about why they reacted in a certain way during a discipline encounter. After the first few sessions I found that the resistance to an expectation of new knowledge and new behavior vis-à-vis their children subsided.

In summary, the findings of the present study showed that a relatively short (ten-week) training intervention has a significant impact on parent *and* child development. One important limitation of the study was that it involved middle class parents, who were predominately college graduates. Therefore, the results cannot be generalized to other socioeconomic groups. Another limitation is that the course was designed to address the developmental needs of early adolescents and their parents. Its effectiveness with younger children or older adolescents must be tested.

So far, moral education studies involving parents have focused on the older child and the adolescent. Parents and teachers of children in the primary grades can give many convincing arguments why moral education interventions are needed with the young child. An intervention designed to help children attain Stage 2 moral reasoning would be an interesting and important contribution.

PART IV
CONCLUSIONS

21

MORAL EDUCATION:
THE NEXT GENERATION

Ralph Mosher

This concluding chapter is being written in the last month of the last year of a decade. Retrospectives are so common as to be clichéd. Tom Wolfe on "Good Morning America" sees the 1970s as "wilder" than the 1960s. His first example is co-ed college dorms where young people "whose juices are at maximum flow are allowed to cohabit, like terriers in the park. We're numb in the face of such moral changes." Watergate is another example: "Both its heroes and its villains cash in. Books by John Dean, Mo Dean, Judge Sirica, Richard Nixon. Even Senator Sam Erwin, the hero of Watergate, with the ability to cut through the persiflage: 'I'm just a down-home country lawyer but I know the difference between right and wrong' winds up on a television ad: "Do you know me?" Is that why he protected the Constitution, to appear in an American Express card advertisement?" The issue for Wolfe is not only one of a changed morality, but also of propriety, of what is socially acceptable in conduct or speech.

That a leading American author is numbed by the moral changes he observes at home and school describes the social context in which the moral education reported in this book flourished. That society sneezes and the schools contract pneumonia is a point made relentlessly. And if American society is deeply afflicted morally? A decade that began with the terrible social, moral, and generational divisions over Vietnam reached new political lows in Watergate's assaults on the Constitution, ends with the first visit of the Pope to America, a woman Nobel Laureate's call for social justice for the poor and the child in utero, and Americans held hostage by a fanatical Iranian Ayatollah.

The book pales in significance by contrast to this larger play of values, cultures, and *real politik*. Moral education is in danger of being, after economics, the second most dismal of the social sciences. Its curricular abstractions of real life seem dull, sometimes intentionally so. How does Heinz compete with Khomeini as a moral educator? The fact that publishers will bring out yet another book on moral development and education, that American capitalists think there is money to be made in morality, documents the fact that the social context of our work gave it topicality, an audience and even a modest market.

THE CASE FOR THE FIRST GENERATION

Not that there is anything wrong, even in academe, with being topical — it's just not one's accustomed state. This book, however, is written to be used by school administrators, curriculum directors, teachers, and counselors as well as researchers. It is intended to influence subsequent practices in moral education, but the book and its content of moral education have merit in their own right. It seems important to summarize the merits and the limitations of what we have learned as a guide to the next generation. Point one is that the book is based on the leading contemporary theory of moral development. Both Piaget and Kohlberg say that the essence of morality is our thinking about right and wrong. Further, our moral understanding can grow in its complexity and expression of ethical principles. Despite the limitations of this psychological explanation of morality — for example, its heavy and rather touching belief in reasoning as the key to moral decisions in human beings and their institutions, the uncertain connection between knowing what is right and doing it, and the philosophical disputes about justice as the ultimate virtue — Kohlberg's theory offers benchmarks for understanding how and why our children think as they do plus a strong psychological case for moral education.

The book also is unequivocal about why we educate people. We do so to promote their further development as human beings. The education described here is a modern restatement of John Dewey. Indeed, as Kohlberg points out in Chapter 2, its philosophical lineage is much older; but a concern that education should promote human thinking, moral reasoning, justice in individuals and in our schools permeates these chapters. If that isn't substantial or ambitious enough there is a common effort to stimulate other dimensions of children's growth. For example, their ego development or knowledge of themselves, their ability to effect their environment (to decide school rules, grading policy, to govern their classroom, to cooperate socially).

Another contribution of this book is to report what happens when the theorists (in this case Kohlberg, Mosher, and their colleagues) go into the arena. Not all of the gory details, incidentally, but gladiators regularly get killed in the arena and the spectators pay to see that occur. Indeed, many come to cheer for the lions. If funny things happen on the way to the forum, very unfunny things happen in it. Some gladiators live to fight, more wisely and well, another day. That is the case for those whose early bouts are described here.

Stated less metaphorically, practice does alter theory. Kohlberg describes how his conception of moral development was affected by Blatt's (1970) finding that reasoning could be stimulated by Socratic discussion in classrooms. Yet classroom education for justice was undermined by prisons or schools that were unjust. In effect, Kohlberg's idealized conception of an education for justice was progressively adjusted to Stage 5 and then Stage 4 translations of that ideal by the experience of trying to vitalize it in the interactions of teachers and students in an alternative school. A Socratic model was supplanted by an idea of moral education relying much more on collective normative thinking and action plus teacher advocacy or indoctrination in the values of being a good citizen and a good community member. Mosher describes a somewhat parallel odyssey between practice and theory. He moved from a Kohlberg view of classroom moral education to Dewey's conceptions of political and social democracy in schooling. His ultimate concern was the promotion of all-around student development and the contributions democratic participation in school make to that.

The research and development in moral education reported here was done with reasonable care. Homesteaders, however, shouldn't be judged by the standards of ornamental gardeners. This record of research has the virtues and the vices of its genre and times. The latter are acknowledged later in this chapter, but by and large our claims were modest. We didn't even set out to write a book. Only later did we become authors in search of a common theme (or failing that, an uncommon publisher). Perhaps the greatest expectations created were for the "just community" studies. The findings that students' moral growth in such "natural" social units is not appreciably greater than in response to good Socratic classroom teaching puts that claim in perspective. Looking beyond gains in the students' moral reasoning, however, there is evidence of important moral, social, and political behavior associated with participation in democratic schooling. That finding has been made with both adolescents and children.

Further, the studies reported here *are* consequential in their cumulative evidence as to the effect of carefully conceived moral education. One swallow doesn't make a spring, 21 of them building nests on the wall of the Mission certainly look like the rites of spring. Indeed, most enterprises in public education flourish on the basis of no more substantiated claims to be teaching children to think. Certainly the book reports the largest body of coordinated if diverse formative research on moral education in the schools done during the 1970s.

The collective efforts of the authors created a base for moral education within the curriculum and not simply as a Tuesday afternoon "add-on" in social studies. Rather, new content and emphasis were created in existing disciplines, for example, in American history, social studies, law, and psychology. Practitioners have taken on expanded roles. Many counselors, for example, taught moral education. Elementary school teachers systematically have changed what they do to permit children a greater voice and participation in formulating the conditions of their schooling. The research and development clearly both has recognized and acted upon the moral nature of schools and classrooms. Moral education, all the more powerful because it is "hidden," is embedded in the tacit values of the curriculum and the school. For example, the most worthy/ valued student in Brookline High School is the one who achieves early admission to Harvard on a full scholarship. How few can accomplish this is obvious. Yet teachers, counselors, and parents put great, albeit subtle, pressure on the many to do likewise. Sarason (1971) has told us that teachers think of this as business as usual, certainly not as moral education. Yet its normative force is enormous if one listens to students in their senior year. What the research has attempted is to make some schooling more just, democratic, or, at least, examined so that it may enhance, rather than simply socialize, student development.

Further, teachers and counselors were accorded a full partnership in all of this. They were respected as capable of developing curriculum and materials for moral education, of training other teachers to go and do likewise, and to alter the conditions of childrens' participation in governing and cooperating in the classroom. While many were called and few chose, those who did confirmed the assumption that teachers, too, are competent to do and to grow.

Reliance upon "tenant ownership and management" by teachers, counselors, and administrators in Brookline and Cambridge was a key element of a modest strategy for educational change explicit in this research and development. As noted, teachers were assumed at first to be most interested in modifying their own curricula and teaching to incorporate moral education. They were helped to do so (by no means fully enough, as a matter of fact). Ownership and title to the materials was clearly in the teacher's name. Where indicated, the teacher was encouraged to publish his or her curricula and pedagogy. Several of the chapters in the book attest to this. Teachers also were encouraged to be the trainers of other teachers in moral education. A significant number in Brookline and Cambridge have done so actively and effectively. All of these means to improved curriculum and teaching, staff development, and the democratizing of schooling seem generalizable to many systems.

What is less immediately generalizable to teacher development elsewhere is the special town-gown relationships between Brookline, Cambridge, Boston University, and Harvard. Many faculty members in both school systems were attracted to graduate study in connection with the on-going research and development on moral education and school democracy. Indeed, most of the authors of this book, now academics, are former employees of the two public school systems. Where they have left the schools proper they have moved to positions of continued leadership in public education. Their leadership will be one of the enduring legacies of the work reported here. In a similar way in the school, democracy research, students, and teachers become co-owners of the governance and social construction of the school. That hands over the keys to change to the people most intelligent to make it and most affected by it. Once people have the franchise there is a greater likelihood they will continue to exercise it.

Two other strengths of this research will be lumped together. One is that it has been done with children and adolescents at all ages, except preschool. While predominated by findings from children who are white and middle class (if not proper Bostonians), much diversity of race, creed, ethnicity, and social class is represented in Brookline and Cambridge and in these chapters (see particularly Kohlberg, Lickona, Paolitto, Stanley, and Wasserman). This is not to claim that the demographic waterfront is covered by two small East Coast cities. Both, however, became much more urban, racially diverse, poor, and cultural melting pots as the decade progressed.

Finally, several chapters (Azrak, Grimes, Stanley) recognize the critical role parents have in the moral education of their children. They report what happens to parents and the moral development of their children when jointly they discuss moral issues in the home and school. Ironically, perhaps the hardest and least successful part of our whole enterprise has been to give away to parents what we know about childrens' moral development and how best to teach them right from wrong. Yet the promise of that audience is as compelling as ever.

THE SINS OF THE FATHERS

The younger generation often has its limitations pointed out to it. In doing so, their elders forget (or exploit?) the fact that the young are painfully aware of their inadequacies. Every pimple, every D in calculus, every inch added to the hips or subtracted from one's height hurts deeply. The research and development reported in this book is admittedly a first generation of moral education, if that phrase is not too pompous or precious. Its limitations are manifest, yet they should be balanced by an important consideration. Two recent annual bibliographies of work in the field of moral education report over 383 citations (Cochrane 1978, 1979). Of these only six, or less than two percent, test the curricular effectiveness of a particular approach to moral or values education. "Current study in this field is dominated by writing advocating or explicating a particular approach. In addition, one finds an abundance of analytical examinations, often critical, of assumptions behind such approaches . . . At some point, however, the researcher must join the cheerleaders and the critics if educators are to develop broad-based and informed judgments concerning the worth of the approaches being proffered" (Leming 1979). So criticism, as usual, is cheap. Nor are philosophical analyses that offer no practical solutions (beyond themselves) especially useful. The very hard work of carefully formulating and testing classroom practices in moral education is understandably as rare as $1.00 a gallon gasoline. Over 90 percent of this book describes and evaluates such practices. Merits or demerits shouldn't be assessed without weighing how much is being attempted.

On Icarus, and Flying Too High

First children also educate their parents and pay a price for so doing. In one sense, the studies reported here were highly ambitious ones. Without laboring the metaphor that, too, may be a characteristic of the young. They were intended to stake out the ground of moral education. Children in first grade to 18-year-old seniors in high school were studied. This means the research encompassed age and developmental levels from school entry, moral Stage 1, to young adulthood and moral Stage 5. Teacher training and parent education also were undertaken.

Our ambitious nature is further reflected in the variety of educational experiences analyzed. These ranged from classroom discussion of moral dilemmas in the work of Ladenburg and Grimes; moral education jointly involving parents and their children (for example, Grimes and Stanley); studies of classroom democracy (Rundle, Lickona); to creating and evaluating the effects of a just community and a democratic high school on adolescents' moral growth. Indeed, Kohlberg was serious about making schools just institutions. I was willing to settle for more sharply etched shadows on the walls of School-Within-A-School rather than the Platonic ideal. Add the fact that we tried and tested curricula that ran the gamut from the conventional (Ladenburg) to the unconventional (Alexander, DiStefano) to the relatively radical (Kohlberg, Mosher, Lickona) and we really did have a lot of balls in the air. That we dropped some (for example, comprehensive measures of other aspects of student development than moral reasoning) and fumbled others egregiously (for example, longitudinal research) is understandable if not forgivable.

Was Anyone in Charge Here?

As noted, the studies were intended to sink test wells, to get some sense of the potential of the field. A phrase used in curriculum development in the 1960s, "post-holing," is descriptive. The research and development were not orchestrated by a master plan in my office or Larry Kohlberg's. Such a blueprint for a second generation is now feasible. Of that, more later. At the same time, we didn't, like Topsy, just grow. Kohlberg's theory pointed the way. It said, for example, that discussion of moral issues, exposure to higher-stage thinking, the experience of social cooperation or helping others, making actual moral choices, particularly in "natural" social settings (for example, schools, families) where the child experiences the consequences of such decisions, and so on, would contribute to moral development.

Thus there was an organic, if not a consecutive, quality to the way these studies built on one another. For example, Grimes, following Blatt, focused on the added effectiveness of mothers, in contrast to teachers, as moral educators; Rundle on the impact of classroom democracy in the elementary school on children's moral reasoning; Paolitto on role-taking experiences in junior high school and their relationship to moral growth; Stanley on education to enhance the moral interaction of parents and their adolescents; Azrak on the education of parents alone as moral educators. Thus religious school moral discussion was extended to public elementary school and to parents; the Kohlberg, Hickey, and Scharf research in prisons was adapted to classroom democracy in the fifth grade (and, à la Bruner, to young children) and in two alternative high schools. Whether role-taking, in practice as in theory, was a precursor to moral development was tested with poor children in junior high school; parents' effectiveness as moral educators was studied in the natural unit of the adolescents' family and as a more traditional form of adult education. Clearly, these are not unrelated studies. The Rundle research, as a further example, was to be a precursor to all of the development activity in classroom democracy reported by Lickona and Paradise. Parallel research and development was being conducted at the high school on classroom moral discussion, the just community school, and democratic alternative schooling.

So, too, were there pedagogical consistencies. Many of the curricula (Alexander, DiStefano, Sullivan, Wasserman) incorporated common experiences, for example, peer counseling, designed to increase the adolescents' empathy or role-taking ability. Experiences in social service, in acting to apply formal learning, for example, by teaching moral education to younger students, were common to several curricula. The discussion of moral dilemmas, hypothetical and personal, occurred in all of the work. How Socratic or "pure" these discussions were undoubtedly varied and so, one suspects, did their effects on the students' thinking. The problem with multiple experiences within and across such curricula, however, was the inability to parse them, to decide which made a difference to the outcome. That is a clear limitation in interpreting the results. One really doesn't know what to keep and what to throw out: The recurrent personal introductions? Peer counseling? Town meetings?

Funny Things Happen on the Way to Commencement

A major qualifier of these studies is that they have the strengths and the failings of doctoral and practitioners' research. We were not a massively funded, 1960s style, curriculum development project (viz the Biological Sciences' Study Group, of which I had personal experience). The research typically was done by individual professors and graduate students, working alone or in small teams. That, incidentally, is a powerful way to get development accomplished. Like the marines, we needed only a few good men and women. But funds, time, and samples of students were limited. Doctoral research, even when it is orchestrated by the faculty members' theory or concepts, will be characterized by topics that are *ad hominem*. The idiosyncratic interests and experiences of the particular researcher, rather than the imperatives of the theory or progress in practice, will be reflected.

Since Ed.D.s don't tend to stick around after commencement, their research characteristically isn't longitudinal. Therefore, we are unable to answer Lockwood's question about the long-term stability of the treatment effects found. I personally do not doubt that these gains are permanent. The Cluster School and SWS data suggest that progress in moral development, while slow, is steady, although only for about 60 percent of the students who attended. Why that may be so is a separate problem for the next round of research. Similarly, we don't have adequate data as to the average moral development in high school against which to compare the apparent greater maturity of students who participate in moral education programs. Longitudinal follow-up of both control and experimental subjects of the kind done by Blatt, Kohlberg, and Erickson is imperative for further research.

Doctoral students also are more knowledgeable and interested in moral development theory, theory generally, and various moral education practices than are regular classroom teachers. They are more invested in inquiry concerning practice. Their degree of sophistication (and, therefore, effect?) realistically is unlikely to be matched by teachers who participate in large-scale dissemination programs in moral education. Interestingly enough, however, only three of the authors in this book with Ed.D. after their names were teachers by trade; the others were counselors. Such on-the-job pedagogical training might be expected to depress their effectiveness. That all of them were highly motivated to produce "results" in children's moral reasoning cannot be denied.

The limitations of research done in the natural laboratories of schools and classrooms are much commented on in the literature but little experienced — understandably so! Review by capricious research and testing committees, to say nothing of school boards; the impossibility of random assignment of subjects; the forgetfulness and groans of students asked to take the Kohlberg Moral Maturity Scale: "Again?"; the thousands of hours spent as a participant observer in classrooms or town meetings; the cost and the delays involved in scoring and data analysis of the MMS echo between the lines of many chapters. Collectively, these factors must affect the findings. My opinion is that they depress rather than inflate the results. Yet the data, collectively, fall out in the same direction — on the side of growth; and there is the distinct smell of school reality about this book.

Similar realities may have affected the research originating with the Brookline teachers. It is impressive for its curricular richness, but its measured effects on adolescents' moral reasoning were negligible. As Higgins points out, content goals undoubtedly were first in the teachers' minds. Development was a strong second. What all of them produced were lively, sophisticated curricula, stimulating or moving for children but with nominal developmental effects. This cannot be other than sobering for those who plan dissemination of programs of classroom moral education. I am reminded of an earlier generation of educators who found that high school physics teachers could be taught more physics but not the view that physics can contribute to the general education of adolescents rather than their academic winnowing out.

The Frailties of the First Generation in Summary

Let me add my own summary to Higgins' and Lockwood's critique of the genre of curriculum research represented in this book. I preface it by an article of faith. If we are as objective and candid as we can be about what we know and don't know we make a maximum contribution to the next generation in this field. That is the ethic of science. *Veritas,* as we know it, is our most important legacy. That being the case, the principal limitations of the curricular studies reported here were their ad hoc and ad hominem character. They were insufficiently consecutive and replicated. In another sense, they lived and died with the evolving interests and careers of their authors. As courses, they were unevenly integrated into the permanent curricula of the schools. They suffered from a lack of longitudinal follow-up, a logical requirement of any developmental research. Insufficient data were collected on other factors (for example, the Piagetian, cognitive stages of the students' development or the growth of political and social attitudes among SWS students, which might explain some of the changes associated with the interventions). Insufficient teacher training was given in Brookline to the pedagogy of classroom moral discussion and to the elements known to contribute to its effectiveness. We tried to do too much, too quickly. We were incautious in our claims as to the effects of such programs; at times, inexcusably so. Telling people (foundation officers, reporters) what they and we wanted to believe may be good funding politics but it is bad science.

The latter comments pertain especially to the just community and school democracy studies. Here Kohlberg and I had to invent the idea (in my case, at least, reinvent Dewey), work out the practices, and concurrently settle on the research design. Speaking for myself, if one is not sure where he is going it is a little difficult to know when he has gotten there. I faulted Reimer and Kohlberg for reductionism in their singular focus on moral stage change and the evolution of group norms in such schools. Yet I opposed, personally, at first, any research as premature. The mixed evidence we have on these dimensions from two alternative "schools" (one at its end, little larger than a California high school classroom, the other with 100 students) is heuristic at best. Only with a second generation of such research will we know more fully the effects of democratic schooling. Such schools have to be studied longitudinally for four to five years, too, before we will know much. The disquieting problem is that they keep going under. A "successful" operation in which the patient dies is not one a prudent man will elect.

As a transition to a commentary on what, then, we have learned from this decade of research and development in moral education a quotation from Nathan Gage (1978, p. 233) may offer some comfort in a bleak New England December:

> So far as I know, the invulnerable price of research in any field of the behavioral sciences is nonexistent. Seldom does a research worker

anticipate all criticisms. And the problems of doing research in the schools may in any case undo his sophistication.

Thus the path to increasing certainty becomes not the single excellent study that is nonetheless weak in one or more respects, but the convergence of findings from many studies that are also weak in many different ways. The dissimilar or nonreplicated weaknesses leave the replicated findings more secure. Where the studies do not overlap in their flaws but do overlap in their implications, the research synthesizer can begin to build confidence in these implications.

WHAT HAVE WE LEARNED FROM A DECADE OF APPLIED RESEARCH IN DEVELOPMENTAL AND MORAL EDUCATION?

Frank Brown characterized the 1970s in American public education as a decade of the bland leading the bland. *Au contraire!* Moral and value education has been a particularly active field of research and development. The work in Boston reported in this book has produced strong echoes in many parts of the country, though maybe echoes is too patronizing a word. Several programs, for example the Tacoma Public Schools' "Ethical Quest," have far surpassed Brookline and Cambridge in their scale. Thus in summarizing what we have learned about moral education I do not suggest that it is from these studies alone. In identifying, to say nothing of rank-ordering, the results of a decade I am very conscious of the fact that beauty is in the eye of the beholder. In so doing I speak as editor and for myself, not for the authors or for the movement.

First and foremost we have found that we can promote moral reasoning. Moral judgment — the ability to think critically about what is right and wrong, one's obligations and rights — is an important part, although by no means all, of morality. Which part is a still unsettled issue. Kohlberg was persuaded of the effect of moral education by Blatt's pioneering research. There have been enough studies now to persuade me that moral reasoning can be stimulated through classroom curriculum and teaching: in American history, social studies, English, law, psychology, special courses on the Holocaust, and so on. Children or adolescents who participate in school or classroom governance, who cooperate in building social community in school also grow morally, and in other equally important ways. Finally, in those rarer instances where we have been able to give away to parents what we know about children's moral development and how to promote it, the children benefit.

Nor do I think this consistent evidence of moral growth in response to education is a fluke. Echoing Gage, it has been found too many times in too many different groups of school children (and in too many parts of the country) to be explained as a Hawthorne (or Blatt) effect,* scorer unreliability, or teaching to the Kohlberg test. That moral reasoning can be promoted in public schooling without detriment to "academic" achievement and that we can say so with our own good consicence is no small accomplishment for one decade. Indeed, this is probably the most important thing we have achieved as a movement. What we have as a result is a body of evidence that we are not out on a very hollow limb as, for example, is the values clarification movement.

Knowledge from Practice

Along the way to establishing that a basic component of human development can be promoted by education we have learned much else. One group of findings has to do with educational research and development per se. That it is possible, if hard, to do respectable formative research in schools is an example. Town and gown can cooperate and with benefit to both. Teachers can be significant partners in creating the curriculum and pedagogy of moral education. Much interesting curriculum has been developed and field tested with children. Most of it is indigenous and properly so, some of it has been published commercially for wider use.

A rather precise (in the editor's view, too precise) pedagogy for classroom moral discussion has emerged. It is the subject of much of Fenton's writing. A great deal has been learned about staff development for moral education. Films, filmstrips, workshop materials, and a national consortium of trainers of moral educators, centered at Carnegie-Mellon University in Pittsburgh, are in place. They constitute the critical mass for a major teacher training and dissemination effort at the secondary school level in the near future. In a related way, the next generation of leadership for moral and developmental education has been educated. The contributions of many of them to this book (and that of their peers to other books on moral education) document rites of passage. The About the Contributors list at the end of the book indicates the leadership roles in education to which they have already moved.

This book furthers a way of generating knowledge from practice. In Chapter 1, I described the concept of "clinical" research in education. While it has limitations and needs fine tuning, a few of us would propose abandoning this fundamental *modus operandi*. It involves hard thinking about the particular students who are our clients; what we want them to become, do, or learn; informing our educational aims with all the philosophical and psychological theory available; the further construction of those theories by using them in creating innovative curriculum, teaching, classrooms or schools, and the complementary staff development; testing the effects of such innovative education

---

*The Blatt effect is the finding that one-fourth to one-half of the students in one semester of moral discussion groups would move (partially or totally) to the next stage up.

comprehensively and longitudinally (to speak of "fine tuning"); and revising our ordering of ideas and practices as a result. In addition to generating applied knowledge we educate teachers and professional leaders in this way.

The epistemology of the book has the most to say about educational practices (and not just in moral education). It is intended to do that. But my view is that we learn much, in the process of improving education, about the underlying strands of human growth (for example, morality, ego) we want to promote. For example, immigrant adolescents are not behind American students in moral or ego development; ego development is much more subject to stimulation by education than Loevinger believed was possible; developmental stages are related to social behavior in classrooms; developmental stages very much influence how students and faculty will understand and practice democracy or justice; theories of development are not theories of education, and so on. Similarly, the capacity of adolescents and very little children to decide the rules by which they will live together in school and generally to act accordingly has been amply illustrated in these practices. Among other things, that underscores how much developmental norms reflect the current opportunities our children are given to learn such competencies in the home and school.

New Understanding of School and Its Effects on Children's Development

Finally, by going into the arena of school and classroom, we have begun to synthesize the concepts from educational philosophy, political science and psychology that can inform major applied research on how schools as institutions affect the cognitive, moral, ego, and sociopolitical development of children. An equally important applied challenge is whether that effect can be enhanced by giving students greater political and social participation in their schooling. Does it contribute to childrens' development to hand them prepackaged rules, sanctions, social arrangements for learning, curriculum, pedagogy, institutional forms? Higgins, in Chapter 5, says no, emphatically. To the contrary, where moral education entails thinking about and deciding upon real issues in the lives of children, classrooms, schools, or families, its effects are greatest. That does seem to be the clear message of the research of Grimes, Rundle, Stanley, and Sullivan. The data from the Cluster School are more equivocal; but we haven't studied enough democratic schools. The particularity of our focus to date on gains in moral reasoning and collective moral norms has distracted us from other effects. Deeper thinking about one's education, politics, and society and more disposition to participate actively in all three were outcomes stumbled upon at SWS. Thus the ordering questions, if not the answers, for a next generation of applied research become progressively clearer.

Kohlberg's writing about how justice evolves in individuals and in schools; Reimer and Clark's analysis of how group norms about right and wrong come to be and in turn affect the individual student; Kohlberg's case for advocacy or indoctrination in being a good citizen and a good member of society as an antidote to adolescent privatism and alienation are a large part of the dialectic. (How indoctrination in a vision of true community or justice differs from indictrination in patriotism or a religious code is moot. Nor do students exist to vindicate theories. It is the other way around.) Mosher's restatement of Dewey's ideas about political and social participation in school as a way to grow, the assertion that the aim of education is to promote all-around student development in democratic institutions and the cautions (à la Piaget) about pushing young people to grow too fast (or too much like us and our theories) are revisionist. Purpel (1979) would say they are conservative. So, too, is Lickona's idea that systematic education in social cooperation for children is a vital precursor to morality and citizenship later in life. Out of this kind of dialectic between theories of development, theories of education, and the hard mother of school practice can come an elaborated vision of humane and democratic education for the 1980s and beyond. This is the ideological portent of this book.

RESOLUTIONS FOR A NEXT GENERATION

Even the moderately attentive or discerning reader will have recognized the miles we have to go before we sleep. In conclusion, I want to suggest some of the things we most need to learn in a next generation of research and development. My first comment concerns the definitional question of what we mean by successful moral education. Then I will examine some of the findings to date. Unresolved issues in curriculum and teacher development follow. Finally, I argue that it is time to "mainstream" moral education, to further our efforts as part of a psychology and an education for all-around human development.

First, what is a "successful" moral education program? One that promotes normal development of morality? Accelerated development? Prevents children from falling behind in moral understanding? A program for children who elect it? All students? An education in understanding the moral and social conventions of the family, church, and state; in understanding why one should keep promises, tell the truth, care about others, act responsibly? Or is such an education covert indoctrination? An education that promotes autonomous moral thinking? Principled thought? An education for moral action as well as judgment? By what means? Classroom discussion, participation in schools or families that are experienced as moral, teachers "like Durkheim's priest of society," facilitation of democratic process in the classroom?

I raise these questions intentionally. My abbreviated answers are an education that permits more growth and by any reasoned means, other than indoctrination or punishment, that promote moral autonomy. I believe our moral actions as teachers speak as loudly as our words. To date, however, moral educators have tended to define success as anything that promotes slightly accelerated development in moral reasoning in one-half the students in experimental classes. Clearly our answers in the 1980s will need to be more sophisticated than that.

This leads to three conundrums in our data to date:

The average moral growth effected by "one-shot" (that is, semester-long) courses in moral education is one-fourth or less of a Kohlberg stage in approximately one-half the children who participate. Why this is the case is puzzling. Perhaps it results from our present largely intuitive (and, therefore, for many pupils random) match of educational material and developmental stage. Is it simply easier to promote growth in those students already in transition? Do some students, by reason of intelligence, verbal ability, or class participation simply learn more, as they typically do in other "subjects"? The questions aren't hard to come by. The answers will take a little longer. There are related problems. A relatively small proportion of the children in any school have been included in such experimental classes. Also, we have more cumulative evidence of gains in moral reasoning in adolescents than we do in elementary school children. Yet there are indications that the effect of systematic moral education may be greatest on younger children and those at a "natural" point of transition (for example, adolescents moving from Stage 2 to Stage 3). The evidence of longitudinal studies is skimpy but encouraging. It suggests that a little bit of moral education can go a long way. Once triggered, growth in moral reasoning may have considerable momentum. These are educated guesses in need of much careful study.

Our present data indicate that the best curriculum and teaching seems as effective as the best "just community" school in promoting growth in moral reasoning. Students in the Cambridge Cluster School averaged a gain of one-fourth of a moral stage (22.5 points) per year over two years. Some 40 percent of the students did not grow, or regressed; the principal movement was from Stage 2 to Stage 3. No control data are available as to how much of this growth is natural and how much is the result of the school's programs. The average development of Cluster School students was essentially equivalent to that found in the best Stone Foundation moral discussion classes (Chapter 2). By "best" classroom moral education is meant the following: well-articulated moral dilemmas are discussed within existing or innovative subject matter; approximately 20 class periods are devoted to such discussions; the teacher is able to recognize moral stages in the students' talk and is effective in probing their thinking; a cross section of moral stages exists among the students. The Brookline teachers included in this book did not achieve the effects found in the Stone Foundation study. I think that was because we concentrated more on curriculum development and too little on the requisite pedagogy. Nonetheless, educating teachers to provide such conditions for moral growth, while anything but simple, probably is more immediately practical and will require less absolute effort than to democratize classrooms and schools. Both kinds of experience, however, are necessary to any comprehensive moral education program.

The practical consequences, in school or out of it, of the growth in children's moral reasoning induced by moral education are largely unknown. One reason is that we have concentrated on measuring increases in moral thought as a be-all and end-all. Increments, even small ones, in human thinking unquestionably are important per se, but we badly need to know what, if anything, goes with an average gain of one-fourth stage in moral reasoning. From Travers' unrelated research, I learned that SWS students think more critically about their education and want to participate in formulating its conditions; are more concerned about local, state, and federal government and participate far more extensively in political and social action in the community than do any other group of students at Brookline High School. Masterson's data in Chapter 10 say that a student's stages of moral and ego development are related to how he will behave toward classmates and the teacher and who influences whom in classrooms. Fenton has found that school grades improve in civic education programs. Admittedly, these are all straws in the wind. Of one thing I'm sure, however: As we accumulate such evidence concerning the practical consequences of children's moral growth for them, the school, or the home, our constituency will enlarge.

Let me turn now to some of the curriculum and teacher development tasks that face us. In previous comments, I've already edged into these matters. How to create a coherent, progressive program of moral education for children, adolescents, and young adults will be the central curriculum challenge of the years ahead. Class meetings to decide upon rules and discipline in Grade 5, discussion of the Holocaust in Grade 8, role playing the constitutional debates in American history in Grade 11, and political action on behalf of local candidates for office in Grade 12 are not a coherent, systematic education for the moral choices facing young people. They are essentially ad hoc and determined more by what teachers volunteer than by any overall conception of moral growth or an education for it. Yet even these patchwork experiences are much more than we offer young people currently. The point is that we need to coordinate curriculum, teaching, and student participation in school governance with parent, family, and religious education if we are to promote moral growth comprehensively.

The need to draw other curriculum areas in the secondary schools (for example, the sciences, mathematics, health, physical education, athletics) into moral education is apparent. Or is it vice versa? Morality is too important to be left to social studies teachers. I don't doubt they feel the same way. Many of the moral issues (for example, nuclear power, endangered species, abortion) that preoccupy young people are the "subject matter" of science; the playing fields of America (if not Ohio State) have always claimed to build character.

Similarly, a major effort to involve elementary school teachers in moral education is required. My experience is that they are very much attuned to children's development and education to promote it. Morality obviously can't wait until high school. Furthering teachers' own development as the aim of their professional education is a promising innovation of Sprinthall at Minnesota and Parsons at Utah. However, no teacher training effort commensurate with that planned by Fenton for high school teachers is underway, or even talked about, for elementary schools. Years ago, Gross said the principal was the key to change in the school. A few pioneering studies of how to promote administrators' moral thinking have been done. More need to be.

Making children's moral development the responsibility of the school as a whole (and of the home and the church) is essential for several reasons. Primary among them is the evidence that moral growth seems to occur in small but progressive increments. No more than children's mental health can be left to school psychologists can morality be left to any one group of teachers (or, for that matter, to the schools alone); and teachers haven't stayed with moral education programs. Kohlberg says that only 1 of 20 teachers in the Stone Foundation study in the Boston area was still teaching moral dilemmas a year after the project ended. He cites this as an example of a successful operation in which the patient died. In Brookline, which I know best, the attrition of active project teachers and counselors since 1973 has been heavy. More than half of the original participating faculty are gone — many to major leadership roles elsewhere. If drop out is one teacher malaise, "burn out" is another. Cumulative fatigue because of the unusual demands made of faculty time and energy in alternative democratic schools unquestionably was a very real problem for teachers and the institutional stability of the Cluster School and SWS.

"Administrative support" (that is, tangible financial and educational backing by the superintendent, school board, or principal); the opportunity for project teachers to disseminate their curricula or to train other teachers; larger-scale teacher training such as that being organized by Fenton at Carnegie-Mellon may all contribute to the staying power of second-generation programs in moral education. Having them wholly owned by the school system and its teachers seems to me to be of the essence. Nonetheless, the attrition facing such programs and their key personnel, especially when the soft money runs out, is apparent. Widening the membership may be part of the solution.

My final general point is that we need to "mainstream" moral education in the years ahead. I will argue for this in several ways. A number of us now are saying that we must look for the effects of what we are doing on more aspects of the child's development than gains in moral reasoning. Is the child's behavior in the class or out of it different? How? Masterson, as noted, has found that one's stage of development does affect how he behaves toward both classmates and the teacher. Is the child's social behavior different? Travers' findings are that it is. Does the adolescent's ego development, a broader strand of growth than any other, move in tandem with moral growth? The tentative answer seems to be yes, only more so. Does the student's sense of competence grow in any way because of moral education or participation in school democracy? I have observed greater student self-assurance in chairing meetings, in speaking publicly, in serving on committees to hire new faculty, in assuming leadership, in confronting faculty and peers on the part of many adolescents in SWS. However, our singular pursuit of gains in moral reasoning at the .01 level, or "the moral atmosphere" of the school, have distracted us from many of the other effects we may, or may not, be having. It is time to open the lens through which we view and measure our world.

There is a converse. A decade ago, I first bumped into moral development as a by-product of teaching counseling to high school students. It was a serendipity. Only later did I understand how teaching empathy was related to morality. Gains in moral reasoning or development similarly may come where we least expect, or aren't trying for, them. Social education, aesthetic education, drama, womens' studies, and so on, may all be carriers of unacknowledged effects on morality. Part of casting a wider net is to search out such effects. Taking an even wider view, I believe we ought to be as concerned to understand and educate for all-around child development as for morality. To do so is a moral imperative for me as an educator. In so doing we probably will promote character development too. Growth seems as holistic as particularistic. Stimulation on one strand of the developmental helix (for example, the self or ego) spills over onto another (morality) through interconnections we only partly understand.

CONCLUSION

My final point is really a summary statement. Personal growth happens in small, progressive steps. It does not take quantum leaps, even when we try very hard to make it do so. Piaget can relax about Americans' obsession with accelerating human development. They'll try, but they can't. What is feasible by education is to help people to actualize more of their personal potential and competence. If that is so, the task is to give the psychology of moral development and education away to as many teachers, administrators, parents, and interested others as possible. That will begin to make morality a common cause rather than the special mandate or burden of moral educators. It is time, also, to recognize morality as but one competency among the many: rationality, social cooperation, love that makes our development as humans complete. The study of moral judgment needs to rejoin the larger body of the psychology of general human development. Similarly, it is time to "mainstream" moral education as one means to enhance overall human capability. This field has led a modest neoprogressivism in American public education. What we have learned can be very helpful in promoting other dimensions of human growth. If we are to avoid being the last hurrah for progressivism, then we need to turn our understanding and energy to collaborative endeavors to promote cognition, ego, affect, social competence, vocation, a sound body, the spiritual as well as character in all people. That is the ultimate meaning of a moral and a democratic education.

BIBLIOGRAPHY

CHAPTER 1

Biddle, B. J., and W. J. Ellena. 1964. *Contemporary Research on Teacher Effectiveness.* New York: Holt, Rinehart, and Winston.

Dewey, John. 1964. "The Need for a Philosophy of Education." In *John Dewey on Education: Selected Writings,* edited by Reginald Archambault. New York: Random House, pp. 1-15.

Kohlberg, Lawrence. 1971. "Humanistic and Cognitive-Developmental Perspectives on Psychological Education." *Counseling Psychologist* 2, no. 4: 80-82.

Miller, G. Dean, editor. 1976. *Developmental Education.* St. Paul: Minnesota Department of Education.

Mosher, Ralph L., editor. 1979. *Adolescents' Development and Education: A Janus Knot.* Berkeley: McCutchan.

Mosher, Ralph L. 1974. "Knowledge from Practice: Clinical Research and Development in Education." *Counseling Psychologist* 4, no. 4: 73-82.

Mosher, Ralph L., and Norman Sprinthall. 1970. "Psychological Education in Secondary Schools: A Program to Promote Individual and Human Development." *American Psychologist* 25 (October): 911-24.

Schaefer, Robert. 1967. *The School As Center of Inquiry.* New York: Harper and Row.

Schwaab, Joseph J. 1972. "The Practical: A Language For Curriculum." In *Curriculum and the Cultural Revolution,* edited by David E. Purpel and Maurice Belanger. Berkeley: McCutchan, pp. 79-99.

CHAPTER 2

Blatt, Moshe. 1969. "Studies on the Effects of Classroom Discussion upon Children's Moral Development." Ph.D. dissertation, University of Chicago. Ann Arbor, Mich.: University Microfilms.

Blatt, Moshe and Lawrence Kohlberg. 1975. "Effects of Classroom Moral Discussions upon Children's Levels of Moral Judgment." *Journal of Moral Education* 4: 129-62.

Candee, Daniel, Richard Graham, and Lawrence Kohlberg. 1978. "Moral Development and Life Outcomes." Report to the National Institute of Education. Grant no. NIE-6-74-0096. Cambridge, Mass.: Harvard University, Center For Moral Education. Mimeographed.

Clark, E., D. Edmonson, and C. Dondineau. 1954. *Civics for Americans*. New York: Ginn.

Dewey, John. 1966. *Democracy and Education*. New York: The Free Press.

_____. 1964. In *John Dewey on Education: Selected Writings,* edited by Reginald Archambault. New York: Random House.

Durkheim, Emile. 1961. *Moral Education*. New York: The Free Press.

Fenton, Edwin, editor. 1976. "The Cognitive-Developmental Approach to Moral Education." *Social Education* 40 (April): 4.

Fenton, Edwin, Ann Colby, and Betsy Speicher-Dubin. 1974. "Developing Moral Dilemmas for Social Studies Classes." Mimeographed. Cambridge, Mass.: Harvard University, Center for Moral Education.

Hartshorne, Hugh, and M. A. May. 1928-30. *Studies in the Nature of Character*. New York: Macmillan.

Hunt, D. 1973. "Education for Disciplinary Understanding." *Behavioral and Social Science Teacher* 1, no. 1.

Keniston, Kenneth. 1968. *Young Radicals: Notes on Committed Youth*. New York: Harcourt, Brace, and World.

_____. 1965. *The Uncommitted: Alienated Youth in American Society*. New York: Harcourt, Brace, and World.

Kohlberg, Lawrence. 1979. *Meaning and Measurement of Moral Development*. Worcester, Mass.: Clark University Press.

_____. 1976. "This Special Section in Perspective." In "The Cognitive-Developmental Approach to Moral Education." *Social Education* 40 (April): 4.

_____. 1973. "Moral Education and the New Social Studies." *Social Education* 37 (May).

_____. 1971. "Cognitive-Developmental Theory and the Practice of Collective Moral Education." In *Group Care: The Education Path of Youth Aliyah,* edited by M. Wolins and M. Gottesman. New York: Gordon and Breach.

_____. 1970. "Educating for Justice: A Modern Statement of the Platonic View." In *Moral Education,* edited by Theodore Sizer. Cambridge, Mass.: Harvard University Press.

_____. 1969. "Stage and Sequence: The Cognitive-Developmental Approach to Socialization." In *Handbook of Socialization Theory,* edited by D. Goslin. New York: Rand McNally.

Kohlberg, Lawrence, and D. Elfenbein. 1975. "The Development of Moral Judgments Concerning Capital Punishment." *American Journal of Orthopsychiatry* 45(4).

Lasch, C. 1978. *The Culture of Narcissism.* New York: Norton Press.

Mead, George H. 1934. *Mind, Self, and Society.* Chicago: University of Chicago Press.

Newmann, Fred. 1980. "Political Participation." In *Political Education in Flux,* edited by D. Heater and J. Gillespie. London: Sage Publications.

_____. 1978. "Visions of Participation to Guide Community Learning." Paper read at the Banff Conference on Community and the School Curriculum, University of Alberta. Mimeographed.

_____. 1977. "Alternative Approaches to Citizenship Education." In *Education for Responsible Citizenship.* New York: McGraw-Hill.

Parsons, Talcott. 1964. *Social Structure and Personality.* New York: The Free Press.

Piaget, Jean. 1965. *The Moral Judgment of the Child.* New York: The Free Press.

Power, Clark. 1979. "The Moral Atmosphere of a Just Community High School: A Four-Year Longitudinal Study." Ed.D. dissertation, Harvard University. Ann Arbor, Mich.: University Microfilms.

Rawls, John. 1973. *A Theory of Justice.* Cambridge, Mass.: Harvard University Press.

Reimer, Joseph. 1977. "A Study in the Moral Development of Kibbutz Adolescents." Ed.D. dissertation, Harvard University. Ann Arbor, Mich.: University Microfilms.

Rest, James. 1979. *Development in Judging Moral Issues.* Minneapolis: University of Minnesota Press.

Riesman, David. 1952. *The Lonely Crowd.* New Haven, Conn.: Yale University Press.

Ringer, R. 1977. *Looking Out for Number One.* New York: Fawcett Books.

Whyte, William H. 1956. *The Organization Man.* New York: Simon and Schuster.

CHAPTER 3

Argyris, C. 1962. *Interpersonal Competence and Organizational Effectiveness.* Homewood, Ill.: Dorsey.

Blatt, Moshe, and Lawrence Kohlberg. 1975. "Effects of Classroom Moral Discussions upon Children's Levels of Moral Judgment." *Journal of Moral Education* 4: 129-62.

Bruner, Jerome S. 1960. *The Process of Education.* Cambridge, Mass.: Harvard University Press.

Goodman, Ellen. 1979. Boston *Globe,* May 8, p. 17.

Havelock, Ronald G., and Alan Guskin. 1969. *Planning for Innovation through Dissemination and Utilization of Knowledge.* Ann Arbor: University of Michigan Press.

Kohlberg, Lawrence, and Ralph Mosher. 1977. "Classroom Moral Education," *Annual Report 1974-77.* Danforth Foundation Grant. Cambridge, Mass.: Harvard University, Center for Moral Development. Mimeographed.

League of Women Voters. 1976. "A Report on Moral Education in the Public Schools of Brookline." Brookline, Mass. Mimeographed.

Miles, M. D., editor. 1964. *Innovation in Education.* New York: Teachers College Press.

Mosher, Ralph L. 1975. "Funny Things Happen on the Way to Curriculum Development." In *Guidance: Strategies and Techniques,* edited by H. Peters and Roger Aubrey. Denver: Love Publishing.

Peters, Richard S., and P. Hirst. 1970. *The Logic of Education.* London: Routledge.

Paolitto, Diana P., and Richard Hersh. 1978. "Moral Development: Implications for Pedagogy." In *Readings in Moral Education,* edited by Peter Scharf. Minneapolis: Winston Press, pp. 140-46.

Reimer, Joseph, and Lawrence Kohlberg. 1977. "First Year Report to the Ford Foundation." Cambridge, Mass: Center for Moral Education, Harvard University.

Scharf, Peter, editor. 1978. *Readings in Moral Education.* Minneapolis: Winston Press.

Selman, Robert, and Dan Jaquette. 1978. "To Understand and to Help: Implications of Developmental Research for the Education of Children with Interpersonal Problems." In *Readings in Moral Education,* edited by Peter Scharf, pp. 124-34.

Sullivan, Paul. 1975. "A Curriculum for Stimulating Moral Reasoning and Ego Development in Adolescents." Ed.D. dissertation, Boston University.

Temkin, S. and M. Brown. 1964. *What Do Research Findings Say About Getting Innovations into Schools: A Symposium.* Philadelphia: Research for Better Schools, Inc.

Weiss, Iris R. 1978. *Report of 1977 National Survey of Science, Mathematics, and Social Studies Education: Report to the National Science Foundation.* Report No. 038-000-003-64-0. Washington, D.C.: U.S. Government Printing Office.

CHAPTER 4

Arredondo-Dowd, Patricia. 1978. "A Moral Education Program for Bilingual, Bicultural Adolescents." Ed.D. dissertation, Boston University.

Bruner, Jerome S. 1960. *The Process of Education.* Cambridge, Mass.: Harvard University Press.

Felton, Louise. 1974. "Teaching Counseling to Adolescents and Adults." Ed.D. Dissertation, Boston University.

Goodman, Ellen. 1979. Boston *Globe,* May 8, p. 17.

Harris, D. 1976. "Psychological Awareness and Moral Discourse: A Curriculum Sequence for Moral Development." Ed.D. dissertation, University of Wisconsin.

Lockwood, Alan. 1978. "The Effects of Values Clarification and Moral Development Curricula on School-Age Subjects: A Critical Review of Recent Research." *Review of Educational Research* 48 (Summer): 325-64.

Peters, Richard S., and P. Hirst. 1970. *The Logic of Education.* London: Routledge.

Selman, Robert. 1973. "Progress Report: Social Cognitive Development in Children Ages 4-10." Cambridge, Mass.: Harvard University. Mimeographed.

Weiss, Iris R. 1978. *Report of 1977 National Survey of Science, Mathematics, and Social Studies Education: Report to the National Science Foundation.* Report No. 038-000-003-64-0. Washington, D.C.: U.S. Government Printing Office.

CHAPTER 5

Alexander, Robert. 1977. "A Moral Education Curriculum on Prejudice." Ed.D. dissertation, Boston University.

Arredondo-Dowd, Patricia. 1978. "A Moral Education Program for Bilingual, Bicultural Adolescents." Ed.D. dissertation, Boston University.

Azrak, Robert. 1978. "Training Fathers and Mothers in Psychological Discipline Strategies: A Curriculum to Effect Attitudes toward Child Bearing and the Moral Development of Early Adolescents." Ed.D. dissertation, Boston University.

Blatt, Moshe, and Lawrence Kohlberg. 1975. "The Effect of Classrooms' Moral Discussion upon Children's Level of Moral Judgment." *Journal of Moral Education* 4: 129-61.

Colby, Ann. 1975. "The Relation between Logical and Moral Development." Cambridge, Mass.: Harvard University. Mimeographed.

Erickson, V. L. 1975. "Deliberate Psychological Education for Women: From Iphigenia to Antigone." *Counselor Education and Supervision* 14: 297-309.

Felton, Louise. 1974. "Teaching Counseling to Adolescents and Adults." Ed.D. dissertation, Boston University.

Grimes, P. 1974. "Teaching Moral Reasoning to Eleven Year Olds and Their Mothers: A Means of Promoting Moral Growth." Ed.D. dissertation, Boston University.

Harris, D. 1976. "Psychological Awareness and Moral Discourse: A Curriculum Sequence for Moral Development." Ed.D. dissertation, University of Wisconsin.

Kohlberg, Lawrence. 1977. Preface. In *Readings in Moral Education,* edited by Peter Scharf. Minneapolis: Winston Press.

Lieberman, Mark. 1979a. "Teaching the Holocaust." Paper presented at the Annual Meeting of the American Educational Research Association in San Francisco.

_____. 1979b. "Issues in the Analysis of Data in Developmental Interventions." Paper presented at the Annual Meeting of the American Educational Research Association in San Francisco.

Lockwood, Alan. 1978. "The Effects of Values Clarification and Moral Development Curricula on School-Age Subjects: A Critical Review of Recent Research." *Review of Educational Research* 48 (Summer): 325-64.

Loevinger, Jane. 1976. *Ego Development.* San Francisco: Jossey-Bass.

Paolitto, Diana. 1975. "Role-Taking Opportunities for Early Adolescents: A Program in Moral Education." Ed.D. dissertation, Boston University.

Power, Clark. 1979. "The Moral Atmosphere of a Just Community High School: A Four Year Longitudinal Study." Ed.D. dissertation, Harvard University.

Rundle, Louise. 1977. "The Stimulation of Moral Development in the Elementary School and the Cognitive Examination of Social Experience: A Fifth Grade Study." Ed.D. dissertation, Boston University.

Selman, Robert. 1973. "Progress Report: Social Cognitive Development in Children Ages 4-10." Cambridge, Mass.: Harvard University. Mimeographed.

Sprinthall, Norman. 1976. "Learning Psychology by Doing Psychology: A High School Curriculum in the Psychology of Counseling." In *Developmental Education,* edited by G. Dean Miller, St. Paul: Minnesota Department of Education.

Stanley, Sheila. 1976. "A Curriculum to Affect the Moral Atmosphere of the Family and the Moral Development of Adolescents." Ed.D. dissertation, Boston University.

Sullivan, Paul. 1975. "A Curriculum for Stimulating Moral Reasoning and Ego Development in Adolescents." Ed.D. dissertation, Boston University.

Walker, L. J. 1979. "Prerequisites for Moral Reasoning Development." Vancouver: University of British Columbia, Mimeographed.

CHAPTER 6

Beyer, Barry K. 1976. "Conducting Moral Discussions in the Classroom." *Social Education* 40 (April): 196.

Dewey, John. 1966 (1916). *Democracy and Education.* New York: The Free Press.

Dewey, John, and J. McLellan. 1964. "The Psychology of Number." In *John Dewey on Education: Selected Writings,* edited by Reginald Archambault. New York: Random House.

Galbraith, Ronald E., and Thomas Jones. 1975. "Teaching Strategies for Moral Dilemmas: An Application of Kohlberg's Theory to the Social Studies Classroom." *Social Education* 39 (January): 16-22.

Nevins, Allan. 1947. *The Ordeal of the Union,* Vol. II. New York: Charles Scribner's Sons.

Whitehead, Alfred North. 1956. *The Aims of Education.* New York: Mentor Books.

Woodward, Kenneth L., and Mary Lord. 1975. "Moral Education." *Newsweek,* March 1, p. 74.

CHAPTER 7

Adorno, T. W., E. Frankel-Brunswick, D. J. Levinson, and R. N. Sanford. 1950. *The Authoritarian Personality*. New York: Harper and Row.

Alexander, Robert C. 1977. "A Moral Education Curriculum of Prejudice." Ed.D. dissertation, Boston University.

Clark, K. 1955. *Prejudice and Young Children*. Boston: Beacon Press.

Davidson, F. H. 1975. "Ability to Respect Persons Compared to Childhood Ethnic Prejudice." Cambridge, Mass.: Harvard University Center for Moral Education. Mimeographed.

Erikson, Erik. 1959. "Identity and the Life Cycle." In *Psychological Issues,* edited by George Klein. New York: International Universities Press.

Frenkel-Brunswick, E. 1951. "Children's Attitudes." *Journal of Orthopsychiatry* 21: 543-58.

Kleg, M. 1971. "Attitudinal Change in White Students after Interaction in an Ethnic Relations Unit." Paper read at the Annual Meeting of the American Educational Research Association. ERIC no.: ED049338.

Lockwood, Alan. 1972. *Moral Reasoning: The Value of Life*. Middletown, Conn.: American Educational Publications.

Loevinger, Jane. 1976. *Ego Development: Conceptions and Theories*. San Francisco: Jossey-Bass.

Piaget, Jean and A. M. Weil. 1951. "The Development in Children of the Idea of Homeland and of Relations with Other Countries." *International Social Science Bulletin* 3: 561-78.

Report of the National Advisory Commission on Civil Disorders. 1968. New York: New York Times Company.

Schuman, H., and J. Harding. 1964. "Prejudice and the Normal of Rationality." *Sociometry* 27: 353-71.

_____. 1963. "Sympathetic Identification with the Underdog." *Public Opinion Quarterly* Summer: 230-41.

Trager, H. and M. Radkee-Yarrow. 1952. *They Learn What They Live*. New York: Harper and Row.

CHAPTER 8

Block, J. H. 1973. "Conceptions of Sex Role." *American Psychologist* 28 (June): 521-26.

Byrne, D. 1973. "The Development of Role-Taking in Adolescence." Ed.D. dissertation, Harvard University.

Douvan, E., and J. Adelson. 1966. *The Adolescent Experience.* New York: John Wiley.

Gilligan, Carol, Lawrence Kohlberg, J. Lerner, and M. Belenky. 1970. "Moral Reasoning About Sexual Dilemmas: The Development of an Interview and Scoring System." Washington, D.C.: President's Commission on Pornography and Obscenity.

Goethals, G., and D. Klos. 1970. *Experiencing Youth, First Person Accounts.* Boston: Little, Brown.

Havighurst, R. 1948. *Developmental Tasks and Education.* New York: David McKay.

Kohlberg, Lawrence. 1966. "A Cognitive-Developmental Analysis of Children's Sex-role Concepts and Attitudes." In *The Development of Sex Differences,* edited by E. Maccoby. Stanford, Calif.: Stanford University Press.

Kohlberg, Lawrence, and Carol Gilligan. 1971. "The Adolescent as a Philosopher: The Discovery of the Self in a Post Conventional World." *Daedalus* 100 (November): 1051-86.

Lickona, Thomas. 1973. "A Cognitive-Developmental Approach to Interpersonal Attraction." In *Perspectives on Interpersonal Attraction,* edited by T. L. Huston. New York: Academic Press.

Loevinger, Jane, and R. Wessler. 1970. *Measuring Ego Development: Construction and Use of a Sentence Completion Test.* San Francisco: Jossey-Bass.

Mussen, P., J. Conger, and J. Kagan. 1969. *Child Development and Personality.* New York: Harper and Row.

Selman, Robert. 1975. "The Development of Social-Cognitive Understanding: A Guide to Educational and Clinical Practice." In *Morality: A Handbook of Moral Development and Behavior,* edited by Thomas Lickona. New York: Holt, Rinehart, and Winston.

Sullivan, Henry S. 1953. *The Interpersonal Theory of Psychiatry.* New York: W. W. Norton.

Ullian, Dora. 1973. Qualifying paper. Cambridge, Mass.: Harvard Graduate School of Education.

CHAPTER 9

Beck, Clive. 1972. *Ethics*. Toronto: McGraw-Hill.

Beck, C., E. Sullivan, and N. Taylor. 1972. "Stimulating Transition to Post-conventional Morality: The Pickering High School Study." *Interchange* 3:28-37.

Blatt, Moshe. 1970. "Studies on the Effects of Classroom Discussions upon Children's Moral Development." Ph.D. dissertation, University of Chicago.

Carkhuff, Robert. 1969. *Helping and Human Relations: A Primer for Lay and Professional Helpers*. New York: Holt, Rinehart, and Winston.

Dowell, R. C. 1971. "Adolescents as Peer Counselors: A Program for Psychological Growth." Ed.D. dissertation, Harvard University.

Frankena, W. K. 1963. *Ethics*. Englewood Cliffs, N.J.: Prentice-Hall.

Griffin, A. 1972. "Teaching Counselor Education to Black Teenagers." Ed.D. dissertation, Harvard University.

Grimes, Patricia. 1974. "Teaching Moral Reasoning to Eleven Year Olds and Their Mothers: A Means of Promoting Moral Development." Ed.D. dissertation, Boston University.

Hospers, J. 1961. *Human Conduct: An Introduction to the Problems of Ethics*. New York: Harcourt, Brace, and World.

Kohlberg, Lawrence. 1973. "Scoring Manuals." Cambridge, Mass.: Harvard University Center for Moral Education. Mimeographed.

Kohlberg, Lawrence, and E. Turiel. 1971. "Moral Development and Moral Education." In *Psychology and Educational Practice*, edited by G. Lesser. Chicago: Scott, Foresman.

Lockwood, Alan. 1972. *Moral Reasoning: The Value of Life*. Middletown, Conn.: American Educational Publications.

Loevinger, Jane, R. Wessler, and C. Redmore. 1970. *Measuring Ego Development*. San Francisco: Jossey-Bass.

Mackie, Peter. 1974. "Teaching Counseling to Low Achieving High School Students." Ed.D. dissertation, Boston University.

Mosher, Ralph L., and Norman Sprinthall. 1971. "Psychological Education: A Means to Promote Personal Development through Adolescence." *The Counseling Psychologist* 2: 3-82.

Mosher, Ralph L., and Paul Sullivan. 1976. "A Curriculum in Moral Education for Adolescents." In *Moral Education: It Goes with the Territory*, edited by David Purpel and K. Ryan. Berkeley, Calif.: McCutchan.

_____. 1975. "A Curriculum in Moral Education for Adolescents." *Journal of Moral Education* 4.

_____. 1974. "A Curriculum in Moral Education for Adolescents." In *Challenge in Educational Administration,* Department of Educational Administration. Edmonton, Alberta: University of Alberta.

Rawls, J. 1971. *A Theory of Justice.* Cambridge, Mass.: Harvard University Press.

CHAPTER 10

Bales, Robert F. 1970. *Personality and Interpersonal Behavior.* New York: Holt, Rinehart, and Winston.

_____. 1968. "Interaction Process Analysis." In *New International Encyclopedia of the Social Sciences.* New York: Macmillan.

_____. 1958. "Task Roles and Social Roles in Problem-Solving Groups." In *Readings in Social Psychology,* edited by Eleanor Maccoby, Theodore M. Newcomb, and Eugene L. Hartley. New York: Holt, Rinehart, and Winston, pp. 437-47.

_____. 1956. "Task Slaters and Likeability as a Function of Talking and Listening in Decision-Making Groups." In *The State of the Social Sciences.* Chicago: University of Chicago Press, pp. 148-61.

_____. 1950. *Interaction Process Analysis: A Method for the Study of Small Groups.* Reading, Mass.: Addison-Wesley.

Blasi, Agusto. 1971. "Experimentation in the Study of Development: A Training Experiment on the Development of Responsiblity." Ph.D. dissertation, Washington University.

Cox, Nell. 1974. "Prior Help, Ego Development, and Helping Behavior." *Child Development* 45 (August).

Donivant, Noel. 1975. "Moral Judgment, Psychological Development, Situational Characteristics and Moral Behavior: A Mediational Interactionist Model." Ph.D. dissertation, University of Texas-Austin.

Frank, S., and Quinlan, D. 1976. "Ego Development and Female Delinquency." *Journal of Abnormal Psychology* 85 (August).

Hahn, J., M. Smith, and J. Block. 1968. "Moral Reasoning of Young Adults: Political-Social Behavior, Family Background, and Personality Correlates." *Journal of Personality and Social Psychology* 10: 183-201.

Hoppe, Carl. 1972. "Ego Development and Conformity Behaviors." Ph.D. dissertation, Washington University.

Kohlberg, Lawrence. 1973. "Continuities and Discontinuities in Childhood and Adult Moral Development Revisited." In *Collected Papers on Moral Development and Moral Education*, edited by Lawrence Kohlberg. Cambridge, Mass.: Harvard University Center for Moral Education.

Kohlberg, Lawrence, and R. Mayer, 1972. "Development as the Aim of Education." *Harvard Educational Review* 42: 449-96.

Krebs, R., and Lawrence Kohlberg. 1975. "Moral Judgment and Ego Controls as Determinants to Resistance to Cheating." In *Recent Research in Moral Development*, New York: Holt, Rinehart, and Winston.

McNamee, S. 1972. "Moral Behavior, Moral Development, and Needs in Students and Political Activists." Ph.D. dissertation, Case Western Reserve University.

Masterson, Mark. 1979. "Structures of Thought and Patterns of Social Behavior; Stage of Ego and Moral Development and Their Relationship to Interpersonal Behavior." Ed.D. dissertation, Boston University.

Milgram, S. 1963. "Behavioral Study of Obedience." *Journal of Abnormal and Social Psychology* 67: 371-78.

Mischell, T. 1969. *Human Action, Conceptual and Empirical Issues.* New York: Academic Press.

Rest, James. 1975. "Comprehension Preference and Spontaneous Usage in Moral Judgment." In *Recent Research in Moral Development*, edited by Lawrence Kohlberg and E. Turiel. New York: Holt, Rinehart, and Winston.

Saltzstein, H. D., R. M. Diamond, and M. Belenky. 1972. "Moral Judgment Level and Conformity Behavior." *Developmental Psychology* 7: 327-36.

Turiel, E. 1966. "An Experimental Test of the Sequentiality of Developmental Stages in the Child's Moral Judgment." *Journal of Personality and Social Psychology* 3: 611-18.

CHAPTER 11

Blatt, Moshe, Ann Colby, and Betsy Speicher. 1974. "Hypothetical Dilemmas for Use in Moral Discussions." Cambridge, Mass.: Harvard University Center for Moral Education. Mimeographed.

Blos, P. 1970. *The Young Adolescent: Clinical Studies.* New York: The Free Press.

———. 1962. *One Adolescence: A Psychoanalytic Interpretation.* New York: The Free Press.

Byrne, D. F. 1973. "The Development of Role-Taking in Adolescence." Ed.D. dissertation, Harvard University.

Erikson, Erik. 1968. *Identity: Youth and Crisis*. New York: W. W. Norton.

Kohlberg, Lawrence. 1973. "Continuities in Childhood and Adult Moral Development and Adult Moral Development Revisited." In *Collected Papers on Moral Development and Moral Education*, edited by Lawrence Kohlberg. Cambridge, Mass.: Harvard University Center for Moral Education.

_____. 1969. "Stage and Sequence: The Cognitive Development Approach to Socialization." In *Handbook of Socialization Theory and Research*, edited by D. Goslin. New York: Rand McNally.

Kohlberg, Lawrence, and E. Turiel. 1971. "Moral Development and Moral Education." In *Psychology and Educational Practice*, edited by G. Lesser. Chicago: Scott, Foresman.

Martin, E. C. 1971. "Reflections on the Early Adolescent in School." *Daedalus* 100: 1087-1103.

Mosher, Ralph L., and Paul Sullivan. 1974. "Moral Education: A New Initiative for Guidance." *Focus on Guidance*, January.

Paolitto, D. P. 1975. "Role-Taking Opportunities for Early Adolescents: A Program in Moral Education." Ed.D. dissertation, Boston University.

Piaget, Jean. 1972. "Intellectual Evolution from Adolescence to Adulthood." *Human Development* 5: 1-12.

Selman, Robert. 1971a. "The Relation of Role-Taking Ability to the Development of Moral Judgment in Children." *Child Development* 42:79.91.

_____. 1971b. "Taking Another's Perspective: Role-Taking Development in Early Childhood." *Child Development* 42: 1721-34.

CHAPTER 12

Bernstein, Richard J. 1978. "Thinking on Thought." *New York Times Book Review*, May 28: 1-2.

Bronowski, Jacob. 1973. *The Ascent of Man*. Boston: Little, Brown.

Campbell, Donald, and Julian Stanley. 1963. *Experimental and Quasi-Experimental Designs for Research*. Chicago: Rand McNally.

Friedlander, Henry. 1979. "Toward a Methodology of Teaching About the Holocaust." *Teachers College Record* 80 (February).

_____. 1973. *On the Holocaust*. New York: Anti-Defamation League of B'nai B'rith.

Ginnott, Haim. 1972. *Teacher and Child*. New York: Macmillan.

Kohlberg, Lawrence. 1969. "Stage and Sequence: The Cognitive Developmental Approach to Socialization." In *Handbook of Socialization Theory and Research*, edited by D. Goslin. New York: Rand McNally.

Lieberman, Marcus. 1979. "Teaching the Holocaust." Paper presented at the Annual Meeting of the American Educational Research Association, San Francisco. Mimeographed.

Loevinger, Jane. 1966. "The Meaning and Measurement of Ego Development." *American Psychologist* 21: 195-206.

Pate, Glen S. 1978. "The Teaching of the Holocaust History: Inadequacies in Textbooks." *Patterns of Prejudice* 12 (September-October): 1-5.

Raskies, Diane K. 1975. *Teaching the Holocaust to Children: A Review and Bibliography*. Boston: KTAV Publishing House.

Sartre, Jean Paul. 1948. *Anti-Semite and Jew*. New York: Schocken Books.

Selman, Robert . 1974. "A Developmental Approach to Interpersonal and Moral Awareness in Young Children: Some Theoretical and Educational Perspectives." Paper read at the Montessori Society National Seminar, Boston.

Strom, Margot Stern. 1980. "Lessons of Genocide." Paper presented at the Brookline, Mass. Public School Workshop. February 7.

Strom, Margot Stern, and William Parsons. 1979. "Facing History and Ourselves: Holocaust and Human Behavior." Curriculum development and inservice project funded by ESEA Title IV, Part C. Brookline, Mass. Mimeographed.

_____. 1976. "Facing History and Ourselves: Holocaust and Human Behavior. A Personal Introduction." Brookline, Mass. Mimeographed.

CHAPTER 13

Beck, C., E. Sullivan, and N. Taylor. 1972. "Stimulating Transition to Post-conventional Morality: The Pickering High School Study." *Interchange* 3: 28-37.

Blatt, Moshe. 1968. "Studies of the Effect of Classroom Discussion upon Children's Moral Development." Chicago: University of Chicago. Mimeographed.

Blatt, Moshe, and Lawrence Kohlberg. 1971. "The Effects of Classroom Discussion on the Development of Moral Judgment." In *Recent Research in Moral Development,* edited by Lawrence Kohlberg and Eliot Turiel. New York: Holt.

Grimes, Patricia. 1974. "Teaching Moral Reasoning to Eleven Year Olds and Their Mothers: A Means of Promoting Moral Growth." Ed.D. dissertation, Boston University.

Kohlberg, Lawrence. 1976. "This Special Section in Perspective." *Social Education* 40: 213-15.

Kohlberg, Lawrence, Elsa Wasserman, and N. Richardson. 1975. "The Just Community School: The Theory and the Cambridge Cluster School Experiment." Harvard University. Mimeographed.

Lieberman, Marcus, and Robert Selman. 1975. "Moral Education in the Primary Grades: An Evaluation of A Developmental Curriculum." *Journal of Educational Psychology* 67: 712-16.

Mosher, Ralph L. 1975. "A Funny Thing Happened on the Way to Curriculum Development." In *Guidance: Strategies and Techniques,* edited by H. Peters and Roger Aubrey. Denver: Love Publishing Co., pp. 149-70.

Rundle, Louise. 1977. "The Stimulation of Moral Development in the Elementary School and the Cognitive Examination of Social Experience: A Fifth Grade Study." Ed.D. dissertation, Boston University.

Sarason, Seymour B. 1971. *The Culture of the School and the Problem of Change.* Boston: Allyn and Bacon.

Schaefer, Robert. 1967. *The School as Center of Inquiry.* New York: Harper and Row.

Wasserman, Elsa. 1976. "Implementing Kohlberg's Just Community Concept in an Alternative High School." *Social Education* 40: 203-07.

CHAPTER 14

Bessell, H. 1972. *Human Development Program.* El Cajon, Calif.: Human Development Training Institute.

Carroll, J. 1974. "Children's Judgments of Statements Exemplifying Different Moral Stages." Ed.D. dissertation, University of Minnesota.

Cooney, E. and Robert Selman. 1978. "Children's Use of Social Conceptions: Toward a Dynamic Model of Social Cognition." In *New Directions for*

Child Development, edited by W. Damon. San Francisco: Jossey-Bass, pp. 23-44.

Dinkmeyer, Donald. 1973. *Developing Understanding of Self and Others.* Circle Pines, Minn.: American Guidance Services.

Festinger, L. 1962. *A Theory of Cognitive Dissonance.* Stanford, Calif.: Stanford University Press.

Flavell, J. H. 1968. *The Development of Role-Taking and Communication Skills in Children.* New York: John Wiley.

Focus on Self-Development. 1973. Chicago: Science Research Associates.

Gordon, I. J. 1968. *A Test Manual for the How I See Myself Scale.* Gainesville: Florida Educational Research and Development Council.

Guidance Associates. 1976. *First Things: Social Reasoning.* Pleasantville, N.Y.

_____. 1974. *First Things: Values.* Pleasantville, N.Y.

Johnson, R. C., and J. D. Kalafat. 1969. "Projective and Socio-Metric Measures of Conscience Development." *Child Development* 40: 651-55.

Kiddle, H., and A. S. Schem. 1877. *The Cyclopedia of Education.* New York: E. Steiger.

Kohlberg, Lawrence, and Robert Selman. 1976. "Teacher Training in Values Education: A Workshop." Pleasantville, N.Y.: Guidance Associates.

Lortie, D. C. 1975. *Schoolteacher: A Sociological Study.* Chicago: University of Chicago Press.

Ojemann, R. O. 1967. *A Teaching Program in Human Behavior and Mental Health.* Cleveland: Educational Research Council of Greater Cleveland.

Rest, James. 1974. *Manual for Defining Issues Test: An Objective Test of Moral Judgment Development.* Minneapolis: University of Minnesota.

Sarason, J. B. 1972. *The Creation of Settings and the Future Societies.* San Francisco: Jossey-Bass.

Science Research Associates. 1973. *Focus on Self Development.* Chicago, Ill.: Science Research Associates.

Selman, Robert L. 1976. "Social-Cognitive Understanding." In *Moral Development and Behavior,* edited by T. Lickona. New York: Holt, Rinehart, and Winston.

_____. 1974. "The Development of Conceptions of Interpersonal Relations: A Structural Analysis and Procedures for the Assessment of Levels of Interpersonal Reasoning Based on Levels of Social Perspective-Taking." Cambridge, Mass.: Harvard University Center for Moral Education. Mimeographed.

Selman, Robert L., and D. Byrne. 1974. "A Structural-Developmental Analysis of Levels of Role-Taking in Middle Childhood." *Child Development* 45: 803-06.

_____. 1972. "Manual for Scoring Role-Taking Stages in Moral and Social Dilemmas." Cambridge, Mass.: Harvard University Center for Moral Education. Mimeographed.

Selman, Robert L., D. Jaquette, and D. Lavin, 1977. "Interpersonal Awareness in Children: Toward an Integration of Developmental and Clinical Child Psychology." *American Journal of Orthopsychiatry* 47: 264-74.

Shure, M. B., and G. Spivack. 1972. "Means-Ends Thinking, Adjustment, and Social Class Among Elementary-School Aged Children." *Journal of Consulting and Clinical Psychology* 38: 348-53.

Thomas, W. L. 1969. *The Assessment of Self-Concept Values Among 4-9 Year Old Children: The Thomas Self-Concept Values Test.* Detroit: Educational Testing Service.

Turiel, E. 1966. "An Experimental Test of the Sequentiality of Developmental Stages in the Child's Moral Judgments." *Journal of Personality and Social Psychology* 3: 611-18.

CHAPTER 15

Kohlberg, Lawrence, and Ann Higgins. 1978. "Progress Report to the Danforth Foundation." Cambridge, Mass.: Harvard University. Mimeographed.

Levinson, Daniel. 1978. *The Seasons of a Man's Life.* New York: Knopf.

Power, Clark. 1978. "The Moral Atmosphere of the School: A Method for Analyzing Community Meetings." Qualifying paper, Harvard University.

_____. 1977. "Scoring Manual." In "The Development of an Alternative High School Based on Kohlberg's Just Community Approach to Education," by Elsa Wasserman. Ed.D. dissertation, Boston University.

Wasserman, Elsa. 1977. "The Development of an Alternative High School Based on Kohlberg's Just Community Approach to Education." Ed.D. dissertation, Boston University.

CHAPTER 16

Candee, Daniel, Richard Graham, and Lawrence Kohlberg. 1978. "Moral Development and Life Outcomes." Report to the National Institute of Education. Grant no. NTE-6-74-0096. Cambridge, Mass.: Harvard University, Center for Moral Education. Mimeographed.

Dewey, John. 1968a. *Democracy and Education*. New York: The Free Press.

_____. 1968b. *Problems of Men*. New York: Greenwood Press.

Erikson, Erik. 1959. "Growth and Crises of the Healthy Personality." In *Identity and the Life Cycle*, by Erik Erikson. New York, International Universities Press.

Fenton, Edwin. 1977. "The Pittsburgh Area Civic Education Project: A Report to the Danforth Foundation for the 1976-77 Fiscal Year." Pittsburgh: Carnegie-Mellon University.

Friere, Paulo. 1970. *The Pedagogy of the Oppressed*. New York: Herder and Herder.

Greene, Maxine. 1978. "The Humanities and Emancipatory Possibility." Paper read at the Center for Curriculum Reform, University of North Carolina, Greensboro. Mimeographed.

Mosher, Ralph. 1978. "A Democratic High School: Damn It: Your Feet are Always in the Water." In *Value Development . . . As An Aim Of Education*, edited by Norman A. Sprinthall and Ralph Mosher. Schenectady, N.Y.: Character Research Press, pp. 69-116.

Newmann, Fred M. 1972. *Education for Citizen Action: Challenge for Secondary Schools*. Berkeley: McCutchan.

Peters, R. S. 1973. *Authority, Responsibility, and Education*, rev. ed. London: George Allen and Unwin.

Purpel, David. 1979. "Adolescents' Development and Education: A Janus Knot: A Review." In *Moral Education Forum* 4, no. 3 (Fall): pp. 29-31.

Robb, Christina. 1978. "Teaching the 3R's +2." In *New England*. Boston: *Globe* Newspaper Co. November 19, pp. 38-40.

Robert, Henry M. 1973. *Robert's Rules of Order*. New York: Pyramid.

Sarason, Seymour. 1971. *The Culture of the School and the Problem of Change*. Boston: Allyn and Bacon.

Scharf, Peter. 1977. "School Democracy: Promise and Paradox." In *Readings in Moral Education*. Minneapolis: Winston.

Selman, Robert. 1977. "A Structural-Developmental Model of Social Cognition; Implications for Intervention Research." In *Counseling Psychologist* 6, no. 4: 3-6.

Travers, Eva. 1980. Swarthmore College, Swarthmore, Pa. Interview, 3 January.

CHAPTER 17

Argyris, C., and D. Schon. 1974. *Theory in Practice: Increasing Professional Effectiveness*. San Francisco: Jossey-Bass.

Coleman, James S. 1961. *The Adolescent Society*. New York: The Free Press.

Dewey, John. 1968. *Problems of Men*. New York: Greenwood Press.

Kohlberg, Lawrence. 1971. "Stages of Moral Development as a Basis for Moral Education." In *Moral Education: Interdisciplinary Approaches,* edited by C. M. Beck, B. S. Crittendon, and E. U. Sullivan. Toronto: University of Toronto Press.

_____. 1969. "Stage and Sequence: The Cognitive-Developmental Approach to Socialization." In *Handbook of Socialization Theory and Research,* edited by D. A. Goslin. Chicago: Rand-McNally.

Kohlberg, Lawrence, and E. Turiel. 1971. "Moral Development and Moral Practice." In *Psychology and Educational Practice,* edited by G. S. Lesser. Glenview, Ill.: Scott, Foresman.

Mosher, Ralph. 1978. "A Democratic High School: Damn It: Your Feet are Always in the Water." In *Value Development . . . As An Aim of Education,* edited by Norman A. Sprinthall and Ralph Mosher. Schenectady, N.Y.: Character Research Press, pp. 69-116.

Piaget, Jean. 1967. *Six Psychological Studies*. New York: Vintage Books.

Power, Clark. 1979. "The Moral Atmosphere of a Just Community High School." Ed.D. dissertation, Harvard University.

Power, Clark, and Joseph Reimer. 1978. "Moral Atmosphere: An Educational Bridge between Moral Judgment and Moral Action." In *New Directions for Child Development,* edited by William Damon. San Francisco: Jossey-Bass.

Reimer, Joseph. 1977. "A Study in the Moral Development of Kibbutz Adolescents." Ed.D. dissertation, Harvard University.

Scharf, Peter. 1973. "Moral Atmosphere and Intervention in the Prison." Ed.D. dissertation, Harvard University.

Wasserman, Elsa. 1977. "The Development of an Alternative High School Based on Kohlberg's Just Community Approach to Education." Ed.D. dissertation, Boston University.

CHAPTER 18

Bussis, A., E. Chittenden, and B. Amarel. 1976. *Beyond Surface Curriculum.* Boulder, Colo.: Westview Press.

Cole, P., and T. Farris. 1979. "Building a Just Community at the Elementary School Level." *Moral Education Forum,* Summer: 12-19.

Damon, William. 1977. *The Social World of the Child.* San Francisco: Jossey-Bass.

Dewey, John. 1968. *Problems of Men.* New York: Greenwood Press.

Enright, R. 1980. "An Integration of Social Cognitive Development and Cognitive Processing: Educational Applications." In press.

Gordon, T. 1975. *Teacher Effectiveness Training.* New York: Peter Wyden.

Jaquette, D., and Robert Selman. 1980. "Group Meeting and Developmental Peer Therapy: An Interpersonal Problem-Solving Approach to Remedial Social Development." *Applied Developmental Psychology,* in press.

Kubelick, C. 1977. "A Study of the Effects of a Social Skills Intervention on the Cognitive-Moral Development of 8, 9, and 10-Year-Olds." Ph.D. dissertation, University of Pittsburgh.

Lickona, Thomas. 1980. "Beyond Justice: A Curriculum for Cooperation." In *Moral Education for Parents and Teachers,* edited by Dr. Cochrane and M. E. Manley-Casimer. New York: Praeger.

_____. 1977. "Creating the Just Community with Children." *Theory into Practice,* April: 97-104.

Lightfoot, S. 1973. "Politics and Reasoning: Through the Eyes of Teachers and Children." *Harvard Educational Review,* May.

Piaget, Jean. 1965. *The Moral Judgment of the Child.* New York: The Free Press.

Rundle, Louise. 1977. "The Stimulation of Moral Development in the Elementary School and the Cognitive Examination of Social Experience: A Fifth-Grade Study." Ed.D. dissertation, Boston University.

Sarason, S. 1971. *The Culture of the School and the Problem of Change.* Boston: Allyn and Bacon.

Selman, Robert. 1979. "A Structural Approach to the Study of Developing Interpersonal Relationship Concepts: Research with Normal and Disturbed Preadolescent Boys." In *Tenth Annual Minnesota Symposium on Child Psychology,* edited by A. Pick. Minneapolis: University of Minnesota Press.

Selman, Robert, and Marcus Lieberman. 1974. "The Evaluation of a Values Curriculum for Primary Grade Children Based on a Cognitive-Developmental Approach." Paper presented to the American Educational Research Association, Chicago, April. Mimeographed.

Shure, M., and G. Spivack. 1972. "Means-End Thinking, Adjustment, and Social Class Among Elementary-School-Age Children." *Journal of Consulting and Clinical Psychology* 38: 348-53.

Witherall, C. S., and V. L. Erickson. 1978. "Teacher Education as Adult Development." *Theory into Practice,* June: 229-38.

CHAPTER 19

Bandura, A., and R. H. Walters. 1963. *Social Learning and Personality Development.* New York: Holt, Rinehart, and Winston.

Brofenbrenner, U. 1967. "The Split-Level American Family." *Saturday Review* October 7, pp. 60-66.

Carkhuff, Robert. 1971. "Training as a Preferred Mode of Treatment." *Journal of Counseling Psychology* 18 (March): 123-31.

Dinkmeyer, Donald, and G. D. McKay. 1973. *Raising a Responsible Child.* New York: Simon and Schuster.

Dowell, R. C. 1971. "Adolescents as Peer Counselors: A Program for Psychological Growth." Ed.D. dissertation, Harvard University.

Dreikers, R. et al. 1959. *Adlerian Family Counseling.* Eugene: University of Oregon Press.

Dreikurs, R., S. Gould, and R. Corsini. 1974. *The Family Council.* Chicago: Henry Regnery.

Gaylin, N. 1971. "The Family is Dead — Long Live the Family." *Youth and Society* 3 (September): 66-67.

Gordon, T. 1970. *Parent Effectiveness Training.* New York: Peter Wyden.

Hoffman, M. L. 1963. "Childrearing Practices and Moral Development: Generalization from Empirical Research." *Child Development* 34: 295-318.

Hoffman, M. L. and H. D. Saltzstein. 1967. "Parent Discipline and the Child's Moral Development." *Journal of Personality and Social Psychology* 5: 45-57.

Holstein, C. 1969. "Parental Determinants of the Development of Moral Judgment." Ed.D. dissertation, University of California-Berkeley.

Kohlberg, Lawrence, Peter Scharf, and J. Hickey. 1972. "The Justice Structure of the Prison: A Theory and Intervention." *Prison Journal* 51: 3-14.

Kohlberg, Lawrence, and E. Turiel. 1971. "Moral Development and Moral Education." In *Psychology and Educational Practice,* edited by G. S. Lesser. Glenview, Ill.: Scott, Foresman.

Peck, R., and R. Havighurst. 1960. *The Psychology of Character Development.* New York: John Wiley.

Peterson, B. 1969. "Parent Effectiveness Training." *School Counselor* 16: 367-69.

Rawls, J. 1971. *A Theory of Justice.* Cambridge, Mass.: Harvard University Press.

Shoffeitt, P. G. 1971. "The Moral Development of Children as a Function of Parental Moral Judgments and Childrearing Practices." Ed.D. dissertation, George Peabody College for Teachers.

Skolnick, A. S., and J. H. Skolnick. 1971. *Family in Transition.* Boston: Little, Brown.

Stanley, Sheila. 1978. "Family Education: A Means of Enhancing the Moral Atmosphere of the Family and the Moral Development of Adolescents." *Journal of Counseling Psychology* 25 (March): 110-18.

CHAPTER 20

Azrak, Robert. 1978. "Parental Discipline and Early Adolescent Moral Development." Ed.D. dissertation, Boston University.

Blos, P. 1971. "The Child Analyst Looks at the Young Adolescent." *Daedalus* 100: 961-78.

_____. 1970. *The Young Adolescent: Clinical Studies.* New York: The Free Press.

_____. 1967. "The Second Individuation Process of Adolescence." In *Psychoanalytic Study of the Child,* vol. 22. New York: International Universities Press.

_____. 1962. *On Adolescence: A Psychoanalytic Interpretation.* New York: The Free Press.

Bowerman, R., and P. Kinch. 1959. "Changes in Family and Peer Orientation of Children between Fourth and Tenth Grades." *Social Forces* 37: 206-11.

Brittam, C. 1963. "Adolescent Choices and Parent-Peer Cross-Pressures." *American Sociological Review* 28: 385-91.

Brofenbrenner, U. 1958. "Socialization and Social Class through Time and Space." In *Readings in Social Psychology,* edited by E. Maccoby. New York: Henry Holt.

Cross, H., and G. Kawash. 1968. "A Short Form of the Parental Attitude Research Instrument to Assess Authoritarian Attitudes toward Childrearing." *Psychological Reports* 23: 91-98.

Elder, G. 1963. "Parental Power Legitimation and Its Effect on the Adolescent." *Sociometry* 26: 50-65.

_____. 1962. "Structural Variations in the Childrearing Relationship." *Sociometry* 26: 241-62.

Gecas, V., and I. Nye. 1974. "Sex and Class Differences in Parent-Child Interaction: A Test of Kohn's Hypothesis." Paper presented at the Annual Meeting of the National Council of Family Relations, St. Louis.

Grimes, Patricia. 1974. "Teaching Moral Reasoning to Eleven Year Olds and Their Mothers: A Means of Promoting Moral Development." Ed.D. dissertation, Boston University.

Hoffman, M. L., and H. Saltzstein. 1967. "Parent Discipline and the Child's Moral Development." *Journal of Personality and Social Psychology* 5: 45-57.

Kohlberg, Lawrence. 1975. "Scoring Manual — Revised." Cambridge, Mass.: Harvard University Center for Moral Education. Mimeographed.

_____. 1973a. *Collected Papers on Moral Development and Moral Education.* Cambridge, Mass.: Harvard University Center for Moral Education. Mimeographed.

_____. 1973b. "Scoring Manual." Cambridge, Mass.: Harvard University Center for Moral Education. Mimeographed.

_____. 1969. "Stage and Sequence: The Cognitive Developmental Approach to Socialization." In *Handbook of Socialization Theory and Research,* edited by D. Goslin. New York: Rand McNally.

Kohn, M. L. 1959. "Social Class and Parental Authority." *American Sociological Review* 24: 352-66.

Manthei, D. 1972. "Disengagement from Childhood in Late Adolescent Females." Ed.D. dissertation, Boston University.

Rest, James, E. Turiel, and L. Kohlberg. 1969. "Level of Moral Judgment as a Determinant of Preference and Comprehension of Moral Judgments Made by Others." *Journal of Personality* 37: 225-52.

Stanley, Sheila. 1976. "A Curriculum to Affect the Justice Structure of the Family and the Moral Development of Adolescents." Ed.D. dissertation, Boston University.

Turiel, E. 1974. "Conflict and Transition in Adolescent Moral Development." *Child Development* 45: 14-29.

_____. 1966. "An Experimental Test of the Sequentiality of Developmental Stages in the Child's Moral Judgments." *Journal of Personality and Social Psychology* 3: 611-18.

CHAPTER 21

Blatt, Moshe. 1970. "Studies on the Effects of Classroom Discussions upon Children's Moral Development." Ph.D. dissertation, University of Chicago.

Cochrane, D. 1978. "Annual Bibliography of Work in Moral Development and Education. *Moral Education Forum* 2: pp. 3-10.

_____. 1979. "Annual Bibliography of Work in Moral Development and Education." *Moral Education Forum* 3: pp. 3-12.

Gage, Nathaniel L. 1978. "The Yield of Research on Teaching." *Phi Delta Kappan,* 60, pp. 229-35.

Leming, J. S. 1979. "Curricular Effectiveness in Moral/Values Education: A Review of Research." Carbondale: Southern Illinois University. Mimeographed.

Purpel, David. 1979. "Adolescents' Development and Education: A Janus Knot: A Review." In *Moral Education Forum* 4, no. 3 (Fall): pp. 29-31.

Sarason, Seymour. 1971. *The Culture of the School and the Problem of Change.* Boston: Allyn and Bacon.

ABOUT THE CONTRIBUTORS

ROBERT ALEXANDER, Associate Professor of Human Services, State University of New York College of Technology, Utica

ROGER AUBREY, Professor of Psychology and Education, and Chair, Department of Human Development Counseling, George Peabody College of Vanderbilt University

ROBERT AZRAK, Cognitive Educational Specialist, Hall-Mercer Children's Unit, McLean Hospital, Belmont, Massachusetts

ANN DISTEFANO, Assistant Professor of Education, Director of Human Services Program, Graduate Institute of Education, Washington University

ANN HIGGINS, Research Associate, Center for Moral Education, Harvard University

LAWRENCE KOHLBERG, Professor of Education and Social Psychology, Harvard University

THOMAS LADENBURG, history teacher, Brookline High School, Brookline, Massachusetts

THOMAS LICKONA, Associate Professor, Department of Education, State University of New York at Cortland.

MARK MASTERSON, Director of Guidance, Masconomet Regional High School, Topsfield, Massachusetts

DAVID MIRON, Director, Human Resources Management, Owens-Illinois, Toledo

RALPH MOSHER, Professor of Education, School of Education, Boston University

DIANA PRITCHARD PAOLITTO, Assistant Professor of Counseling Psychology, Boston College

MUFFY PARADISE, Director, Teacher Center, Brookline Public Schools, Brookline, Massachusetts

CLARK POWER, Research Associate, Center for Moral Education, Harvard University

JOSEPH REIMER, Assistant Professor of Education, School of Education, Boston University, and Research Associate, Center for Moral Education, Harvard University

LOUISE RUNDLE, Associate Director, Counseling Center, Simmons College, Boston

ROBERT SPERBER, Superintendent of Schools, Brookline Public Schools, Brookline, Massachusetts

SHEILA STANLEY, Psychologist, Central New Hampshire Community Mental Health Services, Concord, New Hampshire

MARGOT STERN STROM, Project Director, "Facing History and Ourselves," Brookline Public Schools, Brookline, Massachusetts

DAVID STUHR, Psychologist, Central New Hampshire Community Mental Health Services, Concord, New Hampshire

PAUL SULLIVAN, Associate Professor of Education, College of Education, University of Montana

ELSA WASSERMAN, Educational consultant, Cambridge, Massachusetts

HENRY ZABIEREK, Director of Social Studies, Brookline Public Schools, Brookline, Massachusetts